Agriculture,

economics,

and growth

Agriculture, economics, and growth

second edition

Milton M. Snodgrass
California State Polytechnic College,
Pomona

Luther T. Wallace
University of California,
Berkeley

APPLETON–CENTURY–CROFTS

Educational Division

MEREDITH CORPORATION

New York

Preface

The prime objectives of this book are (1) to combine historical and institutional material into a meaningful context of economic growth and development, (2) to provide a brief, easy-to-read exposition of the more widely used and discussed economic principles and tools of analysis, (3) to give an analytical presentation of some of the physical and human resource adjustment problems resulting from our economy's development, and (4) to provide relevant data for meaningful analysis. This book is intended for use as a beginning text in agricultural economics, but should also be useful in rural economics, resource economics, and other introductory courses in which an applied problem-solving approach is normally used.

This work is directed more toward the beginner in economics and related courses than the intermediate or advanced student. It is designed for easy reading and understanding. No attempt is made to make a sophisticated approach to economics by using highly technical presentations. Appendices are used to entice the better student to delve deeper. Language used in the text has been kept to everyday speech, as we feel that this approach is more likely to stimulate the beginning student's interest in economics.

The focus of this book is on economic growth and the adjustments of people and productive resources within a growth context. An attempt is made to impress the student with the dynamics of economics, the breadth and scope of the subject, and the excitement, stimulation, and personal satisfactions that come from its study. For these reasons we refer quite often to the interrelationships evident in the economy, such as those between the agricultural and industrial sectors, population and food supply, government policies as they affect agriculture, and the household as it is influenced by the growth process. Throughout the text we attempt to offer some explanation of the historical development of economic life.

We have divided our book into six parts. Such a division allows us to place the elements, description, theory, management, and policies of economics in proper perspective. Part I provides the setting for economic growth. It deals with the substance of economics and the process of economic growth. The interrelationships of agricultural and nonagricultural industries are evolved in chapters on the development of economic life. Separate chapters emphasize the role played by the labor force, natural resources, technology, and capital in the process of economic growth.

Part II includes descriptive chapters on the nature of production, marketing, and consumption of food in the United States, with some comparisons with other economies. Part II presents pertinent data needed to study agriculture, agricultural economics, and economic growth.

Part III describes the basic principles and tools of economic analysis. No attempt has been made to include all of them. This leaves the teacher with the task of carrying the student through whatever refinements of the basic principles are considered desirable. Concepts of a production function and simple input-output analysis, including factor-factor, factor-product, and product-product relationships, are explained. The notion of supply is derived together with a discussion of production, while the idea of demand is developed with a discussion of consumption. Price discovery and determination in pure and imperfect market situations are presented. A study of the principles of profit maximization concludes the presentation of principles.

Part IV uses economic principles in applied decision-making for managers. One chapter concerns the management of the farm firm while the other deals with the management of an agribusiness firm. Incorporated into these chapters are the rudiments of farm records and business accounting.

Part V provides an overview of the world agricultural situation. One chapter examines world food needs; the other chapter discusses the potential for increasing world food supplies. Resource availability, the "package of technology" concept, infrastructure, and research and education are topics which are woven together with the material covered in the preceding chapters.

Part VI begins with an introduction to the problem-solving approach. It draws on the material in the previous parts to discuss relevant policy issues of resource development, farm price and income policy, and international trade. A brief discussion of other persisting problems, including the future of family farms and some of the issues involved in regulation, taxation, and land use, concludes the book.

Acknowledgments

We remain indebted, for this revised edition, to all who helped us in writing the first edition. Their help has been, and continues to be, invaluable to us. In addition to those to whom we were first indebted, we would like to express our gratitude to R. W. Taylor and L. P. Fettig, who have made suggestions for improvements based on their class use of the text.

L. T. W.

M. M. S.

Contents

PART II

PART III

PART IV

PART V

PART VI

Agriculture,

economics,

and growth

part I

An introduction to economics, agricultural economics, and economic growth

THE WHY AND WHAT OF ECONOMICS

Why study economics?

There are many reasons why people study economics. Perhaps the biggest single reason is that everyone makes economic decisions throughout their entire lives whether they know it or not. Although everyone is a practicing economist, the old adage "practice makes perfect" does not usually come true unless economic decisions are accompanied by an awareness and understanding of the basic fundamentals of the social science of economics. From the day one gets his first penny to spend or save, he is involved in making economic decisions. Studying economics helps a person make better decisions about spending and saving money, about using his time, and about making a living for himself and his family. In fact the functioning and well-being of our entire democratic and capitalistic society depend to a large extent upon the degree to which the citizenry is well informed and economically literate. These are some of the reasons people study economics.

What is economics?

All social sciences concern human behavior. While the physical scientist deals with inanimate objects and the biological scientist is concerned with living plants and animals, the social scientist is interested in people and their reactions to different situations. Social sciences include psychology, for example, which is concerned primarily with individual behavior, and sociology which devotes more time to group activities. Economics is the social science concerned with how individuals and society choose to allocate their scarce resources (means) among different ends over time.

Becoming proficient in the use of economics is an art that draws heavily on personal insight, training, and judgment. An exceptional economist is one who can combine an excellence in identifying relevant economic questions, an excellence in the understanding of economic theory, and a proficiency in solving problems and interpreting the results.

Any definition of economics includes certain basic notions:

1. The idea of *allocation*—of putting resources (synonymous with inputs, raw materials, and factors of production) or products (synonymous with output or goods) to some use.
2. The idea of *scarcity*—that there simply are not enough inputs to make enough goods to satisfy the nearly insatiable wants of all the individuals and groups in the world.
3. The idea of establishing *goals* or *ends* or *objectives*. Human wants (desires) are unlimited for us as individuals and groups. This necessarily means that *wants compete* for the scarce resources. Because of this competition, we must decide on a priority among our competing wants, and do our best to get the most satisfaction from those chosen.
4. Lastly we must include some reference to *time*. This permits flexibility between short and long time periods and allows for changes in the entire system of goals over time.

The following incorporates these ideas into a definition of economics: *Economics is the allocation of scarce resources between competing ends for the maximization of those chosen ends over time, with provision for maintaining and modifying the system of choice.* (Figure 1-1 illustrates the general subject matter underlying the study of economics.)

The nature of human wants

Everyone can think of something that he would like to have more of. Little children want "just one more" drink of water before they go to bed at night. The head of the family wants more money than he now makes so he can give his family more. A mother wants a little more time to make her house clean and neat. We want just a little more time to enjoy life and not to be so rushed. All of us as individuals and as parts of groups of people within society want things we do not have. Church groups want more churches. Civic groups says we need more schools, better roads, and more of the "right kind" of local government. State governments have long lists of things they need. National governments are the same way. Congress is always considering legislation that the entire society and special interest groups want. Remember any election platform you can think of and check off all the "planks" listing items where improvements were promised.

Unlimited or insatiable wants are not restricted only to economic material things. You may want to be a better artist or piano player just for your own personal enjoyment. Or you may want to help out at Sunday school or in a volunteer children's group. These things bring satisfaction to you, and in making you aware of this satisfaction they make you want more.

There are at least five broad groupings of human wants. A desire for the essentials of life (food, clothing, and shelter) command first priority on man's productive efforts. All people in all societies and countries are alike in this respect. When a family has only a bare minimum of these essentials it can be said to exist at a subsistence level.

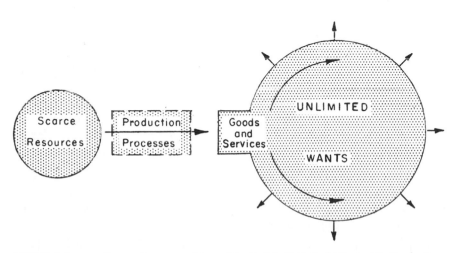

FIGURE 1-1:   Scarce Resources Attempt to Satisfy Unlimited Wants Via Production.

The relative importance of the remaining four groupings of human wants varies among individuals and societies. These groupings are: a desire for self-expression and development, a desire for recognition and approval by others, a desire for power, and a desire for the welfare of others. By attending college, one develops his own mental capacities and communicative skills. Perhaps you have already won public recognition and approval by winning a scholarship. Everyone yearns for social acceptance; some seek it from the masses, while others seek discriminating praise from a select few. Economic wealth can bring you a degree of power over other people. Being captain of a winning team may also satisfy this desire. You can observe a desire for the welfare of others easiest within the family group. Some parents willingly make financial and other sacrifices so their children can attend college. Other people devote their lives to missionary and social work. Our local, state, and federal governments give aid to the needy.

The economizing process

An understanding of the economizing process helps solve the conflict between unlimited wants and scarce resources. The best way to understand this process is in terms of a resource-product or input-output relationship. This relationship simply describes the amount of product produced from a certain set of resources. Essentially the economizing process is used to improve on this input-output relationship. Improvement can be made in one of three ways:

1. Getting more from the same amount of resources by holding inputs constant and increasing output. Example: A greater amount of corn may be obtained from sowing the same amount of seed by using an improved hybrid variety.
2. Getting the same amount of product but using less resources by decreasing inputs while holding output constant. Example: Fewer total dollars may be required to produce an automobile if certain pieces of automatic equipment are used.
3. Getting more product by using relatively less resources by increasing input while increasing output relatively more. Example: A department store manager may more than double sales by doubling his sales force.[1]

The economizing process is useful in analyzing many questions found in everyday living. Automation is an effort to implement the economizing process, as is the situation where a farmer buys a self-propelled combine and no longer needs a hired man.

[1] Point 3 is really a matter of selecting the correct point on a production surface at which to operate.

The basic questions every society must answer

Every society the world over has been confronted with four basic questions. These are: *What* should be produced? *When* should it be produced? *How* should it be produced and distributed? *Who* should receive the income from its sale? We as individuals must also answer these questions. By answering these questions again and again, we continually go back to the basic conflict which gives rise to economics—limited resources and unlimited wants. The answers we find also point out the role each person plays in the economy: producer, consumer, citizen, and planner.

What goods and services shall be produced? Limited resources do not permit a society to have all the goods and services all the people want. However, a society needs some mechanism to guide the use of limited resources into the production of goods and services that will satisfy as many of the people's wants as possible. In our private enterprise economy we rely on our commodity pricing system and the buying habits of all individuals taken together to be the mechanism that determines the amount and the kinds of goods that will be produced. Every time a person purchases a candy bar he is essentially voting for the use of some resources in the production of candy bars. Historically, when people began to use more automobiles than horses for transportation, fewer buggy whips and carriages were bought. Society discontinued its votes for whips and carriages and, accordingly, fewer resources were allocated for their production.

Some goods and services in our economy, such as national highways and defense protection, are consumed collectively by all the citizenry. The decisions of how much and what kind of goods are to be consumed collectively and the amount of resources that are to be used in their production, are made by elected and appointed officials of county, municipal, state, and federal governments. This is often referred to as the public sector of the economy. By voting for representatives to state and national legislatures (the State Senate, State House of Representatives, or Congress), we essentially have a voice in what goods will be produced by the public sector. One may also vote on local issues, such as whether or not to build a new school. In these ways each individual in society helps decide what use, public or private, will be made of the limited resources at hand.

When shall goods and services be produced? The question of *when* to produce a good or service is important because society's output must satisfy both immediate wants and wants that exist over a long period of time. Decisions made now must be based partially on what we want for the present and what we expect in the future. A decision facing a newly married couple is *when* to build a house. Even though they will not build the house themselves they help make the decisions as to when houses are built by deciding when they can afford to buy a house.

Another example of the *when* question is: Should there be a crash program to produce a commodity quickly (such as a cancer cure), should there be a gradual program of orderly research, or should there be no program at all? In this instance, as before, the spending habits of people (market voting), commodity prices, and policies of chosen and appointed government officials guide the decision as to when goods will be produced.

How shall goods and services be produced and distributed? We have already said that it requires scarce resources to produce any good or service. Common sense tells us to attempt to economize on these scarce inputs since they cost money. A producer must decide *how* to produce his product. He will try to utilize the latest technology possible. He will try to combine the proper amounts of each of the inputs necessary for production so that he can produce at as low a cost as possible. The *how* question thus is solved or decided upon by entrepreneurs (producers) as they attempt to find the least cost way (minimum use of resources) in making the product. They search for the best way because other competitors are after their markets and they want to realize as much return as possible from their efforts.

Once the product is made the manager must decide how to get it into the hands of the people who want to use it. Should he send it by truck, rail, air, or water? Should he store it in warehouses in various parts of the country? What should be his inventory policy based on his probable production and the anticipated desire for the product? These are the kinds of production and marketing questions each business manager, each farmer, and every government agency must ask and answer.

Who should receive the income from the sale of the goods and services produced? This question could be illustrated in the following way: When a homemaker buys a loaf of bread for 23 cents, how many of the 23 pennies should go to the farmer who produced the wheat, how many to the grain elevator that stored the wheat, how many to the railroad or truck agency that transported the wheat to the milling company, how many to the milling company, how many to the bakery, and how many to the retailer who sold the bread? This is a difficult question. In our relatively free enterprise economy, where individuals are able, for the most part, to own the factors of production, we believe that each scarce resource should bring a "fair" return to its owner.

However, when viewing the total economy we realize that not all people in our society are able to contribute inputs to the production processes. Should any of the income generated in the economy go to those who do not participate in production? Certainly family breadwinners use their income to care for the members of their family who are not producers in the same sense. But above that, the humanitarian drive in most of us says that people sometimes deserve income even though they supply little or no inputs. For example, many people give money to various charities. Those suffering from flood or fire disaster, or those unemployed for long periods of time are given aid. The question of *who* essentially resolves around how the total income pie will be cut; how big a piece of money income should each member of society receive?

Economics in theory and practice

The study of economic theory and economics in action provides a meaningful analytical framework designed to help answer the *what, when, how,* and *for whom* questions. These basic questions faced by any society do not change as an economy grows. Plato asked the same questions in his writings over 2,000 years ago. However, the answers change as man evolves a more mature understanding of himself, his wants, and the people and cultures which pervade our earth.

An economic theory is a valid generalization or principle concerning economic behavior derived by observation and logical reasoning. An economic theory of consumption, for instance, is that people will buy more steak if the price is lowered. Theory or principle formulation is one of the most practical things man has. You do things a particular way because you know what will happen if another way is chosen instead. You eat meals pretty much on schedule because if you do not you would be hungry or you might have to cook your own. Again, look around you and observe how many things you do consciously or subconsciously that are based on theory, and how often you think, "if I do not do this or act in this way, then these will be the consequences." Theory is a practical guide in almost every phase of our human existence.

Using economics to solve problems. Economics utilizes the problem-solving approach in situations now found in real life or in possible future situations. By understanding economic theory we are better able to identify problems that are occurring within our economy now and might occur as our country grows. After a problem is identified, theory is used to choose the most meaningful alternative ways of solving it. Policymakers then choose the alternative which they feel will best solve the problem. This procedure has been called the "alternative-consequence" approach to problem solving through economics. This approach is equally applicable to an individual or a group.

The dynamics (changing nature) of the economic growth process enable us to see how one part of our economy is related to another. For example, one can trace the consequences of people moving out of farming into manufacturing and service jobs. One can predict and test what the economic results of a particular course of action will be by identifying and describing the problem situation in meaningful terms, and analyzing it with the problem-solving "alternative consequences" approach.

The economist is placed in a unique position by being trained to be aware of the various roles played by business firms, government agencies, and consumers in our interrelated economy. Because of his training to seek cause and effect, to discover the "why" of decision making, he can help formulate courses of action, or policies, that society deems desirable. He can also help in the adjustment of resources and people in a dynamic economy.

Summary

Economics involves all of us personally. We all make decisions that concern the use of resources and the attainment of certain goals over time. Economics is a social science interrelated with, and influenced by, other social disciplines.

Economics approaches the conflict of unlimited wants and limited resources with an analytical input-output framework based on theory, judgment, and experience. This framework can be applied to the basic and enduring questions of production and consumption faced by any individual or society. The economizing process is used to improve on the input-output relationships. Because of the perspective and focus which the study of economics provides, the practicing economist is in a unique position to help formulate and evaluate policies which attempt to maximize resource efficiency while at the same time attempting to fulfill society's needs and wants over time.

The study of economics increases our awareness of the total economy in which we live. It helps us see what happens when limited resources are applied to the various goals generated from the insatiable wants of all groups and individuals. It makes us more conscious of the society around us and of the reasons people act the way they do. It promotes a curiosity about how and why people make decisions the way they do. It develops our insights and decision-making ability as we observe others making decisions about limited means to achieve desired consumption levels of goods and services.

AGRICULTURE AND AGRICULTURAL ECONOMICS [2]

The word *agriculture* has long been associated with the industry of basic food production known as farming. Agriculture and farming were synonymous before farmers began selling their products on a commercial

[2] Data taken from "There's a New Challenge in Agriculture," prepared by a special committee of the Resident Instruction Section, Division of Agriculture, American Association of Land-Grant Colleges and State Universities, undated, but approximately 1962.

market. However, in today's modern agriculture, producing food and fiber (farming) is only one part of scientific agriculture. Modern agriculture also includes the farm supply industries (feed, seed, machinery, pharmaceuticals, etc.) as well as the product processing and distribution industries which convert the raw food into the form consumers want and move it to them (Figure 1-2). Often, these are referred to as agriculturally related industries or agribusinesses.

Farming sector of agriculture (on-farm)

Farming is a big and expanding business, requiring continually increasing amounts of capital, technology, and management. However, as the efficiency of scientific farming increases, fewer and fewer operators and workers are needed each year to feed our growing population. This fact has caused farming to be referred to as a declining industry by some people.

Productivity per farm worker is currently at an all-time high, and this is one of the factors that has allowed a doubling of our national population and large increases in per capita disposable income since 1910. Continued increases in the productivity of farm workers in the 1970's will result in more food raised on less land with less labor.

Modern farming is dynamic and requires men and women with scientific knowledge, skill, and ambition. Knowledge of engineering, chemistry, pathology, entomology, genetics, nutrition, and economics is necessary to successful farming. Farmers are key men in the nation's economy and the opportunity for outdoor living and self-employment are privileges few others enjoy. Because of the ever increasing efficiency in farm production however, fewer and fewer job opportunities will be available on the farm.

Off-farm or agribusiness sector of agriculture

Farm supply industries. Farmers purchase a greater share of their inputs today than ever before. A common example is the farmer who grew oats as fuel for horses which he had also raised. Today the farmer buys gas and oil to fuel a tractor purchased from a farm equipment manufacturer. The farm supply industries include feed, seed, fertilizer, agricultural pharmaceuticals, machinery, pesticides, and lime—for which the farmer spends over $25 billion a year. Government related farm credit institutions and commercial banks lend money capital. Credit is an essential input for food production and hence could also be classified as a part of the farm supply industry. Farm supply industries already employ more people (about seven million) than are employed on farms. While job opportunities are fewer on the farm, employment in farm supply industries is expanding.

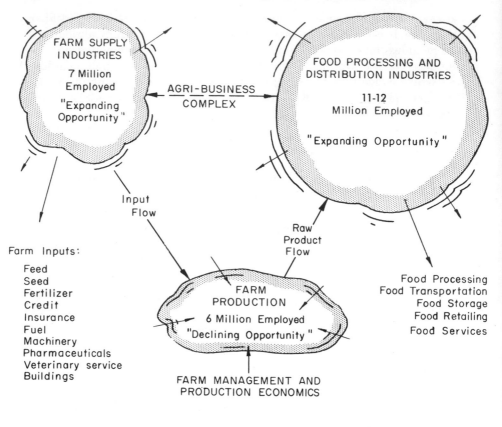

FIGURE 1-2:   Scope of Modern Agriculture.

Food processing and distribution industries. Specialized agricultural industries process, package, and move the food and fiber products to the consumer. Included in these industries are dairy plants, food freezing firms, drying and canning operations, meat-packing plants, fats and oil manufacturing plants, lumber mills, and grain mills. Every type of industry that processes and transports the raw food produced on the farm is included in this category. These industries are expanding and already employ between eleven and twelve million people, or twice the number that is in farming.

Other service industries related to agriculture

Education. More than 2,000 new teachers each year go into positions in high schools, agricultural college staffs, adult teaching with the agricultural extension service, and vocational agriculture. In addition, agricultural education for foreign students is an area that has recently expanded and promises much for the future. Both public and private agencies are increasing staffs of qualified people to teach up-to-date agricultural technology in other countries. The need for teachers in vocational agriculture will likely decline because fewer and fewer students are going back to the farms. The role of extension educators has expanded from demonstrating techniques used to show new agricultural technologies (new seeds, the use of fertilizer, different methods of field cultivation) to issues of farm price and income policy, foreign trade, and urban-industrial development.

Communications. The service industry of agricultural communications is expanding. Widespread dissemination of information concerning agricultural technology, prices, and cost of production is essential to the continued productivity of our agricultural sector. Interviewing farmers, scientists, and industrialists, attending conventions, demonstrations, and legislative sessions, and reporting new research developments are all part of agricultural communications. Colleges, extension services, market reporting agencies, newspapers, farm publications, and television and radio stations all report on agricultural services to farmers and to the general public. These agencies need writers, broadcasters, television and motion picture producers, and photographers.

Research. Research in agricultural industries needs at least 1,500 college graduates each year. Agriculture looks to researchers for new ideas in farm equipment, nutrition of livestock, genetics, disease control, processing, marketing, and economics. There are some 8,000 research scientists in the agricultural experiment stations, 8,000 more in agricultural industries, and 6,000 in the United States Department of Agriculture. Research work usually requires people with advanced college degrees.

Government services. Government agencies on a national, state, and local basis serve agriculture through many service agencies. Communications and research have already been mentioned. Regulatory agencies act to protect farmers in their purchases of inputs relative to quality and quantity. Public health is safeguarded through food inspection and grading. Nursery inspection requires particular specialists in entomology, pathology, botany, and horticulture. Local activities of community planning and recreation agencies are other examples. Foreign service opportunities with the federal government are expanding.

Summary

Agriculture employs nearly 40 percent of the labor force in the United States and at its present rate of growth needs 15,000 new college graduates each year. Employment needs of the agribusinesses of agriculture are expanding, while those of the farm segment are declining. The three segments of agriculture (farm production, farm supply industries, and food processing and distribution industries) are interdependent and their combined scope is of vital importance in the total economy.

Agricultural economics

Agricultural economics is an applied phase of the social science of economics in which attention is given to all aspects of problems related to agriculture. The development of agricultural economics as an applied social science in the United States extends back to about 1900 when the discipline began as a study of farm management, which in turn had its roots primarily in agronomy and horticulture.

At the beginning of the twentieth century interest in economic issues related to agriculture erupted in several educational centers. The depression of the 1890's had hurt agriculture severely and organized farm groups, particularly the Farmer's Alliance, had stirred considerable interest in farm problems. This new field of agricultural interest, later to be designated as agricultural economics, attracted professors of agriculture who formerly labored only in such technical areas as agricultural chemistry, agronomy, and horticulture, as well as general economists and business leaders.

By 1910 about 20 men were identified as agricultural economists. Thomas F. Hunt is recognized as a pioneer in agricultural college and agricultural experiment station work. He was an agriculturist who recognized the physical, biological, and economic aspects of farming and their interdependence in promoting good farm management practices. Courses in the agricultural economy, rural economy, farm management, and agricultural history grew rapidly in the early 1900's. Work in farm management in the United States Department of Agriculture was started by William J. Spillman in 1902. In the early years farm management work was directed toward such questions as how to choose a farm, how to choose the proper enterprises for a farm, how intensive the cultivation should be on farms, and how large farms should be.

After World War I, interest in the marketing of farm products was spurred by the expansion of commercialized farming, surplus farm production, and the subsequent farm depression. Orderly marketing was the objective and considerable attention was given to the importance of marketing cooperatives in marketing farm products more successfully. Staff members of the National Bureau of Agricultural Economics and the agricultural colleges studied general marketing problems, prices, foreign competition, transportation, city produce markets, and market statistics. Over 50 commodities received their attention.

Since the 1920's, farm price and income policy have received considerable attention by agricultural economists as a natural outgrowth of surplus farm production, marketing problems, and depressed farm incomes. Agricultural policy is a course of action decided upon and followed in the field of agriculture. Most people associate it with debates about parity prices, agricultural price supports, production allotments, or with the merits or faults of some national agricultural act. However, it has grown much broader. Agricultural policy analysis is also directed toward such topics as the reasons for the creation and development of the land-grant colleges, the issues in public reclamation and development of irrigated lands, the basis of conflict between persons advocating free trade and those supporting protections in international trade, the merits of the family farm, soil conservation issues, tax issues, education, planning and zoning, and economic development.

Agricultural Economists. Professional agricultural economists are typically classified as working in production economics, farm management, agricultural marketing, and agricultural policy. Specialists in farm finance, farm work simplification, and land economics are more closely allied with farm management. In marketing, agricultural economists may be specialists in any of the commodity areas, such as grain, dairy, poultry, livestock, fruits, and vegetables. In the policy area, agricultural economists may concentrate on price and income policy, land policy, marketing policy, and local government. Recently, there has been increased attention given to international agricultural policy questions, including the Common Market in Europe, the economic development of less developed nations, and the commodity and price implications of domestic farm policies. Agricultural price analysts contribute to all phases of agricultural economics. With the recent emphasis on management problems in the agribusiness segment of agriculture, business management specialists are appearing within the scope of agricultural economics. These men may work principally in finance, production, marketing, or policy in the agricultural supply, food processing, or distribution industries.

ECONOMIC GROWTH

One of the reasons students attend college is to increase their earning power in later years. The increased earning power will enable them to buy more goods and services and enjoy what is often called a "higher standard of living." Just as most individuals want to increase their wealth, so do most countries. With the emergence of many new independent nations in the 1950's, the establishment of the European Economic Community, and the Cold War between the Communist countries and the Free World, the process of economic growth and development is receiving concentrated attention.

Definition of economic growth

Defining economic growth or measuring a rate of growth is a difficult task. By far the most common approach is to measure the total output of goods and services produced by the economy and divide the output by the number of people.

$$\frac{\text{physical output of goods and services (national product)}}{\text{population}} = \frac{\text{national product}}{\text{per capita}}$$

National product can be expressed in dollars by multiplying the total amount of each good or service produced in the economy times its average retail market price. National product in money value becomes national income and our growth measure is converted from physical goods and services to dollars, a more appropriate measure:

$$\frac{\text{national income (dollars)}}{\text{population}} = \text{national income per capita}$$

Two problems arise. First, an increase in the price level (inflation) can be mistaken for a change in the rate of growth. To avoid this problem, any misleading influence of a price change can be removed by adjusting the national income for given years to a rise or fall in the general level of prices. For example, in 1929 the money national product was $96 billion, and in 1933 it was $48 billion. However, during this period the price level dropped by 25 percent, dropping from an index of 100 down to an index of 75 based on 1929 prices. As a result, when priced using the 1929 price level, the real national product fell from $96 billion to only $64 billion ($48 ÷ 75 x 100 = $64).

Second, part of the production of goods in any economy must be allocated for replacing worn out equipment, buildings, and other capital goods. Otherwise the capital stock or wealth of an economy at the end of the year would be less than at the beginning. In national income statistics, capital consumption or depreciation allowances for depletion of capital stock accounts for the difference between gross national product and net national product. In computing national product (income) per capita for use in measuring growth and growth rates, the net national product should be used. In order for an economy to show growth the increase in net national product must be greater than the increase in population.

Factors affecting the rate of economic growth

There is no one theory that fully explains the process of economic development. Certainly a country's growth rate is influenced by social, political, institutional, and economic factors. To isolate the influence of one is most difficult. And the importance of a particular factor in the economic growth rate of the United States may have little or no bearing on the situation in some other country.

Much attention is now being focused on "underdeveloped" nations. In the sense of utilizing all its resources to gain the largest national product possible, however, no country can ever be fully developed except in theory. The measure of national product in determining a country's state of development relegates social or political development to a minor role. Perhaps the ancient Roman or Greek empires were more highly developed in a cultural sense than many of today's "developed" nations.

What are the economic factors conducive to a country's achieving a high growth rate? The following four are frequently cited and shall receive detailed attention in later chapters. It should be emphasized again that although these factors are important, they do not fully explain economic growth by themselves.

First, there are natural resources (Chapter 4). A country that is fortunate enough to be endowed with a large supply of natural resources will find its growth potential aided materially. A high quality soil resource and basic raw materials such as iron ore, natural gas, bauxite, coal, and oil, are conducive to economic development.

Second, there is the human resource—people—which provides the inputs of labor and management (Chapters 5 and 6). The larger a country's population the more mouths there are to feed. On the other hand, the larger the population the greater is the potential labor and management supply and hence, a greater growth potential exists in the economy.

The productive labor force consists primarily of those persons 14 to 65 years of age, although labor laws in many countries prohibit the amount that persons aged 14 to 18 may work. The quantity aspect of the labor force varies (a) seasonally (July is the high month in this country and January the low month), (b) with the number of people, including women, who choose to work, (c) with the average length of the work week, (d) with the number unemployed either for voluntary or involuntary reasons, and (e) with the number of students in school. A second aspect of the labor force is quality. The higher the quality of a person's labor or management input, the greater his efficiency and productivity per hour of input can be in the economy. The primary influences that increase a person's potential contribution to the national product are education, training, and experience.

Third, a country's capital vitally affects its growth potential (Chapter 7). Capital includes all business structures and producers' durable equipment, farm and nonfarm residential structures, inventories of raw and finished goods, and assets abroad owned by a country's populace.

Fourth is the resource of technology—the accumulation of knowledge about production that helps increase output per unit of input and lowers costs of production (Chapter 8). In this context, technology improves the productivity of land, of labor, of capital, and of management.

That a lack of any one of these resources can be restricting is apparent in the world situation today. Brazil, for example, has many natural resources but lacks capital and skilled labor. China has lots of labor but little capital. Egypt has little fertile land and other natural resources. Economic growth in some countries of Europe was relatively slow until outmoded capital destroyed by war was rebuilt with new technologies. It is true that to some extent one group of factors may be substituted for another. This is most true for labor and capital. Producers are always searching to find the least-cost combination of factors that will produce a unit of output. But substitution can only go so far before other problems are encountered. For example, witness the immense social and economic problems created as automated technology and machines replace workers in coal mines.

Social and political institutions may also hinder economic progress. Political instability, particularly evident in Latin America, discourages investment capital from outside sources. It is evident that many interrelated factors influence the rate of economic growth in any particular country.

Variation in national income per capita among countries

Using per capita income as an indicator of standard of living or of the degree to which an economy is developed, one is impressed by the disparity that exists between countries. In the 1950's most of the people in Asia and Africa were living at levels lower than the standard of living in the Western countries before the Industrial Revolution in the 1850's. Kuznets estimates that growth rates in the first half of the twentieth century have been averaging about 1 percent a year in France and England, 1.6 percent in Canda and the United States, and 3 percent in Sweden.[3] With data lacking, it is difficult to say much about the very poor nations, but estimates made by the Center for International Studies at Massachusetts Institute of Technology suggest the following per capita incomes in 1957:

United States	$2108	U.S.S.R.	$500
Canada	1472	Italy	404
Sweden	1171	Japan	252
United Kingdom	955	India	64
France	720	China	64

[3] Simon Kuznets, "Quantitative Aspects of the Economic Growth of Nations: I," *Economic Development and Cultural Change,* Vol. 5, 1956, p. 25. The rate of growth in percentage terms varies within each country for shorter time periods and depends also on the base period selected.

The disparity may grow less with time but with the rates of population growth high in the poorer countries, their struggle will be an extremely difficult one. Thoreau has postulated that a person's happiness is equal to his material consumption divided by desire. One of the major problems in maintaining happiness in the modern world arises because rapid communications bring the news of Western comforts to the poor. This probably helps to explain the revolution and resurgence of much of mankind for new freedom and independence in the mid-twentieth century.

2

Development of
economic life

The purpose of this chapter is to trace the development of economic life from a subsistence economy to a complex industrial society. The reader will note the importance in the economic growth process of specialization and trade, with the resulting increase in interdependence between sectors in the economy.

We live in an exciting age surrounded by a rapidly changing environment. Some scientists believe that more technological developments have taken place since 1900 than in all previous time in man's known history. Yet if all of man's past were represented by a 24-hour day, the twentieth century would represent only 1/1000th of a second.

An advanced economic system like that of the United States is of recent origin. Throughout the world one can find countries which exhibit large variations in kind and amount of economic and social development. Problems concerning agriculture are evident in all stages of any country's development and receive the main emphasis in this book.

PRINCIPAL STAGES OF ECONOMIC DEVELOPMENT IN HISTORY

Man's advancement in his control over nature to satisfy his material wants closely follows his progress in developing tools. As man slowly came to the realization that he was different from other animal life, he also became aware that he was in competition with them for nature's limited food supply. Anthropologists study the physical characteristics which link man to animals, his social organization, and his skills. Economists are interested in man's ability to organize and increase production in order to satisfy his wants.

The hunting or collectional economy

In the collectional economy man was essentially a parasite and lived from the gifts of nature. This period accounts for 98 percent of man's known history. Man was fortunate in that he developed as a "generalized," or easily adaptable, animal. Most scientists agree that man's erect posture was the one feature which allowed him to make gains in learning to control his environment. Even with hands free to grasp things or kill, man found himself only a collector of nature's various gifts. Although his environment offered him the means of survival it required most of his time to gather his daily food.

As man's intelligence gradually increased he changed from a wielder of randomly acquired weapons to a crude toolmaker. Increased efficiency in hunting and collecting allowed time for other activities, such as transmitting knowledge through language. Man's natural sociability together with his language development provided the means for cultural progress.

The Ice Age, which took place some 700,000 years ago, was a vital factor in man's development. Long-range fluctuations between polar and tropical weather about every 100,000 years changed the physical nature of the world, which forced man to learn to adapt to his environment or die. As thousands of feet of ice in glaciers put much of the world in a deep freeze only to be followed by searing droughts, man's adaptive processes were tested and forced to improve.

The development of the human brain gave man the ability to meet the many challenges and bring him safely through the Ice Age, which lasted some 200,000 years. Although hundreds of animal species, many physically stronger than man, perished during the Ice Age, stamina and development of physical skills along with crude weapons gave man an edge on the hunting grounds of Europe and Asia.

Man migrated with the animals across natural land bridges formed by the glaciers. Apparently it was during one of the glacial periods that the men who became American Indians reached the New World by way of the land bridge from Asia over the Bering Strait.

Man continued as a hunter throughout the entire Old Stone Age from 500,000 B.C. to 8,000 B.C. His progress in technology over this period was limited to slow changes in basic stone instruments. With the vast nuclear power of the twentieth century, one easily forgets that during nine-tenths of man's existence his only tools were chipped stones and simple shafts of wood. Man had learned to make most of his fundamental tools by the end of the Old Stone Age. He still had only one form of power—his muscles—and he knew nothing of farming. It is not clear when man learned to harness fire for his own good. It most likely took a longer time for him to learn to make fire than to use it to provide warmth in his cave shelters and for crude cooking. Fire also aided man as a hunter. Since animals were afraid of fire, it could be used to guide them into traps and over mountain precipices. Bones of an estimated 100,000 horses found in France give evidence of cooperative hunting where, with the aid of fire, the horses were driven up a slope to a cliff from which they fell to their death. As the Stone Age closed man had learned to provide himself with shelter and clothing which, together with his more finely wrought weapons and aggressive intelligence, made him better equipped to hunt.

The pastoral stage

Some 20,000 years ago, when the great glaciers mysteriously began receding as they are today, the landscape began to change. Trees took root and rivers and lakes were formed. The Middle Stone Age, which began about 8,000 B.C., found man beginning to use bow and arrow to stalk the smaller, swifter game of deer and wild pig, necessary because many of the larger beasts had become extinct. He trapped fish in large quantities, dried the surplus, and stored it for future use. He also learned to store other foods which appeared seasonally, such as seeds, nuts, and fruits.

In the New Stone Age, estimated as beginning between 6,000 and 7,000 B.C., man discovered the secret of the relationship between seed and plant. Farming was born. He also began to domesticate some animals. These two developments were decisive factors in agricultural development during the pastoral stage. Improved stabilization in the food supply enabled man to gain the necessary leisure time to engage in wars, religion, and the arts.

The pastoral stage included the culture of Neolithic man and was characterized by man's domestication of cattle, sheep, goats, and pigs as animal sources of food. The dog was trained both as a working companion and a pet. Polished stone implements, particularly the stone ax, were developed, although unpolished stone implements were still used. The women spun and wove fibers into cloth. Progress in cooking methods prompted pottery utensils. Although man was still nomadic toward the end of the pastoral stage, he tended to settle in a more fixed abode and to spend more time on farming and less on hunting.

The agricultural or settled village economy

With the disappearance of the nomadic life villages began to grow. Economic life in these local communities centered around the daily tasks of farming. Relatively speaking, growth in this period was rapid. The first urban civilization dawned only 3,500 years after farmers began sowing seeds and reaping their own harvests. It arose in a Middle East region called Mesopotamia, in the Tigris and Euphrates river valleys. The first village people were probably united by bonds of kinship. The concept of property was born through individual family settlements on specific plots of ground. In the process, social intercourse was enriched, group religious observances took form, economic trade was initiated, and a crude form of government evolved as a logical consequence. Thus began the evolution of man's social institutions.

Life in the early villages was full and active and quickly resulted in a higher standard of living. Labor specialization contributed to a longer life span. Older people were freed from such strenuous tasks as hunting, and became useful in performing tasks which required little physical effort. Children could do simple chores like tending animals. Women found never-ending work in milling grain, baking bread, weaving cloth, and fashioning utensils.

The transition of man from a food collector to a food producer was one of the longest steps toward a stable society that mankind has ever taken. It was no coincidence that the first cultivation of plants occurred in the sun-drenched hills that stretch eastward through Asia Minor—the biblical Garden of Eden. The climate there was warm and dry with natural meadows of wild wheat and barley. Rainfall was adequate and the area was also adapted to man's first domesticated animals.

Grain cultivation may have begun when discarded seeds in the garbage dump sprang forth luxuriantly into growth. As a result man experimented by sowing seeds in the soil and watched to see what the next year would bring forth. Over time, rough fields of man-made grain wove patterns across the land. The art of cultivation spread swiftly throughout the Fertile Crescent, an area bending north from Egypt through Palestine and Syria and turning south again through the Tigris and Euphrates river valleys.

While some food problems were solved, some conservation problems were created. By altering the natural environment through soil tillage and forest clearance, man set processes in motion that wasted the soil and created deserts and wastelands. Man overcame these problems with creative genius. Dikes were built to hold the swollen rivers and ditches were dug to carry water to fields for irrigation. Cattle were trained to pull the newly invented plow. The substitution of animal power for human labor constituted a revolution in food production methods. With the invention of the sailboat he turned the broad rivers into highways, and a great up-surge in trade and commerce was then possible. Towns developed along the river banks where farmers could trade their goods.

The stage was then set for the development of the great civilizations of Europe and Asia. The elements of a civilized society usually include pursuit of knowledge and the arts, a high level of political organization, a complex social and economic order, true specialization in crafts and skills, and the adherence of individuals to the impersonal requirements of the state. The ability to write, record, and convey information is a neces-sary skill in such a society.

Three important civilizations in the history of the world were Greece, Rome, and Britain. Unlike Egypt, soil conditions in Greece were not favorable to farming. There was no river like the Nile to provide water and aid in maintaining soil fertility by depositing silt during flood periods. Thus, the Greeks were obliged to either fertilize or resort to letting their land lie idle every other year.

Population pressures and wars forced the Greeks to establish colo-nies. Olive oil and wine were the principal agricultural exports. Slave labor dominated the situation both in agriculture and in the rest of the early village economies. These slaves were often skilled craftsmen work-ing side by side with free men for the same wages. As trade and com-merce flourished, Greece rose to her height about 400 B.C. With the death of Alexander the Great in 323 B.C. the Grecian Empire split into several parts, most of which were taken over by the Roman Empire.

The Romans were not a commercial people. Their genius lay prima-rily in the political realm. They were the greatest organizers and adminis-trators of all antiquity, providing stability to the world for the years between 200 B.C. and 200 A.D. As the population of Rome, the city which grew into an empire, increased to unparalleled proportions, immense im-ports of food became necessary. The burden of paying for grain imports (money raised by taxation) fell heavily, curiously enough, on those in agriculture. The government felt itself politically obliged to sell grain to the city population at less than cost, or to actually give it away. Ironi-cally, the Roman cultivator found himself heavily taxed to pay for grain which competed in this unfair way with his own production.

The ruling class was not blind to the dangers involved in depending so heavily on imported grain. The situation got so serious that Roman citizens were attached to the soil, becoming serfs but not quite slaves. By the end of the fourth century practically no one in the Empire was legally free to move from his place of origin. The growth of large estates and government interference were notable features of Rome's rural decline.

Lessons learned in the early years of Roman rule resulted in some striking changes in the administration of the later Roman provinces established in the West (in Spain, France, and England). The strong central government of Rome maintained military order but allowed these provinces to make limited economic progress. In order to control outlying areas, Roman armies provided protection for trade and communication over improved roads.

The decline in Roman power began in the third century when it lacked the power to repress internal revolts, to repel the inroads of barbarians from the North, and to maintain communications with outlying provinces. The situation deteriorated to such an extent that the provincials could no longer look to Rome for protection and development stimulus. The motives for commerce grew weaker, culture diminished, and obstacles to trade were compounded. Piracy and robbery became commonplace. The "Fall of Rome" occurred in 476 A.D., and the last remnants of Roman progress disappeared as the European world passed into the Dark Ages.

One must understand the methods employed in Roman governmental organization in order to understand why feudalism developed. Cities in the provinces were linked to Rome by a communicative network of roads and highways. Taxes collected by provincial officials and reports of all kinds streamed to Rome while official orders and instructions flowed in the opposite direction. This system became increasingly difficult to use as Roman power fell. Roads were destroyed and journeyers robbed. As a result, few taxes reached Rome and the government no longer had the means to pay its bills. Finally the time came when Rome had to recognize the change in conditions and adopt quite different methods. Basically, the man who previously was a salaried official found that he had to support himself from land revenues which formerly went to Rome for taxes. In reality however, the state split into little self-regulating units and the central government in Rome lost all control over its provinces.

The provincial officials became little kings or lords who enclosed the land they supervised into a self-sufficient community known as the feudal manor or vill. It is estimated that perhaps 10,000 or more of these communities were established. While the peasants or serfs were not fully slaves, they certainly were not free. The serfs, however, did gain protection by living in the manor.

The economic life of these small village groups, perhaps consisting of less than 100 people, was highlighted in their self-sufficiency. A large majority of the people in each manor were necessarily farmers who raised a minimal food supply. Crude methods were used which were often wasteful. The livestock was of such a poor breed that a grown ox was little larger than a present day calf. Stock were few in number and often it was necessary to kill some at the beginning of winter from lack of fodder to feed them. Intensive cultivation on limited land without sufficient fertilizer exhausted the land's productive capacity quickly. A yield of six bushels of wheat per acre, of which two bushels had to be retained for seed, was probably normal.

Houses were constructed of forest materials, clothes were made from flax and wool, and furniture and implements were likewise fashioned within the manor. Nearly every vill had a mill run by water, some had a carpenter, but few special artisans were to be found.

Such a self-sufficient system with little commerce resulted in alternate periods of waste and want. There was no market for any surplus grain harvested in a good year and it was not possible to import any in a bad year. Little economic growth could come about as long as everything had to be produced on the spot and used by the manor people themselves. Feudalism was prevalent throughout Western Europe for over 600 years.

The town economy

The decline of the manor system began about 1000 A.D. in northern Italy. As chaotic conditions lessened, towns began to spring up; they have been aptly described as "isles of freedom in a sea of serfdom." A town was a group of people who settled closely together and maintained themselves chiefly by manufacture and trade. Probably they were the younger, more aggressive, and fearless people who tired of manor living and risked escape. For a while they continued to pay some taxes to nearby manor lords for appeasement and protection. Town population grew as the custom was established that a serf who escaped from his manor lord and lived a year and a day in a town was free. Consequently, manor lords were forced to lighten their requirements to discourage people from leaving. The Black Death, or Plague, which was to ravish the European countries for several centuries to come, also contributed to the decline of the manor system.

Towns brought a new era in commercial production and manufacturing became a profession. The result was specialization of labor bringing increased production income and a higher standard of living. The country people could devote themselves entirely to farming and could exchange their surplus for a profitable exchange with town artisans.

The revival of trade took place first between towns in the same country and eventually between countries. The town was the unit for regulating trade. Each town had its custom tariffs and national regulation was subordinated by municipal laws. The economic life of the town was closely regulated by the *guild*, the forerunner of today's labor unions. All merchants and craftsmen (manufacturers) were organized in guilds. Trading merchants banded together for protection in their journeys to other towns and had to follow guild rules or pay a fine. Often guild members were obliged to carry armor and fight for mutual protection.

Craftsmen also had guilds which established regulations designed to prevent fraud and maintain quality of workmanship. Every town felt a community of interests among its inhabitants and a sense of competition with other towns. Trade flourished and the period centering about the year 1500 was marked by many rapid changes. These changes affected not only the intellectual life of Europe (the Renaissance) and its religious life (the Reformation), but they also caused a revolution in the world of politics, industry, and commerce.

The collapse of feudalism occurred at widely different times in different countries. It has been well summarized as follows:

> It was the collapse of feudalism before the onslaughts of central governments, the liberation of serfs, the development of markets, and the growth of specialized farming for the market which so changed and diversified the manors that a generalized institution was no longer visible. Villeinage sharply declined in England during the fourteenth century and slowly died out afterward. The French crown serfs were all freed by about 1350. As in England, those on private estates gained their freedom by individuals or groups, or were able to rid themselves of particular servile disabilities until the last vestiges were swept away in 1789. The last German villeins were freed by decree during the Napoleonic Wars, but it was several decades before this was fully effective in fact. Those of Russia were emancipated between 1861 and 1866, though vestiges of lordly exploita tion and oppression lingered on.[1]

The industrial economy

The industrial economy began with the Industrial Revolution, which can be simply defined as the emerging of the factory system in the production of goods. It originated in England in the last third of the eighteenth century. While the large factories with tall smokestacks that skirt the edge of many American cities are familiar to everyone, the process of their development is an exciting story in economic history. Needless to say, as one considers the world situation it is quickly noted that some countries have not experienced any such revolution, and it is probably incomplete even in the United States as we now eye a new atomic age era.

The primary object of industry is the production of goods desired by people. The factory system concentrates and multiplies the means of production so that output can be both accelerated and increased. Ma-

[1] M. M. Knight, H. E. Barnes, and Felix Flugel, *Economic History of Europe* (Boston: Houghton Mifflin Co., 1928), p. 182.

chinery with remarkable precision and rapidity performs the most complicated and the heaviest tasks. Intricate machines and skilled men to run them form the mainspring of industrial production.

Once manufactured, goods must be sold. The immense stimulus given to production by the factory system immediately affects the distribution system for the goods. An increased quantity of goods on local markets means lower prices, which puts the nearby consumer in a more favorable position. As transportation methods improve, the effects of increased production extended from individuals to regions and to nations.

Two fundamental facts, closely interwoven, infinitely varied in their consequences but always the same in principle, govern the evolution of economic life. These are the exchange of commodities and the division of labor. Every extension or multiplication in the exchange of goods makes use of an ever more elaborate and effective division of labor by throwing open more channels to production. The division of labor also implies cooperation between interdependent specialized jobs which necessarily involve large numbers of people.

The woolen industry in England was probably the most characteristic and complete example of an early system of manufacture. The first instance of extreme specialization in agriculture was in the sheep industry in England. As the feudal system collapsed, small fields were combined into larger acreages for pasturing sheep. There was a good market for wool across the English channel in Belgium and France. After the Norman conquest, Flemish artisans crossed to England and taught the English how to use some of this wealth themselves and textiles became the predominant type of manufacture.

The domestic system. Before we proceed any further let us take a look at the nature of the cloth manufacturing industry which immediately preceded the factory system. The Domestic System, as it was called, was so named because the manufacturing of cloth took place in the homes of the workers.

The necessary apparatus for weaving was simply a loom, hand cards, and a spinning wheel, all inexpensive machinery. If a weaver had a large family, some specialization and division of labor was possible and the family could handle all the necessary operations. Many times however, a weaver distributed wool for spinning into other homes to keep enough thread available for looms. It was in this way that specialization first came about outside the family circle. There were houses where only spinning was done. In others, several weaving looms were gathered together and the weaver, while still remaining an artisan working with his hands, had a small number of hired laborers under his supervision. In this system the weaver, in his cottage which was both a dwelling place and workshop, controlled production. He was not dependent upon outside capital since he owned both the tools and raw materials.

The same weaver who managed the production phase also marketed the cloth, usually in the nearest town. At Leeds in England, the market was held in the High Street with long counters on each side. The market opened at a specified time and cloth merchants would walk up and down among the tables making purchases.

However, domestic industry of such a nature could continue to exist only as long as local consumption absorbed local production. When production increased beyond this point, the manufacturer was forced to come to some agreement with the cloth merchant or trader who bought goods for resale either in another home market or abroad. The trader now became an indispensable middleman. This new market element soon reacted on the production phase of the industry.

As it was common for the weaver to deliver the cloth in unfinished form, it was necessary for the merchant to employ workmen to dress and dye the cloth. This was the first stage in the gradual transformation of commercial capital to industrial capital. In fact, it became quite common for the merchant to buy the raw wool and have it carded, spun, woven, fulled, and dressed at his own expense.[2] The workmen thus became employees performing tasks for remuneration by an employer.

The workmen in the domestic industry were much different from those employed in a modern factory of today. Most lived in the country and earned some of their income from farming. For most, spinning and weaving were additional occupations for supplementary income. As a result, the workers produced more goods in the winter when there was less farm work to do, and very little goods at planting or harvest time.

The advantage to the merchant capitalist was that he needed no building in which to house equipment. The disadvantages were, of course, that he could exercise no supervisory control over his employees in their private home "factories." Distribution of raw materials and the collection of small amounts of widely scattered manufactured cloth were costly. Pilferage and other problems also plagued the merchant manufacturer.

To some people, the early domestic type industry was "the golden age" where craftsmen, either in country or small town, lived a simpler and healthier life than workmen in today's modern industrial centers. He worked at home, cultivated a few acres, and produced according to his own time, needs, and strength. His moral fiber was thought to be enhanced by good family life and he was considered a respectable member of society.

But as capital was separated from labor and the workman became only a wage earner, he was more at the mercy of his employer. Spinning, usually done by women and children, commanded the lowest pay and as the industry passed from simple to more complicated production proc-

[2] *Report on the State of the Woolen Manufacturer*, p. 8, Parliamentary Debates, II, 668.

esses labor specialization grew at a fast pace. As the domestic system was replaced by the factory system and the Industrial Revolution continued, the lot of the laboring classes was not necessarily improved.

The factory system. These problems asociated with the domestic type industry confronting the capitalist played a major role in the establishment of factories. In factories the workers could all be kept under the eye of a supervisor and specialization of labor could more easily be accomplished.

The factory system evolved slowly. Between the small craftsman, who was his own master, and the wage earning factory workman are many intermediate stages with varying degrees of independence and subjection of workers. Until 1775, workers in the coal mines and salt pits of Scotland were serfs in a full legal sense. They were bound for life to the mines and could be sold with the mine. They even wore a visible sign of their slavery in the shape of a collar, on which was engraved the owner's name.

Complaints of today's factory workers are little different from those echoed by English workers of the eighteenth century. Low wages, unemployment, long working hours, poor working conditions, are a few on the list of grievances. As a result, workers of various kinds banded together and a renewal of the town guilds, now more appropriately named *labor unions,* had their birth. Wool combers were among the first to succeed in organizing themselves. Their work was done by hand, required considerable skill, and there were few of them. These characteristics create favorable conditions in organizing an effective labor union.

The progress of industry and the development of commerce are closely interwoven and mutually influence each other. It was natural for England to try to protect her established textile industry from foreign competition. The extent of this protection seems brash indeed when at one point an effective economic blockade of Ireland was legalized by English law and a fleet of gun boats was deployed to assure success. But at the same time England found herself needing additional markets for her goods. The mercantilists who pushed for expanding exports with little imports were interested in building the gold supply; to them this was the most important source and indication of wealth. The realization that trading among various countries has many advantages to all was slow to develop. Exchange of goods among countries stimulates competition and search for new efficiencies in production. Free trade no longer requires commercial development to precede industrial progress. Development in transport enables the producer to increase the extent of his market beyond the known wants of a localized market.

It is difficult to summarize in a short space the evolution in industry during the period of time described as the Industrial Revolution. Its successive stages are bound together by barely perceptible changes, and the woolen industry has been used for purposes of illustration. First, it was in the hands and under the control of small, independent producers where family, home, and workshop were one and the same. Then followed industry carried on by merchant manufacturers with various degrees of production and marketing coordination. Finally, production was centralized into factories with more distinction between management and labor. As the fruits of the evolving system were reflected in increased output, market development and commercial expansion were necessitated outside of the home country. The disadvantages of attempting to protect home industries became evident and Britain had to adopt a policy advocating freer trade. The next chapter will continue this brief history of economic development, but the physical setting will be changed to the new world discovered in the Americas.

3

American economic development

Emigration from the Old World to the New was spurred principally by the love for adventure, the hope of material or financial gain, and the desire for political and religious liberty. The discovery of the Americas in 1492 opened a new pioneering era. The economic development of the New World was inevitable. Interest in sailing West soon rivaled the zeal to discover a waterway to Asia, and the return of the Spanish and Portuguese with gold and silver from the new lands spurred the race for colonization in the New World. While Spain, Portugal, and France preceded England in journeys to the New World, it was for the British to plant the first permanent settlement on what is now the eastern coastline of the United States.

COLONIAL AMERICA—1607 TO 1776

After peace was established between England and Spain around 1600, England was able to turn more attention to developing new colonies. While an earlier attempt had failed, the King of England granted a charter which created two joint-stock companies known as the London Company and the Plymouth Company in 1606. The main purpose of the companies was to make profits by exploiting the new lands. A second

aim was to carry Christianity to the Indians which would hopefully induce people to buy stock in the company out of a sense of Christian duty.
Stockholders were of two kinds; there were the "adventurers," who bought
shares and remained in England, and the "planters," who ventured to
the new land and who received stock for agreeing to "adventure his
person." Later a grant of 50 acres was given to each immigrant who paid
his way across the Atlantic. This procedure became the basis of the Virginia land system known as the "head right" system.

The first pioneers built a settlement on the James River and named
it Jamestown. While the area appeared lush with good land and wild
berries, extreme difficulties were faced as winter came and food supplies
were low because the settlers were not adept in the cultural practices
necessary to grow food in the new land. Despite food shortages and sickness Jamestown grew and prospered, with the result that Virginia became
the first of the royal colonies.

Soon after the establishment of Jamestown a group of discontented
Protestants called "Puritans" were granted rights to sail to the new world
and settle in the Virginia colony. On the voyage, the famous "Mayflower"
ran off course and landed her passengers on the shores of Cape Cod late
in 1620. With winter at hand the Pilgrims were fortunately forced to stay
in a quite desirable location. Native population had been destroyed by
the Plague and there was a satisfactory harbor, good water, and much
cleared land. Since they were far from the Virginia colony the men drew
up the "Mayflower Compact," forming a "civil body politic" where each
man pledged to submit to the will of the majority. Thus, the Plymouth
colony became a little republic with a remarkable democratic spirit. To
pay their debts to English capitalists who financed their trip, they established fishing stations and posts for trading with Indians on the New
England coast. Although half the settlers did not survive the first winter,
Plymouth Colony survived and gradually increased in stature.

Massachusetts Bay Colony was founded a decade after the Pilgrims
landed. It was successful and influential enough in its early development
for Massachusetts to be considered the mother colony. Connecticut soon
followed and the seventeenth century found the establishment of colonies
at virtually all points on the eastern coast of what is now the United
States.

Colonial agriculture

The two most important characteristics of colonial agriculture were
its self-sufficiency and the extensive nature of food production. Most of
the original "planters" were to continue the pursuit of agriculture in the
New World, both from experience and necessity. The occupation of farming offered the best prospect for a self-sufficing economy. However, to

retire English debts and pay English taxes it was also necessary to diversify production into those lines which would permit exports. New England possessed great advantages for the export of furs, fish, and lumber, while tobacco was a chief export item for the southern colonies.

Continuing in the European tradition, farmers lived in hamlets surrounded by arable fields. Few plows were used in the seventeenth century and tillage systems were crude. Most often the seed was poked into hills along with a herring for fertilizer, and cultivation was done with handmade tools. Stock raising was as unscientific as crop growing. The limited supply of arable land, the necessity to provide exports, and the proximity of the sea led to a rapid growth of the fishing industry.

The creation of one industry fostered the growth of others. Fishing prompted an industry of shipbuilding. The use of horse power in early agriculture spurred the trade of blacksmithing. Woodworking, spinning and weaving, and shoemaking trades grew to satisfy domestic requirements. Commercial development originated in much the same fashion as it did in Europe.

In the southern colonies of Virginia, Maryland, and the Carolinas, natural resources promoted a different type of economic activity. The tobacco industry fulfilled both domestic and export market needs. The supply of labor was even less adequate than in the New England colonies and indented servants were also more numerous. It was not until the eighteenth century that Negro slavery eclipsed indentured white servitude on the plantations. Large plantations owned by rich men were not characteristic of seventeenth-century Virginia.

Eighteenth-century development

Little westward expansion had taken place by 1700. However, inroads were beginning, particularly along the rivers. To the frontiersman most land was abundant and cheap and individuals could reap a harvest from all they could till without sharing with any landlord.

Natural resources were inherently productive, and as farmers employed improved crop production practices output of the native Indian crops increased. Even today about one half of the food produced in the United States comes from crops native to the land cultivated by the American Indian in a crude, inefficient manner.

A one-story house of logs was typical in this self-sufficient agriculture. It was unpainted and unheated except for a fireplace in the room which served as kitchen, dining and living room, and in cold weather as a bedroom. Homespun garments were the rule; books probably included only the Bible and almanac; and infrequent trips to town served as a social event as well as for trade.

The eighteenth century was also a period of rapid industrial development. The northern colonies of New England had a growing fishing industry and, with cheap lumber near at hand, shipbuilding became a principal item of manufacture. From New York and Philadelphia the furs, grain, and flour of the middle colonies went to markets in southern Europe and the West Indies. Among the non-English inhabitants were many mechanics who established small-scale manufacture of stoves, iron-work, glass, paper, and other similar products which exceeded that of either New England or Virginia and the southern colonies. In contrast to the commerce of the northern and middle colonies, the chief trade of the southern colonies was in tobacco, indigo, and rice and was carried on primarily with England.

The life of the interior frontiersmen contrasted sharply with those living on the coast. The coastal inhabitants welcomed the westward settlement of lands as a protection against Indians, but those in political power took care to keep the interior communities subordinate to the minority on the seaboard. The men of the back country did not meekly accept their position of inferiority and soon pushed to get more liberal and representative government.

During the first half of the eighteenth century France continued her explorations south from Canada into the vast interior along the Mississippi River. The fur trade was one of the principal incentives and the English watched French progress with jealous eyes. Rivalry between the French and English from Quebec to New Orleans was revealed in undercutting fur prices, minor skirmishes, and finally in war. By the treaties of Paris in 1763, France yielded Canada and all claims to territory east of the Mississippi River to Great Britain, with France retaining only two small islands of importance to fishermen in the St. Lawrence.

The original goals held by British mercantilists in promoting the colonization of the New World were not realized. The American colonies were never able to provide the quantity and kind of goods which would free England from dependence on other countries. However, in the attempt to exploit the American colonies, greater and greater controls were imposed which soon drove the colonists to rebellion. Additional coercive acts raised the ire of the colonists. A minor incident in April of 1775 in Lexington and Concord precipitated the Revolutionary War.

THE TRANSITION PERIOD—1776 TO 1865

The change from self-sufficient agriculture (Colonial period) to commercial agriculture (typical after the Civil War) took approximately one century and is called the Transition Period. As the United States was ushered into the company of nations upon victory against the British, Europeans looked cynically upon the new country and few believed that the feeble bonds of union would hold the states together for long. Virginia was first to frame a constitution, several weeks prior to the Declaration of Independence in 1776. Soon all thirteen colonies achieved statehood under a new federal government led by George Washington.

It was a demanding task to set up an economic and political structure not dependent on the British Crown. Economic self-sufficiency was necessary in the readjustment period since commerce with Europe was interrupted and trade boycotts were employed. In 1783 an act of Parliament renewed trade with the United States and the preference for British over French goods soon brought the United States and England into close trade relationships. By 1793 one-fifth of all British exports found their way to American shores.

Land policies

Notwithstanding all the political discontent and physical hardships, America was stirred to increase its population and expand into new areas at the close of the Revolution. Cessation of rights by states to land west of the Appalachians paved the way for an organized and planned settlement of the interior. The Ordinance of 1784 divided the whole region extending between these mountains and the Mississippi into 18 regions, which were to become states when their population equalled that of the smallest of the original states. The Land Ordinance of 1785 delineated the method for a system of surveys which became known as the "rectangular" system. By this method a "base line" was first laid out running due east and west. North and south across the base line, meridians were marked off at intervals of six miles. Similar lines at six-mile intervals were laid off parallel to the east-west base line, creating blocks of 36 square miles known as "townships." Each township was subdivided into square mile sections.

Besides the survey system, the Ordinance laid down the terms regarding land sales. Following an old New England practice, section 16 in each township was set aside for supporting schools and the remainder was to be sold at auction to the highest bidder in the minimum quantity of one section and at the minimum price of one dollar per acre. The public Treasury needed funds and urged Congress to deal with the public lands as a source of revenue. However, $640 was a considerable fortune for the poor frontiersmen who became the first settlers. Although Congress expected groups to purchase large plots of land, speculators were often the chief buyers at the auctions. Land sold very slowly under the Ordinance and eventually compelled the government to forego revenue in order to get the land settled. Private land ownership was the dominant aim of congressional land policy. After a series of plans offering liberalized credit had failed to promote private settlement, the historic Homestead Act was signed by Lincoln in 1862.

Under the Homestead Act a man would be given ownership of a tract of 160 acres (quarter section) if he would establish a home on it, attempt to improve its productivity, and stay five years. Under this act the penniless settler now had an incentive to settle the free land. Thousands quickly took advantages of the opportunity. While there were some who gained land title illegally by not meeting the requirements, the Homestead Act stands by itself as an historic landmark in national land policy. One needs only to look at other individual countries where private land ownership by the masses is not encouraged, to see the problems that arise.

A census map of 1830 shows a population of 13 million with all but three percent east of the Mississippi. With the purchase of the Louisiana Territory in 1803 and of Florida in 1819, the annexation of Texas in 1845, the Northwest Treaty of 1846, and the acquisition of Mexican Territory (California, Nevada, Utah, Arizona, and part of New Mexico) in 1848, present day boundaries of the United States were almost complete. Each succeeding decade saw successive waves of population move westward.

State of agriculture. The relative abundance of land contributed to wasteful use of land in the extensive agriculture. An observer said in Missouri in 1849, "Farming is here conducted on the regular skinning system . . . most of the farmers in this country *scratch* over a great deal of ground but *cultivate* none." [1] Handicapped by a lack of markets, the frontier farmer could easily support his family with food but had little incentive to produce commercially. The attempt to profit through land speculation and rising land values was often more dominant than through agricultural production.

In the South, where tobacco was the principal crop in the eighteenth century, a new competitor, cotton, had a meteoric rise in importance in the early 1800's. Mechanical inventions in cotton manufacture culminating with Eli Whitney's cotton gin in 1793 revolutionized the industry and opened vast new markets for raw cotton at home and abroad. The increasing importance of cotton also helped to open up the Southwest as prospective growers expanded westward in search of new rich soils, pushing Indians, Spaniards, and cattle ranchers ahead of them. By the period between 1850 and 1860, New Orleans had displaced Charleston and Savannah as the commercial center for cotton. Rice, sugar cane, and hemp were additional commercial crops produced in the southern states.

Further north, different problems were encountered as settlers pushed west. The tough prairie soil of the Midwest was first mistakenly

[1] *Cultivator,* New Series VI, 1849, p. 302.

thought not to be very rich and trees were relatively scarce to provide lumber for buildings. Soon however, it was learned that the soil and climate were adaptable to cereal grain production and to raising livestock.

Effect of industrial revolution

After the turn of the century the effects of the Industrial Revolution were beginning to transform New England into a manufacturing center. The urban population, constituting about a third of the total in New England by 1860, became dependent on the farmer and thus provided a market for food products.

In 1830, cities (New York was largest with 200,000) were practically without water systems, gas, electric lights, well-paved streets, paid fire departments, or effective police forces. Hardly two dozen miles of railroad had been constructed; it took 36 hours to go from Boston to New York by stage and steamboat and to go overland from Boston to California took as many months as it now takes days by train. Anthracite coal was beginning to be used as a fuel but coal stoves were a rarity and virtually no furnaces existed. However, by 1850 railroads were rapidly being built, gold had been discovered in California and helped to boost food prices, and farming was well on its way to becoming a scientific industry.

An improved plow in 1819, a mowing machine in 1831, and McCormick's reaper in 1834 were additional boosts in improving the productivity of the farming industry. Improved breeds of cattle were imported and knowledge of these superior breeds, new inventions, and improved tillage methods were disseminated by agricultural societies, fairs, schools, and farm periodicals.

Education. Public school education was in a generally deplorable condition. In the South, private family tutors provided the means of education for children of the rich but the common people were left without adequate instruction. Education was in a somewhat better condition in New England, but as late as 1940 nearly one person in twenty in the white adult population over 20 years of age was illiterate. In 1830, there were some 60 colleges, 400 instructors, and 5,000 undergraduate students.[2]

Agricultural education started with specialized instruction in existing schools. The first institution of a distinctive agricultural character was established at Gardner, Maine in 1822. The state of Michigan appropriated money for a state school of agriculture in 1850 followed by Maryland and Pennsylvania two years later. Congress passed the Morrill Act in 1862 which founded the land-grant college system, resulting in the establishment of at least one state-supported college in each state to be devoted to the development of the agriculture and mechanic arts. In the same year

[2] Statistics from the *American Almanac,* 1831.

the United States Department of Agriculture was established, although national aid to agriculture had begun in 1839 when a Patent Department was initiated to collect statistics and make investigations for the promotion of agriculture.

Agriculture in transition. In summarizing the state of agriculture in the Transition Period between the Revolutionary War and the Civil War, several crucial developments are apparent. One was the expansion of the farming area to encompass the Mississippi Valley, which made America one of the largest farming regions of the world. Another was the transition from self-sufficient agriculture to commercial agriculture. This change was spurred by the mechanization of farm production and by the Industrial Revolution, which created an urban population dependent upon the farmer for its food. Since the change was gradual, it is impossible to specify exactly when agriculture in America became "commercial," but it is generally accepted to be since the Civil War.

COMMERCIAL AGRICULTURE SINCE 1860

Volumes have been written on the significant industrial advances made in the last half of the nineteenth century which almost obscured agricultural developments of equal magnitude. Certainly the industrial and agricultural revolutions reinforced each other and it is impossible to separate many of the cause-and-effect relationships. The half century after 1860 saw the rapid adoption of newly invented agricultural machinery and scientific tillage methods. The interest of the national government has already been noted with the passage of the Homestead and Morrill Acts and the establishment of the United States Department of Agriculture. In this half century the number of farms increased from two to six million and over 500 million new acres of land were brought under cultivation. Even though expansion was great this period was characterized by farmer discontent and uncertainty. The Civil War had caused inflated prices and when these collapsed, the farmer in a debtor position was hurt.

The businesses engaged in the processing and distributing of food products were growing very large. Virtual monopolies in the meat-packing and milling industries were often able to hold farm prices artificially low on the buying side while profiting also by charging high prices to consumers. In addition, holders of patent monopolies were often able to overcharge the farmer for farm supplies. "There are three great crops raised in Nebraska," said one of the farmers' papers in 1890. "One is a crop of corn, one is a crop of freight rates, and one is a crop of interest. One is produced by the farmers who by sweating and toil farm the land.

The other two are produced by men who sit in their offices and behind their bank counters and farm the farmers." [3]

The feeling of bitterness over exploitation speeded the organization of farmer societies to unify farmer effort in alleviating this situation. The first of these groups organized in 1867 and was called the National Grange. It has persisted as a major farm group. The Grange promoted the development of cooperative buying and selling organizations and farmers' insurance companies. In 1887 Congress created the Interstate Commerce Commission to regulate trade among states, and in 1890 passed the Sherman Antitrust Act to prevent business from exercising monopoly powers on the public. The Pure Food and Drug Act in 1906 was another milestone in protecting the consuming public from unethical business practices.

In 1887 the passage of the Hatch Act established the Agricultural Experiment Stations in conjunction with the land-grant college system and provided funds for research on agricultural problems. However, it was not until 1914 and 1916 that the Smith-Lever and Smith-Hughes Acts were passed, the first establishing the Agricultural Extension Service and the second providing vocational agricultural training in high schools.

In general, the history of American agriculture until the turn of the century was chiefly the opening of new lands to food production. Farming was still primarily extensive in nature until just before World War I. With the turn of the century, increases in rural population and acreage of productive farm lands slowed down.

The twenty-five-year period before World War I has often been called the Golden Era. Total production increased some thirty percent and strong domestic and foreign demands made for the most prosperous quarter century for farmers in our history. The period from World War I to the present day is incorporated in Part VI, in which the federal government's participation in agriculture is discussed from a policy viewpoint.

---

[3] *Farmers Alliance*, August 23, 1890.

4

Role of natural resources in economic growth

Ask any junior high school student what factors make a country great and his reply is likely to be "natural resources." Natural resources can be divided into the general classifications of land, water, and minerals. Natural resources are distributed throughout the various parts of the world in a rather uneven fashion. For example, the small country of Malaysia produces one third of the world's tin. However, man has learned to stretch the supply of natural resources so they can be used almost anywhere in the world. Transportation facilities on both land and water facilitate resource distribution almost everywhere.

LAND

Excluding the new states of Hawaii and Alaska, the land area in the United States is 1,904 million acres.[1] Fortunately, however, the productivity of land depends not on its area but on man's ability to apply his labor, management, capital, and technology to it. More productive tech-

[1] The definition of "land area" in the United States includes land temporarily or partially covered by water: marshes and swamps, river flood plains, estuaries, streams and the like less than an eighth mile in width, and lakes and reservoirs covering less than 40 acres.

niques are rapidly being developed and there is every prospect that more will be forthcoming. This challenge is not easy, however. Adapting the use of our land to a dynamic civilization and to the increasing demands of a growing population will continue to tax the resourcefulness of man for all time.

Land is a resource base for virtually all kinds of production. Besides producing food, lumber, and other products from cropland, grasslands, and forests, land also provides space for the things man builds, such as cities, highways, airports, recreation areas, and schools. Although no two

TABLE 4-1: Land Utilization: United States, 1959.

Major Use	48 Contiguous States		All 50 States	
	Millions of acres[1]	Per-centage	Millions of acres[1]	Per-centage
Agricultural				
Cropland	457	24	458	20
Crops and related uses[2]	(391)	(21)	(392)	(17)
Used for pasture only	(66)	(3)	(66)	(3)
Pasture (excluding cropland pasture)	630[3]	33	633	28
Forest land[4]	614	32	746	33
Commercial	(488)	(26)	(530)	(23)
Noncommercial	(126)	(6)	(216)	(10)
Farmsteads, farm roads	10	1	10	5
Total agricultural	1711	90	1847	81
Nonagricultural				
Special-purpose uses	129	7	147	7
Urban and other built-up areas	53[6]	3	54[6]	3
Primarily for recreation or wildlife	47	2	62	3
Forest land[5]	(25)	(1)	(27)	(1)
Nonforest	(22)	(1)	(35)	(2)
Public installations and facilities	29	2	31	1
Miscellaneous land	191	10	424	19
Total land area	1902	100	2271	100

[1] Acreages rounded to nearest million.

[2] Cropland harvested, crop failures, cultivated summer fallow, soil improvement crops, and idle cropland.

[3] Open permanent pasture and range in the 48 contiguous states comprises 473 million acres and 157 million acres of federal grassland range used for grazing.

[4] Includes forested grazing land or range, including federal forest range used by permit. The combined acreage of forest land including areas limited primarily to recreation or wildlife use (the 25 and 27 million acres shown under special-use purposes and embracing reserved forest land in parks, wildlife refuges, wilderness, and related areas) totals 639 and 773 million acres in the 48 and 50 states respectively.

[5] Less than one percent.

[6] Rounding to the nearest million accounts for part of the difference between totals for the 48 and 50 states.

Source: U.S.D.A., "Land and Water Resources — A Policy Guide" (Washington, May 1962), Table 1, p. 9

pieces of land are exactly alike, many differences are small and can be changed by man. Air conditioning, heating, and electricity can alter the temperature or hours of light, bulldozers can alter topography, drainage and irrigation projects can modify water availability, and highway construction can change spatial relationships by reducing the time needed to get from one location to another.

In a free enterprise economy the uses of most land are determined by the market. Land use patterns in the United States are not the result of a centralized plan of allocating land sites to uses which might be best from a physical viewpoint. Cities are built on some of the most productive farm land and people try to raise crops on land that would perhaps be better used for grazing or recreation.

The potential uses of land and the resulting output of goods and services from it change with the passage of time, and while its physical location remains always the same, its location in an economic sense can change. As distances shrink from newer and faster modes of transportation, land areas expand in potentials. Today nearly all physically productive land in the United States can contribute products to an international market. As a result, land uses shift and the number of uses increase accordingly. The mobility of people with money to spend for travel now makes the land area of Yellowstone National Park accessible to many thousands of people and thus much more productive in terms of fees charged and output measured in recreation satisfaction. Its spatial relationship from an economic viewpoint has changed, as has its economic potential.

The United States encompasses six percent of the world's land area which lies almost wholly in the temperate zone, an area with climate favorable to most animals and plants. This land area has different population densities which range from 88,000 per square mile on Manhattan Island to 750 in Rhode Island, to less than two in Nevada and about .05 in Alaska. The average is 100 persons per square mile. Our concern will be principally with land use, however, since there is no necessary relationship between population density and the rate of economic growth experienced in an area.

Land use for food and fiber production

Land for food production is a key resource in view of feeding future populations even though we continually learn how to get a larger output per acre. One-fifth of the land in our fifty states is used as cropland; this was some 458 million acres in 1959. Another fourth of the land is pasture and range. The additions of Hawaii and Alaska as states increased the total land area by one-fifth with the largest increases in forest land and waste lands (Table 4-1).

TABLE 4-2: Major Classes of Land by Use and Ownership, 1959.

Ownership States	Cropland 48	Cropland 50	Grassland Pasture and Range 48	Grassland Pasture and Range 50	Forest Land 48	Forest Land 50	Special Use and Other Land 48	Special Use and Other Land 50	Total 48	Total 50
					(Millions of Acres)					
Federal	0.8	0.8	157.1	159.1	198.5[1]	323.9[1]	50.6	281.2	407.0	765.0
State and other public[2]	1.9	2.0	40.0	40.4	33.3	34.6	43.8	44.0	119.0	121.0
Private	454.3	454.8	433.0	433.5	406.7	414.3	81.8	82.7	1375.8	1385.3
Total	457.0	457.6	630.1	633.0	638.5	772.8	176.2	407.9	1901.8	2271.3
					(percent of use total)					
Federal	0.2	0.2	24.9	25.1	31.1[1]	41.9[1]	28.7	68.9	21.4	33.7
State and other public[2]	0.4	0.4	6.4	6.4	5.2	4.5	24.9	10.8	6.3	5.3
Private[3]	99.4	99.4	68.7	68.5	63.7	53.6	46.4	20.3	72.3	61.0
Total	100.0	100.0	100.0	100.0	100.0	100.0	100.0	100.0	100.0	100.0

[1] Includes reserved forest in parks and other special uses, and Indian forest.
[2] Excludes State grant land in process of transfer from the Federal public domain to the state of Alaska.
[3] Includes Indian cropland, pasture and range, special uses, and other land.
Source: U.S.D.A., "Land and Water Resources – A Policy Guide" (Washington, May 1962), Table 3, p. 12

Even though the percentages of acreage in cropland, grassland pasture, and range have not changed much, there have been marked changes in land use. Particular strides forward are evident in the improvement of land for crops and grassland pastures due to drainage systems, flood control, irrigation, and brush clearing. Substantial shifts have occurred among regions. Cropland is concentrated on fertile, more level areas while grass and trees are generally planted on hilly land subject to erosion.

Virtually all of the cropland is in private ownership. Of the total land area in the 48 states, 72.3 percent was privately owned in 1959, 6.3 percent was owned by state and municipal governments, and 21.4 percent by the federal government. Most of the public domain land is in the new state of Alaska and when all 50 states are included, the percentage of the total land owned privately is reduced to 61 percent. About one-half of the forest land and about one-third of the grassland pasture and range is owned by the federal government (Table 4-2).

Cropland used for crops. The physical acreage from which crops were harvested was nearly the same in 1960 as in 1900. But since the average acre yield in 1960 was two-thirds greater than in 1900, the equivalent increase in the land supply for crops was nearly 250 million acres. In addition, over the same period the substitution of machine power for animal power on farms released some 80 million acres for nonfeed uses. By 1960 less than two percent of the cropland used for crops was needed to provide feed for horses and mules, as compared to 25 percent needed in 1920. Since 1942 the increase in total farm output has been more rapid than the increase in population.

Cropland harvested in 1961 was just under 300 million acres, a decline of 16 percent since 1949. Acreage in irrigated crops increased 28 percent or eight million acres during the same period. There is considerable regional variation in land use within the United States. The Corn Belt, Mountain, and Pacific States show increasing acreages in cropland while all the others have declined. Over one-half (fifty-seven percent) of the total land area in the Corn Belt States is in cropland while the Mountain States contain only eight percent. In the Southeast, 63 percent of the land area is in forest and woodland as opposed to only three percent in the Northern Plain States.

Cropland used for pasture and soil improvement. In 1960 one acre of every six of cropland was used for pasture. Cropland in pasture is estimated to be five to six times more productive than the average for all grassland pasture.

Spurred by the Conservation Reserve and Feed Program legislation, about 53 million acres of cropland (11.6 percent) were used in soil improvement crops that were neither harvested nor pastured. The Conservation Reserve began in 1957, and some 28 million acres have been in the program every year since. Of this total, 25 million acres were in soil im-

TABLE 4-3: Distribution of Cropland Use in the United States by Major
Crops, 1950 to 1959, 1960, and Projections for 1980 and 2000.

Use	1950-59[1]	1960[1]	1980[2]	2000[2]
		(Percent)		
Feed grains	29.6	28.4	23.6	26.3
Wheat	11.9	9.8	7.2	8.4
Cotton	4.0	3.4	3.4	4.2
Soybeans	3.8	5.1	7.7	9.2
Hay	15.7	14.8	20.9	24.8
All other crops[3]	6.0	5.1	5.8	6.5
Total crops harvested	71.0	66.6	68.6	79.4
Cropland pasture	14.9	16.8	16.0	12.2
Total crops and pasture	85.9	83.4	84.6	91.6
Fallow, idle, failure	12.8	11.7	9.6	8.4
Excess cropland acreage[4]	1.3	4.9	5.8	——
Total Cropland	100.0	100.0	100.0	100.0

[1] Historical data for crops based upon U.S.D.A., *Crop Production, Annual Summary*, 1960, 1961.
  Pasture, fallow, etc., and total cropland are estimates based upon Census of Agriculture 1950, 1954.
[2] See Table A 18-9 (in source below).
[3] Includes fruits and nuts.
[4] Obtained as residual.
SOURCE: Hans H. Landsberg and others, *Resources in America's Future* (Baltimore: The Johns
  Hopkins Press, 1963), Adapted from Table A 18-8, p. 987. Published for Resources for
  the Future, Inc.

provement crops and three million were planted to trees. The remaining
25 million acres in 1961 were in the feed-grain program which provided
for voluntary reduction of corn and grain sorghum acreage.

Use of cropland by individual crops. Feed grains were raised on 28.4
percent of the cropland in 1960. Wheat acreage accounted for one acre
in ten, and hay one acre in seven. Soybeans have increased rapidly during
recent years (5.1 percent in 1960) and output is expected to double by
the year 2000. Acreages of wheat, feed grains, and cotton are expected to
decline relatively to 1980, then increase at the expense of cropland pasture
(Table 4-3).

Yields per harvested acre showed no major increases until 1940
when gains were registered in most crops. Medium projections for the
year 2000 predict percentage gains for wheat, corn, cotton, and hay yields
per harvested acre to be 41, 88, 79, and 70 percent respectively over the
figures for 1960 (Table 9-11).

Pasture and range (grazing land)

Of the 878 million acres in total pasture and range in the United
States in 1959, 72 percent is considered grassland and range while 28
percent is classified as forest, woodland pasture, and range. Of the 243

million acres of federal range, 92 percent is used by permit and the remaining eight percent is under leases. Most of the land grazed by permit is in national forests and grazing districts.[2]

Grazing takes place on many kinds of land. In the majority of cases there is little incentive for the individual to increase the productivity of grazing land, particularly if the land grazed is owned by someone else. Therefore, even though range acreage is large it produces only about one-third of the livestock feed. Most of the grazing lands are in the Mountain and Pacific States where federal range is a vital element in livestock production. For purposes of comparison, 160 million acres of average western land provide approximately the same number of feed units per acre per year as eight million cropland pasture acres or only three million acres of corn.

Permanent farm pasture land is of greater importance for the future because this category holds the greatest hope of increasing yields per acre. The 474 million acres of privately owned grassland pasture and range were equivalent to about 80 feed units produced per acre.[3] If yields were doubled, which is considered a definite possibility, the equivalent of 80 million acres of cropland pasture would be added to the farm economy.

Projections of farming uses for land [4]

By the year 2000, total cropland needed by the United States will be 418 million acres (Table 4-4). This projection assumes that sources of plant foods from yeast cultures or the ocean will not be important contributors to total output although the success of new technologies is difficult to predict. After consideration is given for roughage needs and yield increases, medium projections indicate that cropland available may be about six million acres short of combined pasture and crop requirements by the year 2000 (Table 4-4).

Land used for forestry

The North American continent has a much greater and richer variety of forest species and types than any other part of the temperate world regions. There are over 100 native conifer and hardwood species compared to less than a dozen such in Europe. The virgin forests were a

---

[2] Hugh H. Wooten and others, "Major Uses of Land and Water in the United States," Agricultural Economic Report No. 13, U.S.D.A., E.R.S. (Washington, D.C.: July, 1962), pp. 7-8.

[3] Hans H. Landsberg and others, *Resources in America's Future* (Baltimore: The Johns Hopkins Press, 1963), p. 349. Published for Resources for the Future, Inc.

[4] Medium projection. See Hans H. Landsberg and others, *op. cit.*, Chapter 18.

TABLE 4-4: Projected Needs in the United States for Land Use in Future Selected Years Compared to 1960.

	1960	1970	1980	1990	2000
	Land Required, (Millions of Acres)[1]				
Feed grains	133.6	102.6	109.6	118.4	124.6
Wheat	45.8	35.1	34.3	36.4	39.5
Cotton	15.7	15.4	16.4	17.8	19.9
Soybeans	24.3	30.2	36.3	41.2	44.0
Hay	67.6	82.5	97.8	110.4	118.3
Total for above crops	287.0	266.0	294.4	324.2	346.3
Total cropland harvested[2]	313.0	290.0	323.0	353.0	378.0
Crop failure, idle, fallow	55.0	50.0	45.0	43.0	40.0
Total cropland required	368.0	340.0	368.0	396.0	418.0
Acreage in excess of requirements based on 470 million acres of cropland	102.0	130.0	102.0	74.0	52.0
	(Billions of Feed Units)[3]				
Roughage required from pasture	241	254	287	306	317
Roughage available from pasture other than cropland	144	155	165	181	193
Roughage required from cropland pasture	97	99	122	125	124
	(Feed Units Per Acre)[3]				
Cropland pasture yield	1230	1410	1620	1830	2120
	(Millions of Acres)				
Cropland pasture required	79	70	75	68	58
Cropland in excess or short of combined crop and pasture requirements	23	60	27	6	− 6

[1] Based on medium assumptions for both demand and yields. See Chapter 18 of reference below for explanation.
[2] Equivalent to 109% of 5 crop total, based upon historical records.
[3] A feed unit has the "feeding efficiency" of one pound of corn, and will vary from animal to animal.
Source: Hans H. Landsberg and others, *Resources in America's Future* (Baltimore: The Johns Hopkins Press, 1963), pp. 979, 980, 982. Published for the Resources for the Future, Inc.

natural resource estimated to have contained 7,500 billion board feet of timber. Only about one-fourth of this timber remained in 1960.[5]

Commercial forestry. Three-fourths of the total forest land in the United States is considered commercial. Commercial forest lands amounted to 525,500, and 484 million acres respectively in 1900, 1920,

[5] Marion Clawson and others, *Land for the Future* (Baltimore: The Johns Hopkins Press, 1960), p. 281. Published for Resources for the Future, Inc.

and 1950.[6] Thirty-six percent of the land is in the North, 39 percent in the South, and 24 percent in the West. In 1953 there were some 2,057 billion cubic feet of live saw timber available in all regions, 80 percent of which was softwoods. Another 517 billion cubic feet were in growing stock. Virtually all timber in the Mountain, Pacific States and Alaska are softwoods, while hardwoods comprise 80 percent of the total in the Northern states. The South has about half hardwood and half softwoods. Nearly two-thirds of the forest land in the 48 states is privately held— slightly over half when 50 states are included.

The amount of land devoted to commercial forestry in the future is expected to remain relatively stable at slightly under 500 million acres. Whether there will be sufficient timber to meet the country's needs will depend upon its productivity per acre. To date, the productivity status of much forest land is far below its potential but management practices of farmers and commercial loggers have materially improved since 1950.

Use of noncommercial forest land. About one-fourth of the forest lands are used for noncommercial purposes, principally recreation and wildlife enhancement. Approximately 27 million acres of forest land in the 50 states (2 million acres are in Hawaii and Alaska) are in parks, wildlife refuges, and wilderness areas.[7]

Urban uses of land [8]

For those living in Los Angeles or New York City it may seem as though cities are rapidly eating up the land area in the United States. With 70 percent of the population living on 1 percent of the land area, the United States is now essentially an urban economy. This situation has an important effect on land use patterns.

A city uses land directly for its physical occupancy area, indirectly for transport and water supply, and usually demands some land area for recreational purposes. The urban population was estimated to occupy some 11 million acres in 1950, but total land reported by incorporated cities of populations over 2,500 includes 13 million acres. Total area withdrawn for city use was estimated to be 17 million acres or just less than one percent of the total land area in the United States, excluding Hawaii

---

[6] Originally, there were some 830 million acres of what would now be called commercial forest land in the area now included in the United States. Of the timber volume standing when the white man landed, some 10 percent is left in the East and about two-thirds in the West.

[7] Hugh H. Wooten and others, *op. cit.*, p. 2.

[8] Marion Clawson and others, *op. cit.*, p. 95. Their estimates show that perhaps one-third of the land within city boundaries is idle, particularly in the smaller cities. This land is held for expansion purposes and is often used quite uneconomically. From a land use viewpoint, the total land withdrawn from alternative uses is the more important criterion.

and Alaska. By 1980 and 2000 a medium projection estimates land withdrawn for urban use to climb to 30 and 41 million acres respectively. As a nation we take about one million acres per year permanently out of any farm production potential for urban development. An additional 10 million acres will likely be needed for transportation use, recreation use, and water control by cities.

Special uses of land

Recreation. Recreation is a rapidly expanding industry in the United States where per capita incomes are rising and working hours per week are declining. There is no evidence that the trend will be reversed.

Of the land area in national forests, some 14 million acres were estimated to be primarily used for recreation purposes in 1956. In addition, all of the land in the national park system (24.4 million acres) is set aside for recreation; there are an additional 5.1 million acres in state parks and 700 thousand acres in municipal parks. TVA reservoirs add an additional 200 thousand acres, and Corps of Engineer reservoirs contribute another 3.3 million acres to recreational oriented land areas. Hunting and fishing pursuits occur on many additional lands.[9] Estimates are that the total demand for outdoor recreation by the year 2000 will be five to fifteen times greater than it was in 1956.[10]

Transportation. Although small in terms of total volume of land required, transportation uses are highly specialized and can easily preempt other uses of land. Railroad rights-of-way now use about eight million acres and although freight volume may increase, improved efficiences will probably allow the increase to be carried on existing trackage. Highways for automobiles now occupy some 16 million acres. This amount of land is estimated to increase by an additional three million acres by the end of the century. Airports and landing strips occupy nearly 1.5 million acres, a figure which may double by the year 2000. Total land needed for transportation uses will be in the neighborhood of 30 million acres by 2000.[11]

Wildlife refuges. While man shares all his land with birds and animals, certain areas are set aside strictly for wildlife refuges. About 15 million acres are now given over for wildlife uses and an additional five million acres may be added by the year 2000. The latter will be principally wetlands used for the benefit of waterfowl.[12]

Water reservoirs. Some 12 million acres in the United States have been inundated by dam-created storage reservoirs or artificial lakes. With

[9] *Ibid.*, p. 150.
[10] *Ibid.*, p. 186
[11] *Ibid.*, pp. 421-422.
[12] *Ibid.*, pp. 427-430.

increased demand for water for consumer and industrial uses, almost another eight million acres will be covered by the end of the century.[13]

Other miscellaneous uses. The remainder of the land area not covered in the preceding discussion is in mineral production, sand dunes, bare rock, deserts, mountain tops, and swamps. These uses comprised about six percent of the total area in 1960, but will decline as land is reclaimed or adapted to other more productive uses in the future.

Multiple uses of land

Throughout the preceding discussion land has been classified and discussed with reference to its primary use. Some land serves two purposes well, such as wildlife and recreation, forestry and recreation, or farm land and hunting. Urban land serves the varied interests of its residents.[14]

WATER

Water is a vital element to virtually all production processes. Too little or too much water in the soil severely limits plant life. Other water uses on farms include stock watering, sanitation, spraying, drinking, and fire protection. Industry is increasing its demands for water each year and the human consumption demand for water will be intensified by the continuing rise in population, outdoor recreation, and growth of cities.

Approximately 300 billion gallons of fresh water were used daily in homes, factories, steam generating plants, or on irrigated farm land in 1960. Other large quantities are utilized without being withdrawn from their natural habitat for such purposes as boating, swimming, supporting inland navigation, turning generators of hydroelectric plants, carrying wastes, and providing scenery. Total use is expected to double by 1980.

The water from rainfall and that which already exists in oceans, lakes, rivers, and streams constitutes the natural resource of water. Using water in various ways to improve its efficiency in production processes converts water from a free good to an economic good.

Two characteristics of water demand present unique problems. The first is a quality problem. Some uses of water affect the acceptability of water for other uses. Stream pollution from toxic home and industry waste products drastically reduces the demand for the resulting polluted water. Continued high demand for fresh water, however, has led to many technical refinements in overcoming water pollution in streams and lakes.

[13] *Ibid.,* pp. 422-424.
[14] For a table depicting the physical compatibility for all possible combinations see Marion Clawson and others, *op. cit.,* p. 449, Table 52.

A second unique characteristic of water is the significance of its regional distribution. The commercial value of water is relatively low because its physical characteristics make transport costly over long distances except in times of emergency. One region of the country may experience severe limitations of economic activity because of a water shortage while other regions may have large quantities of fresh water flowing into the ocean. Therefore, to think in terms of a national market for water or of supply and demand for water on a national basis, is of limited significance.

The overall water picture in the United States

Water supply originates with rain and snow. If the quantity falling on the United States in an average year were spread evenly, it would stand about 30 inches deep. Seventy percent (21 inches) returns to the atmosphere via evapo-transpiration—a part of which supports cultivated crops, forests, and native grasses. The remaining nine inches constitute the manageable water supply. In the 1950's three inches of the manageable supply was withdrawn for use, one inch of which returned to the atmosphere and two inches of which returned to the stream network. The other six inches of manageable supply simply flowed into the ocean via the streams and rivers.[15]

Annual precipitation varies widely within the United States. Arizona, Nevada, and New Mexico receive an average of less than 10 inches per year while Alabama, Louisiana, and Alaska receive over 50 inches annually.[16] The run-off from rain and snow, or manageable water supply, varies with the amount of precipitation. The East has a relatively high average annual run-off of 14.7 inches per year and accounts for seventy-two percent of the run-off in the country. For the most part, the rainfall is fairly well distributed so that crops can be cultivated without irrigation. The West, composed primarily of arid and semi-arid regions comprising over half of the total geographic region, averages only 2.3 inches per year of run-off. This amount is only sixteen percent of the average run-off for the country. Most of the run-off originates at high altitudes from snow. In the Pacific Northwest the run-off averages 11.7 inches per year, constituting 12 percent of the country's run-off.[17]

The use made of water is related both to population density and kind of use. For example, more water is used in the heavily populated Ohio River region than in the less populated Missouri River region, even though the latter has four times as much land area. Some uses consume

[15] U.S. Senate Select Committee an National Water Resources, 86th Cong., 2nd sess., Committee Print No. 3, "National Water Resources and Problems" (Washington, D.C.: Gov't. Printing Off.), pp. 3-4.
[16] *World Almanac*, published annually by the *New York World-Telegram*.
[17] Hans H. Landsberg and others, *op. cit.*, p. 380.

more water than others. Boating, for example, consumes no water during use but irrigation may evaporate 60 percent of the water used. Industry on the other hand, requires huge volumes of water but evaporation claims about only two percent of it. Water is used primarily for irrigation in the West and for industry in the East.

For purposes of discussing the various kinds of demands for water, three classes of demands will be considered: (a) withdrawal uses in which water is actually removed from sources of supply, (b) flow uses, such as hydropower generation, recreation, and waste carrying, and (c) on-site uses, such as maintenance of wetlands for wildlife habitat and land treatment measures for soil conservation.[18]

Withdrawal uses of water

There are four principal categories of withdrawal uses of water. These include municipal, industrial, thermal-electric power, and irrigation uses. Of very minor importance in terms of volume is the water withdrawn from rural household supplies, livestock watering, and mining operations. As noted earlier, withdrawal amounts to three inches (ten percent) of average annual precipitation in the United States, of which less than one-half is actually consumed or used up. The remainder is returned to streams.

Municipal use. Only five percent of total water withdrawn is for municipal uses. This amounted to some 14 billion gallons per day in 1960 and included water used by urban residents for washing, cooking, drinking, lawn watering, and air cooling. These uses averaged about 60 gallons per capita per day in 1960.

Residential use is influenced mostly by income levels, climate, and use of household devices. Pronounced regional differences occur resulting from differences in climate, size of city, degree of industrialization, and many other factors. States having high temperatures with relatively low rainfall show higher per capita usages due to such factors as air conditioning and lawn watering.

Commercial and industrial uses accounted for 65 gallons per capita per day in 1960, of which 26 gallons were supplied to commercial establishments connected to public supply systems. Another 25 gallons per capita per day go for purely municipal public uses like street cleaning and fire protection.

Total municipal needs in the future are difficult to estimate. Exclud-

---

[18] A classification system developed by Nathaniel Wallman who was a staff member of Resources for the Future 1959-60 while on leave from the University of New Mexico. The following discussion draws heavily from Hans H. Landsberg and others, *op. cit.*, Chapter 14, pp. 258-276. Also Senate Select Committee on National Water Resources, *op. cit.*, Committee Print No. 7.

ing industrial use of municipal supplies, some evidence suggests that per capita requirements may diminish owing to the increasing prevalence of apartment living and other multi-family dwellings. On the other hand, further increases in the use of automatic appliances, air conditioning units, and swimming pools suggest much higher per capita uses. Assuming a population of 330 million by 2000 and current per capita usage rates, the total municipal requirement by 1980 and by 2000 could be 29 and 43 billion gallons per day, respectively.

Industrial use. Since 94 percent of the industrial use of water is for cooling, industry is largely a nonconsumptive user of water. In addition, saline water can be used for about one-sixth of the cooling processes in industry. Most cooling water is discarded after one using, but some industries, such as petroleum, recirculate water an average of four times.

In 1960, manufacturing establishments were using about 78 billion gallons per day. The primary effect of industry use of water is the degradation of quality as effluents are discharged with the water, giving rise to waste carriage and other disposal problems. Six major groups use over 60 percent of the total water used by industry. These include in order of importance: iron and steel, chemicals, pulp and paper, food products, aluminum, and copper—the first three accounting for 90 percent of the six industry total. Since new technology tends to reduce water needs in some industries (e.g. substitution of air for water cooling in petroleum industry) while others are expanding their water needs, making water use projections is difficult. However, an eight-fold increase in water usage by the six principal industries is quite likely by the year 2000.[19]

Thermal-electric power use. Thermal-electric power generation was using water at a rate of 89 billion gallons per day in 1960. This use was second only to irrigation. Virtually all water used for steam-electric generation is for condenser cooling, and although more electric power is developed with steam than with hydropower, the latter requires more water. Both have little effect on water supply since the temperature of the water is all that is changed.

About one-fifth of the water used for thermal-electric cooling is recirculated. The main factors determining whether or not water is recirculated are the relative costs of water and of additional equipment. Saline water is used as a substitute for fresh water for cooling purposes particularly in coastal regions, but high-priced noncorrosive equipment is needed. In 1954 saline water represented 20 percent of total use. Water needs for thermal-electric power generation by the year 2000 may increase four times over the 1960 level.

Irrigation use. Irrigation is the largest use of fresh water (121 billion

---

[19] Senate Select Committee on National Water Resources, *op. cit.,* Committee Print No. 8.

gallons per day in 1960). Irrigated land in farms increased from some 15 million acres in 1929 to nearly 35 million acres by 1960, about one acre in twelve. In the 17 western states there were 25.7 million acres of irrigated land in 1960; 80 percent of the total water withdrawn for irrigation was used on this land. Half of the irrigated cropland was used for livestock feeds (hay, sorghum, corn, oats, and other grains), with the major part in hay and pasture land. Small gains (wheat, rice, and barley) account for 16 percent with the remaining one-third in tree fruits, vegetables, potatoes, vineyards, cotton, seeds, and sugar beets.

In the other 31 states located in the more humid areas, only 2.3 million acres were irrigated in 1959; 1.3 million acres were in the Delta States of Mississippi, Arkansas, and Louisiana where rice, cotton, and soybeans are major crops. In the Eastern states, high-value specialty crops such as vegetables, citrus, potatoes, tobacco, berries, and nursery crops predominate on irrigated lands.

Irrigated acreage in the East (using a medium projection) is expected to increase to 6.2 million acres by 1980 and to 9.6 million acres by 2000. Projections for the West are 34.2 and 43.2 million acres, respectively, for 1980 and 2000. Total water requirements would advance to 135 and 170 billion gallons per day for 1980 and 2000, and increase 11 and 41 percent, respectively, over 1960 usage levels. There is little doubt that irrigation use will continue as a major demand for fresh water.

Flow uses of water

Quantitative analysis of flow uses is exceedingly more difficult than of withdrawal uses since a stream or lake often has a multi-purpose use. The principal flow uses include hydroelectric power, navigation, provision of habitat for aquatic life and fishing, swimming and boating, and waste carriage and disposal.

Hydroelectric power. Flowing water has been used as a source of power for many centuries. Hydro-capacity doubled from 1950 to 1960 but output of electricity increased only 50 percent. The share that hydropower contributes to total power will likely decline in the future, from about 18 percent in 1960 to approximately 8 percent in 2000, even though capacity and output generated will continue to rise.

Navigation use. Inland waterways were important arteries of commerce and communication which were developed early in the nation's history and then declined in relative importance due to the advent of railroads and the telephone. Since World War II waterway navigation has experienced a major comeback. Ton miles per year increased 500 percent each year from 1940 to 1957. Successful navigation requires certain minimum water levels in the channel. Of the 20,153 miles of commercial inland waterways in use in 1960, 65 percent were over 9 feet in depth and 33 percent were over 12 feet.[20] The federal government has improved over 90 percent of the inland waterways in recent years.

Petroleum and petroleum products, bituminous coal and lignite, sand, gravel, and crushed rock account for over 70 percent of the tonnage carried. Waterways carrying over 3 million ton-miles per mile of waterway annually make up about one-third of the total miles of waterway.[21] For purposes of comparison, the average main-line railroad carried about 2½ ton-miles of freight per mile of road in 1957.[22]

Aquatic life habitats and water recreation. Principal flow uses of water in lakes and streams are the maintenance of aquatic life and the provision of recreation in the form of boating, swimming, and fishing. Present water recreation facilities are generally overcrowded and national park visits are expected to increase by the years 1980 and 2000 three times and over six times, respectively, above the 1959 level of 63 million visits. With one third of all households having one or more members who engage in hunting and fishing and with family incomes higher and more leisure time available, the demand for water for wildlife and recreation will increase rapidly. The demand for total outdoor recreation is estimated to increase ten times between the years 1960 and 2000. Maintenance of water quality will do much to aid in preserving adequate waters for recreational uses.

Waste disposal use. Water is needed for waste disposal primarily to dilute the waste material so that its harmful effects are diminished. Waste disposal is an extremely complex problem. Many kinds of pollutants get into water courses. Sediment from soil erosion, agricultural pesticides washed off fields, chlorides for ice control washed off highways, salt leached from the soil by irrigation water, organic wastes from households, and both organic and inorganic compounds from industry are some of the more important examples. Warm water returned to streams after its use for cooling purposes may speed up the metabolism of microbes and facilitate more rapid breakdown of organic wastes but it also has harmful effects on fish, as the oxygen saturation level is lowered. However, the major problem of water pollution continues to arise from organic wastes from homes and industries.

The ability of a stream to handle waste materials depends on the quantity of flow, rate of flow, temperature, and chemical content. Another important variable is the extent to which waste is treated before being discharged into the streams. A measure used for the organic pollution

[20] Waterways of less than nine feet in depth are essentially antiquated for commercial uses.

[21] Senate Select Committee on National Water Resources, *op. cit.*, Committee Print No. 11.

[22] Annual Reports of U.S. Interstate Commerce Commission: "Transport Statistics in the United States, Part 1, Railroads."

load is Biochemical Oxygen Demand (BOD) which indicates the rate at which dissolved oxygen is used up in waste-receiving water. The U.S. Public Health Service estimates that waste loads from municipalities and industries prior to any treatment will increase from 304 million population equivalents of BOD in 1954 to 894 million population equivalents in 2000.[23] Laws vary widely with regard to the discharge of wastes into streams, but regulation of stream flow to provide more water during low flow periods is considered to be the least costly means of supplementing waste treatment measures to maintain water quality for most areas.

On-site uses of water

On-site uses are of two principal kinds: the provision of wetlands and swamps for wildlife habitat, and the provision of farm ponds and other soil conservation measures. Swamps and wetlands deplete water supplies through evapo-transpiration. Farm ponds slow water run-off.

Waterfowl require wet and marshy lands with many small ponds to maintain their populations. Future needs of these lands will increase as the population of hunters increases. Most waterfowl are migratory. This means that satisfactory environmental conditions are required on both ends of their migration. The United States has several major flyways (East Coast, Mississippi Valley, and West Coast) that run from Canada to Mexico and the Caribbean. There have been major efforts to protect winter and summer nesting and feeding areas in these countries and along the flyways.

Soil conservation practices have been a major federal program since the 1930's. With federal assistance the number of farm ponds have increased rapidly to aid in watering stock, retarding erosion, and for recreation purposes. Ponds deplete only modest quantities of water and do not constitute a major use of fresh water.

A summary of the water demand outlook

Demand on fresh water will continue to increase simply from increases in population and industrial activity. However, the demand is intensified because of the boom in outdoor recreation and by the need to dilute an increasing amount of organic wastes. The latter use constitutes a relatively new problem since only fairly recently has the concentration of people and industry pushed pollution beyond the point of tolerance for most communities. Although irrigation will continue as the major

[23] U.S. Senate Select Committee on National Water Resources, *op. cit.*, Committee Print No. 9. One "population equivalent" is the amount of BOD exerted, on the average, by the domestic organic wastes generated by one individual.

source of water depletion, municipal and industrial uses will rise. Net loss
from withdrawal uses is likely to double the 1960 levels by the year 2000.

MINERAL RESOURCES

Minerals differ from land and water as natural resources in that they
are not only exhaustible but are also not reproducible. It has been noted
how man can rejuvenate worn out soil and develop reservoirs to capture
more water, but man participates only in the exhaustion of minerals.
Mere existence of huge mineral deposits does not in itself assure a high
rate of economic development. It is knowledge in utilizing minerals
which lays the foundation for progress. An appropriate example is the
Indians who occupied the area that is now the United States and received
relatively little benefit from the minerals deposited in the area.

Mineral resources can be classified in several ways. Metallic and
nonmetallic, or basic and contributory, are two classifications.[24] Basic
minerals include coal, iron, and copper. Among the contributory minerals
the ferro-alloys, particularly chromium, nickel, molybdenum, and manga-
nese are important. Although used in small proportions, they improve the
character of iron and steel. Other contributory minerals, especially plat-
inum, function as catalysts in chemical synthesis. Petroleum and natural
gas serve to supplement coal as a source of energy. The importance of
energy derived from coal is rapidly declining. Nuclear power may also
soon compete favorably as an energy fuel.

The fertilizer minerals (potash, phosphate, and nitrate) form another group. The precious metals are in a class by themselves because
they are valued chiefly as the basis of our currency.

The three major classes considered here will be mineral fuels, metals,
and nonmetallic nonfuel minerals. In terms of expendability, the mineral
fuels of coal, oil, and natural gas are essentially used up. This is in contrast to metals which have some degree of salvage value after use. Nonmetallic nonfuel minerals are also for the most part expendable.

Mineral fuels [25]

Heat and power requirements for homes, industry, and commercial
establishments accounted for 19.9, 20.2, and 8.5 percent of the energy requirements in the economy, respectively, in 1960. Transportation claimed

[24] Metallic minerals include aluminum, antimony, chromite, copper, iron, lead, manga-
nese, mercury, nickel, tin, tungsten, and zinc. Nonmetallic minerals include asbes-
tos, barite, cluna clay, coal, fluor spar, graphite, gypsum, magnesite, mica, nitrate,
petroleum, phosphate, potash, pyrites, sulphur, talc, and soapstone.
[25] Data taken from Hans H. Landsberg and others, *op. cit.*, pp. 184, 277-292, 388-421.

another 20.2 percent and the remainder of 16.2 percent was distributed among other public uses. Potential natural fuel sources are coal, oil, and natural gas. These natural fuels plus hydro water power are used in the production of electricity, as intermediate products vital as an energy source in homes, industry, and commercial uses. Of the total consumption, electricity accounted for about 20 percent of the total and consumed fuels for the remaining 80 percent in 1960.

Coal. Coal resources of the United States are in the order of 1.7 trillion tons.[26] With the projected demand over the 40-year period 1960 to 2000, at 25 to 35 billion tons, it is clear that coal reserves are more than adequate, providing a cushion capable of absorbing large chunks of industrial energy demand should gas and oil use become limited. The bulkiness of coal makes transport costly, increasing total cost an average of 70 percent over the value at the mine. This transport cost factor encourages electric generating plants using coal to be located near the mining area, although the contruction of pipelines to carry a slurry of coal and water over relatively long distances permits generating plants to be located several hundred miles away from their sources of fuel.

In 1960 one-half of the coal mined was used for electric power generation. Also, coal comprised 50 percent of the total energy sources used in electricity production. Coal is expected to decline in relative importance in all end uses (residential, commercial, industrial, and public), and by 1980 and 2000 is expected to provide only 19.9 and 13.3 percent, respectively, of the total source of energy (Table 1 5).

Oil. Throughout the 1950's annual crude oil production in the United States was between 2.0 and 2.5 billion barrels. Oil reserves are established mainly by inference and the commonly used quantitative measure is "proved reserves" which have averaged about 12 times ordinary annual production for some time.[27] The figure of 12 years is about the average life expectancy of a new well and companies tend to gear their exploration activities to maintain about 12 years of reserves. Therefore, the figure is erroneous if used to indicate the potential supply of oil remaining as a natural resource. Estimates of oil awaiting future recovery or potential availability range up to 500 billion barrels. The percent of this amount that will be recoverable is largely dependent upon advances in technology, but a recovery figure of between 50 and 60 percent is not unreasonable to expect in the future even though current recovery is nearer one-third. About 20 percent of total oil used in the United States is imported. This situation will likely continue.

[26] See U.S. Geological Survey Bulletin 1136 and Department of Interior Report to Joint Committee on Atomic Energy, Vol. 4, of *Review of the International Atomic Policies and Programs of the United States* (2 McKinney Report), Joint Committee Print, 86th Congress, 2nd session, October, 1960.

[27] From Committee on Petroleum Reserves, 1961 Report to the American Petroleum Institute, March 10, 1961.

TABLE 4-5: Changes in Energy Service Patterns, 1940, 1960, and Medium Projections for 1980 and 2000.

	1940	1960	1980	2000
		(Quadrillion BTU's)		
Coal	13.0	11.1	15.8	18.0
Oil	8.2	17.7	29.5	54.8
Natural gas	3.4	13.2	24.2	33.9
Natural gas liquids	0.2	1.6	3.4	6.8
Hydro	0.9	1.6	2.6	2.8
Nuclear	——	——	3.7	19.0
All electricity	3.0	9.3	20.8	37.0
		(Percent of Total)		
Coal	50.4	24.5	19.9	13.3
Oil	31.8	39.1	37.2	40.5
Natural gas	13.3	29.2	30.6	25.1
Natural gas liquids	0.9	3.6	4.3	5.1
Hydro	3.6	3.6	3.4	2.1
Nuclear	——	——	4.7	14.0
All electricity	11.6	20.5	26.2	27.4

SOURCE: Adapted from Hans H. Landsberg and others, *Resources in America's Future* (Baltimore: Johns Hopkins Press, 1963), p. 291.

Oil is expected to decline considerably (29.2 to 9.8 percent) as a direct energy source of heat and power for residential use. Industrial use is expected to be maintained over the next 40 years (about 20 percent) and commercial uses may increase slightly. Of the total energy produced, oil will comprise about 40 percent in the future (Table 4-5).

Natural gas and natural gas liquids. The commonly used measure of "proved reserves" also is used for natural gas. Seventy-five to 80 percent of gas supplies are economically recoverable and estimates of potential supplies are based on ultimate oil reserves and a gas/oil ratio. In 1960 13.3 trillion cubic feet of natural gas were withdrawn for use and proved reserves at the end of the year were 263.8 trillion cubic feet, or about 20 times the amount withdrawn.[28] Assuming that only one third of the 500 billion barrels of oil potential is recoverable and that a gas/oil ratio of 7000 cubic feet of gas per barrel exists,[29] gas reserves would be in the neighborhood of 1,200 trillion cubic feet or about 100 years' supply at 1960 use rates. However, a medium projection of use in 2000 is estimated at about 35 trillion cubic feet and the maintenance of proved reserves at

[28] Report of the Committee on National Gas Reserves of the American Gas Association, for year ending December 31, 1961.

[29] The ratio is not a true relationship of the occurrence of gas and oil in nature. It is a factor based upon different types of experience and is conditioned by assumptions made in the commercial evaluation of the occurrences. It should be noted that increasing the recovery rate of oil will not necessarily increase the recoverable gas supply.

20 times production would require a recoverable supply of 1,700 trillion cubic feet in the year 2000, which is the upper limit of current estimates. Two possible sources of imports are available: pipelines from Canada and Mexico, and shipment by tanker. The first is already a reality but of little importance, and the latter method, initiated by Great Britain, appears to be economically feasible.

Natural gas is expected to maintain its relative importance in residential and industrial uses. In 1960 about one-seventh of the natural gas produced served as energy to produce electricity. The emergence of nuclear energy will affect gas use in the future but natural gas will still provide one-fourth of total energy requirements at the end of the century (Table 4-5).

Natural gas liquids, such as methane, ethane, propane, and butane, are increasingly used in the manufacture of chemical products. Although they are of minor importance except in industrial use, by the year 2000 they are expected to provide one-sixth of the total energy. In terms of our total energy sources natural gas liquids will comprise only 3.6 percent in 2000 (Table 4-5). Natural gas liquids are not truly an additional fuel reserve, as they are stripped components from natural gas with the typical yield of 10 to 20 percent on a volume basis.

Hydropower. The limits of hydropower were discussed to some extent in the previous section on water. Hydroelectric capacity is determined by the average flow of streams and the vertical descent of the water. Potential for the United States has been estimated to be no less than 230 and no more than 390 million kw.[30] Much of this potential cannot be developed from an economic viewpoint. The Federal Power Commission recently set the potential hydro capacity at 127 million kw.[31] Installed capacity in 1960 was 31.9 million kw. and it is unlikely that additional capacity will be developed to exceed three times this amount. Hydropower is used exclusively to manufacture electricity and in 1960 provided about 20 percent of the total energy used in electricity production. As a source of total energy used in 1960, hydropower accounted for only 3.6 percent and this percentage is estimated to decline to 2.1 percent by 2000 (Table 4-5).

Nuclear energy. Nuclear power used for generating electricity is expected to gain rapidly in importance after 1970. Supplies of fissionable material (uranium and thorium) are adequate to provide energy equal to 1960 total requirement at current level of technology. With a more highly developed technology, energy potential of up to 100 times the 1960 requirements has been estimated. It seems clear that the use of

[30] Sam H. Schurr and others, *Energy in the American Economy* (Baltimore: Johns Hopkins Press, 1960), p. 476. Published for Resources for the Future, Inc.
[31] Federal Power Commission, *Hydroelectric Power Resources of the United States Developed and Undeveloped, 1960* (Washington: undated).

nuclear energy will be determined more by the state of reactor technology than by the reserves of fissionable materials.

By 1980 one-half or more of new electric generating capacity put into use may be nuclear-powered. Estimates of the share of total electric power output that will be produced by nuclear energy in 1980 range from about 20 to 40 percent. The share that nuclear energy sources may contribute by 2000 to total energy sources at a medium projection would be 14 percent (Table 4-5).

Metals.[32] A medium projection estimates the growth in the demand for metals to be 3.1 percent annually from now to the year 2000. Metals originate in the earth in the form of ores, some of which are used directly in the form in which they are extracted. More commonly, the ore is processed to isolate the metal and purify it. Once the metal is extracted it may be further refined, alloyed, or changed in chemical or molecular structure for particular industrial, commercial, or artistic purposes.

Metal ores are natural resources vital to the development of any economy. The adequacy of this resource base depends upon (a) consumption requirements, (b) known ore sources, (c) ore sources undiscovered, (d) improvements in extractive technology, (e) possibilities for ore importation. Since the end of World War I the United States has been relying to a greater extent on imports. For example, iron ore imports as a percentage of apparent consumption jumped from three percent in 1940 to 32 percent in 1960. Imports came primarily from Venezuela and Canada.

Nonmetallic nonfuel minerals

While the metal and fuels account for the major part of minerals in terms of their value, another group is also important. Three of these minerals (lime, phosphate, and potash) are of vital use in agriculture. Others, such as salt, sand, stone, and quartz, are in sufficient abundance so that concern over reserves are unwarranted. For example, between 15 and 20 percent of the surface of the United States is underlaid by limestone and there is no indication that this resource will be depleted. Sulphur deposits are less than the foreseeable demand but discoveries in the past have tended to keep up with demand. New technology has permitted sulphur to be recovered from gas and oil deposits, and this will help considerably.

Phosphate. Total phosphate consumption was about 17 million tons in 1960, with a phosphate content of 5 million long tons. Half of the consumption went into commercial fertilizer for farm production, with a large amount of the remainder used in the chemical industry. The growth rate

[32] Data taken from Hans H. Landsberg and others, *op. cit.*, pp. 293-316 and 427-482.

for demand for phosphate is estimated at 2.5 percent per year. World reserves are adequate with 25 percent of them in the United States, particularly in Florida. The sea provides a new source which may be commercially feasible in the near future.

Potash. Potash demand increases faster than that for phosphate in agricultural use and an annual 3.7 percent growth rate would require 200 million tons for the 40 years from 1960 to 2000. Crops currently remove some five million tons of potash from the soil annually, and if crop output doubles requirements would be more nearly 300 million tons for the 40 year period. Ninety percent of deposits in the United States come from New Mexico. Even if these deposits become depleted reserves in Canada and Germany are huge.

Summary

Natural resources contribute greatly to a nation's economic growth if the state of technology allows their extraction and use in an increasing number of production processes. Concern over the adequacy of natural resources and their conservation is legitimate. The degree of scarcity of a natural resource in economic terms varies not only with the size of demand but with the technology used in its extraction and processing. As a result, physical existence cannot be equated with economic availability. The limitation is the cost of separating the resource from its environment so that it can be used in desired production processes.

In the past century the "real cost" of natural resource products measured by their prices in comparison with the general price level has shown no marked change except in isolated cases. For example, the minimum grade of copper ore mined in 1940 was about three percent, while in 1960 ore with 0.7 percent copper was being profitably mined without any relative price increase in refined copper. Clearly, technology made a major cost-reducing contribution.

Extractive or mining industries along with farming account for continually decreasing employment and gross national output as a nation's economic development takes place. With the nuclear age on the horizon the future needs and uses of natural resources are uncertain, but when one looks at the century between 1850 and 1950 and notes that fuelwood as a source of energy decreased from 90 to less than 5 percent of the total source of energy, exciting developments are certainly in store. The policy aspects dealing with natural resource development are discussed in Part V.

5

Population and economic growth

A LOOK AT POPULATION

The study of population is a fascinating and intriguing subject. There is frequent speculation and continuing interest regarding man's ability to feed an ever increasing population. History is rich with stories of starvation, and even today an adequate food supply is of primary concern for about 80 percent of the world's population.

Population classification

The human population of a country or area is made up of all the people living in the country or area at any one time. There are many ways to classify this population for purposes of description and analysis. Population is commonly classified by sex, age, and race. Although these three classification systems are closely interrelated, each class can be analyzed separately for different purposes.

Other classifications include geographic distribution, population density, place of residence, nationality, language, religion, occupation, income, health, and marital status. Two populations (country, state, county, town, etc.) may be compared and the differences noted, using any of these classifications. These differences will provide insights into their respective

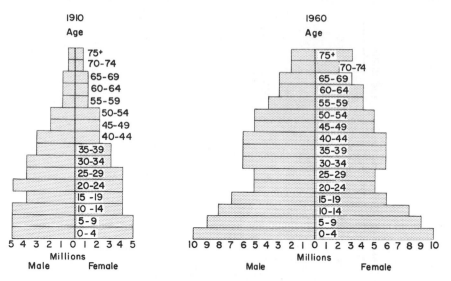

FIGURE 5-1:   Population Pyramids for United States, 1910 and 1960. United States
Census of Population.

rates of growth, their economic and cultural well-being, and will also
offer an indication of possible future problem areas. For example, differences in urban and rural population growth may lead to problems related
to taxation, political representation, schools, and education.

Population pyramid

Demographers are people who study population. They use an analytical tool called a "population pyramid" to portray a population picture
in an area at a given point in time. A pyramid separates the total number
of people by sex and age and shows the profound influence of births and
deaths on a population's age structure. A comparison of the pyramids for
the United States in 1910 and 1960 (Figure 5-1) shows the changes in
age composition. The 1960 pyramid illustrates a population including
relatively more young and old people.

World and U.S. population

World population has been estimated by many different people over
the ages. Some countries conduct incomplete censuses of population or do
not take any at all. Thus, any estimate of people living in these countries
is necessarily an educated guess. World population approximated three
billion in 1960, with an annual rate of increase approaching two percent
(Table 5-1). Although it has taken the human race approximately 200,000

TABLE 5-1: Estimated World Population by Continent, Selected Years, 1650 to 1960 and Projections for 1970 and 2000.

	Year (Millions)										
	1650	1700	1750	1800	1850	1900	1940	1950	1960	1970	2000
North America	1	1	1	6	26	81	143	168	197	225	312
Middle America	6	6	5	10	13	25	42	51	206	265	592
South America	6	6	6	9	20	38	89	112			
Europe	100	110	140	187	266	401	543	393[1]	424[1]	457[1]	568[1]
Asia	330	400	479	602	749	937	1,186	1,380[2]	1,620[2]	1,980[2]	3,870[2]
Africa	100	98	95	90	95	120	157	199	237	294	517
Oceania	2	2	2	2	2	6	11	13	16	19	29
Soviet Union[3]	—	—	—	—	—	—	—	181	215	254	379
Total	545	623	728	906	1,171	1,608	2,170	2,500	2,920	3,500	6,280
Average Percent Increase Per Year.	—	0.29	0.33	0.48	0.58	0.74	0.87	1.33	1.70	1.80	1.90

[1] Excludes European part of Soviet Union.
[2] Excludes Asian part of Soviet Union.
[3] Asian and European parts combined.

SOURCE: Woytinsky, E. S. and W. S., "World Population and Production" (New York: Twentieth Century Fund, 1953), p. 34 and *Population Bulletin* (Washington: Population Reference Bureau, Inc., Vol. 15, No. 2, March 1959), p. 20.

years to achieve its present population level, if current growth trends continue the number of people in the world will double within the next 40 years, rising from three to six billion people.

Population in the United States reached 200 million in 1970, with an annual rate of increase similar to the world rate (Table 5-2). Population

TABLE 5-2: U.S. Population, Amount and Percent of Increase by Decades, 1650 to 1960 and Projections to 2000.

Year	Population (Thousands)	Increase (Thousands)	Average Percent [1] Increase Per Year
1650	52		
1700	275	223	3.4
1750	1,207	932	3.0
1800	5,297	4,090	3.0
1850	23,261	17,964	3.0
1900	76,094	52,833	2.4
1920	106,466	30,372	1.7
1940	132,122	25,656	1.1
1960	179,325	27,642	1.5
1970	206,039	26,714	1.4
1980	235,212	29,173	1.3
1990	270,770	35,558	1.4
2000	307,803	37,033	1.3

[1] Percentages calculated using midpoint population in each interval as the basis.

Source: *Historical Statistics of the United States, Colonial Times to 1957* (Washington: Bureau of the Census, 1960) p. 7; and "Population Estimates," Series P-25, U.S. Department of Commerce, March 14, 1968, p. 36.

data on the United States are reliable because a census has been taken systematically every ten years since the birth of the nation.

FACTORS INFLUENCING POPULATION GROWTH

The total number of people living in a geographic area at any one time is the result of the number of people born, the number of people dying, the number of people moving out of the area (emigration) and the number of people moving into the area (immigration). Population growth for the world is simply the excess of births over deaths. Population growth for an area is the excess of births over deaths *plus* the difference between people moving into and out of the area.

Let us work through an example in order to more clearly show the relationship between birth rate, death rate, and annual rate of population increase (often called the natural rate of increase). The birth rate is simply the number of babies born per 1000 population in a year's time. The

TABLE 5-3: Birth and Death Rates for Selected Countries and Years.

Country	Birth Rates (per thousand population)					
	1911-19	1920-30	1931-38	1941-47	1948-50	1959
United States	24.3	21.3	17.2	21.5	23.8	24.1
England and Wales	22.0	18.8	15.0	17.0	16.7	16.5
France	15.2	19.0	15.9	16.7	20.8	18.4
Sweden	22.1	18.0	14.2	18.9	17.4	14.1
Germany	24.0	20.5	17.5	–	16.7	17.1
Spain	30.0	29.6	27.0	21.3	21.4	21.8
Japan	33.0	34.2	31.2	29.2	31.5	17.5
Australia	27.0	22.6	17.1	21.3	23.1	22.6
Burma (towns)	–	–	–	–	36.1[3]	37.6
Mexico	–	36.7[1]	44.1[2]	–	44.4[3]	47.0

Country	Death Rates					
	1911-19	1920-30	1931-38	1941-50	1950-54	1959
United States	14.3	11.9	10.9	10.1	9.5	9.4
England and Wales	14.5	12.2	12.0	12.5	11.6	11.6
France	18.6	17.0	15.8	15.5	12.8	11.3
Sweden	13.1	12.2	11.6	10.5	9.8	9.5
Germany	15.4	12.6	11.2	13.2	11.7	13.1
Spain	23.0	19.6	16.3	13.4	10.2	9.0
Japan	20.0	21.0	17.9	16.2	9.4	7.4
Australia	10.7	9.5	9.1	10.5	9.4[4]	8.9
Burma (towns)	–	–	–	–	20.8	17.7
Mexico	–	–	–	17.4[3]	15.5	11.9

[1] 1927
[2] 1937
[3] 1946-49
[4] 1953-54

SOURCES: Woytinsky, E. S. and W. S., "World Population and Production" (New York: Twentieth Century Fund, 1953), pp. 144-165. *Population Bulletin* (Washington: Population Reference Bureau, Inc., March, 1962. *Population Index*, Office of Population Research Princeton University, Vol. 27, No. 1, January 1961), pp. 278-282.

death rate is the number of people who die per 1000 population in a year's time. The difference between the two rates divided by 1000 and expressed as a percent gives the annual rate of increase excluding immigration and emigration. For example:

Birth rate   24
Death rate   10
Difference $\overline{14}$
Annual rate of increase 1.4%

Factors influencing birth rates

Currently the world birth rate is approximately 35, ranging from a low of under 20 in Europe to a high of nearly 50 in tropical Africa and parts of Latin America (Table 5-3). The relative importance of factors influencing birth rates varies between countries as well as regions within a country. However, the following list of factors is generally applicable in most countries.

1. Number of marriages.
2. Age at which females marry.
3. Divorce rate.
4. Diseases affecting reproductive capacity.
5. Use of contraceptives and abortion.
6. General business conditions.
7. Cultural and religious influences.
8. Education.
9. Governmental policies.

Most societies prescribe some type of marriage ceremony before a couple may legally have children. The number of marriages in a country then has a direct bearing on the potential number of children born. Age at which females marry also influences the potential number of children. It is a general rule that more children are born in families in which the mother begins childbearing at an early age rather than later in life. The divorce rate also influences the birth rate because it tends to postpone a lasting marriage and thus indirectly has the same effect as marrying at a later age.

Diseases affecting reproductive capacity usually concern temporary or permanent sterility. Proper medical treatment, diet, and sanitation are removing much of this negative influence. The prevention of conception through the use of contraceptives is gaining attention throughout the world. Medical technology has done much to provide information on this subject, particularly in cases where childbearing would impair the potential mother's health. Abortion has also been increasingly resorted to, notably in Japan, to slow down the rate of population growth.

General business conditions are closely associated with birth rates. An economic depression or pronounced retreat from an established level of living tends to be highly correlated with a decided drop in the birth rate (see Table 5-3, birth rate for 1930-40). Cultural and religious influences sometimes encourage and sometimes discourage high birth rates. Cultures that foster early marriages combined with religions that prohibit the use of contraceptives act to enhance the birth rate; cultures that encourage marriages later in life and religions that do not discourage contraceptive practices tend to reduce birth rates.

The level of education in a country is also associated with birth rates; the higher the general level of literacy and formal schooling the lower the birth rate. In general, couples with lower education and income levels have more children than couples possessing higher education and income levels. Also, differential birth rates within and between cultures are often caused simply by the freedom of married couples to decide to have children or not to have them. Freedom of choice pertaining to children is a comparatively new consideration for mankind.

Governmental policies can exert an overt influence on population by encouraging or discouraging early marriages. Offering free medical help for expectant mothers and providing low cost housing opportunities for young couples whose financial status prevent marriage are other examples. The state's influence on birth rates has been recognized since the days of Herodotus and Plato. In recent years governmental efforts to increase the birth rate have been notable in Germany under Hitler and in Italy under Mussolini. Efforts to discourage the birth rate include the legalization of abortion and government supported clinics to disseminate birth control information and provide free sterilization. Japan and India provide examples of national efforts of these kinds.

Factors influencing death rates

The world death rate currently averages about 18, ranging from a low of about 9 in the more developed economies to a high over 25 in parts of Asia and Africa. Although death rates are primarily influenced by the level of medical technology, the acceptance and practice of that technology is also crucial. In many countries the causes of death lie largely in areas in which present medical knowledge is relatively inexpensive and adequate to reduce mortality substantially (malaria, typhoid, tuberculosis, respiratory and intestinal infections, measles and whooping cough).

The infant mortality rate (deaths under one year of age per thousand live births) is considered one of the most sensitive indicators of death rates. In some of the more underdeveloped areas of the world deaths of infants account for over 50 percent of the total deaths. This is particularly true in a high birth rate nation. Infant mortality ranges from a low of about 20 in Sweden, the Netherlands, and Iceland, to nearly 200 in parts of Africa. The United States rate is 26.4.

Longer average life span is due to lowered infant and child mortality and reduced mortality of the older population. Mortality rate reductions are in turn due primarily to the innovation and adoption of medical technology, sanitation, and nutrition. Life expectancy at birth appears to have been about 20 years in Rome at the height of the Roman Empire. Average life expectancy now ranges from Norway's expectancy of between 71 and 75 years to India's average of 32 years. In general, females live longer than males. However, life expectancy for both males and females is increasing in all parts of the world.

POPULATION AND ECONOMIC GROWTH POTENTIAL

Countries can be classified into three groups according to population growth and economic development (Figure 5-2). The high growth potential countries have a high birth rate and a high death rate. Countries in this category contain approximately three-fifths of the world's people. These countries are Africa, much of Latin America and the Caribbean nations, and all of Asia except Japan. The standard of living is extremely low in these countries where man is constantly forced to fight for physical survival. Agricultural productivity is also low, with the vast majority of people necessarily engaged in food production. Little effort or time remains for the bulk of these people to consider longer-range economic and social problems. Most of their energy is simply devoted to the task of finding enough food to stay alive.

Countries in the transitional growth stage make up about one-fifth of the world's population. Some countries in eastern and southern Europe and parts of Latin America are examples. In this stage, although the birth rate is falling, use of medical technology has caused a correspondingly faster drop in the death rate. This exerts even a greater population pressure on the resources of the country, particularly on the food supply.

It is in the transitional stage that a society is faced with other immense problems of social, institutional and economic change. Political instability, revolution rather than reform, and rigidly planned economic and social guidance are prevalent at this time. Potential opportunity, uncertainty as to the economic and social outcome of change, limited education, and a wide divergence between those who own and control property and those who do not lead to resistance to change.

In the incipient decline group of countries there is a low birth rate and a lower death rate. Population may be expanding in these countries at a rate equal to those in the high growth potential group. To test your understanding of this point compare the vertical distance between the birth and death rate in Figure 5-2 for these two groups. The incipient decline countries currently have about one-fifth of the people in the world and examples would include the advanced economies of the United States, Canada, Northwestern and Central Europe, Australia, and New Zealand. These economies have become relatively stable and political and social change is more orderly.

One can anticipate large population increases for several reasons in countries where birth rates are greater than death rates. One reason is that declining mortality rates raise the fertility level of the population

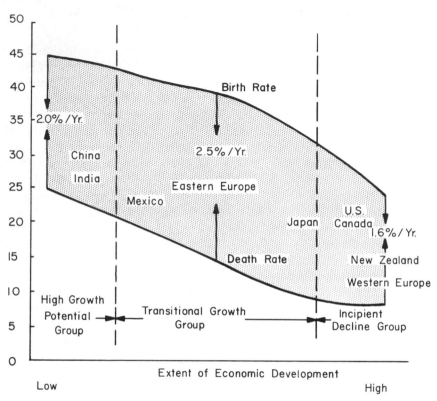

°Rate of population increase: birth rate minus death rate divided by 1000.

FIGURE 5-2:   Relationship Between Birth Rates, Death Rates, and Extent of Economic
Development.

because a comparably larger portion of the population pyramid is located in the fertile age group. Despite some encouraging birth rate control factors, the world will be faced with an additional 3 billion persons to feed by the year 2000. Most of this increase will be in areas presently the least able to cope with their present population-food pressure problems. This inability, in addition to sheer increases in the numbers of people, includes other reasons such as low food production, inadequate transport, poor food distribution methods, and low-level food merchandising. While we have experienced a very real challenge concerning helping feed the world's millions, the most serious impact pressures are yet to come.

THEORIES OF POPULATION GROWTH

There are two main schools of thought in this area, each of which generates its own theories of population growth. One school is based on a naturalistic, almost mechanistic, approach to population. Factors considered by this school as limiting population include the biological capacity of women to produce children (fecundity), the actual number of children born (fertility), the inability to reproduce (sterility), natural ecological conditions affecting food and physical resources, economic goods and standard of living, and the geographical density of population. The other school of thought is based on a sociological approach. This school believes that reproductive behavior is derived from a pattern of human custom based on institutions devised by human beings. Population growth is considered a social rather than environmental phenomenon. This latter school attempts to explain population growth in terms of the influences of cultural patterns and social behavior.

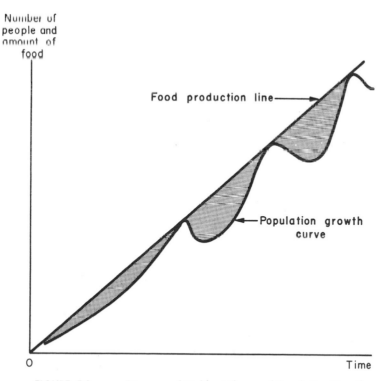

FIGURE 5-3:   Diagram of Malthus' Theory of Population Growth.

Naturalistic theories of population growth

In the late 18th century an Englishman named Malthus formulated a theory of population growth. His principal contention was that nature is limited in its capacity to produce plant life and meat, while mankind's prolificacy is not bounded by anything but himself. Malthus observed that food production increased in an arithmetic ratio (1, 2, 3, 4, ...) while population increased in geometric ratio (1, 2, 4, 8, ...). He concluded that human population growth is ultimately limited by the amount of food the world can produce and if population grows faster than food production natural checks of famine and pestilence will soon bring the population level into balance with food production (Figure 5-3). History shows that whenever the population curve attempts to rise above the food production line it becomes subject to "natural" pressures which reduce population to at least the subsistence level.

Criticism of Malthus centers around two main points: that he neglected the influence of man's inventive abilities to produce more food on less land, and that man might devise culturally acceptable ways to control the birth rate.

Other naturalistic theories include: (a) Sadler: fecundity varies inversely with the geographic density of population; (b) Doubleday: fecundity varies inversely with the abundance and variety of available food; (c) Spencer: fecundity varies inversely with the complexity of life—an overtaxed brain has deleterious effects on the ability to reproduce; (d) Gini: combined a biological interpretation of population growth with a social one by saying that different social strata have different rates of fertility, and that the higher the strata the lower the rate.

Social theories of population growth

In this school many theorists point to the decisions man has made concerning himself and population growth. Some of these decisions stem from overt institutional influences, such as religion, law, and medicine. Other decisions stem more from a socio-cultural background. Theories in this school involve such factors as the place of the children in family life goals, the influence of women working outside the home, and parental motivation concerning childbearing. The explicit decision to use medical technology to prevent births is another example.

Some of the theorists in this school include: (a) Henry George: a "single-tax" plan was envisioned that would enable men to return to the land and produce food for a greater population than could now be fed; (b) Marx: thought capitalism would cause both poverty and a decline of population; (c) Dumont: fertility varies inversely with social mobility—a rigid caste system promotes a high fertility while a culture which permits an easy transition from one job and social strata to another results in a lowered fertility; (d) Carr-Saunders: man is free to choose an "optimal" level of resources and population; hence population growth is determined by man's notion of the most economically and socially desirable number of people under current living conditions.

POPULATION CHECKS AND BALANCES

Malthus differentiated between two types of checks on population growth. One type was composed of "natural" checks such as famine, disease, violence, vice, and misery. The other type included "preventative" checks of late marriage, abstinence, and celibacy. The natural check was attributed to population outrunning available food supply; the second comprised socially acceptable modes of population restriction imposed by individuals. Other restrictive methods of population control include infanticide, cultural taboos of various kinds, "mercy" killing, and colonization.

Public goals relative to population may be designed to: (a) slow up or prevent an increase in population numbers, (b) encourage an increase in numbers, (c) increase the "quality" of the population (eugenic selections) and (d) secure a "better" distribution of people relative to the resources devoted to their support. In addition, sterilization of those judged medically to be permanently insane is legally practiced in several countries, including the United States. One of the reasons governments established colonies throughout the world was to attain a better ratio of people and resources. For many years the western frontier in the United States acted as a continual colonization area, capable of absorbing easily the population increase associated with the transitional growth stage.

POPULATION MOBILITY

Immigration and emigration

Movements of people into and out of an area (immigration and emigration) depend to a large extent on the relative economic and social attractiveness of the area. Lack of jobs and food or escape from political repression may actually push people out of a specific area. On the other hand, high paying jobs, plentiful food, and political security may attract people. There may be movements of people between (inter) nations or

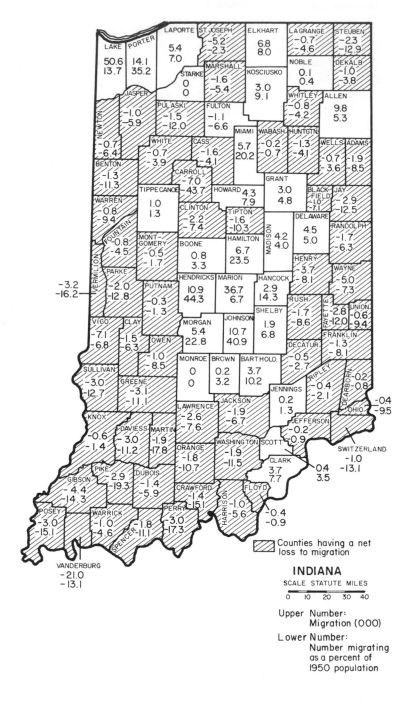

FIGURE 5-4:   Net Migration of Indiana Population, 1950-1960.

there may be movements within (intra) a country. In either case the motivations for migration are usually similar.

Signs of population pressure on a country's resources are evident primarily from its efforts to obtain food. Elaborate terracing and highly intensive cropping systems designed to utilize the last possible bit of land tend to indicate the degree of the food-population crisis. Extremely low wages in agriculture and industry also show that labor is plentiful relative to the demand for it. A low value set on human life is another characteristic of population pressure.

The results of extreme population pressure on the food resources of a country from which emigration is slight can usually be identified in the death rate and the causes of death. Malnutrition and famine are usually felt sooner by the young and the old. However, lowered levels of nutrition also mean a lowered resistance to disease and hence a raised incidence of death from ordinarily preventable sicknesses.

European and Far Eastern history relates accounts of waves of emigration from areas when food production fails. The history of the United States and Europe shows that when agricultural productivity is high enough labor tends to migrate from farm to nonfarm jobs. This is a basic factor underlying urbanization. However, in times of economic depression and severe dips in the business cycle, some people move from the city back to the farm where food is cheaper to obtain.

Increased mobility of people can lead to a buildup of the rural non-farm population. The growth of unincorporated suburbs is an example of this development. Many of the rural nonfarm residents can be characterized by special circumstances: often they are low-skilled, retired, or members of the un- or underemployed "stranded" population groups. Their incomes are sometimes low and uncertain. However, with improvements in highways and commuter accessibility to public transport, an increasing number of salaried workers and higher paid wage earners are moving to the country from urban areas.

Besides immigration and emigration, people move continually within a country. Changing residences within a country can be explained in terms of economic and/or social betterment. Leaving the farm for city work, community to nonfarm jobs from a rural area, and retirement close to one's family in town are all evident in today's society.

The concept of a "net migration" allows people interested in economic growth and agriculture to analyze local trends closely. Fertility and death ratios coupled with census counts provide part of the data necessary to help determine relative rates of economic growth. Suppose the 1960 census of population indicated that there were 10,000 people in one county and that natural increase would be expected to add 2,000 additional people by 1970. If in 1970 only 11,000 people were actually living there, the areas shows a net loss to migration of 1,000 people.

Example: 1960 actual   10,000 people
          1960-70 natural increase   2,000 people
          1970 expected   12,000 people
          1970 actual   11,000 people
          1960-70 net loss to   1,000 people
          migration

If in 1970 the actual population was over 12,000 there would be a "net gain to migration." Typically, a net loss to migration means there are not enough job opportunities in the area to provide employment for everyone who wants to work; likewise, a "net gain to migration" may indicate a surplus of nonfarm jobs which induce labor from outside the area to move in. For an actual example, see the net migration map for Indiana's population, 1950 to 1960 (Figure 5-4).

This chapter has included the necessary concepts about population which are essential to discuss the labor force and economic growth. The following chapter will complete the discussion.

6

The role of the labor
force in economic growth

THE LABOR FORCE

Economic growth and development was defined earlier in terms of people and the production of goods and services. In order to better understand economic growth and development, it is necessary to study the relationship between the population and the size and quality of the labor force.

The labor force is not the same thing as the population. A nation's population is all the people who are citizens of the country and who live within the national boundaries of that country or are included in its embassies or its armed forces outside of the country. A population includes many people who, for one reason or another, are unable to work. Children going to school, youngsters who are too young to begin school, sick people, old people, and people who have retired are among those who are usually not employed.

The labor force of a country is described most generally by age. There are many other characteristics of a labor force (sex, education, occupation, income, etc.), but they all apply to the group of people classified by an age description. In the United States those constituting the labor force are described as any people between the ages of 14 and 65 years of age who are physically and mentally able to work. Although 65 years has been accepted for a long time as an upper limit, it was only around 1920 that the lower limit was raised from 10 years to 14 years. Children have long been exploited for their labor, and as a result the institution of child labor laws and legislation affecting mandatory school attendance were primary causes for raising the lower age limits of the labor force.

Although all the population benefits from the growth of our economic system, it is the labor force that constitutes the labor input in production processes. The labor force contributes the two catalytic agents of labor and management to the factors of land and capital. The whole population, as consumers, help decide what the labor force will produce, how it will produce it, and who will share in the profits.

EMPLOYMENT

The employment status of the United States labor force shows that the farm labor force in 1967 was less than that of 1850 (Table 6-1). While

TABLE 6-1: U.S. Employed, Selected Years, 1820-1967.

Year	Total Employed (thousands)	Agricultural (thousands)	% Agricultural	Nonagricultural (thousands)	% Nonagricultural
1820	2,881	2,069	71.8	812	28.2
1850	7,696	4,901	63.7	2,795	36.3
1900	29,073	10,912	37.5	18,161	62.5
1920	37,371	11,592	31.0	25,779	69.0
1930	45,480	10,340	22.7	35,140	77.3
1940	47,520	9,540	20.1	37,980	79.9
1950	59,748	7,497	12.5	52,251	87.5
1960	66,681	5,723	8.6	60,958	91.4
1965	72,179	4,585	6.4	67,594	93.6
1967	74,372	3,844	5.2	70,527	94.8

Data 1820-1920 includes persons over ten years of age; data 1930-1967 includes persons 14 years of age and over.

SOURCE: Data 1820-1920, U.S. Dept. of Commerce, *Statistical Abstract,* USGPO (Washington, 1959). Other data *Supplement to Economic Indicators,* prepared for the Joint Economic Committee by the Office of Statistical Standards and the Bureau of the Budget, USGPO, Washington, 1962), and *Manpower Report of the President,* U.S. Department of Labor, April 1968, p. 233.

the labor force on farms rose until 1920 and has fallen steadily since, the labor force in nonfarm employment has increased steadily since 1820. There are many reasons for changes in employment and the labor force. Probably the primary causes for shifts in demand for farm labor are secular changes in commodity prices, new technology, and the relative ease with which a farmer can substitute capital for labor.

Changes in employment

The economic development of a country or area can usually be traced from the growth of its trade patterns. Channels of commerce and trade change over the ages and correspondingly, so does the country's or area's development. For example, in the United States early settlers established a north-south coastal pattern based on cotton. Dependence upon cotton as a "one crop economy" dictated shipment to the cotton mills in the North and export to England. Advancing technology in communications, the advent of the railroad, and an attitude of "manifest destiny" toward the undeveloped West began to exert an east-west trade pattern. The Civil War with its ensuing depression in the South, the boom of the industrial North, and the expansion westward combined to swing the bulk of trade into an east-west trade pattern which dominated the north-south pattern. People began to move from the comparatively disadvantaged South to the North and West.

Employment pattern changes with growth

Economic development of a country or area can usually be measured by adjustments in three sectors of employment: *primary employment—* people employed in extractive industries of farming, forestry, fishing, and

TABLE 6-2: Percentage Distribution of Employment by Major Groups in the United States, Selected Years, 1919-1959.

Year	Primary (Agriculture[1] and Mining)	Secondary (Contract Construction and Manufacturing)	Tertiary (Transportation, Trade, Finance, Selected Services, and Government)
1919	28.5	29.4	42.1
1925	26.8	27.7	45.5
1930	25.8	26.6	47.6
1935	26.6	25.5	47.9
1940	22.6	27.6	49.8
1945	17.8	32.4	49.8
1950	14.8	32.5	52.7
1955	12.0	32.9	55.1
1959	10.3	31.5	58.2

[1] Henderson has used agriculture in the same context as farming.
SOURCE: J. P. Henderson, *Changes in the Industrial Distribution of Employment,* 1919-1959, University of Illinois, Bulletin 87.

mining; *secondary employment*—those people having jobs in the manufacturing industries, processing or fabricating materials into semi-finished and finished goods; *tertiary employment*—people whose job it is to service the needs of the other two employment sectors as well as providing much of the maintenance of the total economy (finance, education, transportation, construction, government, etc.). Using these three employment categories, let us trace the typical economic growth pattern.

Historically, the economic growth of a country goes through three phases. In the first phase the economy is almost solely dependent upon primary employment. Typical productivity per farm worker is quite low and the vast majority of the population must engage in farming for survival. The second phase is introduced by an increase in farming productivity which permits a movement of some workers from employment on farms to various types of nonfarm work. The first migrants out of farming generally manufacture materials and utensils for use on farms. Increases in secondary employment bring increases in both the size and quality of the labor force and in number and quality of manufactured goods. The technology contained in the use of the new agricultural implements is reflected in the continued movement of people from primary to secondary employment. As the number of people in secondary employment grows over time, there is a more than proportionate increase in the number of people employed to service the needs of the primary and secondary sectors. Fewer and fewer people are needed in farming. Technology permits more food to be raised by fewer people. Workers can thus move from producing food to the production of other goods and services desired by society.

Even during a recent 40-year period one can see the process of economic development through the employment changes in this country (Table 6-2). The primary industries have declined from over one-fourth of all the employment in the United States in 1919 to just barely 10 percent of the total in 1959. Both secondary and tertiary employment have increased. Their growth came from two sources: the migration from agriculture and mining, and the new entrants to the labor force provided by natural population growth. It is interesting to note (Table 6-2) that manufacturing and construction were able to keep up with the material nonfood needs of a growing population without much increase in the employment; but the demands of a growing society and a need to service a growing commercial and industrial sector of the economy necessitated almost a 40 percent increase in tertiary employment in 40 years. Similar changes in employment among primary, secondary, and tertiary industries occur in other countries as economic development takes place.

When specfic industry groups are analyzed (Table 6-3) further effects of economic growth on employment are noticeable. For example, numbers employed in manufacturing increased by almost 60 percent be-

TABLE 6-3: Estimates of Employment by Industry Division, Selected Years 1919-1959.

Year	Farming		Mining and Contract Construction		Manufacturing		Transportation and Public Utilities		Government		Other[1]		All Industries	
	No.	%	No.	%	No.	%	No.	%	No.	%	No.	%	No.	%
1919	10,749	25.7	2,785	6.7	10,649	25.5	3,500	9.3	2,671	6.4	11,017	26.4	41,771	100.0
1920	10,903	25.9	2,659	6.3	10,649	25.3	4,193	9.9	2,603	6.2	11,142	26.4	42,149	100.0
1923	10,684	24.8	3,136	7.2	10,265	23.8	4,075	9.4	2,611	6.0	12,438	28.8	43,209	100.0
1925	10,581	24.3	3,304	7.5	9,891	22.7	4,016	9.2	2,802	6.4	13,015	29.9	43,609	100.0
1928	10,301	23.0	3,478	7.8	9,891	22.1	4,014	9.0	2,996	6.7	14,021	31.4	44,701	100.0
1930	10,340	23.5	3,213	7.3	9,510	21.6	3,841	8.7	3,149	7.1	14,070	31.8	44,123	100.0
1933	10,090	26.6	2,255	5.9	7,327	19.3	2,829	7.4	3,167	8.5	12,307	32.3	37,975	100.0
1935	10,110	24.4	2,484	6.0	8,896	21.7	2,943	7.1	3,477	8.4	13,397	32.5	41,397	100.0
1938	9,690	22.4	2,606	6.0	9,351	21.6	3,018	7.0	3,876	8.9	14,767	34.1	43,309	100.0
1940	9,540	20.5	2,904	6.3	10,907	23.4	3,200	6.9	4,202	9.0	15,732	33.9	46,485	100.0
1943	9,080	16.4	3,122	5.6	17,535	31.5	3,785	6.8	6,080	10.9	15,983	28.8	55,585	100.0
1945	8,580	16.2	2,549	4.8	15,476	29.2	4,006	7.5	5,944	11.2	16,514	31.1	53,069	100.0
1948	7,960	13.7	4,173	7.2	15,504	26.7	4,338	7.5	5,650	9.7	20,446	35.2	58,073	100.0
1950	7,497	12.9	4,268	7.3	15,161	26.2	4,180	7.3	6,026	10.4	20,845	35.9	57,977	100.0
1953	6,555	10.5	4,648	7.4	17,440	28.0	4,437	7.1	6,645	10.7	22,574	36.3	62,299	100.0
1955	6,718	10.7	4,809	7.6	16,748	26.6	4,268	6.8	6,914	11.0	23,566	37.3	63,023	100.0
1958	5,844	9.3	4,547	7.2	15,648	25.1	4,096	6.5	7,893	12.6	24,579	39.3	62,607	100.0
1959	5,836	9.1	4,656	7.3	16,345	25.4	4,096	6.4	8,126	12.7	25,045	39.1	64,104	100.0

[1] Includes Wholesale and Retail Trade, Finance, Insurance, Real Estate, and other Selected Services.

SOURCE: John P. Henderson, *Changes in the Industrial Distribution of Employment, 1919-1959*, University of Illinois, Bulletin 87.

tween 1919 and 1959, but this sector's share of total employment of all industries was about the same in 1959 as in 1919. During the same time an approximate 50 percent drop in numbers employed in farming induced a drop of almost 16 percent in its share of total employment. Government employees advanced the fastest as a single category, but most of these employees were at the state or local level; furthermore, almost half of this increase was for public school teachers.

LABOR FORCE CHARACTERISTICS

It is virtually impossible to talk about the labor force as if it were a single homogeneous mass. The labor force is dissimilar in some respects and similar in others. In order to discuss the working people of this nation with any degree of understanding, there have been several characteristics developed by which the people in the labor force may be described. In general, these characteristics are qualitative in nature. The most common characteristics include: occupation, sex, place of residence and urbanization, mobility, productivity, income, part-time and full-time work, unemployment, race, and education. Each of these characteristics will be discussed briefly to give a perspective of their relevance and meaning.

Women and the labor force

For many years it was commonly thought that the woman's place was in the home. It was somehow not quite respectable for women to work in the same way as men did for their livings, despite their need. In 1880, for example, there were only 2.6 million women employed; in 1960, there were approximately 23.6 million women employed, or about a third of the total labor force.[1] Changing family pressures, younger marriages, increased mobility for young people, and a change in the social perspective on the "material necessities" of life have all helped to lessen the social stigma attached to working women.

In the more recent years between 1947 and 1967, the role of women as active participants in the labor force has increased significantly (Table 6-4). It is interesting that employed single women enjoyed slightly more employment stability than single men; that married women with husbands alive doubled their number employed while employment of single women fell slightly; and that women who had been married but were divorced or widowed also increased in the numbers employed.

Women workers have generally been paid less than men who do

[1] Committee for Economic Development, "Economic Growth in the United States," February, 1958, p. 30.

TABLE 6-4: Employment Status of the Population by Marital Status and Sex, Selected Years, 1947-1967 (thousands of persons 14 years of age and over).

Marital Status and Year	Male				Female			
	Population	Labor Force Total	Em- ployed	Unem- ployed	Popu- lation	Labor Force Total	Em- ployed	Unem- ployed
Single:								
1947	14,760	9,375	8,500	849	12,078	6,181	5,991	190
1952	12,868	7,836	7,254	444	11,068	5,532	5,360	168
1958	14,331	8,174	6,959	1,122	11,822	5,365	5,078	287
1962	15,708	8,121	7,134	922	13,134	5,481	5,096	385
1967	17,754	9,001	8,151	706	15,311	6,323	5,958	365
Married (Spouse Present):								
1947	33,389	30,927	29,865	837	33,458	6,676	6,502	174
1952	36,510	33,482	32,222	464	36,510	9,222	8,946	266
1958	30,182	35,327	32,283	2,267	30,182	11,826	10,993	833
1962	41,218	36,396	33,883	1,605	41,218	13,485	12,716	769
1967	43,225	37,596	35,964	792	43,225	15,908	15,189	719
Other Marital Status:								
1947	4,201	2,760	2,546	211	9,270	3,466	3,309	157
1952	4,186	2,602	2,422	140	10,456	4,058	3,928	130
1958	4,949	2,903	2,524	354	11,780	4,810	4,474	336
1962	5,203	2,989	2,629	355	12,814	5,012	4,681	331
1967	5,525	3,027	2,819	190	14,551	5,724	5,472	251

SOURCE: Manpower Report of the President and a Report on Manpower Requirements, Resources, Utilization, and Training, U.S. Dept. of Labor, March, 1963.

similar work equally well. Recent legislation has changed this situation, and henceforth women will draw equal pay for equal work. There is a long history of women's efforts to engage in employment in the professions such as medicine and law, education, and also in manufacturing and the service industries.

Urbanization

As noted elsewhere, population and the labor force move about primarily in response to the relative productivity and income differentials between farm and nonfarm employment opportunity. Throughout the world, migration is motivated by an effort either to escape the unevenness of fluctuations in food production or to gain access to greater income opportunities out of farming. It is of historic significance that population growth and economic development do not occur at an equal rate throughout a country or region. Pockets of economically and socially underde-

veloped areas occur in the most developed nations of the world. There is
a constantly changing comparative production advantage between nations
and regions. Such a change is based on changing conditions of production
technology, on the goals of local people and their government, and on
myriads of other political, social, institutional, and economic forces at
work in a society.

The rise and fall of city centers follows much the same pattern described for regions. As cities grow, certain cost economics can be found
for some industries. Creation of nonfarm jobs beckons to farm workers
who are not fully satisfied with rural living, and they eventually move
close to this new source of work. An increased population in turn brings
about an increased demand for goods and services. More jobs are created
by these demands; more rural people come to fill them, and they also
exert further demands on the local economy.

There has been a dramatic urbanization of the United States population over the last 150 years (Table 6-5). In general, urbanization is a
process of population and employment concentration proceeding in two
ways: (a) through an increasing number of towns and cities, and (b)
through an increasing number of people at each of these geographical
concentrations.

There has been quite a rapid decline in the rural farm population
and an increasing number of people living in rural nonfarm areas (Tables
6-5 and 6-6). These areas are the suburbs of tomorrow, offering people
who are not desirous of city life an opportunity to live in the country

TABLE 6-5: U.S. Population, Selected Years, 1790 to 1960, by Place of Residence.

Year	Total (Millions)	Place of Residence		
		Urban	Rural	
		Percent		
1790	3.9	5	95	
1820	9.6	7	93	
1850	23.2	15	85	
1860	31.5	20	80	
1880	50.2	28	72	
1910	92.4	46	54	
			Rural Farm	Rural Nonfarm
1920	106.5	51	30	19
1930	123.1	56	25	19
1940	132.1	57	23	20
1950	151.7	62	17	21
1960	179.9	69	9	22

SOURCE: *U. S. Census of Population*, General Social and Economic Characteristics, U. S. Department of Commerce, Washington, D.C.

while still permitting them to hold nonfarm jobs. An ever increasing number of people seeking the attributes of a rural life by living in the country and commuting to work in the city has caused a closer relationship between rural and urban people. Rural and urban people are becoming more aware of each others' situations, goals, and problems. This awareness is essential if the people of a country are to fully participate in a rapidly growing economy.

For the past two decades the big cities and metropolitan areas throughout the entire country have been growing more rapidly than the small cities and rural towns. Employment trends have followed this same general pattern both in manufacturing and in the service sectors. As cities develop and grow they form concentrations of communications and distribution facilities that provide the impetus for new businesses, expanding industries, and a demand for increasing personnel to service the city center and the nearby city satellites.

During the 1950's the percentage of people living in metropolitan centers rose from 56 to 63 percent. Another way of looking at this urban growth is that 84 percent of all our population expansion took place on about one percent of our land area, that portion of the country contained within standard metropolitan areas.[2] This relatively concentrated growth is not an indication of a lack of space in which to develop; rather it is an indication of the appeal and attractiveness of urban life for many people.

Coincident with the development of urban life has been the development of suburban society. Suburbs are a result of the decentralization of the central cities and often develop at their expense. Part of the urban growth comes about because of annexations by big cities of smaller surrounding suburbs.

The consequences of people leaving rural areas and of rapid urban growth cause differences in approach to employment and land use. In rural areas the employment problems revolve around issues of finding economic uses for land that will help retard the migration, while in the city the problems concern choosing between competing demands for intensive land use.

Mobility and migrant workers

Mobility simply refers to the rate at which people in the labor force change residence. There are also different kinds of mobility; job mobility, for example, refers to the rate at which people in the labor force change jobs.

There has been a trend over the past few decades for men in the

[2] "Recent Population Trends in the United States with Emphasis on Rural Areas," U.S.D.A., E.R.S., Agricultural Economic Report No. 23 (Washington, D.C.: January, 1963).

labor force to be slightly more mobile than men not in the labor force, and for the unemployed to be more mobile than the employed. In general, the longer the period of employment the higher the income earned, and the greater the seniority built up on the job the less mobile a person becomes. The nonwhite population tends to have a greater mobility than the white population.

TABLE 6-6: Population Estimates by Residence and Percentage Ratios of Farm Population to National Totals, Selected Years, 1910-1966.

Year	Farm	Population Nonfarm (Thousands)	Total	Percent that farm is of total
1910	32,077 [1]	60,330	92,407	34.7
1920	31,974	74,492	106,466	30.0
1930	30,529	92,548	123,188	24.8
1940	30,547	101,575	132,122	23.1
1950	25,058	126,625	151,683	16.6
1960	15,635	164,225	179,860	8.7
1966	11,595	184,749	196,344	5.9

[1] 1910-1958 data are under the old definition of farm population; 1960-1966 data are under the new definition.

SOURCE: U.S.D.A., B.A.E., *The Farm Income Situation* (Washington, D.C.: U.S. Government Printing Office, October 1955); *Farm Population*, Bureau of Census, Series ERS (P-27), March 1963; USDA, *Agricultural Statistics*, 1967.

Since 1948 the mobility rate of our entire population one year of age and older has remained at about 20 percent.[3] This means that every year since 1948 one out of five persons has changed residence. More people move within the same county than move between counties, and more people move to another county in the same state than from one state to another.

Mobility rates are particularly high in the young adult ages. For example, 43.6 percent of the entire population ages 20 to 24 years changed residence from 1960 to 1961. However, as people get older they tend to become less mobile; only 9.6 percent of the population 65 years and older changed residence from 1960 to 1961.[4] Married persons have a slightly higher mobility rate than single people, which indicates that family formation and the need to find suitable employment to support the family is a major cause of mobility.

Mobility should not be confused with the migrant or the migratory worker. The migrant worker and the migratory worker both have a de-

[3] "Current Population Reports," Series P-20, United States Bureau of Census, August, 1962.
[4] *Ibid*. Recent information indicates these trends have persisted into the late 1960's.

gree of mobility. A migrant farm worker is broadly defined as a farm wage worker who has left his home country temporarily to do seasonal farm wage work in another country. A migratory worker is commonly understood to be one who follows a crop, planting it, cultivating it, or harvesting it. The Mexican *bracero* who works in this country is an example of a migrant worker. The wheat harvest crews who begin in Oklahoma and follow the ripening crop through into Canada are examples of migratory workers.

PRODUCTIVITY OF THE LABOR FORCE

Productivity of farm labor is largely influenced by (a) applying work methods which emphasize labor efficiency itself, (b) the quality and capabilities of the agricultural worker himself, (c) increased use of particular agricultural inputs, and (d) the adoption of new production, processing, and distribution technologies. While the productivity of nonfarm labor is also dependent upon the same factors, productivity per man hour in farming has increased more rapidly than the nonfarm sector worker since the mid-1940's. From 1929 to 1936 farm productivity per man hour increased only 6.8 percent, compared to an industrial productivity increase of 16.4 percent. From 1937 to 1947, however, productivity in farming rose 51 percent compared to 28 percent in industry, and from 1948 to 1956 the gain in farm productivity was 64.7 percent compared to 28.6 percent for industry. At no time between 1900 and 1929 did farm productivity gains equal those in the nonfarm sector.[5]

Data for the years 1947 to 1967 show the tremendous strides in productivity of the farm labor force even in recent times (Table 6-7). Although total farm output increased relatively more slowly than the output from either the manufacuring or the nonmanufacturing sectors, man hours of labor have been more than halved in farming while they increased in each of the other sectors. In the 20 years between 1947 and 1967 farm output per man hour increased nearly 1½ times. At the same time output per man hour was higher in manufacturing employment than in nonmanufacturing employment.

Increasing productivity in farming has had several consequences upon the total economy. It has first of all freed labor to undertake new jobs off the farm in industry and services. Second, although the productivity increases have not been distributed evenly throughout our agricultural history (hindered partially by wars, depression, and by such natural disasters as flood, drought, plant disease, and insects), they did allow farmers to provide for an ever increasing number of people. In 1820 one

[5] "Agriculture and Economic Growth," USDA, ERS, Agricultural Economic Report No. 28 (Washington, D.C.: March, 1963), p. 17.

TABLE 6-7: Indexes of Output for the United States, Agriculture, Manufacturing, and Nonmanufacturing Industries, Selected Years, 1947-1967 (1957-59 = 100).

Year	Output [1]				Man Hours				Output per Man Hour			
	Total	Farming	Mfg.	Nonmfg.	Total	Farming	Mfg.	Nonmfg.	Total	Farming	Mfg.	Nonmfg.
1947	68.4	81.2	71.1	65.9	96.5	161.8	95.1	85.8	70.9	50.2	74.8	76.8
1950	77.3	92.8	78.3	75.5	95.6	143.4	93.5	88.2	80.9	64.7	83.7	85.6
1952	84.4	90.4	88.4	81.9	99.6	129.4	102.3	93.3	84.7	69.9	86.4	87.8
1954	87.2	97.6	88.1	85.8	97.2	117.0	98.1	93.3	89.7	83.4	89.8	92.0
1956	97.0	100.5	102.1	94.1	103.3	113.8	105.2	100.7	93.9	88.3	97.1	93.4
1958	97.0	100.5	94.2	98.1	97.4	97.6	95.2	98.4	99.6	103.0	98.9	99.7
1960	106.9	104.8	107.1	107.0	101.5	95.9	100.9	102.7	105.3	109.3	106.1	104.2
1962	114.4	107.2	117.3	113.6	100.9	88.0	102.1	102.7	113.4	121.8	114.9	110.6
1964	127.8	107.7	131.2	127.7	104.3	79.5	105.2	108.2	122.5	135.5	124.7	118.0
1967	146.5	116.4	156.5	144.0	111.0	68.0	117.2	115.7	132.0	171.2	133.5	124.5

[1] Output refers to Gross National Product in 1954 prices for years 1947-1962; 1958 prices are used for 1964 and 1967.

SOURCE: Economic Report of the President, February 1968, p. 248.

90

TABLE 6-8: Number of Persons Supplied with Food and Fiber by One Farm Worker in the United States, Selected Years, 1920-1962.

Year	Number of Persons Supported by One Farm Worker
1820	4.1
1910	7.1
1920	8.3
1930	9.8
1940	10.8
1950	15.5
1955	17.9
1958	23.0
1960	25.3
1962	28.6
1966	39.6

SOURCE: Agricultural Outlook Charts, U.S.D.A., 1967.

farmer could supply enough food and fiber for only an additional four persons (Table 6-8). It took one hundred years for him to be able to double this effort and provide for eight people. The number doubled again in only 30 years, reaching 16 by 1950. But by 1966 only 16 years later, one farmer could take care of the food and fiber needs for about 40 people, more than doubling again. Not only has the time required to double productivity of farm labor been reduced substantially, but the number of people provided for has risen rapidly with significantly higher levels of population.

In addition, Morris and Kadlec have shown that the figure of 28 for 1962 is based on a large number of part-time farm workers and the figure reflects an average of only 1370 hours per year. If full-time man equivalents were considered, one worker supplied 66 people in 1962. Furthermore, if only farm workers on farms grossing over $10,000 sales per year are considered, one full-time worker equivalent supplied food for 90 others.[6]

Income

Wage and salaries paid to workers vary with the kind of job and with the capabilities of the person working. Also, wages paid for the same type of job and for the same quality of employee will vary from region to region throughout the country (Table 6-9).

In general, farm workers are not paid as much as nonfarm workers

---

[6] W. H. M. Morris and John E. Kadlec, "An Evaluation and Projection of Output per Man in Agriculture," Journal Paper 2190, Purdue University Agricultural Experiment Station (Lafayette, Indiana: August, 1963).

TABLE 6-9: Median Money Income of Farm and Nonfarm Families by Region and Color, 1960.

	United States	North-East	North Central	South White	South Nonwhite	West
Median Income						
Farm	$2,875	$4,077	$3,109	$2,668	$1,154	$5,242
Rural nonfarm	5,620	6,125	5,893	4,905	1,707	6,735
Urban	5,911	6,089	6,150	5,377	2,773	5,564
Farm income as a percent of:						
Rural nonfarm	51	67	53	54	68	78
Urban	49	67	51	50	42	80

SOURCE: Ruttan, V. W. "The Human Resources Problem in American Agriculture," *Farming, Farmers, and Markets for Farm Goods,* Supplementary Paper No. 15, published by the Committee for Economic Development, November 1962, p. 80.

even though many farmers work seven days a week and up to 18 hours a day during peak labor seasons of planting and harvest. Cost of living differences account for part of the farm-nonfarm differential, as does the fact that many farm people prefer to live in the country and raise their families there rather than in the city, despite the difference in income.

Median farm family incomes are consistently lower than median nonfarm family incomes even though both have shown secular increases. Median farm family incomes rose from $1,963 in 1947 to $4,841 in 1966, while median nonfarm family incomes rose from $2,826 in 1947 to $7,582 in 1966. In addition to differences in family incomes by place of residence, there are differences in income according to race. White families had median family incomes in 1966 of $7,722 for the United States, $8,093 in the North and West region, and $6,773 in the South. These data can be compared to black median family incomes of $4,463 for the entire country, $5,725 for the North and West region, and $3,422 for the South.[7]

Part-time employment

There has been a rapid increase in part-time employment. In fact, many jobs have been modified in an attempt to obtain competent adult women employees, for example, who prefer not to be away from their families all day on a full-time job. Students working their way through school have also helped develop the institution of part-time employment.

Since the numbers of farmers declined drastically during the 1950's, the statistics for those employed in part-time work or in off-farm work of 100 days or more either stayed constant or increased for most states. These part-time jobs became necessary if farmers wanted to stay in the

[7] U.S. Department of Commerce, *Statistical Abstract of the United States,* 1968, pp. 326 and 328.

business of food production. The most common kinds of part-time jobs obtained included custom work on somebody else's farm, driving a school bus, highway jobs, or some type of nonfarm work in town.

There were approximately 12.3 million part-time workers in 1960. By 1970 a 30 percent increase or a total of about 16 million part-time workers is expected.[8] Service and finance, trade, and construction will provide the majority of these jobs. The number of part-time jobs available in farming will continue to decline.

Unemployment and underemployment

An unemployed person can generally be defined as a person who does not have a job. While this definition is not precise since it does not specify such considerations as how long he has been without employment or whether he has to be actively seeking work, no discussion of the definition will be attempted here. There is much controversy about what constitutes legitimate unemployment.

The United States has always had a certain amount of unemployment (Tables 6-1 and 6-4). Economists recognize two broad types of unemployment: frictional and structural. Frictional unemployment takes place when a man changes jobs of his own accord or when he is forced to change jobs because of technology or hiring policies. Structural unemployment occurs as a result of the inability of the entire economy to function at a sufficiently high level so that all the people who want jobs may find them. Since the end of World War II there has been an increasing proportion of structural unemployment in our economy in spite of the unprecedented level of economic growth during this time.

Underemployment is a difficult concept to understand. It is now generally defined as occurring when an employed person produces less than another employed person of equal skill, who does the same kind of work with the same resources. The term does not mean that the underemployed person is not working hard and long hours, nor is it based on the idea of equal pay for equal worth. It essentially means that the worker is not producing the output of which he is potentially capable, either because he does not have a full-time job or because his labor resource is under-utilized in some other way.

Although the number of jobs in the nation has increased rapidly, growth at any one time has not been sufficient to employ all those currently in the labor force plus all the new entrants to the labor force. Unemployment in agriculture has been especially severe. Not only has the total opportunity for agricultural employment been declining, but the seasonal nature of production, disruptions by weather, and the replace-

[8] "Manpower Challenge of the 1960's," United States Department of Labor, 1961.

ment of labor with capital (automation) have all contributed to increasingly fewer people being employed.

Unemployment has almost always been higher among persons under 25 years of age than for those 25 years and older. For example, although people under 25 years of age represented only one-fifth of the labor force in 1962, they comprised over a third of the unemployed.[9] There are good reasons for this situation. Young people just entering the labor force have not usually had time to discover at what job they want to work the rest of their lives; they are not trained in any skilled job and they have not had an opportunity to build up job experience and seniority. As a result, it is the young people who are the last hired and the first laid off.

Unemployment rates are also higher among the nonwhite population than among the white population, regardless of occupation. This situation is particularly true of the nonwhite population under age 20.[10] There is also significantly more unemployment among unskilled or semi-skilled workers than there is among professional or skilled workers, in spite of color.

Education has a direct bearing on employment. Boys and girls who drop out of high school have significantly higher rates of unemployment than high school graduates, and high school graduates have a higher rate than college graduates.

Unemployment and underemployment are not spread evenly throughout the country; they occur in much the same pattern in which economic growth develops, although they are influenced inversely by it. Where economic growth is rapid unemployment rates and underemployment are low. Where economic growth has by-passed an area the numbers of those unemployed and underemployed mushroom if the population living there does not make the necessary migration adjustments.

QUALITY OF THE LABOR FORCE

Education

The illiteracy of our entire population declined from 11.3 per cent in 1900 to 2.4 per cent in 1960.[11] The median years of school completed by all persons 25 years and older has risen steadily (Table 6-10) in all parts of the nation. Public school enrollment in 1880 was 9.9 million persons and 36.2 million in 1960, while the public school days of schooling

---

[9] "Manpower Research," Bulletin No. 2, OMAT, U.S. Department of Labor, March, 1963, p. 9.

[10] *Ibid.*

[11] "Current Population Reports," Series P-23, U.S. Bureau of Census, February 12, 1963.

per enrolled pupil increased from 81 days in 1880 to 160 days in 1960.[12] However, even though illiteracy is falling and more people are attending school and spending more time in the classroom each year, the need for education has intensified as never before in our history.

The average work week for adults and children was about 63 hours in 1880, and by 1960 it declined to about 40 hours.[13] The increase in leisure time has meant several things for workers. First, they could simply relax and enjoy life. Second, they could obtain another job in addition to their initial job (and approximately 25 percent of the workers held two or more jobs in 1966). Third, they could take advantage of the free time to pursue their education and upgrade their job skills. As was pointed out in the section on unemployment, although there has been a persistent lack of jobs for everyone who wants to work in this country, those with education and technical training are not as hard hit by unemployment as those who have none.

The need for education and training is probably highest among the younger population. The age group between 18 and 24 is faced with a difficult task in finding a job, as these people have to compete not only with their peers but also with older people already in the labor force.

There will be an estimated increase of 13.5 million workers by 1970. This is a 20 percent increase above that of 1960. Even though more boys and girls will be spending more time in school, workers under 25 years of age are expected to increase by 40 percent during the 1960's. Of the net increase of 13.5 million workers, 6.4 million will be under 25 and 5.5 million will be 45 and over. The two groups together will then account for seven-eighths of the increase in growth of the labor force in the 1960's. These are the age groups in which employment problems are the greatest. If we construct a labor force balance sheet for the 1960's,[14] we find the following:

		Millions
Number of workers in 1960		73.6
Subtract:		
Withdrawals (deaths, retirement, marriage, etc.)	−15.5	
1960 workers still there in 1970		58.1
Add:		
New young workers	+26.0	
Women returning	+ 3.0	
Number of workers in 1970		87.1

[12] "Economic Growth in the United States," CED, *op. cit.*, p. 29.
[13] *Ibid.*, p. 29.
[14] "Manpower, Challenge of the 1960's," U.S. Department of Labor.

TABLE 6-10: Median Years School Completed by Persons 25 Years and Older for the United States and Regions, 1940, 1950, and 1960.

| | Year | | |
	1940	1950	1960
United States	8.4	9.3	10.6
Regions:			
Pacific	9.7	11.5	12.0
Mountain	8.9	10.7	12.2
New England	8.8	10.4	11.2
E. N. Central	8.5	9.6	10.7
Middle Atlantic	8.4	9.3	10.5
W. S. Central	8.1	8.8	9.9
W. N. Central	8.1	9.0	10.7
S. Atlantic	7.8	8.6	9.8
E. S. Central	7.5	8.3	8.8

SOURCE: U. S. Census of Population, Characteristics of Population, Vol. II, 1960.

The 26 million new young workers added in the balance sheet represent 40 percent more than those added from that group in the 1950's. Furthermore, they came on at the rate of 3 million a year in the late 1960's.

The large number of new young workers will mean that employers:
(a) will find that they have a bigger stake in a sound educational system
(b) will have to employ a larger proportion of young and inexperienced persons
(c) will have to provide more and better training on the job and concentrate on supervision and safety education
(d) will have to expect more turnover
(e) will have to allow for more part-time workers.

Education and training undoubtedly will get more emphasis in the future. High school enrollments increased by nearly 50 percent in the 1960's, a 10 percent greater increase than that of the 1950's. College enrollments increased by almost 70 percent as compared to a 40 percent increase during the 1950's. Our new young workers will thus have more schooling; 70 percent will be high school graduates as compared with 60 percent in the 1950's. And there will be fewer entering the labor force without completing at least 8 grades.

Some people question the emphasis on education, wondering whether or not it actually pays to get a high school diploma or some type of advanced college or professional training. The answer is clearly that it does pay (Table 6-11). For people graduating from high school, average annual earnings were over twice what they were for people who had less than an eighth grade education. For those who had a college degree or

TABLE 6-11: Education and Average Annual Earnings of Males, 45 to 54 Years of Age, 1956 and 1966.

Years of School Completed	Lifetime Income		Annual Average Income	
	1956	1966	1956	1966
Elementary:	($1,000)		(dollars)	
less than 8 years	122	174	2,574	3,520
8 years	66	228	3,631	4,867
High School:				
1 to 3 years	189	270	4,367	6,294
4 or more years	228	320	5,183	7,494
College:				
1 to 3 years	268	381	5,597	8,738
4 or more years	359	520	7,877	11,739

SOURCE: U.S. Department of Commerce, *Statistical Abstract of the United States,* 1968, p. 112.

more, average annual earnings were almost twice those of a high school graduate.

The earnings of the hired farm-working force were not quite as spectacular, although higher wages for both men and women are associated with higher levels of education. The number of days worked by a farm worker also increased as his educational level rose.

EMPLOYMENT OUTLOOK

Looking ahead to the employment needs of the future, the biggest increases in job openings have occurred and will likely continue to occur in occupations requiring the most education and training (Figure 6-1). There was over a 40 percent increase in the professional and technical occupational group from 1960 to 1970. Proprietors and managers, clerical and sales workers, and skilled workers and service workers increased about one-fourth. Semi-skilled workers increased about 18 percent. But no more unskilled workers and fewer farmers were required.

When we match recent training with those future needs, we find that in 1959 professional and technical workers averaged a few months beyond a college degree (Table 6-12). Proprietors and managers, and clerical and sales workers averaged about a half year beyond high school. Skilled, semi-skilled, and service workers averaged about 2 or 3 years of high school.

Farm employment

The employment situation in farming is not one of growth. The total farm population and work force are declining. Only one out of six chil-

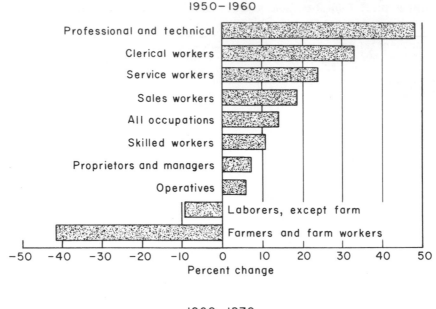

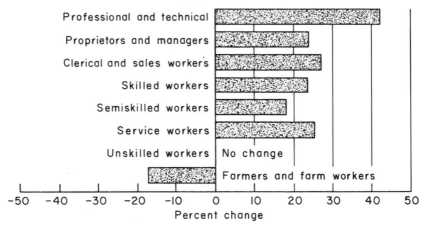

FIGURE 6-1:   Percent Change in Employment by Major Occupational Groups, 1950-
1960 and 1960-1970, United States. United States Department of Commerce,
and "Manpower — Challenge of the 1960's," United States Department of
Labor.

dren born on farms now has an opportunity to enter farming and it is
likely that in 1970 this ratio was closer to only one out of ten. The educational level of the farm work force is low and income opportunities
for the average farmer are not as great as in most nonfarm jobs.

However, those who survive the adjustments in farming will be

TABLE 6-12: Average Years of School Completed for Those Working in 1959, United States.

Occupation Group	Average Years of School Completed
Professional and Technical	16.2
Proprietors and Managers	12.4
Clerical and Sales	12.5
Skilled	11.0
Semiskilled	9.9
Service	9.7
Unskilled	8.6
Farmers and Farm Workers	8.6

SOURCE: "Manpower Challenge of the 1960's," U. S. Department of Labor, Undated.

business managers of considerable skill regardless of how much formal training they may have had. They will control significant amounts of capital and operate an agricultural plant whose productivity is unsurpassed in the history of the world. These men will be specialists in crop and livestock production, grassland farming and timber production, in the use of technical agricultural inputs of fertilizer and water, and in marketing their agricultural output. This is the current challenge in American farming, but the risks are high and the opportunity is limited.

7

The role of capital

in agriculture and

economic growth[1]

WAYS TO DEFINE CAPITAL

There are many definitions of capital. Until the early 1950's most people expressed capital in terms of such tangible items as physical plant and equipment, construction of all kinds, machinery, and producer's inventories. Since 1950 certain intangible items such as education have been added to the physical kinds of capital recognized above.

Much of the recognition of intangible capital is due to the work of T. W. Schultz, who attempted to assess economic growth in America and

[1] See W. G. Murray and A. G. Nelson, "Agricultural Finance," Iowa State Press, 1960, for a definitive discussion of capital in agriculture. Also, see "Capital and Credit Needs in a Changing Agriculture," E. L. Baum and others (Symposium), Iowa State Press, 1961, for a discussion of historical and projected capital and credit needs in agriculture.

abroad. He estimated that between two-thirds and three-fourths of the total output of developed countries was not attributable to the traditional forms of capital investment, but rather to invesment in human beings through education, technical training, and managerial knowledge. It was Schultz's idea that expenditures on education, training, health, and the like, were not consumption expenditures but were really investments of a sort that produced a flow of income over time.[2]

Up to Schultz's time capital had been defined traditionally as all forms of reproducible wealth or goods used directly or indirectly in the production process. A different perspective of capital was provided by the addition of intangible capital items. Capital could still be defined as an input in production which embodies technology; it was still consistent with the definition that capital is produced from goods and services saved from consumption and used by, or as a part of, the human agent in further production. But it went further; it recognized that investment could be made in the human being himself, and that he could produce an income flow directly as a result of this investment. Under this new perspective capital might well be defined as a factor of production which generates a flow of income spread over a certain period of time.

Capital used in agriculture is composed of both equity and debt capital. Debt capital is money borrowed (credit) which can be used to purchase inputs for production processes and which generates money income over time. Credit facilitates the process of economic development by supplementing equity funds when the latter are not sufficient to provide for such capital-consuming necessities as machinery. Equity capital is the capital which is fully owned and free of debt. It is important to distinguish between equity and debt capital (or credit) only insofar as they come from different sources, for they are essentially the same in their capacity to generate income flow.

Capital may also be classified as private or social capital. Any capital such as farm buildings, houses, stores, factories, and even education made by a private individual, partnership, or corporation, can be classified as private capital. These items comprise a major share of the fixed assets of private business. Expenditures of public money made by authorized local, state, or federal public agencies for roads, highways, schools, courthouses, bridges, and parks belong in the social capital category.

As a society grows both kinds of capital grow and constitute the visible form of the country's wealth. A growing population calls for more businesses, for more construction, and for more factories. More people also increase the need for better communications. People also want better roads, better schools, and more parks and zoos.

[2] T. W. Schultz, "Investment in Human Capital," AER (Vol. 51, March, 1961, No. 1), pp. 1-16.

WAYS TO MEASURE CAPITAL

The total amount of capital can be measured in three general ways. One way is to simply total the accumulation of funds spent on plant and equipment over a certain period of time. A second way is to total all expenditures. The third way is to enumerate and evaluate the production of all physical goods. Each method has certain advantages and disadvantages. Much depends on the purpose for which the particular measurement is being made.

CHARACTERISTICS OF CAPITAL

Physical capital items have several distinguishing characteristics. One of these characteristics is durability. Most physical capital items like plant and equipment, housing, barns, and dams, are things that will last a relatively long time. Another characteristic is that these items usually involve large expenditures of money and are often put in a fixed location. A final characteristic is that there is usually quite a long time between the time the project is initiated and the end of construction.

Note that these characteristics also apply to education and technical training. An education lasts for one's lifetime and can be constantly supplemented; it involves considerable costs of time, money, and effort; it is fixed in the individual, who in turn may teach someone else; and it generally takes a minimum of 16 years of formal education to get a bachelor's degree from college.

EVAULATION OF CAPITAL

There are three general methods of evaluating capital items. One is to capitalize the anticipated income stream over its expected life time.[3] This method can be misleading at times because the capital item may not last as long as expected, or at the end of its expected lifetime it may still be in excellent condition, still generating a stream of revenue.

The second method is simply to record the item's market price. This is perhaps the easiest method. However, market prices are often deceiving because of inflation, variation from one year to the next, and different markets in different parts of the country.

[3] The formula is to divide the annual income stream in dollars by an imputed interest rate. For example, suppose you bought a piece of machinery which would increase your net income $300 a year. If your money is worth 5% a year to you the piece of machinery would be worth $6,000 — capitalized value ($300 ÷ .05).

The third way is to note the initial price and subtract a certain allowance for depreciation. This method can also be standardized by formula, but it is liable to the same difficulties mentioned above in the first method.

All three methods are used widely. However, the evaluation of capital assumes meaning only within a given framework of technology and institutions. For example, even though the looms and cloth markets of Britain during the Industrial Revolution had great significance at that time, both the looms (capital items) and marketing methods (institutions) are obsolete today. Advances in technology have shown new methods of weaving and the innovation of new marketing institutions has opened new and different channels of product distribution.

There is probably more difficulty in measuring and evaluating social capital goods than private capital goods. Part of the reason for this is that the private individual in business is interested in making profits, while this is not generally true for social capital investment. How should one value public harbors, roads, bridges, parks, museums, schools, and utilities? Many of the items like roads and bridges are indispensable for the operation of a dynamic society; some things like museums are priceless outgrowths of a society's cultural development. Does one measure and evaluate social capital expenditures in the same manner that he does a private expenditure? Should the tolls we pay on certain roads and bridges be determined on a maintenance and repair basis or on a profit framework designed to return a "fair" amount to all input factors?

Another difficulty in capital evaluation arises when one attempts to standardize and evaluate either private or public capital expenditures on an international basis. Besides currency differences, different cultures place different emphasis upon different items so that what might be highly valued in one country might have a relatively low value in another.

ROLE OF CAPITAL IN ECONOMIC DEVELOPMENT AND AGRICULTURE

Capital is a critical factor in determining the kind, amount, and quality of a society's total output or production. Use of capital follows the general law of variable proportions (discussed in Chapter 12 under its other name, the "law of diminishing returns") which says (with reference to capital) that output can be increased by adding more capital if capital is the limiting factor in a production process. However, even though economists may be in general agreement with this law, they are not in general agreement on (a) what kinds of capital to add, (b) when they should be added, and (c) into what sector they should be added and through which enterprises they should be introduced into the economy. Most of this disagreement can be traced to different judgments of the relative roles to be taken by the private and public sectors of our economy, in differences in opinion of how capital should be raised, and in differences in viewpoint over rates of repayment.

It has been commonly said that relatively underdeveloped countries and certain areas in the United States lack capital to develop their industry and agriculture properly, and that there is a dearth of both private and public capital immediately available for investment in these areas. However, in many instances it is individuals' attitudes toward credit, toward acquiring capital and using it, and their managerial ability and desire which often constitute the limiting factors and not the availability of capital per se.

In our economy capital has generally been used to increase the productivity of labor in farming. One can see this readily by noting the increasing value of assets per farmworker, a decreasing amount of farm labor, an increasing total farm output, and an increasing output per farm worker (Table 7-1).

TABLE 7-1: Indices of Farm Output and Average Value of Production Assets per Farm Worker, Selected Years, 1940-1967.

	1940	1950	1955	1960	1967
Index of Total Farm Output [1]	70	86	96	106	118
Index of Total Farm Output [2]					
per unit of total input	72	85	94	105	109
per man hour	36	61	80	115	167
Average Value of Production [3]					
Assets per farm worker	$3,326	$9,529	$13,876	$21,304	$41,307
Index of man hours for all					
farm work [1]	190	142	120	92	70

Indices are based on 1957-59 = 100.
[1] USDA, Statistical Bulletin 233, revised July 1968.
[2] Economic Report of the President, USGPO, Washington, February 1968.
[3] USDA, Balance Sheet of Agriculture 1967, Agr. Info. Bull. 329.

Increased use of capital in agriculture has been facilitated by the adoption of yield-increasing technology. These new technologies are usually concerned with an intensive use of capital on farms. Although their adoption generally lowers per unit costs of production, they increase total capital costs per farm.

Total capital investment in farm production

Total investment in physical assets on farms has increased over 10 times in the last century, and has increased five-fold in just the last 25 years (Table 7-2). By dividing capital investment into real estate (land and buildings) and non-real estate, several trends can be separated.

The fixed investment in real estate has increased about 15 times since 1870 and 6 times since 1940, but almost half of this increase has been due to increasing prices. Rising land prices means that the generation of farmers holding real estate will benefit by getting appreciably higher prices for their land than they paid, although they may have done nothing to it but hold onto it, while the generation of farmers which buys land from them assumes a new, higher cost structure for the same land. When analyzing increases in land values, it is well to remember that if one deflates land values to hold them in constant comparable dollars the figures he compares are not the prices that a farmer getting into business today will have to pay—and it is the current land prices in which most farmers are interested.

The net adjustment in livestock capital has been upward, even though the introduction of the gas engine and the electric motor eliminated the need for much of the animal power on farms. The rise in value of implements and machinery capital is consistent with this shift and also with the decrease in farm population and labor force.

Recent data on capital assets in agriculture show large increases in the last 25 years. Since 1940, real estate values have risen about six times, livestock and poultry values have gone up over three times, and investment in machinery and motor vehicles has increased over 9 times (Table 7-2). At the same time farmer's assets in the form of deposits and currency have risen by a factor of 3, and investments in cooperatives has increased by a factor of almost 9.

Capital expenditures for farm inputs of all kinds were only 33 percent greater in 1967 than they were in 1910, but their composition had changed drastically (Table 7-3). About one third the labor was used in 1967 as compared to 1910, but even with the decrease in labor 20 percent more land and buildings were utilized. The use of mechanical power of some type on farms was over five times greater in 1967 than it was in 1910, while the use of fertilizers, feed, seed, and livestock purchases had increased almost ten times. Miscellaneous items such as taxes and interest had just about doubled during the same time.

Greater specialization in farming combined with a trend toward larger farms and fewer farmers has helped cause an increased dependence upon farm inputs produced in the nonfarm sector of the economy. Farmers purchased about three times as many agricultural inputs in 1967 than they did in 1910, and used about half as many farm-produced nonpurchased inputs (Table 7-3).

One should remember that increased productivity per worker and manhour is associated with the quality of resources (inputs) used as well

TABLE 7-2: Comparative Balance Sheet of Agriculture, United States, January 1, Specified Years, 1940 to 1967 (in billions of dollars).[1]

Item	1940	1950	1960	1967 [2]
ASSETS				
Physical assets:				
Real estate	33.6	75.3	129.9	182.0
Non–real-estate:				
Livestock and poultry	5.1	12.9	15.6	18.8
Machinery and motor vehicles	3.1	12.2	22.3	28.9
Crops stored on and off farms [3]	2.7	7.6	7.8	10.0
Household furnishings and equipment	4.2	8.6	9.6	8.5
Financial assets:				
Deposits and currency	3.2	9.1	9.2	10.3
United States savings bonds	.2	4.7	4.7	4.0
Investments in cooperatives	.8	2.1	4.4	7.0
Total	52.9	132.5	203.5	269.5
CLAIMS				
Liabilities:				
Real estate debt	6.6	5.6	12.1	23.3
Non–real-estate debt—				
Excluding Commodity Credit Corporation	3.0	5.1	11.6	21.2
Commodity Credit Corporation [4]	.4	1.7	1.2	1.2
Total liabilities	10.0	12.4	24.9	45.7
Proprietors' equities	42.9	120.1	178.6	223.8
Total	52.9	132.5	203.5	269.5

[1] For 48 States.
[2] Preliminary.
[3] Includes all crops held on farms including crops under loan to Commodity Credit Corporation, and crops held off farms as security for CCC loans. On January 1, 1967, the latter totaled $447 million.
[4] Nonrecourse CCC loans secured by crops owned by farmers and included as assets in this Balance Sheet.

as their quantity. Increased managerial knowhow and improved farm organization also help account for the spectacular productivity increases shown in Table 7-1.

It should be remembered that although these figures are for the entire country and all of its agricultural production, there are regional differences between types of farming regions as well. The data presented here show only the aggregate trend and are not meant to apply to specific regions.

Capital investment per farm. The average capital investment required in modern day farming has increased rapidly during the last two decades (Table 7-4). Those families who stayed in farming between 1940

TABLE 7-3: Index of Total Farm Inputs by Major Subgroups, Purchased and Nonpurchased for the United States, Selected Years 1910-1967, (1957-59 = 100).

Year	Total Inputs	Farm Labor	Farm Real Estate	Mechanical Power and Machinery	Fertilizers and Lime	Feed, Seed, and Livestock Purchases	Miscellaneous	Purchased	Nonpurchased
1910	82	208	88	20	12	16	56	44	162
1915	88	215	92	25	12	15	65	50	166
1920	93	222	92	32	16	23	67	55	174
1925	95	220	89	33	18	27	71	60	169
1930	97	212	91	40	21	26	76	62	170
1935	88	212	91	40	17	23	66	56	150
1940	97	190	92	42	28	45	73	72	142
1945	99	174	88	54	45	72	76	76	140
1950	101	140	97	86	68	72	85	91	119
1955	102	119	100	99	90	86	94	97	111
1960	101	92	100	100	110	109	106	103	96
1967	109	70	106	112	205	140	120	124	81

SOURCE: U.S.D.A Statistical Bulletin No. 233 (Changes in Farm Production and Efficiency).

TABLE 7-4: Average Value of Production Assets per Farm, Current Prices, United States, January 1 for Selected Years, 1940-1967.

Year	Farm Real Estate (dollars)	Livestock (dollars)	Machinery and Motor Vehicles (dollars)	Other (dollars)	Total (dollars)
1940	4,608	608	591	351	6,158
1950	12,003	2,199	1,983	1,193	17,378
1955	18,814	2,357	3,402	1,592	26,165
1960	31,966	3,843	4,860	1,796	42,465
1967	57,198	5,933	7,690	2,299	73,120

SOURCE: Balance Sheet of Agriculture 1967, U.S.D.A., Ag. Info. Bull. No. 329.

and 1967 made an average investment of almost $2,000 per year. Average capital investment on approximately 500 Indiana Farm Account Co-operator's farms rose almost $5,500 each year during the 1950's (Table 7-5). While the capital invested and the production rose on the Indiana farms, the number of men needed to utilize the capital and to manage the increase in production stayed constant at 1.7 persons. Net farm income

TABLE 7-5: Average Capital Requirements, Acres, Production, and Income on Approximately 500 Indiana Farm Record Cooperator Farms, 1950 and 1960.

Items	1950	1960
Acres per farm:		
Total	225	310
Tillable	179	253
In corn	56	122
Bushels of corn produced per acre	58	86
Number of feeder cattle bought	7	23
Number of hogs raised	150	289
Capital invested per farm:		
Real estate	$30,171	$71,662
Machinery and equipment	6,761	10,443
Livestock, feed, supplies	12,896	21,811
Total	$49,828	$103,916
Size of labor force — average	1.7	1.7
Net farm income	$8,405	$10,868
Income to labor and management	5,914	5,672
Rate earned on investment	10.7%	5.4%

SOURCE: *Farm Record Business Summaries*, Cooperative Extension Service, Purdue University, Department of Agricultural Economics, Lafayette, Indiana, 1960.

on these farms rose about $220 per year, while the rate earned on total investment declined by about one-half.

Capital investment varies with the size of the farm and with the type of farming. Differences in capital investment related to size of farm come about principally because there is usually a higher dollar investment associated with more acres and more buildings. Differences in investment associated with types of farming can usually be traced to the number of acres needed for the various enterprises and to the differences in the type of equipment needed. For example, tillable acres tend to be lower on Indiana dairy farms than on the hog-cattle feeding operations.

Studies have shown that the lower risk enterprises which produce frequent and regular incomes are associated with comparatively lower capital investment requirements than high risk once-a-year income enterprises. Poultry and dairy farms prior to 1960 have in general fit the low risk category, as compared to specialized crop and livestock farms (Table 7-6).

Capital accumulation and control in farming

Capital accumulation is generally understood to be capital owned by individuals or legal business entities, such as partnerships or corporations. All capital accumulation occurs because someone or some group

TABLE 7-6: Value of Capital Per Farm, Specified Types of Commercial Family-Operated Farms, 1940 and 1959.

Type of Farm	Average Value 1940	1959	1959 as a percent of 1940
	(Dollars)		(Percent)
Dairy farms, Central Northeast:			
Total farm capital, January 1	9,600	38,750	404
Land and buildings	5,300	20,550	388
Livestock and equipment	3,400	15,430	454
Hog-beef fattening farms, Corn Belt:			
Total farm capital, January 1	20,990	75,420	359
Land and buildings	14,220	48,120	338
Livestock and equipment	4,860	21,100	434
Cash-grain, Corn Belt:			
Total farm capital, January 1	31,470	112,280	357
Land and buildings	26,250	93,930	358
Livestock and equipment	2,900	10,830	373
Cotton farms, Black Prairie:			
Total farm capital, January 1	8,820	34,210	388
Land and buildings	7,240	28,420	393
Livestock and equipment	1,320	5,320	403
Cotton farms (irrigated), High Plains, Texas:			
Total farm capital, January 1	24,120	107,850	447
Land and buildings	18,300	96,300	526
Livestock and equipment	4,900	10,840	221
Southern Piedmont:			
Total farm capital, January 1	4,760	20,430	429
Land and buildings	3,670	17,010	463
Livestock and equipment	880	2,920	332
Tobacco-cotton farms, North Carolina:			
Total farm capital, January 1	6,770	24,530	362
Land and buildings	5,500	20,000	364
Livestock and equipment	1,080	3,790	351
Wheat-small grain-livestock farms, Northern Plains:			
Total farm capital, January 1	10,830	57,610	532
Land and buildings	7,230	33,980	470
Livestock and equipment	2,710	16,840	621
Wheat-pea farms, Washington and Idaho:			
Total farm capital, January 1	35,970	183,810	511
Land and buildings	29,060	155,000	533
Livestock and equipment	4,620	22,020	477

SOURCE: "Capital and Credit Needs in a Changing Agriculture," Symposium, Iowa State Press, 1961, p. 8.

saves. Individual farmers accumulate capital from income which is not all spent on current consumption or maintenance items.

Control of capital on the other hand, means that an individual or legal entity can use capital without necessarily having ownership of it. This is especially relevant in farming where a large initial investment is necessary if a beginning farmer is to make a living on the farm equal to that which he could make off the farm. Acquiring control of capital usually means that a particular individual or group chooses the lending institutions from which to borrow, determines the debt load, and then makes investment decisions concerning a total set of capital assets, both borrowed and owned, as if all capital were owned by him.

Both capital accumulation and control of capital permit the adoption of new technologies and allow their adopters to reap initiator's profits, which in turn are an incentive to adopt other technologies. When capital accumulation is greater than population growth, the nation's stock of capital grows. The more economic growth that exists, the more new technologies are introduced into the production process and the institutional environment. These innovations also lead to further capital accumulation and economic growth.

SOURCES OF CAPITAL IN AGRICULTURE

Capital in agriculture comes from three main sources: from the equity of landlords, from the equity of farm operators, or from credit. The equity sources give rise to capital directly through savings; the credit source gives rise to capital directly through borrowing (although these funds have been saved previously for investment). "Mixed" types of equity and credit sources include gifts, inheritance, marriage, inflation, and certain legal entities such as rental or purchase contracts (including vertical integration), partnerships, and corporations.

The volume of savings is influenced by psychological and social values as well as economics. The desire of the individual to save, his evaluation of the worth of future risk versus the pleasure of current consumption, his expectations of profit, and his personal evaluation of the size of investment all enter into the savings decisions. The current tone of business activity and the outlook for both short- and long-term economic activity also influence the volume of saving and investment.

In many underdeveloped areas the savings level tends to be low because the income level is low. In these situations capital formation may be difficult since the major portion of income is consumed by current necessities.

Capital for loans may come from home or abroad. The rate of interest is both the market price of credit and the investment incentive to which most potential lenders look. The rate of interest and the volume of credit outstanding at any one time both fluctuate. This is true for both short-term and long-term credit. Those seeking capital for investment on farms must compete for borrowed funds in the domestic and foreign capital markets along with all those who seek capital resources for investment in the other sectors of the economy.

The principal sources of farm credit in this country are private individuals, commercial banks, insurance companies, merchants and dealers, authorized government agencies, and the cooperative agricultural credit system. These sources make loans available in one or more of the following ways:

(a) the direct method, in which the loan is made directly from the investor to the borrower without an intermediary of any kind. This is typical of the way most private individuals make loans.

(b) the agency or middleman method, in which the agency or individual who makes the initial loan sells it to another investor who, in turn, holds the mortgage or note.

(c) the pooling or bond system, in which the agency or individual pools all its (his) loans and sells bonds through a broker to investors. However, these investors do not hold the mortgage(s) or note(s), but can only claim title to the bond itself as an income yielding investment.

(d) the indirect method, in which the credit agency borrows from many investors and then lends to farmers without knowledge on the part of the investors of the specific loan into which their funds went. Commercial banks and insurance companies are included in this category.

Repayment plans will vary with the type of loan made, the security given for the loan, the length of time for which the loan is outstanding, the expected risk involved, and the tradition of the lending institution. There are three main types of repayment plans. The straight end payment plan is one in which the borrower pays interest annually or semi-annually, making a principal lump sum payment at the end of the loan period. The second method is the partial payment plan, in which the borrower makes payments which include interest and part of the initial principal, closing the loan with a lump sum payment of the remaining balance plus accrued interest at the end of a designated time period. The third method is the amortization plan in which principal and interest are combined into one constant payment and the payments are kept up at regular intervals until the initial sum is entirely repaid.

Another way to classify the sources of the money used in agricultural credit is to divide them into two groups. One group includes the sources from the private sector of the economy (individuals, banks, merchants, insurance companies, and the cooperative agricultural credit system). The other group includes the public sources of credit (government agencies like the Commodity Credit Corporation and the Federal Housing

Administration which are legally authorized to make loans to farmers). These two broad classifications would apply equally well to short-term loans, intermediate or long-term credit, and to real estate and non-real estate loans.

Private and public sources of loanable funds serve to dampen the effects on farming of the fluctuations caused by the business cycle. For example, in the depression of the 1930's, when the agricultural role of commercial banks declined because of unprofitable loans and shrinking deposits, government-sponsored credit agencies were created to help the farmers. When times are good the role of the private sector of the economy in providing farm credit increases, but tends to diminish in times of recession or depression. On the other hand, the role which the public sector plays in providing agricultural credit increases when the country's economic activity slackens. The two sources tend to offset each other and thus reduce what otherwise might be disastrous effects of credit fluctuation on the people in agriculture.

Individuals

Individuals currently account for over one-third of the loans made to farmers. These loans are usually made directly. Loans are made for real estate, capital improvements, and operating funds. As a result of the person-to-person responsibilities there is no established method of loan supervision (except by legal suit) or loan limit.

Commercial banks

Commercial banks are corporations chartered under state or federal law. They are owned by stockholders and controlled by boards of directors. All the banks are supervised under laws which specify systems of audit and inspection.

Commercial banks are unique among credit institutions for their abilities to create money in the form of bank deposits for purposes of making loans. This ability directly affects the supply of credit available to agriculture. The money used by commercial banks for making loans is, in a sense, not the bank's money. It belongs to the depositors and stockholders and the banks only hold a type of investing trusteeship over these funds.

Although the goal of a bank is to make profits for its stockholders, it must also be responsible for the safety of the depositor's money and the economic soundness of its overall loan policy. The most general criteria used by commercial banks when making farm loans are (a) service to the borrowers involved and (b) satisfactory evaluation of the risk involved in making the loan.

Many of the commercial banks have agricultural representatives attached to their regular staff. These men usually have an agricultural orientation either from their own farming experience or through their college training; they are well acquainted with old and current techniques of farm production and with new production technology that might be adopted by farmers. They are also usually familiar with the geographic area over which the bank makes its loans, and with the people who live in the area. These trained agricultural representatives help to evaluate farm loans from both the bank's point of view and the borrower's viewpoint. They review the purpose of the loan, its expected return to the enterprise, the person(s) to whom the loan is to be made, the interest rate to be charged, the security required to back the loan, the length of time for which the loan is made, and the repayment schedule. Frequently, commercial banks maintain contact with the farmer after the loan is made, providing technical production and finance information when called upon. Banks make both operating and real estate loans. Although each bank has a state-regulated loan limit, the use of correspondent banks makes the financing of loans past these limits possible.

Insurance companies

Insurance companies constitute the largest institutional lender in the farm mortgage field. Their loans generally cover real estate and repayment schedules extend over relatively long periods of time. The loans are generally larger than those made by commercial banks, because real estate loans are usually larger than non-real estate loans.

There are two general types of insurance companies which make loan funds available to farmers. One type is the stock company which is owned by stockholders who provide the capital from which the loanable funds arise; the other type is the mutual company in which loanable funds originate from cooperative associations organized under state law and controlled by boards of directors in much the same manner as banks. They are supervised by state insurance departments who perform audits and inspections.

Loan policies of insurance companies are only slightly different from those of banks. In general, loans must not be too risky, they must be profitable and backed by collateral, and they must also promote goodwill for the company involved. The total loan policy of the company indicates that the total investment portfolio also be of a diverse nature so that there is a certain amount of stability throughout.

The major insurance companies now employ trained agricultural personnel to handle their farm loan business in much the same manner explained earlier for commercial banks.

Merchants and dealers

The majority of merchants and dealers lend capital resources for current production purposes. This is especially true of businesses which manufacture and/or sell agricultural inputs. Feed and seed dealers, distributors of petroleum products, and fertilizer sales agencies are good examples. These businessmen extend credit via notes, open accounts, or chattel mortgages. However, mortgages are used most often when equipment items, such as new tractors or combines, are involved.

The time over which credit is extended by merchants and dealers depends upon many things. In some instances personal friendship is the key to the length of the loan time. In other cases, harvest time determines loan repayment. In areas where livestock and poultry are fed in large numbers, it is not at all uncommon for dealers to extend open account credit for feed bills of $150,000-$200,000 payable when the "feeders" are sold. Company salesmen keep the company management informed of the farmer's progress, his progress with his "feeders," and the approximate time when they can expect repayment. This type of credit is not usually budgeted in the same manner as loans from banks, insurance companies, or the cooperative agricultural credit system.

Commodity credit corporation

The CCC was created by executive order in October, 1933. This credit agency was to make loans connected with farm commodity price support programs. The CCC originated as a corporation wholly owned by the government, with $100 million capital and borrowing authority to obtain additional funds for loans on farm commodities. There is a current borrowing authority limit of $14.5 billion. In July, 1939 the CCC became part of the U.S. Department of Agriculture, and in 1948 it received a permanent federal charter from Congress.

One of the initial objectives of the CCC was to act as a stabilizing influence on selected farm commodity prices. If the loan rate went below the market price, few loans would be made; if the loan rate rose above the market price of a commodity, there would be relatively more loans made. The CCC makes a nonrecourse loan to farmers which is different from the loans made by most lending agencies. In a CCC loan the commodity acts just like cash. Here is how the loan works. The CCC make loans based on the support price of the agricultural commodity in question. However, the borrower is not under obligation to repay the loan in cash. Instead, if the market price goes below the loan rate the farmer can pay off the loan in kind with the commodity he has already mortgaged in order to get the loan. On the other hand, if the market price goes above the loan rate the farmer can sell the commodity and pay off the loan (principal plus interest) in cash. In addition, if the farmer stores the commodity on his farm (particularly in the case of grain), he is paid for storage if the commodity is stored past the first season. Commodity loans may also be made by private agencies, such as banks, under contract agreement with the CCC.

THE FARM CREDIT SYSTEM

There were 31 major pieces of legislation or executive orders affecting farmers' credit between 1916 and 1960. The Federal Land Banks and the Joint Stock Land Banks were established in 1916. Since that time major revisions have included the Federal Intermediate Credit Banks, the Rural Electrification Administration, the Bankhead-Jones Act providing for tenant-purchase loans, the farmer-owned credit cooperatives, the Farm Home Act, provisions for veterans, emergency credit programs, and permission for interagency mergers and incorporation of federal credit agencies into the Department of Agriculture.

The farm credit system was initially a government sponsored attempt to set up a means by which farmers could provide their own cooperative credit. There are three principal parts to the Farm Credit System. They are the Federal Land Banks, the Production Credit System, and the Banks for Cooperatives. Each of these three agencies operates under the supervision of the District Farm Credit Boards which were set up in 12 Farm Credit Districts spread over the entire United States.

Federal land bank system

This system is composed of 12 Federal Land Banks (FLB) and 831 FLB Associations (as of January 1, 1960) scattered throughout the 12 Farm Credit Districts. Each of the 12 FLB's is a corporation chartered under the Federal Farm Loan Act of 1916. Each of the 12 District FLB's is supervised by a Board and each District Board determines its own loan policies. The Federal Land Bank Associations have been completely owned by farmers since 1947, at which time they completely repaid the initial capital given to them by the government.

Under present FLB loan policy, area credit needs are pooled and the funds necessary to handle these loans are obtained by the sale of debenture bonds in the regular capital markets or investment centers of the economy. Loans are made directly to individual farmers at interest rates which will vary depending upon the cost obligations undertaken at the time of the bond sales.

Production credit system

The Production Credit System is made up of the Federal Intermediate Credit Banks (FICB) and the Production Credit Associations (PCA). Chartered in 1923, the 12 FICB's help provide the funds necessary to operate the 494 PCA's (as of January 1, 1960). This system operates under the policies of the District Farm Credit Board in the same manner as do the FLB's discussed above.

The PCA's are the farmers' contacts and make short-term and intermediate term loans. These loans are "budgeted" loans with repayment only on the outstanding balance. This is a specialized type of repayment plan initiated by the PCA's. Trained field personnel discuss the farm budgets, made out as a loan requirement, with the farmers, and offer technical help wherever they can.

The Production Credit System is owned partially by the government and partially by the farmers. The PCA's are almost entirely owned by farmers and it is intended that government ownership be gradually retired as the PCA's absorb the FICB stock.

Sources of funds for the PCA's come from funds borrowed from the FICB, from rediscounting farmer's notes with the FICB, and from rediscounting farmer loans made by other financing institutions. The FICB, in turn, obtains funds to lend to the PCA's by sales of debenture bonds to the investing public. The rate of interest charged by the PCA's depends on what rate of interest they must pay on their debenture bonds plus the cost of operation.

Banks for cooperatives

These banks were chartered under the Farm Credit Act of 1933 in an attempt to provide credit which farmers could obtain to operate their cooperatives. There are 13 Banks for Cooperatives, one in each of the 12 Districts, and one central bank located in Washington, D.C. Each Bank has a Board of Directors which is served by the District Credit Board. These banks are owned jointly by farmers and the government but final ownership will ultimately rest with the farmer through stock acquisition.

Types of loans made by the Banks for Cooperatives include loans for facilities, for operating capital, and for various commodities. Interest charged is variable, depending upon the type of loan, its term, and the cost of borrowed funds.

Sources of loan funds for the Banks for Cooperatives are capital and surplus, sales of debenture bonds on established capital markets, and funds borrowed directly from the FICB, the FLB's, and commercial banks.

Farmer's Home Administration

Despite the cooperative Farm Credit System, many farmers were unable to get adequate financing for their operations. This situation is typical for many beginning farmers and for other farmers with limited resources. The Farmer's Home Administration Act of 1946 created the Farmer's Home Administration (FHA). This agency replaced two other government credit agencies which handled direct loans and emergency loans in the U.S. Department of Agriculture. Under this act, FHA loan services were considerably broadened past the responsibilities of the two agencies it replaced.

The objectives of the FHA were to provide supervised agricultural credit to farmers unable to get adequate credit from other sources on reasonable terms. In order to get a loan from FHA the farmer had to certify that other credit was not available. He also had to agree to re-finance his farm operation until such time as regular commercial credit channels were willing to accept his risk. The second major objective of FHA is to provide emergency credit in times of drought, hail, flood, and other conditions which are beyond the control of the individual.

FHA has a National Office in Washington, D.C. which determines loan policies, interprets legislation, controls budgets, and gives technical training to FHA field personnel. There is also a National Finance Office in St. Louis, Missouri, which handles all the fiscal and business management matters as well as the accounting procedures. There are 43 state FHA offices and about 1450 county offices.

FHA has three main sources of loanable funds; it can borrow from the Federal Treasury, it can use a revolving fund set up by Congress principally to handle emergency loans, and it can borrow from banks.

All applications for loans are made at local county offices and are reviewed by a county committee of three people, at least two of whom are farmers. This committee determines the applicant's eligibility, certifies as to the validity of the loan request, and reviews the borrower's progress. Operating loans are secured by chattel mortgages and farm ownership loans are secured by real estate mortgages.

There are six main types of loans made by the FHA: operating loans, farm ownership loans, soil and water conservation loans, farm housing loans, emergency loans, and watershed loans. Operating loans are available to tenants as well as owner-operators. These loans are designed primarily to enable farmers to make more profitable use of their existing land and labor resources. Loan size is variable, with a ceiling of $20,000. Repayment schedules may not exceed seven years.

Farm ownership loans are given for buying farms, enlarging existing farms, for land developments, and to refinance debts. Repayment schedules extend up to 40 years, but they may be repaid sooner at the borrower's discretion. Soil and water conservation loans are made to individuals and groups of farmers to carry out conservation measures, irrigation developments, and farm water systems. An individual's total indebtedness may not exceed $250,000. Maximum repayment periods are 20 years for individuals and 40 years for groups or associations.

Farm housing loans are made to farmers for the construction and repair of farm outbuildings and farm houses. Emergency loans are made in areas designated disaster areas. These funds may be made for operating loans or to replace fixed capital resources. The size of the loan is variable (averages about $2,500) and the repayment schedule is based on the ability of the borrower to repay. Watershed loans are made to local organizations to finance projects designed to develop and conserve land and water resources in small watersheds. However, loans are made only on the basis of project approval by the Soil Conservation Service, and only specific soil and water organizations are eligible to receive funds.

THE FUTURE OF CAPITAL IN FARMING

What are the trends in capital accumulation and use that might continue in American agriculture? The amount of capital per farm worker and the amount of capital per farm will rise in the foreseeable future. As farmers try to lower per unit production costs and obtain higher incomes, they will increase the size, volume, and specialization of their farm businesses. These adjustments will call forth an increased need for the use and control of capital. Although capital requirements per farm will rise, it is not so clear that the total capital requirements for all of agricultural production will also increase. The reason for this situation is that the rapid decline in the total number of farms may offset the total capital increases needed by the remaining farm units.

The composition of the capital used will probably continue to shift in the direction of its current trends. There will likely be more machinery, livestock, feed, seed, and fertilizer used; and there will probably be relatively less capital investment in land and buildings.

Most of the capital requirements on farms will probably continue to be satisfied from current gross income from farming, but there will be more capital flowing into farming from external sources. Capital used both from within the farm sector and outside of it will undoubtedly provide relatively more non-real estate credit to farmers than real estate credit.

There will be more corporate farming in order to control capital, although corporate members will by no means monopolize the field. There will also be an increase in the number of part owners. These men will be full-time farmers but will own only a small portion of the agricultural assets they use. Farmers in this category will be permanent residents of the farm community, but they will use the land they own primarily as a base of operations for production work in related fields rather than as the principal source of their farm income.

8

The role of technology in economic growth

WHAT IS TECHNOLOGY?

Technology is the knowledge applied by man to improve production or marketing processes. It is reflected in tractors, combines, and cornpickers. It is embodied in hybrid seed corn, improved crop varieties, pesticides, commercial fertilizer, contour plowing, automatic hog feeders, and rural electrification. Technology is in the workshop, chemistry laboratory, barn, field, and office. Its objective is to provide greater output from a given amount of land, labor, and capital resources. Technology is vital to the economizing process.

Technology causes rapid changes in farm production. Within two short decades after hybrid seed corn was developed, it was used on 24 million acres. The estimated increase in yield during that time was 100 million bushels. This great increase in production coupled with a more slowly developing demand resulted in lower corn prices. Mechanization of American agriculture occurred so swiftly that from 1915 to 1940 the tractor, truck, and automobile cut down the human labor force by thousands and resulted in nearly 10 million less horses and mules being needed

[1] "Technology on the Farm," U.S.D.A., B.A.E. (Washington, D.C.: August, 1940).

120

on farms.[1] Hence, as scientific knowledge about improving crops and animals grows and as engineers perfect labor saving machinery, other problems such as unemployment and falling commodity prices may be created.

TECHNOLOGY IS CUMULATIVE

"I entreat you send me thirty carpenters, husbandmen, gardeners, blacksmiths, masons, and diggers-up of trees' roots rather than a thousand such as we have," wrote Captain John Smith in 1609, in a desperate effort to save the settlement at Jamestown, Virginia. Of what significance is this? Simply that technology was a necessary ingredient to survival. The bare necessities of life (food, clothing, and shelter) required the application of man's knowledge of production processes in using the resources on hand. The initial settlement at Jamestown included a majority of traders, goldsmiths, and silversmiths—men who were sent to search for gold and other valuable items—men who knew little about food production. What the New World needed was men who had brainpower oriented toward technical food production processes. The mistake made at Jamestown was not repeated by the Pilgrims of Plymouth, who in 1620 brought skilled husbandmen, artisans, and tools to the first permanent settlement in New England.

Technology passes from father to son, from teacher to student, from generation to generation as knowledge once learned becomes a permanent resource. To say that the new settlers' technology was merely a replica of the Old World would be a grievous error. The native Indians offered much in helping the new white man understand his environment. In 1609 Captain John Smith captured two Indians with the avowed purpose of making them "teach us how to order and plant our fields." Forty acres of corn were planted with the assistance of the Indians, and within five years the Jamestown Colony was planting 200 acres of corn.

The important point is that as time passes, the fruits of technology—increased production at lower cost or better quality produce for the same cost—become cumulative. Not only does the amount of technical knowledge increase but its growth in all directions tends to grow at a continually faster rate. It is probably safe to say that if an Egyptian farmer on the Nile River in 1000 B.C. could be transported through time to an 1850 colonial farm in America, he would not be too surprised by the agricultural technology in use. But should that 1850 colonial farmer be transported to a modern commercial farm, the technology employed would be almost entirely past his understanding. Thus, in a real sense, if technological knowledge is likened to a snowball rolling down a hill, the snowball rolled very slowly and increased in size very little for many years; but currently the snowball's momentum is great and its size is overpowering.

Another important element contributing to the rapid use and implementation of new technology is the advancement in the field of communications. The flow of new technology can be rapidly distributed through the mass media of television, radio, books, and newspapers. The rapid movement of people from one place to another due to developments in transportation also contributes to the rapid dissemination of new technology.

At this time, however, the point should be made that simply disseminating the knowledge concerning new technology does not guarantee its adoption and implementation. Many Americans are so conditioned by living in a country of rapid technological change that they are used to a new production idea being tested quickly and implemented immediately if it proves successful. This is not so in other parts of the world. Foster points out the complexity of the process of technological development.[2] He argues there can be no such thing as technological development in isolation and proposes the term "socio-technological development" instead. The acceptance of technology is a complex cultural, social, and psychological process much more than the overt acceptance of material and technical improvements. The failure of some American technical aid programs overseas is in part due to our lack of understanding that for every technical and material change, there must be an accompanying change in attitudes, values, and beliefs of the people affected by the change. Foster argues:

> . . . . These nonmaterial changes are more subtle. Often they are overlooked or their significance is underestimated. Yet the eventual effect of a material or social improvement is determined by the extent to which the other aspects of culture affected by it can alter their forms with a minimum of interruption. In newly developing countries, for example, the introduction of factory labor brings changes in family structure. If the workers and their families can accept these new social patterns and reconcile their attitudes toward traditional family obligations with new conditions, industrialization need not be disruptive. But . . . reconciliation is often difficult, and the process of development is accordingly slowed.[3]

So we see that the use of new technology is not magical and is indeed a complex process. It is cumulative in its effect and the reservoir of technology is always growing.

---

[2] George M. Foster, *Traditional Cultures: and the Impact of Technological Change* (New York: Harper and Row, Publishers, 1962), p. 2.
[3] *Ibid.*, p. 3.

TECHNOLOGY REDUCES COST AND INCREASES OUTPUT

By definition, if the input-output ratio is improved by the introduction of a new technology it must eventually result in a greater output at a lower per unit production cost. A new cultivation practice may increase output with relatively no change in inputs. Or it may allow the same amount of product to be realized from less inputs. New minimum tillage methods are good examples of the latter.

Technological change, therefore, nearly always has an important effect on the level of agricultural prices. As new technology is introduced and per unit costs of production decline, the quantity and quality of output increases. Under some demand conditions for certain commodities there may be an eventual price decline. Therefore, part of the benefits of technology are passed on to food consumers through lower prices or a better quality product for the same price. Whether the benefits of technology are equitably distributed among the farmers, the marketing middleman, and the food consumer is another question almost constantly under debate.[4] There are many factors that affect farm prices. The generalization that can be made with regard to farming technology is that the application of new technological advancements generally result in lower production costs, expanded output, and lower prices.

The effect of technology on the farmer's gross income is determined largely if and when a new technology is adopted. For example, the farmer who was an "early adapter" and used hybrid seed corn before the majority of his neighbors did was able to increase his gross and net income considerably. With the hybrid seed resulting in higher yields per acre harvested, his dollar return per acre was higher with relatively little additional cost. However, now that practically all commercial corn producers use hybrid seed no individual farmer increases his net income very much as a result of using it; but if a farmer were not to use hybrid seed corn now, his low yields would lower his income. The old adage "the early bird catches the worm" is directly applicable in the case of technology. The producer who adopts the new technology before others do gets higher net returns as a result. After every producer has adopted the technology the income benefits to producers are generally lowered, while all society benefits from increases in the quantity and quality of products available.

The above generalization, however, does not preclude the fact that some technologies are adopted without any influence on dollar income. The intangible return of enjoying greater convenience and satisfaction are

---

[4] The theoretical and technical aspects of technology are examined later in Chapter 12.

often reason enough to adopt some technologies. The use of a tractor instead of manual labor on a farm in certain tasks does not necessarily reduce the cost of producing or handling a crop. But the work can be done more quickly and easily freeing more time and energy for leisure time activities or additional productive effort elsewhere. Much of the technology which influences food preparation time does not reduce the cost of feeding a family, but it does free much of the homemaker's time for other enjoyable activities. Numerous examples are in evidence but these important ideas remain: a new technology will be adopted if the extra return generated as a result of adoption is greater than the added cost of adoption, remembering that returns may be of an intangible or actual dollar nature. As technology changes costs and output, it also influences the level and distribution of income. Further, the use of existing technology and the infusion of new technology are strong stimulants to the level and rate of economic growth.

TWO KINDS OF TECHNICAL KNOWLEDGE

Dennison distinguishes between technological knowledge and managerial knowledge as follows:

> Technological knowledge consists of knowledge concerning the physical properties of things, and of how to make, or combine, or use them in a physical sense. . . . Managerial knowledge consists of advances in knowledge concerning the techniques of management construed in the broadest sense, and in business organization.[5]

Certainly any discussion of advances in productivity and economic growth should recognize both kinds of knowledge and the contribution each makes. Advances in the technological sense are more obvious with the familiar references to the steam engine, telephones, computers, rockets, synthetic fibers, and so on. Less obvious are the effects of better business organization and management procedures embodied in improved inventory control procedure, office building designs, self-service supermarkets, labor-management negotiations, and integration of production and marketing activities as exemplified in the broiler industry.

Some 20 percent of the increase in the measured growth rate of total real national product has been ascribed to the increase of knowledge and its application.[6] To separate the contribution to this total between the components of technological knowledge and managerial knowledge is difficult. In many cases the two are complementary. For example, im-

[5] Dennison, Edward F. "The Sources of Economic Growth in the United States and the Alternatives Before Us," Supplementary Paper No. 13 published by Committee for Economic Development, January 1962, pp. 231-232.
[6] *Ibid.*, p. 230.

provement in inventory control methods was speeded by both managerial knowledge and high speed data processing machines. Integration in the broiler industry was speeded by both new managerial organization methods and machines, buildings, equipment, and genetic strains of broilers which functioned well in a controlled environment.

Another way of viewing technologies is to differentiate between changes in the use of a given bundle of resources compared to changes in the composition of resources used. Under the first grouping the proportion of inputs remain the same while output increases. Timing of operations, organizational efficiency, or new production and marketing procedures are examples of this type of technology. The second grouping includes technology which changes the proportion of resources used. Under this category inputs may be substituted in varying amounts and recombined in such a way that output increases relative to the amount of inputs used.

THE DIFFUSION OF TECHNOLOGY AND TECHNOLOGICAL CHANGE

The fruits of technology are not realized in a society until the new knowledge is utilized. The change that occurs in using technological knowledge is called technological change. Technological change cannot occur until new inventions and scientific discoveries take place.

Knowledge is a universal commodity whose increase depends greatly on a country's level of economic and social development; the greater the development, the more knowledge exists and is applied. The rate at which technological knowledge is adopted by countries and by individuals varies widely. Some of the obstacles to its adoption with regard to culture have already been discussed. Tradition, habit, and general attitude toward change are important factors affecting the use of technology.

What incentive does a person have to be inventive and create a new idea? There are many. Often, people are creative merely for the personal satisfaction it gives to them. Others are spurred by the hopes of large profit. A productive scientist in an academic institution, business, or government job will sometimes find his paycheck increased if he is a productive generator of new ideas. The federal and state governments, as well as private businesses, allocate funds for research and development. The competitive nature of our economy requires commercial and industrial businesses to constantly search for better methods of production of goods and services. Estimates of total funds for performance of research and development and basic research amounted to almost $24 billion in 1967, over twice the amount in 1958.[7] About two-thirds of these funds are

[7] Statistical Abstract of the United States, 1968, p. 525.

used by industry, but over half this money comes from federal sources. In 1967, universities were using about two-thirds of the total funds distributed for basic research. Most of the R & D funds go to improve existing products, or to develop new prototypes capable of being market tested. Funds used solely to improve efficiency in production methods, thereby lowering production costs, play a relatively minor role in industrial research.

Our system of patents also encourage the generation of new ideas, since the owner is protected from other inventors with similar ideas as soon as the patent is given. This means he has exclusive opportunities to make profits for a limited amount of time. Although the number of patents issued is sometimes used as another indicator of the rate at which new knowledge is being generated, it is at best a very rough indicator. Patent statistics indicate that patent applications were higher in the 1920's than at any time since, and the number of patents issued since that time has remained relatively constant at somewhere between 40 and 48 thousand annually, except for the 1940's.[8]

Diffusion of Technology

The rapidity with which technology is actually used in production processes depends on (a) the receptivity of the society to new ideas; (b) the efficiency of the communication or education system; (c) the size of the cash outlay required to use the technology; and (d) the degree of obsolescence of existing production equipment. How receptive the population is to new ideas is a function of many social, economic, and political factors which have already been discussed. There is little impediment to the use of technology from lack of communication in the United States. In addition to a free press and the mass media of radio and television, the Agricultural Extension Service created in 1914 by the Smith-Lever Act established a communications network reaching the "grassroot" farmer in an educational system which is unsurpassed in any part of the world.

When the application of a new technology involves a considerable cash outlay, such as the initial purchase of a tractor or combine or the replacement of existing equipment with an improved model, other considerations become important. The decision depends on the answer to such questions as, "Should I invest my money in a new tractor or should we put it aside for the children's education?" In contrast, whether or not a farmer should use hybrid seed rather than open pollinated varieties is a much easier decision because relatively little cash outlay is required. The

[8] Edward F. Dennison, op. cit., p. 238.

important generalization is that technology requiring a large initial money outlay in order to implement its use is likely to be adopted more slowly than one that requires only a small cash outlay. The rate of depreciation and obsolescence of existing machinery and equipment, the extent of desire to maximize profits, the weights of risk and uncertainty, and the individual's personal preferences and values all also influence the degree to which technology is created, adopted, and used.[9]

Measuring technological progress

Estimates of the impact of the application of technological knowledge on output in agriculture is a complicated and difficult task. The rapid growth in food production in the United States is necessarily the result of an increase in the total level and quality of inputs as well as technology. Dennison estimates that in the 1929 to 1957 period the annual growth rate of total real national income was 2.93 percent. Of this amount, 2 percent was from an increase in total inputs, 0.59 percent from increased knowledge and its application (technological and managerial), and 0.34 from other sources.[10]

Changes in the productivity of labor in terms of output per man hour and output per farm worker have also been used to indicate technological progress, but Ruttan points out that the differences in substitutability of one input for another distorts its use.[11] An example is the extent to which capital can be substituted for physical labor. Not only may this substitution reduce operating costs, particularly when labor costs are high, but it may also provide intangible satisfaction because of the freeing of time for other uses. Thus, in an industry such as farming where the use in labor productivity has stemmed largely from substituting capital for labor, the index of output per man hour overstates the contribution of technology. On the other hand, in an industry such as meat-packing, where technological progress has been primarily capital-saving rather than labor-saving, the indicator of change in labor productivity understates the contribution of technological change to output.[12] If output per

---

[9] In Part III costs will be separated into two categories—fixed and variable—and the significance of this aspect of implementing technology will become better understood at that point.

[10] Edward F. Dennison, *op. cit.*, p. 230.

[11] Ruttan, Vernon W. "The Contribution of Technological Progress to Farm Output: 1950-75," *Review of Economics and Statistics* (Vol. 38, February, 1956, No. 1), p. 62.

[12] Ruttan, Vernon W. "Technological Change in the Meat Packing Industry, 1919-1947," U.S.D.A., Marketing Research Report #59, January, 1954, pp. 8-10.

[13] "Technology and the American Economy," Report of the National Commission on Technology, Automation, and Economic Progress, Vol. 1, February 1966, USGPO.

manhour is used as an index for comparing technology in the farm and nonfarm economies, the farm index moved above the private nonfarm index in the late 1940's for the first time since pre-World War 1.[13] Several other studies indicate that the rate of technological change in farming is about twice that of all manufacturing.[14]

Technology and locational change. When a production process utilizes new technology there are bound to be changes in the location of production, of the input markets, of the markets where the product is sold, or in all three locations at once. For example, when technology was adopted by those in the home arts and crafts industries at the beginning of the Industrial Revolution, it soon became clear that a factory system of production was better adapted to production methods than was the home. Technological improvements usually required machines powered by more than man himself. As a consequence, new inventions in the use of energy through the steam engine, water power, electricity, gas, and atomic power have all been increasingly away from the use of man or animal power to run machines.

Technology led to the use of improved, more costly, and physically larger units of machinery. Increasingly, inputs were used for a more mass-like type of production. For example, improvements in the mining of coal led to cheaper steel and an increased demand for it by other industries that was fulfilled only through the use of massive rolling mills and open hearth furnaces. None of the new steel technology and machinery could be used in the homes of those previously employed in the home craft industries.

When the production process shifted from the home to the factory there was a simultaneous emphasis upon the division of labor and the degree to which it was specialized. Labor was now utilized by the production process in an entirely different way than before. New skills were required and new responsibilities were demanded of supervisors and management. A man was forced to specialize since he could not be fully competent in all phases of the skills required for a top quality production job.

With specialization also evolved the technologies associated with materials utilization and materials handling. One input was made substitutable for another in the production of a good, the amount of substitution depending upon the price of the necessary factors of production. As new inputs were used the markets for inputs widened. Business specialists

---

[14] See R. M. Solow, "Technical Change and Aggregate Production Functions," *Review of Economics and Statistics,* Vol. 39, August 1957, pp. 312-320; and Lester B. Lave, *Technological Change: Its Conception and Measurement,* Prentice-Hall, N.J., 1966.

evolved who were trained in assembling the needed factors of production for various other business and manufacturing concerns.

Improved methods of transfer were evolved. The railroads made new cars that refrigerated or froze the products enroute. Trucking lines established new routes and express schedules, and also instituted new handling techniques including refrigeration. New standards of quality were used and new improved methods of communication relayed the current news about standards.

When the total impact of technology is assessed on location, it simply points up the fact that new processes generally reach increasingly farther into input or final product markets. They bring the country closer together through an improved network of transportation which includes cheaper rates, influences relative input and product prices, changes the locational pattern of distance and time, influences mass production of an item, and also tends to raise the quality of production.

As a consequence of an increased division of labor and specialization, there is an increased sensitivity of the moves of one firm or plant or industry on other firms or industries. This sensitivity is caused by changing responses established in markets and supply areas. Sensitivity to these changes can lead to intense competition between producers and between the suppliers of inputs to these producers.

It should be noted that although new ideas and machines are invented, invention is only the scientific fact—innovation is the economic fact which determines which inventions are used and which are not. There are certain permissive conditions for innovation or for the acceptance of an invention into the production process. In many cases, these conditions resolve themselves into the ability of the labor force to absorb the technical changes brought about by use of the new technology. Although some labor displacement is tolerated socially and politically, extreme unemployment is not tolerable. Automation and the resulting unemployment is an example of a problem in the adoption of technology that is not yet solved.

In addition to the permissive conditions imposed by society, the individual entrepreneur has to be willing to risk the chance of using the new idea. He must be convinced that the potential profits are worth the costs necessarily incurred to put the technology into his production process. Credit institutions must be willing to finance the effort. Distributors must be paid for handling the new product. And finally, the individual household or businessman must be convinced that the new product would be a good thing for him to buy.

There is little doubt that we now live in an era of exploding technology which can contribute rapidly to any country's growth rate if it is utilized in production. The use of atomic energy and major contributions by geneticists in improving plant and animal life are on the horizon.

A BRIEF CHRONOLOGY OF TECHNOLOGICAL DEVELOPMENT IN UNITED STATES FARMING [15]

Many pages have been written about the dynamics of farming methods in the United States. For purposes of discussion here, technological development will be classified as to changes in machines, animals, plants, land use improvements, and food processing methods.

Technology in machines

Beginning with Whitney's cotton gin about 1820, the revolution in agricultural farm machinery began to take place rapidly. The reaper, the mower, the seed drill, the steel plow, and the threshing machine made farming possible on an extensive scale, particularly in the prairie regions of the Midwest. The pioneer colonial farmer was neither the traditional landlord or peasant type typical in Europe. He was enterprising, a pretty good mechanic, and when convinced a machine would aid him he was fairly quick to adopt it.

The steel plow was perfected by John Deere in the 1840's. It evolved from the wood and cast iron plows which failed to scour the moldboards in sticky prairie soils. Corn planters and wheat drills greatly simplified the planting process and the reaper mechanically harvested grain which for centuries had been cut with a hand sickle. The McCormick reaper, patented in 1831, sold rapidly after a Chicago factory opened in 1844. The stationary threshing machine appeared at about the same time. This introduction helped to initiate the construction of grain elevators by Dart, who was given a patent on a granary (grain elevator) designed to be "heat and moisture proof."

But it was probably the tractor more than any other piece of equipment that revolutionized farming, particularly after 1910, when the old cumbersome model was replaced with a lighter machine of a "jack-of-all-trades" sort. "Drawbar power" rapidly replaced "horsepower" and made it much more feasible for farmers to use large equipment in addition to greatly speeding each process. Belt pulleys provided mobile power and the power take-off increased both the efficiency and dependability of mechanical equipment. Tractor numbers doubled on farms in the decade of the 1930's, and the substitution of rubber tires for steel wheels decreased fuel consumption and extended the life of the general purpose tractor.

To complement the all-purpose tractor, tillage implements have be-

---

[15] This material draws heavily from "Technology on the Farm," U.S.D.A., B.A.E., Special Report, U.S. Government Printing Office, 1940, and John W. Oliver, *History of American Technology* (New York: The Ronald Press Company, 1956), Chapter 16.

come lighter (in their relative size groups), more flexible, and more versatile. Erosion control and new fertilization and seeding practices have also influenced tillage machinery developments. The combine and mechanical corn picker were in widespread used by the 1940's, but the perfection of a mechanical cotton picker was more difficult. Mechanical harvesting equipment has been introduced in orchards and for some perishable vegetables.

The list of new equipment technology is long, but the hay chopper, irrigation equipment, power duster and sprayers, and nitrogen fertilizer applicators are a few of the more important ones. While electric power is not machinery in the same sense, it should be noted that scarcely 100,000 rural homes were receiving electric current from power lines in 1919, but 20 years later some two million farms had electricity. By any measure, electric power was a vital technological advance for the commercial farmer.

Technology in animal production

As time passes Americans change their mode of living and eating habits. These changes have prompted biological scientists to search for ways to change animals and plants to meet the desires of food consumers. As a whole, physical labor has been reduced and a larger number of people have more sedentary tasks. As an example, weight consciousness and disease prevention have reduced the desire for animal fats, with the result that hogs and cattle are bred to provide a higher proportion of lean meat. Nutritional studies are often applicable to farm animals as well as humans and new knowledge of insects, pests, germs, and minerals controlling animal disease are in wide use.

Animal feeding research has been directed toward learning the importance and use of such elements as vitamins, forage, and minerals in rations. The results appear in converting feeds to edible meats more efficiently. The broiler is a prime example. In the late 1940's it required some 15 pounds of feed to grow a three pound broiler over a 15-week period. Currently, the figure is more likely to be slightly over 7 pounds of feed input for an 8-week growing period, a conversion factor of 2 pounds of feed for 1 pound of chicken which is produced in half the time.

New knowledge concerning diseases and parasites, the use of progeny testing, crossbreeding within all types of animals, and artificial insemination, have all contributed significantly to an increase in livestock and livestock products.

Technology in plant production

Plant technologists continually battle crop failure, and some of their greatest achievements are in breeding new varieties to withstand drought, disease, and plant parasites, as well as developing higher yielding varieties. Plant innovations make available new species for regions that formerly could not grow them. While much has been already learned about hybrid plants, new research on plant hormones and other growth and food substances continue to bring new revolutionary developments in our forests, fields, and gardens.

Hybrid seed corn, which has been already mentioned, increased corn output by 100 million bushels in the 1930's after the first commercial seed was produced in Connecticut about 1922. In addition to increased output, hybrid varieties may be more resistant to disease and possess better durability, allowing for more efficient use of mechanical corn pickers. While developments in wheat do not show results comparable to corn, new wheat varieties have met the challenge of increased production in the face of depleted land fertility, increasing insect pests, and the extension of grain production into high risk areas. In oats, the contribution of plant technologists has been in perfecting varieties resistant to stemrust, crownrust, and smut. For cotton, an important development is standardization production in single variety communities, a procedure whereby all farmers in a locality grow one improved strain of cotton.

The list of technologies in plants listed is far from complete. Future successes in plant technology are difficult to predict, for the continued onslaught of diseases and parasites, the recurrence of drought in some areas, and continued efforts to produce new market varieties present an almost unlimited challenge in plant development.

Technology in land use

There is a fixed amount of land but technology continually affects its productivity. The merit of good conservation practices of soil and forest resources was firmly established by the formation of the Soil Conservation Service in 1935. The primary objective of conservation is to control soil erosion losses and the depletion of fertility. The use of cover crops and suitable crop rotations together with proper tillage practices are necessary technologies in maintaining the basic soil resource. The stimulus to shift land use from grain crops to legumes and grasses was aided by increased yields which allowed the total grain production needed in the United States to be produced on fewer acres.

Terracing, contour farming, and sod waterways are important technologies which serve to make better use of the land resource and increase its productivity. Terracing and sod waterways provide a system of drainage which conserves water in areas of low precipitation and disposes of excess water in areas of high precipitation. Terraces are used primarily by farmers in the South. Contour farming controls erosion and conserves moisture on regular slopes.

The use of commercial fertilizer gained momentum after World War

I, slowed down during the depression, and has risen continuously since 1937. In conjunction with cropping practices in improving soil productivity, commercial fertilizer has tremendously increased yields. Some plant diseases have been traced to the deficiency of certain trace elements in the soil. These losses have been stemmed or replaced by increased use of commercial fertilizer. Encouraged by agricultural legislation in 1938, the application of phosphate and lime contributed to large increases in hay and forage output as well as in grain yields.

Much of the efforts in improving land use have been from the standpoint of redirecting its use to serve human needs more effectively both for present and future generations. Farm woodlands, for example, are now thought of as commercial farm enterprises, and wildlife management practices have enhanced the recreational value for many areas.

Technology in food processing

New methods in processing, packaging, preparing, and serving foods to the consumer have increased at a rapid rate. Most of these innovations are aimed at giving the housewife more convenience and less difficulty in providing the family with meals.

Frozen food packing. Preserving fruits, vegetables, and meats by freezing is not only more convenient for the consumer, but also provides him with a higher degree of food nutrients, food flavor and aroma, and color than does canning. Proper freezing techniques also retard deterioration and keep the product fresher. Accompanying the rise in frozen food processing were the developments of efficient retail dispensing cabinets to facilitate mass supermarket distribution. Other adjuncts to frozen food packing are freezer lockers, home freezers, and freezing compartment space in refrigerators.

Canning. The canning of fruit, vegetables, and fruit juices was an important technology in preserving foods and it is still growing in importance. Commercial canning began in the United States in 1819 when a firm packed various meats and fish in glass containers. The tin can was patented in 1825; machine-made cans were manufactured after 1847. Early canners experienced difficulty with spoilage losses. While this could be solved by higher sterilization temperatures, a new problem of exploding cans arose. This latter problem was taken care of by the steam retort invented in 1874. Large-scale canning operations are aided by machines such as the pea viner and the bean snipper, which cuts the ends off pods and reduces the cost of canned string beans. Other equipment of importance includes the machine that peels the hard shell of pineapple, removes the core, and cuts off the end in one operation, and the "Iron Chunk," a machine which eviscerates salmon and removes fins, tail, and scales.

Summary

Technology results from man's efforts to make a new piece of equipment, to breed new varieties of plants, or to adapt existing products to new human uses. In essence, technology improves the physical input-output ratio in our production processes and in so doing, promotes efficiency in satisfying human wants from scarce resources. Technology is a cumulative process because knowledge is passed from one generation to another and tends to grow at an ever increasing rate. The rate at which new technology is adopted varies considerably among technologies, producers, and countries. The adoption process is sometimes slowed because of cultural and social factors. Technologies requiring little initial cash outlay will tend to be adopted faster than those requiring large cash outlays. Measuring this contribution of technology to society is a very complex task but it has been estimated to have contributed about 20 percent of the total growth in per capita real national output.

part **II**

9

Characteristics of farms and farm production in the United States

Many changes have taken place in American farming. These changes have implications for the future which merit study and analysis. Although this chapter describes many of the characteristics of the farming industry, some have been left out and may be observed in other chapters.

It is difficult to separate any one farm characteristic for analysis. Although data can be isolated and tabulated, nothing in farming moves by itself. There are many forces within farming and the rest of the economy that moves at the same time. What stimulus causes exactly what response is sometimes extremely hard to discover. For this reason it is to be remembered that farmers do not operate in a vacuum, but do things for reasons that make good sense to them. To find out these reasons, analyze the consequences of them and of the trends in farming, and predict future farmer decisions is a serious challenge.

FARM DEFINITIONS

The first nationwide census of agriculture was taken in 1850. It itemized the number of farms, the land in farms, and the value of land and buildings. The census definition of a farm has changed several times but it basically includes all the land on which some agricultural operations are performed by a person, either by his own labor alone or with the assistance of members of his household or hired employees. Agricultural operations consist of the production of crops or plants, vines, or trees (excluding forestry operations), or the keeping, grazing, or feeding of livestock for animal products, animal increase, or value enhancement. Included as farms are such enterprises as nurseries, greenhouses, hothouses, fur farms, mushroom houses, apiaries, and cranberry bogs. Excluded are fish farms, fish hatcheries, oyster farms, frog farms, kennels, game preserves, and the like. The Bureau of Census in 1964 defined a farm on the basis of a combination of "acres in the place" and the quantity of agricultural resources on the place or the quantity of agricultural products produced. Detailed computer editing specifications on land use, crop and livestock resources, and harvested acres were applied to determine if places of 10 acres or more, or places less than 10 acres were farms.

Family farms

Reference to family farms is often made in discussing American agriculture. Usually a family farm has simply meant a farm operated and managed by the labor of one family, and may include a small amount of part-time hired labor. Some people refer to a family farm on the basis of acreage. However, defining a family farm by size is misleading because farming operations run by one family range from a few acres of intensive vegetable farming to several thousands of acres of cattle range.

Commercial farms

A commercial farm is defined (as of 1964) as any farm with a value of sales from agricultural products of $2500 or more. Farms with less than $2500 sales were counted as commercial only if the farm operator was under 65 years of age, or if he reported less than 100 days of nonfarm work.

RELATIVE IMPORTANCE OF FARMING

The total income from farming during the early 1800's comprised a large part of national income because our society was primarily agrarian. However, with the advent of the Industrial Revolution the relative importance of farm income began declining. A continuing stream of scientific knowledge and applied technology aided a high rate of growth in nonfarm industries. This trend has become more pronounced in recent times. Since 1955 farm income has been less than five percent of total national income (Table 9-1).

TABLE 9-1: National income: Farm and nonfarm, 1930-67.

Year	Farm (Millions of Dollars)	Nonfarm (Millions of Dollars)	Total (Millions of Dollars)	Farm as a percentage of Total
1930	6,218	69,164	75,382	8.2
1940	5,967	75,157	81,124	7.4
1950	16,883	224,191	241,074	7.0
1955	14,500	316,518	331,018	4.4
1960	15,857	398,665	414,522	3.8
1967	19,812	633,055	652,867	3.0

SOURCE: The Farm Income Situation, U.S.D.A., July, 1968.

Despite this dramatic decline in relative income contribution, farming comprises nearly half the total business units. This is remarkable considering that farm numbers have been cut almost in half since 1914, that farm population and the number of farm workers in the labor force has fallen from about a third to only five percent of the total, and that only recently has farm income per capita risen to be more than half of per capita nonfarm income (Table 9-2). No wonder it has often been said

TABLE 9-2: Several Series Showing the Relative Importance of Farming in the United States, Selected Years, 1930-1967.

Year	Number of Farms [2] (millions)	Farm Income as a Percent of Total National Income [1]	Farm Population as a Percent of Total Population [2]	Agriculturally Employed as a Percent of Total Civilian Labor Force [2, 3]	Per Capita Disposable Income All Sources, Farm as a Percent of Nonfarm
1930	6.55	8.2	24.7	—	—
1935	6.81	11.4	25.3	—	44.3
1940	6.35	7.4	23.2	—	36.5
1945	5.97	8.2	18.1	13.3 [4]	56.4
1950	5.65	7.0	16.6	11.5	57.7
1955	4.65	4.4	13.6	9.9	48.2
1960	3.96	3.8	8.7	7.8	54.5
1965	3.34	3.5	6.4	5.9	71.5
1967	3.15	3.0	5.4	5.0	73.2

[1] SOURCE: U.S.D.A., E.R.S. Farm Income Situation, Washington, D.C.: U.S. Government Printing Office, July 1968.

[2] SOURCE: U.S. Department of Commerce, Statistical Abstract of U.S., 1968, Washington, D.C.: U.S. Government Printing Office.

[3] Includes self-employed farmers, hired labor, managers and foremen.

[4] Based on 1947 data.

that farming is a way of life for many people in addition to being a business. However, it cannot be denied that this is becoming less and less so. The management, capital, and technical requirements necessary to earn a good money income in farming call for an increased business perspective of farming. Farming is big business in America and while it is difficult to separate farming as a business from living on a farm, the trend is clearly away from a general family farm to a more specialized, highly efficient commercial farming business.

FARM CHARACTERISTICS

Number of farms

There were approximately the same number of farms in the United States in 1964 as between 1870 and 1880, while total population has increased five times (Table 9-3). When the first census count of farms was taken in 1850 there was one farm for every 16 persons living in the United States. Despite rapid population growth and the movement westward to new lands, there was still approximately the same ratio of farms to population (one farm for every 16.4 persons) in 1920 as there was in 1850. During the next few decades the picture changed so rapidly that by 1964 the ratio was one farm for every 60.8 persons living in this country.

During the late 1800's and early 1900's growth in numbers of farms was stimulated not only because of population growth but also because food was produced in the new territories opening in the West, and transportation was not sufficiently developed to handle either the quantity or the quality of food needed to support the settlers there. Food needed to be produced where the people lived. Limited agricultural technology and reliance on animal power rather than mechanical power also necessitated a growth in farm numbers into the early 1900's if food production was to keep pace with total population.

From 1910 to 1940 farm numbers stayed relatively stable. A downward trend in farm numbers has been evident since 1920 except for a brief increase during the depression years when over half a million families returned to the land. In 1935 the number of farms reached a new high of 6.8 million farms. From 1954 to 1964 farm numbers decreased in all of the 48 coterminous United States.

Farm size and value

The average size of a farm (Table 9-3) was almost the same in 1950 as it was in 1850, while the average value increased approximately

TABLE 9-3: Number of Farms in the United States, Selected Years, 1850 to 1964.

Year[1]	Total Number	Change from previous period: Number	Percent	Average Farm Size Acres	Average Farm Value Dollars (Current)
1850	1,449,073			202.6	2,258
1860	2,044,077	595,004	41.1	199.2	3,251
1870	2,659,986	615,908	30.1	153.3	2,799
1880	4,008,907	1,348,922	50.7	133.7	2,544
1890	4,564,641	555,734	13.9	136.5	2,909
1900	5,739,657	1,172,731	25.7	146.6	2,905
1910	6,366,044	624,130	10.9	138.5	5,480
1920	6,453,991	86,841	1.4	148.5	10,295
1925	6,371,640	− 76,703	− 1.2	145.1	7,764
1930	6,295,103	− 82,992	− 1.3	157.3	7,624
1935	6,812,350	523,702	8.3	154.8	4,823
1940	6,102,417	− 715,551	−10.5	174.5	5,532
1945	5,859,169	− 237,630	− 3.9	194.8	7,917
1950	5,388,437	− 477,007	− 8.1	215.8	14,005
1954	4,782,416	− 599,746	−11.1	242.2	20,405
1959	3,710,503	−1,078,522	−22.6	302.8	34,825
1964	3,157,857	−552,646	−14.9	351.6	50,646

[1] Data for Alaska and Hawaii not included for 1850, 1860, 1870, 1880, 1890, 1925, 1935, 1945, and 1954.
SOURCE: United States Census of Agriculture: 1964, General Report, Volume 2, Chapter 1, p. 15, and Chapter 3, p. 241.

seven times and total farm numbers increased about four times. Farm size reached the smallest average acreage during the middle of this period. It dropped from about 203 acres in 1850 to 134 acres in 1880, rose to 139 acres in 1910, and reached 216 acres in 1950.

In spite of this hundred-year "stability" in farm acreage, there have been relatively large increases since 1935. During the period between 1935 and 1964 average farm size increased 197 acres or 127 percent. The most rapid increase in farm size has been within the last decade, when average farm size increased 109 acres partly due to definition change. Average value of farms also increased the most during this same period.

Consolidation of small farms into larger operating units has been an important cause of the reduction in farm numbers. Consolidation has been aided by the increased use of mechanized technology in farming that has made it possible for one man to handle increasingly larger acreages.

Number of farms by size. While there have been large changes in total farm numbers, there have also been large changes in sizes of farms. Since 1880 farms with 500 or more acres have increased steadily, with

TABLE 9-4: Number of Farms by Acres for the United States, Selected Years, 1880 to 1964.

Year	Less than 10 acres	10-99 Acres	100-499 Acres	500-999 Acres	1,000 or More Acres
1880	139,241	2,069,133	1,695,983	75,972	28,578
1890	150,194	2,289,812	2,008,694	84,395	31,546
1900	268,446	3,030,964	2,290,561	102,526	47,160
1910[1]	335,043	3,356,568	2,494,461	125,295	50,135
1920	288,772	3,488,521	2,456,729	149,826	67,409
1930	361,999	3,377,313	2,315,403	159,723	80,665
1940	509,347	3,080,389	2,255,396	163,711	100,574
1950	488,530	2,527,671	2,068,466	182,297	121,473
1959[2]	244,328	1,471,206	1,658,530	200,012	136,427
1964	182,581	1,179,864	1,439,683	260,437	145,292

[1] Data for Hawaii and Alaska not included.
[2] Change of census definition of a farm contributed partially to the decline.
SOURCE: U. S. Census of Agriculture, 1959, General Report, Chapter V, Table 7; Chapter 3, Vol. 2, 1964, p. 265.

the number of farms of 1,000 acres or more growing more rapidly than farms between 500 and 1,000 acres (Table 9-4).

In 1964 farms of 1,000 or more acres comprised 4.6 percent of all farms, yet accounted for over half of the total farm land. These large farms controlled 24.6 percent of the total cropland, 71 percent of the total pastureland, and 34.2 percent of the total woodland.

Farms with less than 10 acres increased fairly rapidly until 1940, then declined sharply. Farms in the 10 to 99 acre and 100 to 499 categories comprise about 80 percent of the total, showing increases in numbers up to 1920 and declines ever since.

Regional differences in farm numbers and size. Increases and decreases in farm numbers have not been spread evenly across the land. In the East the abandonment of some of the poorer farming land in the mountain and hill regions have led to significant declines in farm numbers. There have been consistent decreases in the number of farms in the Northeast since 1880.

New technology and new legislation affecting land for farms have allowed other areas to increase their farm numbers. In the 17 Western states there were 47,462 (22.1 percent) more irrigated farms in 1959 than there were in 1920. The institution of conservation, drainage, and irrigation districts, and new laws affecting payments for land development projects have contributed to this increase.

The largest decreases in the number of farms, between 1959 and 1964, were in the South where there was a loss of 273,860 farms. Most of these farms were share-tenant and cropper farms that were absorbed into larger operating units. The largest percentage losses in number of farms were in the South Atlantic and New England areas. These areas had almost one-fourth fewer farms in 1964 than in 1959. However, this decrease came primarily from marginal and part-time farms with sales of farm products of less than $2,500.

Even though every state except Alaska reported a decrease in farm numbers, all but one (Rhode Island) reported increases in farm size. However, the average size of a farm covers a wide range. In 1964 the average size of farms varied from 94 acres in Rhode Island to 6,262 acres in Arizona. The reason for this lies primarily in the differences between types of farming: the fairly intensive type of farming in Rhode Island and the extensive dryland range operations in Arizona.

Land in farms and tenure of operator

Total land in farms has little more than doubled from 1880 to 1964 (Table 9-5). From 1880 to 1950 there was a steady increase in the number of acres in food production. However, from 1950 to 1964 there was actually a reduction of over 50 million acres in land in farms. This reduction can be attributed to many things: increased application of farm production technology, participation in land retiring government programs, Social Security, high production costs, low farm income, and the movement of farmers to nonfarm jobs.

Perhaps the most significant trend in tenure and land in farms is the increasing importance of the part-owner. The importance of part-owners is much greater than that indicated by the number of farmers who reported farms operated, particularly since part-owner farms are larger than those operated by full owners or tenants. Although full owners operated about 57 percent of all the farms in 1964, as compared to about 25 percent by part-owners, the latter controlled over 48 percent of the land in farms compared to only 29 percent for full owners.

The fact that part-owners currently control more farm land than any other single tenure group heralds a new approach to the business of farming. Increased capital requirements and high land values tend to restrict a man entering farming from owning his land outright. If he bought very much land he would have too large a percentage of his capital resources tied up in it and would not be left with enough for production operations. Instead, a farm operator may choose to own a portion of the land he farms and rent the rest. Part-owners must be skillful managers if their operations are to be profitable. It takes additional management ability to profitably farm land owned by people other than the operator because fixed rent charges must be paid and the tracts may be far apart. An outstanding example of good part-time management is a situation in Indiana (1963) where one man with one hired worker farmed almost 1500 acres which was owned by 14 different landlords.

TABLE 9-5: Number of Farms and Land in Farms by Tenure of Operator for the United States, Selected Years, 1880-1964.

Year	All Farm Operators	Full Owners[1]	Part Owners[2]	Managers[3]	All Tenants[4]	Full Owners	Part Owners	All Tenants
						Percent of Farms		
			Number of Farms					
1880	4,008,907	na	na	na	1,024,601	—	—	—
1890	4,564,641	na	na	na	1,294,913	—	—	—
1900	5,739,657	3,202,643	451,515	59,213	2,026,286	55.8	7.9	36.3
1910	6,366,044	na	na	na	na	—	—	—
1920	6,453,991	na	na	68,583	2,458,554	—	—	—
1930	6,295,103	na	na	56,131	2,668,811	—	—	—
1940	6,102,417	3,085,491	615,502	36,501	2,364,923	50.5	10.0	39.5
1950	5,388,437	3,091,666	825,670	23,646	1,447,455	57.1	15.3	27.6
1959	3,710,503	2,118,783	811,079	20,668	759,973	57.1	22.0	20.9
1964	3,157,857	1,818,254	781,884	17,798	539,921	57.6	24.8	17.0
						Percent Land		
			Land in Farms (Acres)					
1880	536,081,835	na	na	na	na	na	na	na
1890	623,218,619	na	na	na	na	na	na	na
1900	841,201,546	431,507,203	124,956,065	89,665,821	195,072,457	51.2	14.8	23.2
1910	881,431,469	na	na	na	na	—	—	—
1920	958,676,612	na	na	na	na	—	—	—
1930	990,111,984	(619,179,971)		63,626,120	307,305,893	—	—	31.0
1940	1,065,113,774	382,183,912	300,781,781	68,938,849	313,209,232	35.9	28.3	29.4
1950	1,161,419,720	419,108,646	422,811,633	107,295,661	212,203,780	36.1	36.4	18.3
1959	1,123,587,574	348,596,060	498,274,934	109,848,097	166,788,483	31.0	44.3	14.8
1964	1,110,187,000	318,876,209	533,043,590	113,360,779	144,906,422	28.7	48.0	13.1

na Not available.
[1] Full owners farm only the land they own.
[2] Part owners farm their own land and also land rented from others.
[3] Managers operate land for others and are paid a wage or salary.
[4] Tenants rent all the land they farm.
SOURCE: U.S. Census of Agriculture, General Report Vol. II, Chapter X, 1959, Table 25; Chapter 8, 1964, Tables 1 and 2.

In 1954 part-owners had more land under lease than tenants. And in 1959 the number of part-owners became greater than the number of tenants for the first time in our country's history. Land in part-owner operated farms accounted for 56 percent of the total land in farms in the West, for 46 percent in the North and for 42 percent in the South, in 1964.

There are five main classes of tenants: crop-share, share-cash, crop-

Table 9-6: Number of Farms Reporting Selected Kinds of Livestock, United States, Selected Years, 1900 to 1964.[1]

Year	Cattle and Calves		Milk Cows		Hogs and Pigs		Sheep and Lambs		Chickens 4 Months Old and Over	
	Total	Percent of All Farms	Total	Percent of All Farms	Total	Percent of All Farms	Total	Percent of All Farms	Total	Percent of All Farms
1900	4,730,480	82.4	4,513,895	78.7	4,335,363	75.6	753,518	13.3	—	—
1910	5,284,916	83.1	5,140,869	80.8	4,351,751	68.4	610,894	9.6	5,578,425	87.7
1920	5,358,243	83.1	4,461,296	69.2	4,850,807	75.2	538,593	8.4	5,837,367	90.5
1925	—	—	3,728,587	58.5	3,618,624	56.8	430,738	6.8	5,505,617	86.4
1930	4,803,174	76.4	4,452,936	70.8	3,535,119	56.2	583,578	9.3	5,372,597	85.4
1935	5,480,775	80.5	—	—	3,971,122	58.3	635,384	9.3	5,833,079	85.6
1940	4,843,417	79.4	4,644,317	76.2	3,766,675	61.8	584,935	9.6	5,150,055	84.5
1945	4,688,746	80.0	—	—	3,313,883	56.6	456,986	7.8	4,900,948	83.6
1950	4,063,945	75.5	3,648,257	67.8	3,011,807	56.0	320,314	6.0	4,215,616	78.3
1954	3,650,714	76.3	2,935,842	61.4	2,365,708	49.5	361,001	8.1	3,418,204	71.5
1959	2,672,085	72.1	1,791,729	48.4	1,846,982	46.9	341,897	9.2	2,170,265	58.6
1964	2,282,138	72.4	1,132,589	36.6	1,080,371	34.3	234,746	7.4	1,209,988	38.4

[1] Alaska and Hawaii not included.

SOURCE: U. S. Census of Agriculture, General Report, Vol. II, Chapter VI, 1959, p. 493; Chapter 2, 1964 p. 44.

pers (in the South only), cash tenants, and livestock-share tenants. There are more crop-share tenants than any other group and fewer livestock-share tenants than any other group. Crop-share tenants are most frequent in the cash grain areas and where cotton and tobacco are grown. Livestock-share tenants tend to concentrate where feed grains and livestock production are found. Adjustments in agricultural operations have brought about the biggest share of reductions in farm tenancy. These adjustments include consolidation of farms, the growth of part-owner operated farms, and farm mechanization.

Specialization on farms

The decrease in number of farms and the increase in the average size of the farm has been accompanied by a trend toward greater farm enterprise specialization. Specialization in farming means that one farmer will tend to concentrate production in one enterprise rather than have many different agricultural enterprises on the same farm. For example, rather than two or three milk cows, a hundred chickens, four or five feeders, and 20 sows, the farmer may have only the sows and the land necessary to provide feed for them. Without the other enterprises the farmer is free to attempt more intensive production from his hog enterprise. To gain the production he wants and to fill his time efficiently, he will get more sows and pigs than he used to have under a multi-enterprise farm organization.

Looking at the number of farms reporting cattle and calves, milk cows, hogs and pigs, sheep and lambs, and chickens (four months old and over), the trend toward specialization in livestock and poultry is evident (Table 9-6). The best example is milk cows. In 1900 over three-fourths of all farms had milk cows; by 1964 only about one third of the farms had milk cows. The same situation existed for hogs and pigs and for chickens (four months and older) during this same period.

There is a growth in size of enterprise associated with enterprise specialization. However, in spite of the tendency to specialize and introduce large scale enterprises, the continuing smallness of the average enterprise is noticeable. Large numbers of small enterprises tend to offset the large specialized farm operations that have been so widely publicized. Whether this situation will continue in the future depends on many things. Capital limitations, adjustments in farm organization, management capabilities, technology, and the risk and uncertainty preferences of the individual managers all influence the decision about whether a farm enterprise should be expanded or eliminated from the farm.

There also tends to be a specialization in the production patterns across the country (Figure 9-1). This type of regional production specialization is defined very broadly and the farms in each region are by no means limited only to the major type of farming for that area. However, the climate, markets, topography, soils, and institutional patterns have combined to provide certain areas with certain production advantages.

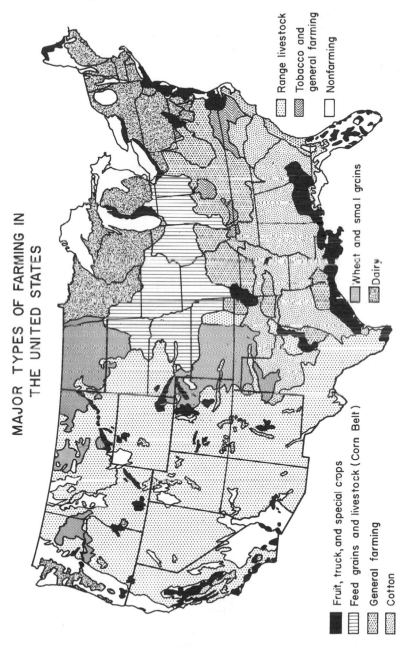

FIGURE 9-1.

Value of production assets per farm and farmworker

There have been large increases in the amount of capital assets needed to carry out enterprise specialization and farm consolidation. While the average value per farm has gone up since 1850 (Table 9-3), the increase has been especially rapid since 1940 (Table 9-7). From 1940 to

TABLE 9-7: Average Value of Production Assets per Farm and Farmworker, United States, Selected Years, 1940-1967.[1]

Year	Per Farm ($)	Per Farmworker ($)
1940	6,158	3,326
1950	17,378	9,529
1955	26,165	13,876
1960	42,465	21,304
1967	73,120	41,307

[1] Alaska and Hawaii not included.

Source: Balance Sheet of Agriculture, 1967 U.S.D.A., Agricultural Information Bulletin No. 329.

1967 the average value of production assets per farm in current prices increased almost 12 times. During this same period the average value of production assets (in current prices) per farmworker increased even more rapidly than per farm—about 1150 percent. In constant 1947 to 1949 prices, the value of assets per farm and per farmworker has more than doubled in the same period.

FARM PRODUCTION, YIELDS, AND EXPENSES

Farm production

Farm production increased 131 percent from 1910 to 1967 (Table 9-8). Livestock and livestock products have increased more rapidly than crops during this period; both categories more than doubled, while poultry and egg production rose fourfold. In crops, the most spectacular increase was in oil crops, rising from an index of six in 1910 to an index of 171 in 1967 on a 1957-59 base. This rapid increase was due primarily to the introduction of soybeans as an oil crop and to increased plantings of peanuts. Tung nuts were introduced in the late 1930's and the tung oil substituted for whale oil as a lubricant for many intricate mechanical parts. Neither feed grain output nor hay and forage output kept pace with the output of meat animals. The reasons include the facts that many meat

TABLE 9-8: Farm Production: Index Numbers of Total Output and Gross Production of Livestock and Crops, by Groups, United States, Selected Years, 1910-67 (1957-59 = 100).

Year	Farm Output	Livestock and Livestock Products[1]				Crops									
	All[2]	All[2]	Meat Animals[3]	Dairy Products[4]	Poultry and Eggs[5]	All[6]	Feed Grains[7]	Hay and Forage[8]	Food Grains[9]	Vegetables[10]	Fruits and Nuts[11]	Sugar Crops[12]	Cotton[13]	Tobacco	Oil Crops[14]
1910	51	49	53	53	33	63	68	70	53	53	52	65	95	64	6
1915	57	55	62	58	34	72	72	80	84	56	70	65	91	65	6
1920	59	52	55	60	34	76	76	82	73	64	72	86	109	86	9
1925	59	58	59	69	41	72	69	73	57	66	66	62	130	78	13
1930	61	64	63	76	45	69	56	66	74	74	73	71	113	95	14
1935	61	59	53	78	41	70	60	82	55	81	90	77	86	76	21
1940	70	71	72	84	49	78	66	85	69	83	93	87	102	84	34
1945	81	86	84	95	74	85	75	93	92	94	89	77	74	114	54
1950	86	88	89	93	78	89	81	89	86	96	98	94	82	117	71
1955	96	99	103	99	86	96	86	95	83	96	99	86	120	127	78
1960	106	102	103	101	104	108	109	103	115	103	98	102	116	112	105
1965	114	111	111	103	124	115	111	112	117	108	106	138	121	107	153
1967[15]	118	117	120	100	138	117	124	115	134	112	115	136	62	116	171

1 Production of livestock products. Horses and mules excluded.
2 Includes clipped wool, mohair, and for 1939 to date, honey and beeswax. These items are not included in the separate groups of livestock and products shown.
3 Cattle and calves, sheep and lambs, and hogs.
4 Butter, butterfat, wholesale milk, retail milk, and milk consumed on farms.
5 Chickens and eggs, commercial broilers, and turkeys.
6 Includes farm gardens, hay seeds, pasture and cover-crop seeds and some miscellaneous crop production not included in separate groups of crops shown. Coverage of seed and miscellaneous crops is more complete for 1939 to date than for prior years.
7 Corn for grain, oats, barley, and sorghum grain.
8 All hay, sorghum forage, corn silage, and for 1939 to date, sorghum silage.
9 All wheat, rye, buckwheat, and rice.
10 Potatoes, sweetpotatoes, dry edible beans, dry field peas, truck crops for processing and truck crops for fresh market.
11 Fruits, berries, and tree nuts.
12 Sugar beets, sugarcane for sugar and seed, sugarcane syrup, and maple syrup.
13 Cotton lint and cottonseed.
14 Soybeans, peanuts picked and threshed, peanuts hogged, flaxseed, and for 1939 to date, tungnuts.
15 Preliminary.

SOURCE: Changes in Farm Production and Efficiency, 1968, U.S.D.A., Statistical Bulletin 233.

animals consumed the feed initially needed for horses, which were replaced by mechanical power, that the number of dairy animals (some of
which were used for meat) was reduced, and that gains in efficiency due
to breeding and nutritional technology were made.

A closer look at livestock production shows that while the number of
animal breeding units was almost the same in 1967 as it was in 1919,
livestock production per breeding unit more than doubled (Table 9-9).
This gain in efficiency can be attributed primarily to gains in the knowledge of genetics and animal breeding. Isolating genetic characteristics
such as animal size, rate of gain, milk production, and conformation in
selected animals to be used for breeding purposes have been keys for
these gains in efficiency.

When the gains in production efficiency are compared for livestock
and poultry, it is easy to see that the gains are not spread evenly through
the various enterprises and that additional feed conversion efficiencies are
likely. For example, from 1935 to 1966 the amount of feed necessary to
produce 100 pounds of broilers was about cut in half, while the amount of
feed necessary to produce 100 eggs remained constant (Table 9-10).
However, in order to get 100 pounds of milk, of cattle and calves, or of
hogs, a farmer actually had to feed more in 1966 than he did in 1935.
When one compares these rates of gain in farm production and feed
efficiencies to population growth it is easy to understand why research
efforts continue in the animal sciences, horticulture, agronomy, soils, and
plant breeding.

TABLE 9-9: Index Numbers of Animal Units of Breeding Livestock and Livestock Production Per Breeding Unit, United States, Selected Years,
1919-67.[1]

(1957-59 = 100)

Year	Animal Units of Breeding Livestock	Livestock Production Per Breeding Unit
1919	97	56
1925	92	63
1930	92	70
1935	86	69
1940	95	75
1945	109	79
1950	102	86
1955	106	93
1960	97	105
1965	100	111
1967[2]	98	119

[1] Excludes horses and mules.
[2] Preliminary.
SOURCE: Changes in Farm Production and Efficiency, 1968, U.S.D.A., Statistical Bulletin No. 233.

TABLE 9-10: Feed Units of All Feed, Including Pasture, Consumed Per Unit
of Production by Different Classes of Livestock and Poultry,
United States, Selected Years, 1910-66.

Year beginning Oct. 1	Milk cows, Per 100 Pounds of Milk (feed units)	Cattle and Calves, Per 100 Pounds Produced[1] (feed units)	Hens and Pullets, Per 100 Eggs Produced (feed units)	Broilers Per 100 Pounds Produced[1] (feed units)	Hogs, Per 100 Pounds Produced[1] (feed units)
Average:					
1910–1914	121	967	56	—	665
1920–1924	119	1,230	61	—	566
1930–1934	100	906	60	508	519
1940–1944	114	1,001	63	467	546
1950	112	966	60	374	531
1955	109	904	56	326	536
1960	115	987	53	287	576
1965	113	1,040	54	302	597
1966 [2]	108	1,026	54	305	555

[1] Live-weight production.
[2] Preliminary.

Source: Changes in Farm Production and Efficiency, 1968, U.S.D.A., Statistical Bulletin No. 233.

Crop yields per acre have tended to increase rapidly since the figures
of 1935 to 1939 (Table 9-11). Before that time the opening of new lands
acted as an inducement to move to better soils rather than increase yields
on existing land. The years of depression during the 1930's also restricted
the amount of technology that farmers were able and willing to buy and
apply to their crop lands. Crop yields projected to the year 2000 show an
approximate doubling of yield from the 1960 level for corn and cotton
from 53 bushels to 100 bushels per acre, and from 446 pounds to 800
pounds per acre respectively. Wheat and hay yields will probably increase
about one third.

Acres harvested

The cropland harvested dropped 15 million acres from 1910 to 1967
(Table 9-12), but an approximate doubling of crop production per acre
filled the needs of our population, which also doubled. Acreage needed to
produce the farm products for one person in this country fell from 2.17
acres in 1910 to 1.18 acres in 1967. The number of acres used to produce
products for export has undergone large fluctuations, from a low in 1940
of 8 million acres to a high in 1965 of 76 million acres.

TABLE 9-11: Yields Per Harvested Acre of Four Major Crops, Selected Periods with Projections, United States.[1]

Years	Wheat (bushel/acre)	Corn	Cotton (lb./acre)	Hay (tons/acre)
1878-82	13.2	25.6	179	1.14[2]
1920-24	13.9	27.2	154	1.21
1925-29	14.1	26.4	171	1.20
1930-34	13.3	23.8	185	1.08
1935-39	13.2	22.5	226	1.24
1940-44	17.1	31.9	262	1.35
1945-49	17.0	35.6	270	1.35
1950-54	17.3	38.5	297	1.43
1955-59	22.1	47.3	429	1.58
1960	26.2	53.0	446	1.76
1970	28.0	70.0	560	2.00
1980	31.0	80.0	640	2.30
1990	33.0	90.0	720	2.60
2000	35.0	100.0	800	3.00

[1] U.S.D.A., *Agricultural Statistics and Crop Production, Annual Summary,* Projection estimates are a medium projection. The way these estimates were made is explained in detail in the source listed below.

[2] Estimated from data on tame hay alone.

Source: Hans H. Landsberg, and others, *Resources in America's Future* (Baltimore: The Johns Hopkins Press, 1963), Adapted from Table A 18-1, p. 972. Published for Resources for the Future, Inc.

Animal power and mechanical power [1]

Much of the productivity of farming in America can be attributed to the change from animal power to mechanical power. In 1910 there were virtually no mechanical aids to help the farmer (Table 9-13). Everything from breaking ground for planting to harvest was done by hand or with animal power, principally horses and mules. The farmer did have a few automobiles and some dairy men had milking machines. By 1960 this situation had just about reversed itself. Horses and mules were down to a fraction of their 1910 numbers, while almost every farm had at least one tractor. Many of the larger farms had three tractors: a large 4 to 6 bottom plow tractor for heavy work, a medium-sized tractor for lighter field jobs, and a small "runabout" tractor to work in the barns and supply power for specialized equipment like augers, hay loaders, and stationary forage choppers and blowers.

The use of trucks on farms grew more rapidly than did the use of combines. Pickup balers and field harvesters also increased rapidly, but neither of these implements was used much prior to the early 1940's. Milking machines on farms increased until the early 1950's, when their

[1] See Chapter 7, "The Role of Capital in Agriculture and Economic Growth" for a supplementary discussion of changes in the use of agricultural inputs.

TABLE 9-12: Acres of Cropland Harvested for Export and Domestic Use, Selected Years, 1910-67.

Year	Cropland Harvested[1] (Millions of Acres)	Total Cropland[2] (Millions of Acres)	Index Crop Production Per Acre (1957-59=100)	Acreage Used for Producing Export Crops[3] (Millions of Acres)	Acreage Used for Producing Products for Domestic Use[4] Total (Millions of Acres)	Per Capita (Acres)
1910	317	330	68	37	200	2.17
1915	332	348	74	49	198	1.96
1920	351	368	74	60	210	1.98
1925	351	370	69	44	238	2.05
1930	360	382	64	39	265	2.15
1935	336	377	66	20	269	2.12
1940	331	368	76	8	290	2.20
1945	345	372	82	42	280	2.00
1950	336	377	84	50	276	1.82
1955	333	378	91	47	283	1.72
1960	317	355	109	64	255	1.41
1965	292	336	122	76	218	1.12
1967.[2]	302	342	122	71	233	1.18

[1] Land from which one or more crops were harvested.

[2] The difference between total acres and cropland harvested is in the number of acres of crop failure or summer fallow.

[3] Acreages for exports relate to exports for year beginning July 1, or month representing beginning of crop season. Acreage includes seeds for crops and feed for livestock that are exported.

[4] Includes products used by our military forces in this country and abroad, and by our domestic civilian population.

[5] Preliminary.

Source: Changes in Farm Production and Efficiency, 1962, U.S.D.A., Statistical Bulletin No. 233, Washington, D.C.

number declined. This decline was due primarily to the reduction in the numbers of dairy farms and farmers.

Farm production expenses

The costs necessary to produce agricultural output have fluctuated over the years, corresponding to the ups and downs of total agricultural income. For example, during the early 1950's agricultural income declined (Table 9-14) and so did the total production expense of farmers (Table 7-3). However, some expenses did not fluctuate as much as others. While expenses for feed, livestock, seed, and hired labor took a relatively large decline, expenses for fertilizer and lime showed only a slight dip. Seed costs have stayed within a fairly narrow range, from 491 to 671 million dollars from 1947-1967, while feed purchases varied almost three billion dollars during the same period.

Costs not associated directly with a level of production, such as taxes and interest charges, have increased steadily since 1940. Rising tax costs reflect the pressure of population on rural areas. More intensive land uses and suburban development projects of all kinds require financing

TABLE 9-13: Horses and Mules, Motor Vehicles, and Specified Machines on Farms, United States, Jan. 1, Selected Years, 1910-1962.[1]

Year	Horses and Mules All Ages (Millions)	Tractors (exclusive of steam and garden) (Thous.)	Motor Trucks (Thous.)	Automobiles (Thous.)	Grain Combines (Thous.)	Corn Pickers (Thous.)	Farms With Milking Machines (Thous.)	Pickup Balers (Thous.)	Field Forage Harvesters (Thous.)
1910	24.2	1	0	50	1	—	12	—	—
1915	26.5	25	25	472	—	—	—	—	—
1920	25.7	246[2]	139[2]	2,146[2]	4	10	55	—	—
1925	22.6	549	459	3,283	—	—	—	—	—
1930	19.1	920[2]	900[2]	4,135[2]	61	50	100	—	—
1935	16.7	1,048	890	3,642	—	—	—	—	—
1940	14.5	1,567[2]	1,047[2]	4,144[2]	190	110	175	—	—
1945	12.0	2,354[2]	1,490[2]	4,148[2]	375[2]	168	365[2]	42	20[3]
1950	7.8	3,394[2]	2,207[2]	4,100	714[2]	456[2]	636[2]	196[2]	81
1951	7.0	3,678	2,325	—	810	522	655	240	102
1952	6.2	3,907	2,430	—	887	588	675	298	124
1953	5.4	4,100	2,535	—	930	630	690	345	148
1954	4.8	4,243	2,610	4,140	965	660	705	395	175
1955	4.3	4,345[4]	2,675	—	980[4]	688[4]	712[4]	448[4]	202[4]
1956	4.0	4,480	2,707	—	1,005	715	—	505	220
1957	3.6	4,570	2,745	—	1,015	740	—	560	240
1958	3.4	4,620	2,775	—	1,030	755	—	600	258
1959	3.2	4,673	2,800	—	1,045	775	—	645	270
1960	3.1	4,684[4]	2,826[4]	3,629[4]	1,040[4]	795[4]	666[4]	680[4]	290[4]
1961	5	4,700	2,850	5	1,035	800	5	715	305
1962[6]	5	4,660	2,875	5	1,025	815	5	735	320

[1] Current Industrial Reports of the Bureau of the Census (formerly Facts for Industry), annual registrations of motor vehicles, and results of enumerative and mailed questionnaire surveys were used in developing estimates for years and machines not covered by census reports. Numbers of horses and mules, which were discontinued in 1960, are from livestock reports of the Statistical Reporting Service. [2] Census of Agriculture, census dates January 1, 1920 and 1945; April 1, 1930, 1940, and 1950. [3] Information for previous years is not available. [4] Census of agriculture, Nov. 1954 and 1959. [5] Estimates discontinued because of insufficient information. [6] Preliminary.

Source: Changes in Farm Production and Efficiency, 1962, U.S.D.A., Statistical Bulletin No. 233.

that is often drawn from the land. For this reason many farmers are paying higher taxes for schools and highways even though they may not use these facilities very much, if at all.

GROSS AND NET FARM INCOME

Gross cash receipts from farm marketings in current dollars have risen almost every year since the mid-1930's, except for a six-year period in the 1950's. However, when the net income of farm operators is adjusted to a constant 1957-59 dollar basis, it shows a decline over the last 20 years of about 3 and one-half billion dollars (Table 9-14). Inflation and the competitive structure of agriculture have contributed to this situation. It takes continually increased amounts of farm sales just to maintain a given level of net farm income.

Realized gross income per farm in the United States tripled from 1949 to 1967, in current dollars. This is what one would expect from con-

TABLE 9-14: Realized Gross and Net Incomes, All Farms and Per Farm, United States, Selected Years 1949-1967.

	United States		Per Farm	
Year	Realized Gross Farm Income[1] (Millions) (Current $)	Operators' Realized Net Farm Income[1,2] (Millions) (1957-59 $)	Realized Gross Income[1,3] (Current $)	Operators' Realized Net Income[1,3] (1957-59 $)
1949	$31,628	$16,054	$ 5,561	$2,806
1951	37,055	15,748	6,876	2,901
1953	34,986	14,586	7,076	2,927
1955	33,138	11,841	7,162	2,544
1957	34,001	10,815	7,866	2,474
1959	37,468	11,250	9,147	2,746
1961	39,771	12,398	10,407[4]	3,244
1963	42,271	12,099	11,870	3,397
1965	44,926	13,078	13,452	3,916
1967	49,061	12,603	15,593	4,005

[1] Includes Alaska and Hawaii after 1960.

[2] Of farm operators.

[3] Realized gross income includes cash receipts from farm marketings, government payments, value of home consumption, and gross rental value of farm dwellings. Realized net income deducts farm production expenses and accounts for net changes in farm inventories.

[4] Per farm estimates prior to 1960 have not been corrected for change in definition of farm.

SOURCE: U.S.D.A., E.R.S., Supplements to FIS 187 and 211, 1962 and 1968; and U.S.D.A., E.R.S., Farm Income Situation, July 1968

tinually increasing receipts from all farm marketings. However, realized net income per farm increased by only about 43 percent. Increasing production costs, falling farm prices, rising fixed costs of owning land and debt, and inflation all reduced the margin of profit.

Number of farms and value of farm products sold

When the number of farms are grouped by the value of farm products sold, several trends become apparent. Since 1939 there have been reductions in the number of farms selling less than $5,000 worth of farm products, and gains in the number of farms selling more than $5,000 worth of products. In addition, the loss in farm numbers is intensified in the lower income scales while relatively large increases in numbers of farms are recorded in high income groups. For example, there was a loss of almost 60 percent in the number of farms selling less than $5,000 worth of farm products from 1949 to 1967. Farms which sold between $5,000 and $10,000 worth of farm products decreased in numbers by only about 38 percent, while the number of farms which sold over $10,000 worth of output increased by about 105 percent.

The percent of farms selling more than $10,000 worth of farm products in 1939 was slightly under 5 percent. By 1949 it had increased to almost 9 percent, by 1959 to over 21 percent, and by 1967 to almost 32 percent (Table 9-15). In 1967 this group, comprising slightly under one-third of all farmers, sold approximately 85 percent of our country's agricultural output.

Ranking of farm products sold

When the farm production is analyzed in terms of income contribution, livestock and livestock products head the list. Field crops and fruit are quite far down the list. This is to be expected because livestock must convert the field crops into meat, eggs, and milk, and the value of these products must be correspondingly higher than the feed which the animals producing them must eat.

One can also pick up the reasons for differences in regional farm incomes from a priority ranking of farm products. The most prosperous states in terms of farm income are those states which produce both the feed and the finished livestock or livestock products. Those states with lower farm incomes are more crop-producing states, or states which produce the cattle and other livestock for finishing elsewhere.

Government payments

Government payments for farmers were first introduced in legislation of the early 1930's. The initial objective was to stabilize incomes and

TABLE 9-15: Number and Percent of U.S. Farms by Value of Farm Products Sold—1949, 1959, and 1967

Value of Farm Products Sold ($)	1949				1959				1967			
	Number and % of Farms by Sales Class		Amount and % of Farm Sales		Number and % of Farms by Sales Class		Amount and % of Farm Sales		Number and % of Farms by Sales Class		Amount and % of Farm Sales	
	Number (thou.)	%	Dollars (bill.)	%	Number (thou.)	%	Dollars (bill.)	%	Number (thou.)	%	Dollars (bill.)	%
10,000 +	484	9.0	11.3	50.9	794	21.5	21.9	71.6	993	31.6	39.0	85.0
5,000–9,999	721	13.4	5.1	23.0	653	17.6	4.7	15.4	446	14.2	3.7	8.1
2,500–4,999	882	16.4	3.2	14.4	617	16.7	2.3	7.5	360	11.4	1.5	3.4
Less than $2,500 [1]	3292	61.2	2.6	11.7	1637	44.2	1.7	5.5	1347	42.8	1.6	3.5
Total	5379	100.0	22.2	100.0	3701	100.0	30.6	100.0	3146	100.0	45.8	100.0

[1] Not fully comparable. The more restrictive definition of a farm used in the census of 1959 resulted in exclusion of approximately 232,000 places that would have qualified as farms under the definition used in the census of 1949. By definition, the farms excluded were small places selling less than $250 worth of farm products. Their exclusion affects total number of farms much more than the total value of farm products sold. For a discussion of the change in the census definition of a farm, see Introduction, Volume 2, 1959 Census of Agriculture.

SOURCE: Statistical Abstract, United States, 1968, U.S. Department of Commerce, p. 596; and U.S.D.A., E.R.S., Farm Income Situation, July 1968, p. 69.

protect against widely fluctuating farm prices. Gradually an income level objective was added to the justification of price supports. This income objective of supports has not been realized for the low income farmers to which it was politically aimed, but this issue will be discussed more fully in Chapter 22.

Payments are made to farmers under a variety of programs (Table 9-16). They are made only to farmers who are legally eligible for compensation and who have filed application or notified the proper officials of their actions.

Government payments, or price supports, are achieved through loans, purchases, and direct payments to producers—all at levels announced by the Secretary of Agriculture. For most commodities loans are made directly to producers. Some commodities may also be purchased directly from producers at the time of loan maturity for the crop. Price-support loans are "nonrecourse," which simply means that farmers are not obligated to make good any decline in the market price of the commodity they put up as collateral. Direct payments are made to producers who participate in certain of the land retirement provisions of the Feed Grain Programs or in cotton acreage diversion programs, or sell wool under the Wool Act.

Government payments have comprised an increasing share of gross farm income since the late 1940's. In 1949 government payments amounted to only $185 million, but rose to $554 million by 1956.[2] The next year they almost doubled, reaching $1,016 million. In 1961 payments hit $1,493 million, and rose to $3,079 million by 1967.

Farm home consumption and rent

The amount of food consumed in farm homes and the rent for the farm dwellings are two items that are not generally accounted for when farm incomes are calculated. It has been estimated that in 1949 the value of food both produced and consumed by farmers was 2,399 million dollars. With the reduction in the farm population this amount had fallen to 745 million dollars by 1967, about one-half what it had been in 1959.

Although the value of food consumed declined, the rental value of farm dwellings increased. In 1949 the gross rental value of farm dwellings was 1,408 million dollars. But by 1967 it had climbed to 2,449 million dollars. This increase is caused primarily by the increased capital investments by farmers in dwellings and in their equipment. Many have made improvements in their houses and have added offices for more efficient farm organization.

[2] See J. V. McElveen, "Farm Numbers, Farm Size, and Farm Income," *Journal of Farm Economics* (Vol. 45, February 1963, No. 1), pp. 4-5.

TABLE 9-16: Government Payments by Programs, Selected Years 1950-1967 (in millions of dollars).[1]

| Year | Conservation | | Soil Bank | Sugar Act | Wool | Feed Grain | Wheat | Cotton[2] | Cropland Adjustment | Total |
	ACP	Great Plains								
1950	246	—	—	37	—	—	—	—	—	283
1955	188	—	—	41	—	—	—	—	—	229
1956	220	—	243	37	54	—	—	—	—	554
1957	230	—	700	32	53	—	—	—	—	1,016
1958	214	1	815	44	14	—	—	—	—	1,089
1959	228	5	323	44	82	—	—	—	—	682
1960	217	6	370	59	51	—	—	—	—	702
1961	230	6	334	53	56	772	42	—	—	1,493
1962	224	6	304	64	54	841	253	—	—	1,747
1963	223	8	304	67	37	843	215	—	—	1,696
1964	227	9	199	79	25	1,163	438	39	—	2,181[3]
1965	215	9	160	75	18	1,391	525	70	—	2,463[3]
1966	220	11	145	71	34	1,293	679	773	51	3,277[3]
1967	225	12	129	70	29	865	731	932	85	3,079[3]

[1] Details may not add to totals due to rounding.
[2] Includes cotton price adjustment and cotton option and producers' pool payments.
[3] Includes milk indemnity payments ($155,000 in 1964, $194,000 in 1965, $150,000 in 1966, and $275,000 in 1967).

SOURCE: U.S.D.A., E.R.S., FIS-211, July 1968, Washington, D.C., Table 21H.

TABLE 9-17: Off-Farm Work by Farm Operators in the United States, Selected Years, 1934-1964.

Year	All Farm Operators[1]	Total	Operators Working Off Their Farms					
			1-99 Days	100 or More Days	Total	1-99 Days	100 or More Days
	Number		Days	Days	Percent	Percent	Percent
1934	6,812,350	2,077,474	1,316,702	760,772	30.5	19.3	11.2
1939	6,101,794	1,749,296	803,902	945,394	28.7	13.2	15.5
1944	5,858,889	1,660,163	529,904	1,130,259	28.3	9.0	19.3
1949	5,385,525	2,092,922	835,672	1,257,250	38.9	15.5	23.3
1954	4,783,021	2,153,737	820,012	1,333,725	45.0	17.1	27.9
1959	3,707,973	1,663,841	556,235	1,107,606	44.9	15.0	29.9
1964	3,157,857	1,462,183	448,983	1,013,200	46.3	14.2	32.1

[1] All farm operators October-November 1959 and 1954; April 1, 1950 and 1940; and January 1, 1945 and earlier.

SOURCE: United States Census of Agriculture, 1964, General Report, Volume 2, Chapter 5, Tables 2 and 5.

Farmer's nonfarm income

With the increase in farmers doing more nonfarm work there has also been an increase in the number of farmers who report income from nonfarm sources to be greater than farm income. In 1954 29.8 percent of the farm operators reported nonfarm income to be greater than farm income. By 1959 this proportion had increased to 35.8 percent, and by 1964 to almost 40 percent.

Farmers and farming continue to be a big business in America. However, there are significant changes going on in production, in farm income, and in the numbers of people who farm. There are problems of agricultural adjustment that will not be solved easily, including not only the quality and quantity of farm production but the number and quality of people who farm. The changes in farms and farmers have come about primarily through the interplay of free market forces and voluntary individual management decisions. What will take place in the future?

FARM OPERATORS

Farmer's age, education, and off-farm work

The average age of farmers in this country has stayed remarkably stable. Since 1945 the average age of farmers has risen only two and one-half years. In 1954 16.6 percent of the farmers were 65 years of age or older, and in 1964 this proportion had risen to 17.4 percent. However, during the same period the proportion of farm operators under 35 years of age decreased from 15.1 percent to 11.5 percent. Two out of every three farmers are now 45 years or older. It seems to take a certain set amount of time for the average farmer to accumulate and control enough capital to farm profitably, and for him to make the decision to stay in farming.

The farmer's educational level has been discussed quite thoroughly in Chapter 6. In general, the level of educational attainment in rural areas is lower than in urban areas. Only a small fraction of boys born on farms can make their living from farming. There is a growing demand for highly trained and skilled people, and farmers who decide to stop farming or youngsters from farming areas who stop school or technical training will be severely handicapped when they look for other employment. This will be increasingly true for the young people in rural areas looking for their first jobs, and for middle-aged farmers who decide to try to shift to non-farm jobs.

The kinds of jobs that farmers have off the farm vary from odd jobs to part-time jobs, such as driving a school bus or holding a regular job with regular hours. Since 1945 the increase in the share of farmers working off their farms is largely the result of an increase in the share of commercial farmers working off their farms. There has also been a significant increase in those farmers who sell between $2,500 and $9,999 worth of farm products, working off the farm 100 days or more.

Although the number of farmers has decreased, the number of farmers working off the farm 100 days or more has increased (Table 9-17). In 1959 over two-thirds of the farmers who worked off the farm reported 100 days or more of nonfarm work, and 26.1 percent of all the farmers worked off the farm 200 days or more.

10

Marketing food products

Commercial agriculture separated the farm producer from the urban consumer, creating the need for a marketing system. Marketing activities arise primarily because of form, distance, and time variables. These variables require that food be processed, transported, and stored. Thus, the job of our marketing system is to get food to the consumer at the proper place, at the proper time, in the proper form, and at acceptable prices.

MARKETING ACTIVITIES ARE CONSUMER ORIENTED

The focus of all marketing activities is to satisfy the consumer. Food processing and distributing firm managers must keep this in mind. Consumer purchases are signals to the marketing men about what is wanted. Every time a housewife buys a pound box of frozen peas, she is in a sense saying to the marketing men "continue to freeze peas and package them in one-pound boxes." In turn, the marketing men pass the signal back to the farmer by placing an order which prompts the farmer to continue pea production. If the consumer stops buying, or voting for, a product with dollar bills at the retail store the production of the item will soon slow down. For example, weight conscious Americans no longer prefer cuts of meats with much fat attached. As a result the signals pass back to the farmer and more lean type hogs are being produced.

Businessmen attempt to influence consumer votes through advertising. The American Dairy Association reminds us to continue to drink milk, and consumers are also bombarded with commercials describing the merits of various brands of cereals, meat products, and ice cream. These efforts have varying degrees of success. Efforts to advertise butter, for example, have failed to stem the tide of consumer tastes changing to oleo.

WHAT SOCIETY WANTS FROM ITS MARKETING SYSTEM

The public wants a marketing system which provides food at the lowest possible cost. While efficient marketing activities also operate within the framework of input-output ratios, in the process of consumption, output is measured in terms of consumer satisfaction. From another viewpoint, society allows those people working in the marketing system a reasonable return for their inputs of property and personal service. The marketing system should also function to find and develop new markets in the sense of making new products or bettering old products for sale at home and abroad.

From the farmer's viewpoint a marketing system that can entice consumers to buy more food is a good one. To make goods continuously available to consumers at prices which allow the consumer to raise his standard of living and increase his satisfaction is a goal that requires much of both the farmer and the marketing man. They are partners dependent on each other.

THE DEVELOPMENT OF OUR MARKETING SYSTEM

As we have already discussed, self-sufficient colonial farmers marketed few of their products commercially. Food was grown, processed, and stored primarily for family sustenance. But with the rapid development of commercial agriculture in the 19th century the business of processing and distributing food grew quickly. The Chicago Board of Trade was founded in 1848 and quickly became the nation's leading grain market. The Union Stockyards of Chicago in 1865, followed by the development of the refrigerated railroad car in 1880, allowed the meat industry to commercialize quickly. About the same time the grain milling industry centered in Minneapolis. New technologies in food containers allowed the canning industry for both fruits and vegetables to develop.

With farms increasing production at a record pace new marketing businesses were under great pressure to move food to markets at home and abroad. Rapid growth led to the use of various unethical business practices, particularly as some of the huge firms wielded monopoly power. By 1900, with federal antitrust legislation passed and regulatory agencies such as the Interstate Commerce Commission established, the situation eased. The steady and regular growth of the marketing system aided the quarter century of agricultural prosperity enjoyed by the farmer before World War I.

THE FUNCTIONAL APPROACH TO MARKETING

A framework is needed in order to study marketing problems. One of the most useful is the functional approach. Marketing functions are synonymous with business activities, and the functional approach classifies each of them into three groups: exchange, physical, and facilitating.

Exchange functions

Buying and selling. The exchange or transfer of title of food as it moves from the farm to the consumer is vital to the marketing system. Buying and selling functions are part of the cost of marketing. Every time a buyer and seller agree to exchange money for goods or goods for money price negotiation takes place. A detailed study of prices will come later.

Buying costs often include the time and effort involved in seeking out sources of supply in addition to the negotiating phase. Selling, on the other hand, may include the cost involved in preparing advertising and promoting a product for sale. Merchandising is a term sometimes used to describe these kinds of costs.

Physical functions

Transportation. Physical functions are those of transportation and storage which are directly associated with the physical handling of the products. To move the raw food production from several million scattered farms to a population of over 200 million consumers domestically and many more abroad is a big job. Transportation activity creates place utility, becoming a major factor with the assembly of raw food at the farm. The network of railways, airways, waterways, and highways are an integral and essential part of our marketing system. In addition to assembly and actual costs in transit, the cost of loading and unloading goods is included in transportation.

Storage. Most farm products are harvested in one season, but because consumers desire to obtain all sorts of foods at any time storage activities which create time utility are another vital element in our marketing system. Storage of perishable commodities is more expensive than storage of nonperishables since costly refrigeration or other equipment may be necessary to maintain proper product quality. The farmer often performs the storage function himself. A farmer who stores grain after harvest through the winter for sale in the spring is creating time utility in the same manner as a large grain elevator would. Owners of commercial storage usually charge a fee based on amount stored and time held.

Facilitating functions

The costs of marketing arising from the facilitating functions of standardization, financing, risk-bearing, and market information are commonly overlooked. These functions do what their name suggests; they facilitate the smooth performance of the market and hold down the costs of the exchange and physical functions. They are the grease that makes the wheels in our marketing system perform easily.

Standardization. Did you ever stop to think how difficult it would be if a bushel of wheat in Kansas was 60 pounds but only 50 pounds in Indiana? This certainly would complicate the exchange of wheat between the two areas. Or what about the complexities that would arise if the criteria for a choice steer in three different livestock markets were all different? Immediately the necessity for a uniform measuring system for quantity and quality becomes apparent. In a complex mass economy such as ours, standardization greatly simplifies the exchange process of buying and selling, and at the same time reduces the cost. You can call your broker, order 5,000 bushels of Number 1 hard red winter wheat and know exactly how much you will get and what qualities it will possess. In other words, accepted and uniform standards allow sale by description and buyers feel no compulsion to see the physical product before purchase.

The nature of standardization requires a regulating agency. This is most often a public body of the local, state, or federal government.

Financing. The financing function creates a cost to the person or agency owning the product because of time lags between purchase and sale. It is impossible to escape this type of cost because someone must always own the product at all times. When a grain elevator buys wheat from the farmer the elevator exchanges money for wheat and must finance the wheat until it exchanges the commodity for money with the miller. The retailer who buys a can of beans and places it on the shelf in his store has money tied up until some consumer purchases the beans, which may be six months later.

Risk-bearing. Another cost associated with ownership is risk-bearing. This function is distinct from financing and includes two kinds—physical risk and market risk.

Physical risk arises with ownership because of the possible deterioration of a product due to excessive moisture, heat, contaminating metals, bacteria, insects, and rodents, and because of possible physical loss from accidents, fire, or theft. There is no escaping this cost, although it may be converted to a different form. Sometimes the owner elects to take out insurance against possible physical loss and pays a premium to a company willing to assume the risk for the premium fee.

Market risk arises with ownership because of a possible decline in the product's price. Whether a commodity is held by a farmer, a warehouseman, a processor, wholesaler or retailer, the risk of a lower market price is always present. Various devices are available to the owner to shift or spread the risk involved. For certain commodities the farmer may be able to get nonrecourse loans from the government. Another method is to sell products now for later delivery. Still another widely used method is to buy or sell futures contracts on the commodities exchange. A grain elevator that purchases corn on October 1st for $1.10 a bushel can "hedge" by selling a futures contract to deliver corn at some future date at some specified price, say $1.20.[1] If the price of corn declines such that the elevator can get only $1.05 a bushel for its corn when sold to a miller two months later, the elevator manager will try to buy a futures contract for $1.15 a bushel at that time. The five-cent loss on the actual corn bought and sold ($1.10 − $1.05) is offset by a five-cent gain on the corn futures contract ($1.15 − $1.20). The gain and loss in this situation would be referred to as a perfect "hedge." Actual grain prices and futures prices generally move in the same direction with a difference that approximates storage costs over the specified period of time.

Market information. It is vital that both buyer and seller possess adequate and up-to-date information about the market conditions when negotiating price. Also, good market information can greatly expedite the physical functions. Jobs in market information include the collecting, analyzing, and disseminating of a large variety of data. As with the standardization function, much of the marketing information is provided by government agencies.

The functional approach—a summary

The functional approach looks at the various activities that are performed to increase the utility of the product as it moves from the farmer to the consumer. It is of considerable help in making cost studies. Some businesses in marketing specialize in one function, such as the owner of refrigerated storage, while others such as a retail food merchant may perform nearly all eight functions.

Although it is impossible to eliminate any marketing function, it may

---

[1] A corn futures contract is a commitment to take (if contract is bought) or deliver (if contract is sold) a specified amount of corn at a specified date in the future. Typically, no actual corn shipments ever take place as a person buying a contract will sell it again before the specified date in the future is reached and vice versa.

be possible to improve its efficiency and thus lower its cost. The farmer who sells his produce via roadside stand (frequently referred to as "direct" marketing) carries the burden and cost of all eight functions.

The functional approach also helps us to understand why one product has a higher marketing cost than another. For example, the cost of the storage function would be higher for eggs than for corn because of the more perishable nature of eggs; they require controlled storage temperatures and involve more risk because of possible breakage. Sometimes the consumer performs marketing functions. When a housewife pushes a grocery cart around the supermarket she simplifies the selling task and reduces the retailer's cost.

THE INSTITUTIONAL APPROACH TO MARKETING

The institutional approach to marketing describes the person who performs the various functions in the marketing system. The business firms that engage in marketing activities vary widely in size and ownership. There are the small concerns owned and operated by individual proprietorships; there are partnership concerns and huge corporations. Cooperatives, owned and operated by farm producers, are also prominent in the marketing of agricultural products. The institutional approach to marketing gives primary emphasis to people and business organizations. The people engaged in performing marketing activities are called middlemen.

Merchant middlemen

Retailers and wholesalers. Some middlemen, such as retailers and wholesalers, are classed as merchant middlemen because they actually take title to and thus own the products they handle. The merchant middleman buys a product, performs functions which add utility to it, and sells it for gain. Hopefully, he will cover the costs of the functions which he performs, and in addition will realize a profit for his efforts. A retailer is the market agency closest to the consumer and in most cases his marketing job is the most complex. Retailers are also the most numerous of marketing agencies.

Wholesalers are more heterogeneous than retailers and generally include those agencies referred to as jobbers, car lot receivers, and country assemblers, such as the local livestock buyer and grain elevator. The wholesaler performs fewer functions than the retailer and usually deals in larger volumes of goods.

Agent middlemen

Agent middlemen act as representatives for their clients and are differentiated from the merchant middlemen by the fact that they do not take title to any products. The principal function performed by most agent middlemen is providing market information in which they become specialists. Their income is generated by fees and charges in exchange for services rendered.

Brokers and commission men. Brokers act to bring buyers and sellers together in negotiating favorable terms of exchange. If either a buyer or seller feels he does not have enough market information to bargain effectively, does not have the time, or wishes to remain anonymous, he can secure a broker to represent him for a fee.

Usually, when products are consigned to a commission firm on a market the commission agent has a relatively broad degree of control. His job is to sell the product at the best possible price with no obligation to check with the owner as to whether the selling price is acceptable. The difference between brokers and commission men is largely one of degree of control. The commission firm normally supervises the physical handling of the product. Conversely, the broker works much more closely with the client and will not buy or sell except at a specific price after consultation with him.

Speculative middlemen. While the word speculation connotes something evil to many people, the speculative middleman is important to an efficient marketing system. Remember the device used by the grain elevator operator in "hedging" against market risk. This hedge merely shifted the responsibility of performing the market function of market risk to someone else—a speculative middleman. A speculator is one who seeks out market price risks and is willing to accept them in the hopes that the price will move in a direction that will afford him a profit. Speculators deal mostly on futures contracts rather than physical goods and most often attempt to earn their profits from short-run price fluctuations.

Facilitative organizations. These organizations do not take part directly in marketing activities, but are important to any market. Examples include the stockyard companies which own the real estate or physical parts of the market and which receive rent and fees for their use. They usually stipulate the trading hours and terms of sale on the market.

Trade associations are also considered a type of facilitative organization. An example is the American Meat Institute. Trade association activities are varied and typically include the gathering and dissemination of market or other information of particular value to their group. Lobbying in state and federal legislative bodies in an effort to influence legislation important to their industry is also an important task.

Food processors. Since about 60 percent of the food consumed needs to be processed to some degree, processors cannot be ignored in the institutional approach. In many cases processing is only one kind of activity of large business concerns which often act as their own buyers, wholesalers, and retailers.

THE COMMODITY APPROACH TO MARKETING

A third way to study marketing is to concentrate on a particular commodity such as wheat and follow it through its various processing stages as each market function is performed by each institutional organization. Actually this combines the two previous approaches in studying the marketing of a single commodity. For those interested in a specific commodity this is probably the best approach. It helps to focus attention on the physical differences of products that result in different marketing costs.

All three approaches to marketing may be utilized to gain a thorough understanding of marketing principles. Moreover, due to the wide variety of technical and physical data necessary to solve many marketing problems, the economist must obtain the cooperation of horticulturists, food technologists, entomologists, engineers, transportation specialists, and many others.

ORGANIZATIONAL ASPECTS OF MARKETING

In addition to the functions and kinds of middlemen, there are organizational aspects among the various market agencies which merit study. A market channel is simply the path of a product from its raw to its finished form. For example, after production on the farm a product may pass through the hands of a local assembler, a food processor, a wholesaler, and finally a retailer before its ultimate destination—the consumer. The nature of the market channel for any product may vary depending upon the region of the country, the season of the year, and the methods employed in handling. Also, one or more channels may be employed to market any single product.

Integration is a marketing organizational feature gaining recent attention. Where various marketing agencies are grouped together under the control of the same management, integration exists. Vertical integration occurs when two agencies at different levels performing unlike market functions are bonded together. If a food processor controls his wholesaler either by contractual agreement or ownership vertical integration exists. Horizontal integration, however, exists when management control is extended over another firm performing like activities or functions. Examples of horizontal integration are the retail chain food stores. A single firm may expand its activities both horizontally and vertically. In the poultry industry feed mills initiated vertical integration by extending control over the farm production phase and in some cases, over marketing agencies as well. More attention to integration will be given later in the chapter.

THE COSTS OF MARKETING FOOD

The marketing bill and its composition

In 1967 consumers spent $85.5 billion for food products at the retail level, more than double the amount spent in 1950 (Table 10-1). The costs

TABLE 10-1: Total Marketing Bill, Farm Value, Consumer Expenditures, and Farmers' Share of Consumer's Dollar, 1947-49, 1957-59, and 1960-67.[1]

| | Total Marketing Bill [2] | Farm Value [3] | Civilian Expenditure for Farm Foods [4] | Farmer's Share of Consumer's Dollar |
	(Billion Dollars)			(Percent)
1947–49	24.5	18.9	43.4	43.5
1957–59	39.9	20.9	60.8	34.4
1960	44.2	21.7	65.9	32.9
1961	45.1	22.0	67.1	32.8
1962	46.9	22.4	69.3	32.5
1963	48.9	22.6	71.5	31.6
1964	51.2	23.4	74.6	31.4
1965	52.1	25.5	77.6	32.9
1966	55.3	28.1	83.4	33.7
1967	58.0	27.5	85.5	32.2

[1] Data for 1960-67 includes Alaska and Hawaii.
[2] Difference between farm value and domestic expenditure.
[3] Payment to farmers for equivalent farm products, adjusted to eliminate imputed value of nonfood by-products.
[4] Market value of food products derived from products produced on domestic farms and purchased by civilian consumers. Imports and seafoods not included.
SOURCE: *Marketing and Transportation Situation,* U.S.D.A., E.R.S., February 1968.

of marketing accounted for two-thirds of the total. The remaining one-third, commonly referred to as the farmer's share (Farm Value, Table 10-1) has been declining as a percent of the total for some time. Factors accounting for the rising marketing bill include an increase in the amount of processing and other services sold with food, an increase in marketing costs per unit sold, and an increase in volume of food sold.

Marketing services sold with food doubled in volume from 1940 to 1966 while volume of food marketed increased 73 percent. Thus, the volume of services per unit of product increased about 16 percent. Product innovations and technologies of processing and transportation have been the basis for much of the increase in marketing services. For example, it is estimated that 55 percent of the food items on the market in 1967 were not in existence 10 years earlier. Furthermore, 8000 items were carried on retail food shelves in 1967 compared to 5000 in 1957.[2] Other reasons for the increase in volume of food marketing services include: increased emphasis on nonprice competition among food marketing firms which often includes more services, increasing amounts of food eaten away from the home, the entrance of more women into the labor force which increases the need for foods which can be easily prepared, and the increasing affluence among the population.[3]

There was a 20 percent increase in the volume of food marketed from 1955 to 1965 which accounts for a rising dollar value of the farm share. Farm prices fluctuated within relatively narrow limits in that period. In 1966 and 1967, however, increases in farm prices also contributed to a larger farm value.

Increases in marketing charges per unit sold (141 percent from 1929 to 1963) reflect increases in wage rates for labor, transportation, and other costs. All major components of the marketing bill have continued to increase since 1951. Total labor costs doubled from 1950 to 1967 and have accounted for nearly half of the total marketing bill for a long time. Hourly labor cost increased 40 percent from the 1957-59 average to 1967, however, due to increased output per man hour, unit labor costs increased only 14 percent in the same period.

Transportation accounts for about 10 percent of the total marketing bill. Most of the increase in this component of the bill since 1958 has resulted from a growth in the volume marketed. Rail freight rates for unprocessed foods declined 10 percent from 1957-59 to 1965.

Profits (before income taxes) earned by corporations from marketing the products included in the marketing bill amount to 5-6 percent of the total marketing bill. While the total dollars of corporate profits have doubled since 1947, due primarily to increased capital investments in plant and equipment, profits remain quite a stable percentage of the total bill.

Depreciation charges make up one of the most rapidly increasing

[2] Marketing and Transportation Situation, U.S.D.A., E.R.S., November 1967, p. 27.
[3] The income elasticity for food marketing services is several times higher than the income elasticity for basic food.

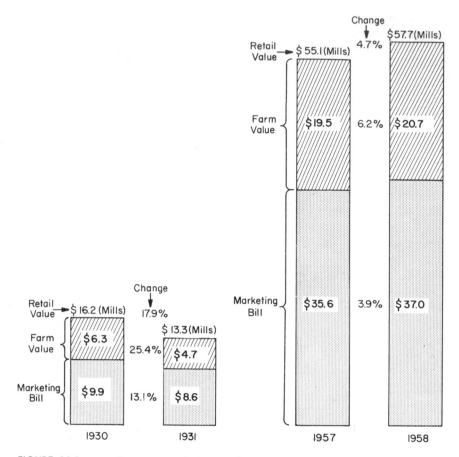

FIGURE 10-1:   Comparison of Changes in Retail Value, Farm Value, and Marketing Bill for 1930-31 and 1957-58. *Marketing and Transportation Situation*, U.S.D.A., E.R.S., M.T.S. 147, November, 1962.

items in the marketing bill. A major cause is the rapid growth in the total value of depreciable assets through replacement, extension, and modernization of plants and equipment. Increases in depreciation rates per dollar of assets is another factor. Advertising, rents, and taxes are other cost components of the marketing bill which have risen faster in the past 20 years than the bill itself, thus taking a larger share of the total.

Another way to view the total marketing charge would be to divide it up among the various important groups of middlemen. Studies in 1939 concluded that retailing took 39 percent of the total farm-to-consumer cost; wholesaling, 11 percent; local assembly agencies in production areas, 6 percent; transportation agencies, 10 percent; and processing firms, 34 percent.[4] In 1955, a study showed that "retailing took about one third of the marketing margin and processing probably accounted for another third."[5] The processor's share has been increasing gradually to 40 percent of the total because of growth in unit processing charges and in the quantity of processed foods. If away-from-home eating places are included with the retail food group, the retail share accounted for 44 percent of the total marketing bill in 1963, about the same as in 1929.[6]

A rising marketing bill, however, is not sufficient reason to reach the conclusion that the marketing system is inefficient. Remember that there were some 50 million more consumers in 1967 than in 1950 and that they continually demanded more services with their food such as packaging, credit, and changes in physical facilities. Efficiency can only be determined if consumer satisfaction is adequately measured and considered.

The farmer's share of the consumer's food dollar

With marketing costs rising relatively faster than consumer's expenditures for food products, the percentage of the total being returned to the farmer has been decreasing, from 42 percent in 1950 to 32 percent in 1967 (Table 10-1). The farmer's share has been given considerable attention by various groups investigating the high cost of marketing. Farm groups point to their declining share and conclude that the middlemen are getting rich at the farmer's expense. Consumer groups use the rising marketing share to justify their conclusion that the marketing middlemen are the cause of high food prices. Each group's conclusion if based solely on this one measure is faulty.

Relationship of retail value to farmer's share and marketing costs

The amount that consumers spend for food products is primarily affected by the level of disposable income. If the general economy is prosperous and there is little unemployment, the public will spend more freely for all goods and services, including food. On the other hand, if the economy is experiencing a depression consumers have less disposable income and hence spend less.

The farm value is the amount left after subtracting total marketing costs from the total amount spent for food (retail value). Two ideas are

---

[4] *Series of Margin and Cost Studies by Commodities,* U.S.D.A. Technical Bulletins 932, 934, 936, and 939, 1946-48.
[5] *Farm-Retail Spreads for Food Products,* U.S.D.A. Miscellaneous Publication 741, 1957, p. 55.
[6] *The Farm Food Marketing Bill and Its Components,* Agricultural Economic Report No. 105, U.S.D.A., E.R.S., January 1967, p. 17.

important: First, changes in the farm value vary directly with changes in retail value, and second, marketing costs fluctuate less than farm value. Marketing costs are slower to change with changing economic conditions and hence might be called inflexible relative to retail value. This characteristic of marketing charges causes the farmer's share to fluctuate widely. For example, when the economy was depressed in the early 1930's, retail value fell 17.9 percent. Marketing charges fell only 13.1 percent. As a result, farm value suffered a 25.4 percent decline. The opposite situation occurred in 1957 to 1958. A 4.7 percent increase in the retail value was accompanied by a 6.2 percent increase in farm value but only a 3.9 percent rise in the marketing bill (Figure 10-1). The statement that farm value fluctuates to a greater degree than retail value can also be made about individual commodity prices. Farm value reflects farm prices times quantities sold, while retail value reflects retail prices times quantities sold. It follows then that farm prices will fluctuate more widely than retail prices.

Marketing costs are inflexible because many of them are based on volume rather than value, particularly those associated with the physical functions. For example, the cost of transporting 100 pounds of beef is the same for the trucking company regardless of whether the meat eventually sells for 50 or 75 cents per pound. Likewise for the storage cost. In the meat-packing plant the labor required to kill the animal and cut it up in hours of time is the same regardless of the meat's final selling price. Rigidities have also been built into the labor cost by labor-management contracts which stipulate pay based on hours worked rather than meat prices.

Are marketing costs too high?

As we have already noticed, marketing is more important today than a century ago. The role of the home and the housewife has changed. Instead of the grocer stocking flour and sugar to be sold for processing into bread and cakes in the home, the grocer today must stock more finished products, many of which require a large amount of prior processing. In addition, the housewife wants to buy in relatively small food units, which increases handling and packaging costs. To provide and offer an increased variety of products in convenient and attractive packages, merchants and distributors have had to assume new risks and take on additional tasks, all of which contribute to costs.

To ascertain whether marketing costs are too high it is necessary to assess consumer satisfactions. Studies dwelling on the duplication of services in the marketing system and the almost maddening drive of merchandisers to add services and promote their product's consumption through advertising may well suggest that costs are too high. However, the fact that consumers buy additional services with food is an indication that a forced sale does not take place and costs are considered reasonable.

This is not to say there are not inefficiencies in the marketing system which require correction and close scrutiny. However, as long as consumers continue to receive higher incomes, marketing costs will no doubt continue to rise as more services are demanded and added.

Marketing costs differ among products

The alert student will already be able to see why marketing costs and farmer's share vary among products. While it has been noted that marketing costs took two-thirds of the consumer's dollar in 1966, they took only 40 percent on the average for choice beef but a whopping 84 percent for canned tomatoes (Table 10-2). The following four reasons can account for such differences:

1. *Amount of processing.* The more processing a product requires the higher the marketing cost will be. Bread and canned foods are good examples.
2. *Degree of perishability.* A perishable product will require more careful physical handling both in storage and during transportation. To prevent deterioration, special kinds of storage facilities and transporting vehicles may be required. Refrigerated railroad cars and fluid milk tanker trucks are examples.
3. *Bulkiness relative to value.* Fresh cabbage is not only a perishable product but it is bulky and takes up a relatively large amount of storage and transportation space. This bulkiness makes cabbage marketing cost high relative to its low retail value.
4. *Seasonality of production.* Consumers want to be able to buy nearly all food products the year around. Some foods can be produced only in certain areas of the United States. While producers attempt to even out the seasonality of production, they are only able to do so within limits. When oranges are out of season their price is seasonally high to defray the costs of storing them until that time.

SOME IMPORTANT TRENDS IN MARKETING

The marketing system is continuously changing to meet new market conditions, as businessmen experiment to find new market channels and new organizations that reduce costs and enhance their competitive advantage. To outline and discuss in detail the developments in marketing

TABLE 10-2: Distribution of Consumer's Dollar and Farm Share of Retail Price, Selected Foods, 1964.

Item	Retail Price	Retailing [1]	Whlsng. & Trans.	Processing	Assembly	Farm Value	Farm Share of Retail Price (Percent)
			(Dollars)				
Butter (lb.)	$.744	$.076	$.082 [2]	$.056	$ —	$.530	71
Turkey (lb.)	.406	.040	.030	.070	.006	.260	64
Choice beef (lb.) [3]	.708	.170	.023	.053	.038	.424	60
Grade A eggs (doz.)	.515	.088	.062	.060	.014	.291	57
Choice lamb (lb.)	.700	.175	.024	.074	.032	.395	56
Veal (lb.)	.781	.209	.026	.104	.036	.406	52
Pork (lb.)	.523	.123	.016	.101	.017	.266	51
Fresh milk: (½ gal.)							
In store	.477	.073	.075 [4]	.098	.014	.217	45
Home delivery	.528	—	.208 [4]	.089	.014	.217	41
Evap. milk (13 oz. can)	.149	.015	.012	.058	—	.064	43
Processed cheese (½ lb.)	.367	.076	.059	.081 [5]	—	.151	41
Fresh fruits & vegetables [6]	1.000	.300	.240	.130 [7]	—	.330	33
Ice cream (½ gal.)	.804	.186	.194	.206	.026	.192 [8]	24 [8]
Oranges (lb.) [9]	.126	.043	.025	.023 [10]	—	.030 [11]	24
Proc. fruits & vegetables [6]	1.000	.210	.140	.440	—	.210	21

White bread (lb.)	.207	.037	.061[12]	.067[13]	.002	.040[14]	19[14]
Apples (lb.) [15]	.233	.088	.051	.052[10]	—	.042[11]	18
Canned tomatoes (#303 can) [16]	.160	.028	.016	.090	—	.026	16
Canned corn (#303 can)	.190	.033	.030	.103	—	.024	13
Breakfast cereals (lb.)	.416	.064	.034	.250[17]	.025[18]	.043	10

[1] In-store costs only. Warehousing, delivery, etc., included in wholesaling.
[2] Includes packaging, 3.5 cents.
[3] More than half of all beef is choice grade, but the exact proportion is unknown.
[4] Delivery and selling by processor.
[5] Includes both cheesemaking and later processing.
[6] A market basket of fruits and vegetables valued at $1.00 at retail.
[7] Packing, selling, and some harvesting and hauling.
[8] Includes sugar valued at 1.6 cents. Net farm value of milk was 17.6 cents, and share of retail value paid to dairy farmers was 22 percent.
[9] For sale in Atlanta, Chicago, and New York.
[10] Harvesting, hauling, packing, and storing.
[11] On-tree value.
[12] Bakers' wholesaling and delivery costs.
[13] Baking and milling.
[14] Includes bakery cost (1.7 cents) of ingredients other than flour. Net farm value of wheat was 11 percent of the retail value of one pound of bread.
[15] For sale in Chicago and New York.
[16] Cream style.
[17] Not including manufacturers' freight and delivery expenses (1.3 cents).
[18] Spread between net farm value of ingredients and their delivered cost to manufacturer.

SOURCE: *Food from Farmer to Consumer*, Report of the National Commission on Food Marketing, U.S.G.P.O., June 1966, pp. 14-15.

over the past century would fill many pages. Only a few of the more important ones will be discussed here.

Market decentralization

The initial developments of the large terminal markets at strategic transportation points in large cities accompanied the development of railroads which could move large loads over long distances. Local markets in the country complemented the terminal market because of their collection and assembly functions. The goods were sold on the central market by commission firms representing the farmer. Processors were usually located near the terminal market (Figure 10-2).

One of the drawbacks of this early market organization was the relatively costly process of concentrating the huge quantities of goods at the central market. To the farmer, the typical deduction of one to two percent from his sales value for sending his goods to the central market seemed large, particularly if these costs could be avoided by selling on a local market.

After World War I, developments in transportation, communications, storage, and retailing favored market decentralization. Decentralization essentially means that the large terminal market is by-passed and goods move from the farmer or local market directly to processors and wholesalers. The relocation of meat-packing plants and other food processors nearer the producing areas was favored by the freight rate structure. More trucking and improved highways also facilitated the assembly of goods in local areas.

Any market must place accurate values on their products, including considerations of quality differentials. Farmers will want to sell on a market only if the price is as high as they could get elsewhere. Buyers want to purchase at a market where products are available at prices no higher than elsewhere. Market information is one of the keys to efficient market pricing. With improvements in the gathering and dissemination of market news information it became possible for buyers and sellers on local markets in producing areas to have as much price information as those buying and selling on the central market. As a result, prices could be established at local markets which would adequately reflect quality differentials. In addition, the development of standards and grades facilitated sale by description. Consequently, since World War I the volume of products moving through the terminal markets has been constantly decreasing. Federally inspected packers in 1950 purchased 75 percent of their cattle, 42 percent of their hogs, and 52 percent of their sheep and lambs at terminal markets. By 1964 the percentages had fallen to 36, 24, and 29 respectively. Also since 1950, there has been a rapid increase in meat packer purchases directly from farmers. While the percentages of live-

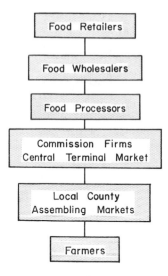

FIGURE 10-2:   Typical Early Market Channel For Farm Products.

stock purchased by packers at auction markets has changed very little, direct sales to packers from producers, feeders, and dealers accounted for 45 percent of the cattle, 32 percent of the calves, 63 percent of the hogs, and 58 percent of sheep and lambs in 1964.[7]

There is considerable controversy over the effects of market decentralization, the majority of problems concerning how "good" competition is and how "efficient" prices are at local markets. Physical presence of buyers, sellers, or products is hardly necessary for competition to exist if telephones are available and product standards are known. However, if decentralization is to be successful market grade and price information must be provided for on a basis comparable with the terminal markets.

Market firm integration

It has already been mentioned that integration of producing and/or marketing firms is an institutional development which revolutionized marketing channels for some products. A marketing firm becomes integrated primarily to try to improve its profits. It attempts to shorten the market channel by reducing the number of agencies owning the product between farm and consumers. One cost advantage is immediately apparent—that of lowering the buying and selling costs, since the product is exchanged fewer times. In addition, spreading the fixed costs

[7] *The Food Marketing Industries—Recent and Prospective Structural Changes*, ERS-295, U.S.D.A., E.R.S., p. 14. (Reprinted from the *Marketing and Transportation Situation*, U.S.D.A., E.R.S., May 1966.

of administration (bookkeeping, accounting, etc.) tends to lower unit costs. When the management input of the integrator is extended to include supervision of the firm being integrated, there may also be savings in the cost of management. However, the opposite may be true if the management of the integrating firm is not qualified to supervise the firm being integrated.

Integration—an industry example. It is estimated that 60-65 percent of the turkeys and 95 percent of the broilers raised in the United States in 1966 were under some sort of integrated program.[8] In the broiler industry it was the feed dealer who initiated integration and contracted with the producer. Usually the producer supplied his labor and physical facilities for broiler production in return for a guaranteed amount per pound of broiler produced. The feed dealer supplied the capital to finance the chicks, feed, and other variable costs as well as other management supervision, including time and conditions of sale. To assure a market the feed dealer would, in addition, also negotiate a contract with a broiler meat processor who would agree to slaughter the broilers at some prearranged price corresponding to a current market quotation at the time of sale. Many times the broiler processor was as anxious as the farmer to enter these agreements, since he then would have a dependable source of supply. However, the contract between the processor and feed dealer does not meet the definition of integration unless management control was extended. Otherwise it would be only a simple contract between two independent parties.

Management control can also be extended by outright ownership. The egg producer who markets his own eggs and thus performs the marketing functions is vertically integrated. Motivations for either ownership integration or contractual integration stem from the same root—an attempt to reduce costs and improve profits. The concentration in food retailing discussed next is a significant factor in causing integration and the shifting organization in marketing firms.

Changes in food wholesaling and retailing

One of the most striking institutional innovations in recent years is the rise of supermarkets and large food retailing organizations. Declining in importance are the small grocery stores which usually waited on each customer, extended credit, and often doubled as a social center for the neighborhood "philosophers." In 1963, supermarkets (if defined as stores with annual sales of one million dollars or more annually) represented 7 percent of all grocery stores but accounted for 53 percent of total sales. Their numbers increased sixfold from 1948 to 1963 while their sales in-

[8] *Agricultural Markets in Change,* Agricultural Economic Report No. 95, U.S.D.A., E.R.S., July 1966, p. 362.

creased more than eightfold. Total grocery store numbers decreased 32 percent in the same period and stores with annual sales under $100,000 decreased 46 percent. This concentration is dramatic because as late as 1940 supermarkets had only 25 percent of the business. The division is one of the large and small groceries, not one of chain stores as opposed to independents as 17 percent of the supermarkets were owned by independent retailers in 1963—up from 13 percent in 1954.[9] Even with the concentration of sales into a smaller number of stores, there is intense competition in the food retailing business. High volume and high turnover are the primary features of a supermarket with typical profits of one cent out of each dollar of sales.

Another development in food retailing is the shift in sales from single-unit firms to multi-unit firms. In 1948, single unit establishments averaging only $42,000 in annual sales did 59 percent of the grocery business. In 1963, however, multi-units accounted for 57 percent of the total. As the multi-unit firms increased their share of total grocery store sales, each multi-unit size category—in terms of number of stores operated—increased its share. For example, firms operating 51 or more stores increased their market share from 29 to 40 percent from 1948 to 1963.[10] Despite this increasing share of total grocery sales, each multi-unit category's share of multi-unit sales remained fairly constant. This means that small multi-units firms with 2-10 stores maintained their share of the market in that period. Between 1963 and 1965, however, trade sources estimate a 10 percent increase in the number of grocery stores operated by all multi-unit firms compared with a 3 percent increase in number of stores owned by firms operating only 2 or 3 stores.[11]

The rise of the self-service, multi-unit food market is both the cause and effect of other trends. Size of stores increased, wages of employees rose, the amount of advertising increased, more items were stocked, and margins fell. The impersonal nature of selling in the supermarket has resulted in changes in the marketing channel. Because the single retailer moves a larger volume of goods than ever before, he has increased his power in negotiating price with food processors and wholesalers. This is particularly true of the chain stores, which may have one purchasing agent for a region or area.

Changes in grocery wholesaling are also significant. In order for the retailer to assure himself of adequate amounts of uniform and quality products when needed, many have acquired their own wholesaling facilities or have vertically integrated the wholesaling functions into the retail-

[9] *The Food Marketing Industries—Recent and Prospective Structural Changes, op. cit.,* p. 46.
[10] *Ibid.,* p. 43.
[11] *Directory of Supermarket and Grocery Chains,* New York: Business Guides, Inc. 1963 and 1965 editions.

ing functions. Others have joined cooperative wholesaling groups or entered into contracts with private wholesaling firms which stipulate a rigid procurement policy.

Thus, affiliated grocery establishments—those sponsoring voluntary groups of retailers and those cooperatively owned by retailers—were a major new force in the general-line wholesale grocery trade in the mid-1960's. Between 1948 and 1963, their sales increased 274 percent with another 20-25 percent increase from 1963 to 1965.[12] Sales of retailer-owned cooperative establishments grew at a faster rate but started from a much smaller base. The growth of affiliated wholesalers has been due to the realization of both wholesalers and retailers that in order to compete effectively, they had to achieve the economies of scale accruing to their chain competitors.

Sponsoring a voluntary group of retailers affords the wholesaler a relatively stable base of loyal customers. In return for this loyalty, the wholesaler provides the retailer with a merchandising and promotional program and the services of specialists in store operation. Moreover, many voluntary group sponsors provide financial assistance, store employee training, and other services to improve retailer effectiveness.

Retailers have also placed new demands on processors. As a result, some have resorted to vertical integration backward toward the farmer. For example, an egg processor by contracting with an egg producer could extend his supervision over the production of eggs on the farm. By integrating, the processor would be assuring a source of eggs as well as more carefully controlling product quality. This would enable the processor to meet the demands of the modern supermarket operator for large quantities of uniform quality eggs. There is a power struggle between large-scale retailers and national processors as to who will control whom. In any event, there are less open market negotiations in the marketing channel as concentration at the retail level has favored vertical integration.

Air transportation [13]

World air freight traffic increased more than 32 times in the period 1946 to 1966, with current annual increase estimated at 20 percent. The volume of fresh fruit and vegetables shipped out of California during the 1965 season included more than 100 carlot equivalents of strawberries (50 percent more than a year earlier), and 180 carlot equivalents of other

---

[12] *The Food Marketing Industries—Recent and Prospective Structural Changes, op. cit.*, p. 41.

[13] Data taken from *Marketing and Transportation Situation*, U.S.D.A., E.R.S., February 1966, p. 19.

items such as fresh figs, cherries, apricots, plums, grapes, asparagus, lettuce, parsley, tomatoes, poultry, eggs, meats, and so on.

The increase in use of air transportation is spurred by decreases in rates per ton mile which dropped sharply from 18-20 cents (from California to East Coast) in 1961 to an average of 12 cents in 1965. The reduction was partly due to more efficient operations plus the use of more cargo-carrying jets. While air rates from San Francisco to Chicago and New York are still considerably above rail freight and express rates, the advantages include less spoilage because of shorter transit times, less expensive packaging, and less risk of physical damage in transit.[14]

Airlines are planning for continuing substantial increases in agricultural commodity air freight traffic. Reasons include reduced operating costs permitting reduced rates, better use of equipment, better packaging, more automation, additional services, greater effort to improve marketing conditions, improved sales promotion plans, increased demand for high quality perishable products, and increased service by airline customers to consumers.

Selling of livestock on a carcass grade-and-yield basis [15]

The number of livestock—particularly cattle—sold on a carcass grade-and-yield basis is increasing. In 1961, about 13 percent of all cattle, 12 percent of all sheep and lambs, 0 percent of calves, and 1 percent of hogs sold direct to packers were sold on a grade-and-yield basis. While comparable data are not available for other years, in a 10-month period beginning June 1965, 27 percent of the slaughter cattle sold by direct sales from interior Iowa and southern Minnesota were on a grade-and-yield basis.

This method of selling has an inherent marketing advantage as it is a more accurate way to determine value. For animals sold on a live basis, only an estimate can be made of carcass quality and weight. However, a disadvantage of grade-and-yield selling for cattle is that a "pencil shrink" is applied to the hot-carcass weight to convert it to cold-carcass weight on which sales are based. This "shrink" may vary from 1.5 to 3 percent among packing plants.

Since grade-and-yield prices are not directly comparable to live prices, the producer has difficulty in comparing and evaluating markets. Until producers gain confidence in procedures used at the packing plants

---

[14] For comparisons, the cost of shipping 100 pounds of peaches from San Francisco to New York in 1965 was $2.07 by rail freight; $4.94 by railway express; and $8.65 by air. Similar figures for strawberries were $2.07, $6.33, and $8.45 respectively while figures for asparagus were $2.02, $4.94, and $7.30. See *Marketing and Transportation Situation*, U.S.D.A., E.R.S., February 1966, p. 19.

[15] *The Food Marketing Industries—Recent and Prospective Structural Changes, op. cit.*, p. 16.

to grade, weigh, and identify carcasses, the use of this method will grow rather slowly despite the economic advantage offered by it.

Other major changes in livestock marketing include a 70 percent drop in cattle shipments by rail between 1948 and 1963 as the growth and development of highways has spurred truck transportation. Also, futures trading in live animals is a recent innovation. Since there is virtually no delivery of livestock on futures contracts, futures trading has not altered directly the way in which livestock are sold but it is an important vehicle for establishing future prices for livestock and for transferring price risks.

Fewer and larger food processing firms [16]

A general trend in evidence throughout the food marketing industry is fewer but larger firms. A notable exception is meat slaughter and packing firms where the four largest firms accounted for 51 percent of the slaughter in 1950 but only 33 percent in 1964 due to the growth of medium size operations. The pattern of changes varies with commodity orientation.

The number of fluid milk bottling plants decreased 53 percent between 1948 and 1965. The distribution of annual volume shows plants bottling over 5 million quarts of milk annually increased their share of total volume from 7 to 36 percent in the 1950-64 period. The number of plants manufacturing dairy products fell 37 percent in the period 1944-61 while the volume of large butter plants (over 2 million pounds annually), for example, increased their share of total butter produced from 26 to 62 percent.

For poultry and eggs, only those egg assembly plants over 4000 cases handled per week increased their relative share of total volume handled in the period 1963-65. While output increased 11 percent from 1962 to 1964 in poultry slaughter plants, plant numbers fell 10 percent and plants slaughtering over 30 million pounds annually increased their share of the total slaughter from 48 to 57 percent.

The number of country grain elevators decreased sharply from 1947 to 1954 but increased 16 percent from 1954 to 1963. Terminal elevators increased 50 percent in the 1954-58 period but decreased nearly 10 percent from 1958 to 1963. The number of plants producing flour and meal decreased nearly 50 percent during 1947-63. Establishments in the blended and prepared flour industry showed a substantial increase in the same period while rice milling and cereal preparations plants declined. Numbers declined sharply in the bread and related products industry while biscuit and cracker companies increased.

In the past two decades, the number of establishments canning

[16] *Ibid.*, pp. 19-40.

fruits and vegetables in the United States declined more than a third. In contrast, numbers in the frozen fruit and vegetable industry has more than doubled; dehydration plants up one fifth. The four largest processors of four canned fruits accounted for more than half of the total production in 1959; a similar situation existed for canned sweet corn, green peas, and tomato catsup. In juices, the top four accounted for 90 percent of the packs of grape and prune juice and 50 percent of tomato and orange juices.

Soybean oil and cottonseed oil are the two major vegetable oils produced in the United States accounting for 90 percent of total production. Both are used primarily in the production of edible commodities. The number of cottonseed processors decreased 40 percent from 1947 to 1963 while the average size of plant increased 80 percent. Soybean processing companies fell 30 percent in number while production doubled in the same period.

In summary, the trend towards fewer but larger firms can be found throughout the food marketing industry. Technological developments such as changes in equipment and improved transportation and communications has intensified the trend. Changes in ownership by purchase or merger also have furthered the movement. A surviving company often concentrates its operations in the most efficient plants, which often were its largest plants.

Market orders

Marketing orders are administered by the state or federal government and specify rates which marketing agencies and, indirectly, producers must follow in marketing certain products. The purpose is to achieve an orderly system of marketing.

"Orderly marketing is defined as the maintenance of a price structure and marketing conditions that are conducive to the uninterrupted flow of product to the market in the desired quantity and pattern." [17] Enabling legislation passed in the middle 1930's with subsequent amendments allows the regulation (with certain restrictions) of milk, tobacco, hops, peanuts, turkeys, turkey hatching eggs, filberts, almonds, pecans, walnuts, honey bees (but not their products), fresh vegetables, and fresh fruits. Milk marketing orders emphasize the pricing aspects, while supply manipulations get more emphasis in fruits and vegetables.

In 1961 some 124 orders were in effect. Cash receipts to the farmers who sold products under these orders accounted for 15 percent of gross

---

[17] E. M. Babb and others, "Federal Market Orders: Present and Potential Uses," Mimeo EC-233, Department of Agricultural Economics (Lafayette, Indiana: Purdue University Cooperative Extension Service, December, 1961).

farm incomes.[18] About 175,000 producers and 2,200 marketing agencies participate in federal milk orders, under which 45 percent of all milk sold at wholesale is marketed. Fruit and vegetable orders are concentrated in the West and involve about 150,000 producers. In addition, 15 states currently have some provision in their statutes establishing state marketing orders as legislation for specific products.[19]

In general, market orders for fruits and vegetables specify that demand conditions will be estimated to see how much produce can be sold at a fair price. Then some control mechanism will be employed to keep production from rising above the stipulated quantity. In addition to achieving orderly marketing as previously defined, unreasonable fluctuation in supply and prices may be avoided and the establishment of better standards for quality and the stipulation of grading and inspection requirements may be attained. Orders may also allow an organized approach to industry promotion and research in market development activities.

In recent years there has been increased experimentation in marketing orders. Orders seem to work most successfully for products with a limited geographical production area. A good example is the walnut order which has been in continuous operation since 1933. Estimating the supply and controlling production of any agricultural product is difficult. Chronic overproduction seems to be the tendency and when a crisis erupts producers are more inclined to try a marketing order. An exception was an order for turkeys which was defeated decisively in June 1962 after a year of disastrously low turkey prices driven down by a production increase of over 20 percent in one year. There are three requirements if a market order is to be successful:

1. The production of the commodity must be such that it can be brought under control. This often means a concentration of production within relatively few hands or limited areas and a control over the entry of new producers.
2. The product itself must be perishable or handled in such a way as to prevent "outsiders" from gaining control of the supply through purchase and storage.
3. The market must be divisible into parts (different uses, qualities, places, times, etc.) that have different elasticities of demand and are relatively protected from the encroachment of close substitutes.[20]

[18] *Wall Street Journal*, XLII, No. 12, October 31, 1961, p. 1.
[19] Sidney Hoos, November 1957, "The Contribution of Marketing Agreements and Orders to the Stability and Level of Farm Income," *Policy for Commercial Agriculture*, Joint Economics Committee, 85th Congress, p. 318.
[20] Kohls, *op. cit.*, p. 197.

AGRICULTURAL COOPERATIVES

About 20 percent of farm products sold by farmers in the United States are marketed through cooperatives. There is nothing magic about a cooperative in the way that it performs marketing functions. Nor is a cooperative always successful. It is only one of the legal types of business organizations, as are partnerships or corporations. The differences between a corporation and a cooperative lie in the way the business is owned and controlled and in the basic objectives and policies for organizing and carrying on business activities.

The old-fashioned husking bee or barn raising was an example of cooperative action to solve tasks by groups for their mutual good. The stimulus for group cooperative action by farmers was often initiated by low market prices or by the inability to buy quality inputs at reasonable prices. Farmers, feeling that perhaps the middleman was taking advantage of his situation, thought that by banding together they could set up a cooperative business to do a better job. Most cooperatives in the United States are among farmers, and with the passage of the Capper-Volstead Act in 1922 the concept of a cooperative as a type of business organization was legally established.

Mutual insurance was the earliest form of organized cooperation in the United States. Benjamin Franklin headed the board of directors of the first one, known as the Philadelphia Contributorship for the Insurance of Houses from Loss by Fire established in 1752. Cooperatives of many kinds have been formed and can be easily classified by tasks performed; there are purchasing, marketing, service, and manufacture or processing associations. There are three distinctive characteristics of a cooperative which differentiate it from other forms of business organization.[21]

1. Ownership and control are exercised by those who patronize the business. While you may own stock in Ford Motor Company and still buy and operate a General Motors produced Chevrolet, this is not so with a cooperative. If you own stock in a cooperative business you use its services; in fact, wanting to do business with the cooperative is the reason you become a part owner in it. To assure that this concept will be maintained, cooperatives usually restrict the amount of business they do with nonmembers to a certain small percentage of the total. In addition, each member in a cooperative has an equal voice—one member, one vote. In a corporation, however, each share gets the privilege of a vote and

[21] Harold Hedges, *Yearbook for Agriculture*, 1954, *op. cit.*, p. 239 and R. L. Kohls, *op. cit.*, p. 383.

one person gaining control of 51 percent of the stock can effectively control the business. In a cooperative, then, there is a patron-owner relationship rather than an investor-owner relationship. Most cooperatives also give control over the transfer of capital stock shares to their board of directors who limit transfers to those utilizing the services of the cooperative.

2. Another basic principle is that the cooperative business will be operated to just cover costs, and any excess will be returned to the patron-owners based on patronage. This is not to say that the desire for profits does not motivate the management to perform in the most efficient manner for its patron-owners. The incentive for ownership is to gain from group action and not to earn a large return on money invested, as the incentive would be in owning stock in a corporation.

3. The third differentiating characteristic in a cooperative is that there shall be limited returns on owner's invested capital. The fact that investors join a cooperative to gain from utilizing its services gives a very distinctive feature to the capital invested in a cooperative. To reduce speculation on capital shares, their transfer is carefully controlled and they are commonly given a top value. To raise new funds for financing an expansion of a cooperative, patronage refunds are often given in stock rather than cash. However, since there is no market where shares can be bought and sold, this method merely forces patrons to increase their capital holdings in the cooperative.

Marketing cooperatives

Marketing cooperatives may be organized to perform one or more of the marketing functions already described. Their objective is to maximize returns to the producers. A cooperative livestock commission may only perform the function of market information. Other cooperatives, such as a grain elevator, may mix and sell feed as well as buy and store grain and thus act as a purchasing cooperative. Unofficial estimates indicate that approximately 60 percent of our citrus fruits, 45 percent of our milk, 40 percent of our grain, and 10 percent of our cotton are marketed by cooperatives.[22]

How cooperatives function

Cooperatives have all the problems associated with performing business activities that private concerns have. They must compete with

[22] R. L. Kohls, *op. cit.*, p. 386.

corporations and all other forms of business organization. They must be able to do a job as well or better than their competitors in order to survive. Many times, farmers are unwilling to meet their competition and try to cut costs by hiring poor management or constructing inefficient physical facilities. This practice eventually leads to failure.

Since business is conducted on a cost basis the cooperative theoretically has no profits, the excess returns above costs being regarded as return payments to patrons and not as profit. In this way they do not pay a tax equivalent to the corporation income tax. This information is used by noncooperative firms as a way to generate public opinion against cooperatives. The public has generally favored cooperatives, particularly in the 1920's when it was felt that cooperatives could achieve orderly marketing and solve "the farm problems."

While cooperatives are not technically outside antitrust laws, the Capper-Volstead Act in 1922 makes prosecution of them unlikely. The act gives the Secretary of Agriculture restricted jurisdiction over cooperatives and a complaint must come from him if a cooperative is to be charged with an antitrust suit for monopolizing or restraining trade. No complaints have ever been issued.

The role of the cooperative must change with the times. Present operational methods designed to serve small farmers probably will not be adequate to meet the challenges associated with larger and more specialized production units. Bargaining cooperatives common in the marketing of milk are diversifying in other products. The concept of countervailing power is important when concentration and integration of firms take place in the marketing channel. The bargaining cooperative is one avenue to offsetting the increased market power of large retailers and vertically integrated market agencies. In any case, the future of cooperatives as a surviving type of business organization rests with the ability of their management to adapt to competitive conditions and to continue to serve their patron-owners in the best fashion possible.

11

Consumption of food

Although man's most persistent efforts have been spent in acquiring food, it has only been in the last century that investigations have been made into food consumption and man's needs for various nutrients. A study of the economics of food consumption centers around what foods man consumes and the factors that influence his choice.

History contains many stories of famine which eliminated large segments of the population. It is only in the industrialized West that man has been relieved of the preoccupation with the all-consuming task of feeding himself and his family. In the "modern" twentieth century two-thirds of the world population finds malnutrition a daily concern. The seriousness of the problem is described in a recent U.S. Department of Agriculture report, "The World Food Budget 1970." [1] The analysis indicates that shortages of proteins, fats, and calories exist in many of the less developed countries, and there is not much chance of alleviating that condition in the near future.

THE CURRENT WORLD SITUATION [2]

To get a picture of the world food situation, the Food and Agriculture Organization classified nations into three groups: the industrialized

---

[1] "The World Food Budget 1970," Foreign Agricultural Economic Report No. 19, U.S.D.A., E.R.S., October 1964.
[2] Data in this part taken from the 1959 Production Yearbook of the Food and Agriculture Organization and U.S.D.A. estimates.

West, the Sino-Soviet bloc, and the less developed countries. Although no two countries are directly comparable and the averages given include some distortions, the data given are the best estimates possible (Table 11-1).

TABLE 11-1: Selected Data of Food Production and Consumption for Three World Areas, 1959.

Item	Industrial-ized West	Sino-Soviet Bloc	Less Developed Countries
World population (%)	18	35	47
World arable land (%)	26	28	46
Starch food output (%)	32	37	31
Grain produced per capita (kilograms)	529	281	169
Daily caloric intake per capita (calories)	3000	2400	2300
Cereal grain per capita of farm population			
(acres)	3.0	0.9	0.5
(metric ton output)	1.7	0.39	0.25
Population in agriculture (millions)	110	615	1000
Population increase over 1935-39 (%)	20	25	50
Cereal grain yield increase over 1935-39 (%)	60	1	3
Cereal grain output per capita change since			
1935-39 (%)	26	−9	−14

Source: Food and Agricultural Organization, Production Yearbook, 1959.

The most striking contrast in the current world food situation is the surplus of food in the West and the shortages that prevail in almost all the less developed countries. This situation results in a great difference in the composition of diets between countries. In the poorer and more heavily populated sections of the world the diet is composed largely of cereal grains. Estimates are that while virtually all types of cereal grains are eaten by man in the poorer areas, nearly 70 percent of the grain production in the United States, excluding sorghums, is consumed by animals. It is easy to see that it takes a rich country to be able to convert its grain into meat. An average of eight pounds of grain is required to produce a pound of meat. In addition, a pound of milled rice contains 50 percent more calories than a pound of beef.

The West has a preponderantly urban population, while the other two areas are mostly rural. The typical farmer in the less developed areas, which comprise 70 percent of the population, rarely produces more food than his own family needs. This leaves the 400 million urban people facing a severe shortage. On the other hand, one farm worker in the United States produced enough food for himself and 27 other persons in 1962. The food situation in the less developed areas has not been im-

TABLE 11-2: Per Capita Food Use in Families of Various Income Levels, Spring Week, 1955, United States.·

Item	Pounds Used Average of All Families of 2 or More	$2000- 3000	Income After Taxes $3000 4000	$6000- $8000	$10,000 and Over
	Pounds Per Capita		Percent of Average		
Meat:	2.93	96	97	105	115
Beef	1.21	86	93	111	131
Pork	1.10	107	98	100	97
Chicken	.61	97	92	102	110
Eggs (doz.)	.59	100	98	95	108
Potatoes	1.75	105	108	95	83
Vegetables:	2.54	99	94	96	120
Fresh	.72	101	108	104	88
Canned	.13	54	92	154	262
Frozen					
Fruit:					
Fresh citrus	1.11	90	94	111	171
Fresh (other fruit)	1.62	94	96	108	123
Canned	.40	80	90	130	143
Frozen	.03	67	67	133	133
Fluid milk (quarts)	3.23	91	95	97	114
Evaporated milk	.28	154	129	71	36
Ice cream (quarts)	.31	58	81	81	139
Cheese	.30	90	93	113	137
Butter	.19	79	79	105	168
Margarine	.14	84	111	100	84
Flour	.78	140	95	49	35
Prepared flour mixes	.18	78	100	111	117
Breakfast cereals	.24	104	100	92	92
Bread	1.37	93	104	110	100
Baked goods	.57	79	102	123	139

SOURCE: Calculated from basic data in "Food Consumption of Households in the U.S.," Household Food Consumption Survey Report No. 1, U.S.D.A., 1956.

proving relative to population. Between 1935 and 1939 the less developed countries actually exported 12 million tons of cereal grain products but by 1960 were importing more than three million tons. With production up only 3 percent and population up 50 percent since 1939, the cereal grain output per capita decreased 14 percent (Table 11-1). At the same time, per capita output increased 26 percent in the West and yields were up 60 percent.

A large part of the reason for the differences in productivity increases is that Western Agriculture uses large quantities of capital while the rest of the world uses mainly human labor. The West has less than one-fourth of the world's cereal grain acreage but possesses nearly three-fourths of the tractors and uses 70 percent of all nitrogenous fertilizers.

While improvements in transportation have effectively reduced the occurrence of famine and starvation by enabling more trade among countries, the lack of adequate food supplies is still shockingly evident today. The famines of 1960 and 1961 in the mainland of China reportedly brought on food riots and widespread starvation. In 1960, as a result of the forced slaughter of millions of draft animals in China, more than 20 million men were recruited from the cities to assist in farm work.[3] This is most certainly a step backward in economic development, since draft animals are a more efficient form of power than human beings and involve a lower maintenance cost.

FACTORS INFLUENCING FOOD CONSUMPTION

Consumer wants and desires

The strategic position of consumers at the end of the marketing process has been discussed. The basis of the consumer's desire for food is rooted in the physiological requirements of the human body. The standards necessary to maintain adequate health have been constantly reviewed by the Food and Nutrition Board of the National Research Council.

In some parts of the world, particularly the industrialized West, the standards necessary to satisfy the physiological requirements are met so easily that it is seldom thought about. People who are "food rich" eat food for enjoyment as well as for nutrition. A person may want a particular food merely because it tastes good or looks good to him.

We are also influenced by our cultures and want to eat the kind of food that is customary. If our neighbors eat a wide variety of foods we want to consume a similar variety. Certain tribes in Africa keep cattle for the purpose of drawing and drinking the blood from them. This is socially unacceptable as a food in most places but each new generation in those tribes not only is willing but desires to consume blood as a food. This example illustrates forcefully the influence of social environment on food consumption.

Physical environment is also important. For example, rice grows well in Southeast Asia; people there are accustomed to eating rice early in life and this habit continues. People in Northeast Asia, where the climate is suitable to wheat production, prefer wheat products.

People's food preferences arising from their social, cultural, and physical environment do not change quickly or often. However, changes are important and some of the more recent examples that can be noted

[3] *The Economist*, June 17, 1961, p. 1212.

TABLE 11-3: Cross-Section Data: Variation of Food Consumption with Income.[1]

Spring 1955	All U.S.	Urban	Income Elasticity Rural Nonfarm	Rural
1. Index per person use of farm foods from all sources[2]	.12	.12	.17	.09
2. Index of per person use of purchased farm foods	.24	.14	.26	.15
3. Value of food marketing services bought with food, per person	.42	.33	.46	.26

[1] Income coefficients derived in linear regressions of logarithms based on spring 1955 food data and disposable money income per person in 1954.
[2] Including home-produced supplies.
SOURCE: Marguerite C. Burk, "Relationship Between Income and Food," *Journal of Farm Economics* (Vol. 42, February 1962, Number 1), p. 122.

in the United States are: (a) the decline in consumer preference for fat meats as compared to lean meats, (b) the decline in consumer preference for animal fats as compared to vegetable fats, (c) the decline in fresh fruits and vegetables as compared to canned and frozen fruit and vegetable products, and (d) the decline in grain consumption as compared to meat consumption.

Consumer income

Consumers spend about 18 percent of their disposal income for food in the United States. This percentage averaged about one-fourth from 1920 to 1950 but has since declined. It was a bit higher during the depression when total family incomes were lower. However, the average covers up the fact that poor families may spend half or more of their income for food while the rich spend a small percent. In 1857 Ernest Engel propounded his famous law of consumption: the poorer a family is the greater the proportion of total expenditures which it must use to procure food.

Economists are vitally concerned with what happens to a family's food consumption pattern when the family's income changes. The change that occurs in consumption of an item when income increases is measured by what is called *income elasticity*. For example, if consumption of food increases one percent as a result of a one percent increase in income, the income elasticity of food would be +1.00. The formula is:

$$\text{Income elasticity} = \frac{\text{Percent change in consumption (dollar expenditure)}}{\text{Percent change in income (dollars)}}$$

Income elasticity for food varies with (a) level of family income,[4, 5] (b) type of product, (c) whether measured at farm or at retail level, or the effect of services added to product in marketing channel, and (d) family residence. The idea of elasticity is an important one which is discussed in more detail in Chapter 15.

Type of product. It has already been mentioned that diets of families in general change from a grain-oriented protein diet to an animal protein diet with more processed foods as income increases. If consumption of a food increases with an income increase it is called a *superior* food (income elasticity coefficient is positive); if consumption decreases with an income increase, it is called an *inferior* food (income elasticity coefficient is negative). Some foods exhibit no particular trend one way or the other and might be called *neutral*. Beef, frozen fruits and vegetables, and ice cream are examples of superior foods while potatoes, evaporated milk, and flour are good examples of inferior foods (Table 11-2).

Measured at farm or retail level. The income elasticity for farm food products is in the neighborhood of 0.2 while the income elasticity at retail runs 0.6 to 0.7. The difference is associated with the high income elasticity (1.0 to 1.3) of the services added by agencies in the marketing channel.[6] Consumers are more willing to purchase added convenience with their food than more basic food. As this trend continues, the income elasticity of food will approach zero as income increases.

Family residence. The rural population consumes more home-produced food than urban consumers do and this influences income elasticity. Excluding services, the quantity of all food consumed per person varies with the level of income from farm to nonfarm to urban, but has quite a low income elasticity (Table 11-3). Burk also concludes that:

> (1) The quantity of purchased foods consumed per person varies much more with level of income among rural families than does the quantity of all foods, which includes home produced supplies, and (2) the value of food marketing services per person bought with food, both in

[4] Rockwell reports the following income elasticities of expenditures for all food and beverages at mean value for nonfarm household groups by income (based on arithmetic regressions of individual observations, per person average): Low income 0.25; medium income, 0.21; and high income, 0.15. See George R. Rockwell, "Income and Household Size; Their Effects on Food Consumption," Marketing Research Report 340, U.S.D.A., A.M.S. (Washington, D.C.: June, 1959), p. 58.

[5] Income elasticity estimates for the United States for specified food groups are: cereals, −0.5; vegetables, 0.25; milk, 0.05; meat, 0.35; eggs, 0.0; and fish, 0.3. In contrast, estimates for India where the per capita income level is only 1/35 of the United States average, income elasticity estimates are: cereals, 0.5; vegetables, 1.0; milk, 1.7; meat, 1.4; eggs, 2.2; and fish, 1.5. See "The World Food Budget 1970," Foreign Agricultural Economic Report No. 19, U.S.D.A., E.R.S., October 1964, Table 8, p. 21.

[6] W. W. Wilcox and W. W. Cochrane, *Economics of American Agriculture,* 2nd ed. (Englewood Cliffs: Prentice-Hall, Inc.), 1960, pp. 315-316.

retail stores and in eating places, varies with level of income two to three times as much as the quantity of food *per se* consumed among families within each urbanization category.[7]

Prices of competing products

If the consumer finds the price of beef high he may substitute pork for it as meat for the family table. It should be apparent that there are various degrees of substitutability among foods. Fruits are not good substitutes for meat, but chicken may be substituted directly because chicken prices are lower than pork.

Supply of products

Basically, whatever food is produced is consumed. If nature cooperates to produce an abundant crop of carrots, per capita consumption of carrots will tend to increase. The increased quantity on the market will drive prices down and induce consumers to purchase the extra large amount. This will be particularly true of perishable foods where storage cannot help even out the variations in annual supplies.

TRENDS AND PATTERNS IN FOOD CONSUMPTION IN THE UNITED STATES

Consumers in the United States are fortunate to have adequate supplies of practically all kinds of food. While poundage of food consumed is not an adequate economic measure of food consumption, the following partial list of foods consumed annually by an average family of four in the United States is impressive.[8]

> 2000 pounds of milk and milk products
> 871 pounds of meat, fish, and poultry
> 572 pounds of flour, cereals, and baked goods
> 442 pounds of potatoes
> 195 pounds of sugar and sweets
> 136 pounds of fats and oils
> 1404 eggs

Because of the changing nature of the average diet, total pounds of food consumed per capita has decreased about 100 pounds since World War II. Curiously enough, with one out of three adults overweight many Americans spend more money losing weight than buying food. Food

[7] Marguerite C. Burk, "Relationship Between Income and Food," *Journal of Farm Economics* (Volume 44, February 1962), p. 122.
[8] "CBS Reports," CBS Television, July, 1962.

abundance is also reflected by the fact that on the average, 600 calories per person per day are thrown away with garbage—almost 20 percent of the total purchased for use.

Over the years, the relative importance of animal products which include fish and livestock products has varied between 55 and 60 percent of the total (Table 11-4). Crop and animal components of the all-food

TABLE 11-4: Per Capita Food Consumption Index (in percent of total): Relative Importance of Major Food Groups.[1]

Food Group	1909–13	1925–29	1935–39	1947–49	1957–59	1963
Meats	27.4	24.0	22.7	24.3	24.3	25.4
Fish	2.9	2.9	2.8	2.3	1.9	1.9
Poultry	4.0	3.9	3.9	4.9	4.2	4.7
Eggs	5.6	5.9	5.3	6.3	4.4	3.9
Dairy Products [2]	13.6	14.9	15.3	16.5	17.4	16.8
Fats and oils [3]	7.5	8.3	8.6	6.5	4.9	4.9
Fruits [4]	6.8	7.3	7.7	7.5	8.6	7.6
Vegetables	9.3	9.8	10.6	9.7	10.3	10.1
Baby food and soup	(5)	0.2	0.5	1.0	1.1	1.3
Potatoes and sweet potatoes [6]	4.0	3.1	2.8	2.2	2.9	3.4
Dry beans, peas, nuts	2.0	2.2	2.5	2.2	1.7	1.8
Cereal products	10.7	9.3	8.5	7.4	7.4	7.1
Sugars and sweetners	4.3	6.0	6.2	6.3	7.3	7.4
Coffee, tea, cocoa	1.9	2.2	2.6	2.9	3.6	3.7
	100.0	100.0	100.0	100.0	100.0	100.0

[1] Individual food items combined in terms of 1947-49 average retail prices through 1954; 1957-59 thereafter.
[2] Excluding butter.
[3] Including butter.
[4] Including melons.
[5] Less than 0.05 percent.
[6] Canned and frozen potatoes and sweet potatoes included with vegetables prior to the revision beginning 1955.

Source: "U.S. Food Consumption," Statistical Bulletin #364, E.R.S., U.S.D.A., June 1965, Table 3, p. 11.

index have varied considerably from year to year. Consumption of crop products rose more sharply than that of animal products from about 1920 to 1950, but animal products have gained relatively since 1950. Major product substitutions have occurred within each of the two groups. Fruits and vegetables have gained while cereals and potatoes have declined. Per capita consumption of dairy products and eggs, which increased in the prewar period, trended downward in postwar years. Vegetable oils have increased and fats of animal origin have decreased.

A recent change in food consumption patterns is the decline in the amount of food consumed from home production. It declined from about

20 percent in the mid-1930's to seven percent in 1959. Most of the decline occurred since 1943.

Changes within major food groups

Meat. From the economic viewpoint meat is the most important food in the average diet of civilians in the United States. Since World War II meat has represented about 25 percent of the total food consumed. Although consumption of pork has been greater than beef consumption in all but nine years between 1900 and 1953, beef consumption has recently gained over pork (Table 11-5). Beef now represents 60 percent of the

TABLE 11-5: Per Capita Consumption of Red Meats for Selected Periods, Primary Distribution Weight with Percentage Comparison [1]

Period	Beef	Pork [2]	Veal	Lamb and Mutton	Total
		(Pounds)			
1909–14	66.2	65.2	6.7	7.0	145.1
1925–29	53.8	56.9	7.3	5.3	133.3
1935–39	55.6	56.5	8.1	6.8	127.0
1947–49	65.6	68.4	9.7	4.8	148.5
1956–59	83.0	64.3	7.7	4.4	159.4
1962–65	95.7	63.2	5.2	4.5	168.6
1967	105.9	63.9	3.8	3.9	177.5
Index (1967 = 100)					
1909–14	62.5	102.0	176.3	179.5	81.7
1925–29	50.8	89.0	192.1	135.9	75.1
1935–39	52.5	88.4	213.2	174.4	71.5
1947–49	61.9	107.0	255.3	123.1	83.7
1956–59	78.4	100.6	202.6	112.8	89.8
1962–65	90.4	98.9	136.8	115.4	95.0

[1] Civilian consumption only since 1941. Calendar year basis. 50 states beginning 1964.
[2] Excluding lard.
[3] Carcass weight.

SOURCE: *Livestock and Meat Situation,* U.S.D.A., E.R.S., May and November 1962, and May 1968.

total red meat consumption. Per capita consumption of veal, lamb, and mutton declined in the immediate post war years, rose between 1952 and 1954, and then drifted downward again. The decrease was sharper for veal than for lamb and mutton.

While separate data are not available, there no doubt have been important changes in consumption patterns of canned and processed meats. Many new meat specialty items have been introduced in the postwar

TABLE 11-6: Per Capita Meat Consumption in Selected Countries, Prewar, 1946-1950, 1951-1955, 1960 and 1961.[1]

Country	Prewar[2]	1946-1950	1951-1955	1960	1961
		(pounds)			
New Zealand[3][4]	212	212	216	227	223
Uruguay	225	219	272	238	212
Australia[3][5]	245	201	214	227	215
Argentina	209	230	222	191	197
United States	127	149	151	161	161
Canada[3]	113	128	129	142	139
USSR	—	—	53	65	64
Italy	38	29	38	58	58
Greece	36	24	25	37	44
Mexico	38	41	41	38	37
Philippines	—	—	15	18	—
Japan	—	—	5	8	10

[1] Carcass meat basis. Calendar year basis.

[2] For years 1935-39 for United States, and Canada; 1936-38 for Greece; and 1934-38 for other countries.

[3] Per capita consumption figures taken into account in commercial stocks. Data for Canada for civilian consumption only.

[4] Years ending June 30; prewar average 1936-37 to 1938-39.

[5] Years ending September 30; prewar average 1937-39.

Source: *Livestock and Meat Situation*, U.S.D.A., E.R.S., L.M.S. 126, September, 1962.

period. Altogether, canned meats represent about six percent of total meat consumption.

The principal factors influencing meat consumption are consumer incomes, consumer customs and habits, and meat production. Essentially, the amount that is produced is consumed. Thus, if cattle numbers are at a peak there will be more beef produced and this will be reflected in per capita consumption. However, improvements in animal production practices and in their application, particularly in environmental control, have tended to reduce the cyclical pattern in beef production.

Income of consumers is among the most important factors affecting the demand for meat. Surveys indicate that beef, veal, and lamb consumption increase with income levels, while pork fluctuates over the income scale.[9] Families with high levels of income also tend to buy more expensive types and cuts of meat.

Custom and habit are also important influences on the type and cut of meat that people consume. These factors change slowly and have a moderating effect on consumption patterns. In the South, pork consumption is higher than in any other region and has not been altered much by rising incomes. Veal and lamb consumption is also highly concentrated

[9] Household Food Consumption Survey Reports For 1955, U.S.D.A.

geographically. Education about nutrition, and food promotion and advertising also have their effects.

The United States was fifth in per capita meat consumption in 1960 (Table 11-6). Fifteen countries enjoy more than 100 pounds of meat per person per year, nine of which are in Western Europe. About half of the 99 billion pounds consumed in the world in 1960, excluding Communist China, was beef and veal, 41 percent was pork, 8 percent lamb, mutton, and goat, and the remainder was horse meat.

Fish. Total fish consumption has been relatively stable at 10 to 11 pounds per capita (Table 11-7). In relation to consumption of all foods between 1947 and 1949, fish consumption reached a high of about three percent in 1929 and again in 1935 to 1938. It declined to two percent of all food consumed in World War II years and has stabilized at that point.

TABLE 11-7: **Per Capita Consumption of Fish and Poultry Products for Selected Periods, Primary Distribution Weight with Percentage Comparisons** [1]

Period	*Fish*				*Poultry*		
	Fresh and Frozen	*Canned*[2]	*Cured*	*Total*	*Eggs*	*Chicken*	*Turkey*
		(Pounds)			*(Number)*	*(Pounds)*	
1909–14	[3]	[3]	[3]	[3]	302	14.8	[3]
1925–29	[3]	3.6	[3]	[3]	330	14.3	[3]
1935–39	5.4	4.9	0.7	11.0	300	13.4	2.2
1947–49	6.0	3.9	0.6	10.5	385	18.7	3.3
1956–59	5.7	4.1	0.6	10.4	357	26.8	5.8
1962–65	—	—	—	—	319	31.2	7.2
1963 [4]	5.7	4.4	0.5	10.6	—	—	—
1967 [5]	—	—	—	—	324	37.5	8.8
	Index (1963 = 100)				*Index (1967 = 100)*		
1909–14	—	—	—	—	93.2	39.5	—
1925–29	—	81.8	—	—	101.9	38.1	—
1935–39	94.7	111.4	140.0	103.8	92.6	35.7	25.0
1947–49	105.3	88.6	116.7	99.1	118.8	50.0	37.5
1956–59	100.0	93.2	116.7	98.1	110.2	71.5	65.9
1962–65	—	—	—	—	98.5	83.2	81.8

[1] Civilian consumption only since 1941. Data on a calendar year basis. Includes available data for Alaska and Hawaii beginning in 1960.
[2] Excludes canned food products containing small quantities of fish such as clam chowder.
[3] Not available.
[4] Preliminary.
[5] Forecast.

SOURCE: Poultry and Egg Situation, U.S.D.A., E.R.S., March, July 1962 and November 1967.

These data reflect only commercial fish. While it is difficult to estimate the extent of game fish caught and consumed, it is estimated to average about 1.2 pounds per capita.

Poultry. Fried chicken for Sunday dinner is no longer a treat for most Americans. Continuing improvements in breeding and rearing methods along with relatively low feed prices have resulted in making chicken one of the least expensive types of meat. Consumption of "ready-to-cook" chicken has nearly tripled since 1939, while consumption of turkey in 1967 was up four times.

Poultry meat output has expanded at a more rapid pace than demand with the result that prices fell drastically. Low prices, in turn, stimulated consumption. Exports of broilers, turkeys, and other fowl tripled in the past five years and amounted to 3 percent of total production in 1960.

Per capita egg consumption reached a peak in 1949, falling steadily since that time. However, per capita egg consumption for 1967 indicates that the decline may have ended. Increased egg output per hen has been spurred by new technologies in breeding and rearing. The result is a sagging egg price. Technologists are searching for new uses for eggs to impede falling consumption, but as yet have not been successful. Breakfast cereals together with declining emphasis on the breakfast meal have had a negative effect on egg consumption.

Fats and oils. While total consumption in the past 40 years has been relatively stable, major shifts have occurred in the use of food fats and oils. Substitution among the three major food fat groups (table spreads, cooking fats, and cooking and salad oils) has continued. The reduced consumption of table spreads, particularly butter, has been offset by increases in other edible oils. Butter consumption in 1966 was only 34 percent of that of 1935-1939, while margarine consumption was nearly four times higher (Table 11-8). The combined consumption of table spreads (butter and margarine) averaged about 20 pounds per capita prior to World War II. In 1946 it was reduced to a record low of 14.4 pounds. Since then, recovery has been slow and it appears stabilized at about 16 pounds. The increased use of mayonnaise and cheese spreads along with declining use of bread and potatoes are factors contributing to the fall in per capita fat and oil consumption.

The rapidly rising role of margarine is largely attributed to a favorable price ratio and the removal of restrictive legislation. In 1959 the price of butter averaged 2.7 times higher than margarine. Also, government purchase programs and price supports have tended to keep butter prices relatively high. Beginning in July, 1950 the federal excise tax of 10 cents per pound on colored margarine and one-fourth of a cent per pound on uncolored margarine was repealed. The same legislation lifted the annual retailer's, wholesaler's, and manufacturer's tax imposed on the margarine

TABLE 11-8: Per Capita Consumption of Fats and Oils for Selected Periods, Primary Distribution Weight with Percentage Comparisons [1]

Period	Total Fat Contents [2]	Butter	Margarine Actual Weight (Pounds)	Lard	Shortening	Other Edible Fats and Oils [3]
1909–14	([5])	17.2	1.4	11.5	([5])	([5])
1925–29	([5])	17.7	2.4	12.5	9.5	([5])
1935–39	45.4	17.0	2.9	11.0	11.8	6.5
1947–49	42.4	10.6	5.6	12.4	9.6	7.3
1955–59	45.5	8.5	8.6	9.6	11.3	10.8
1962–65	46.8	6.9	9.6	6.6	13.7	13.0
1966 [4]	48.6	5.7	10.5	5.6	15.9	14.1
			(Index 1966 = 100)			
1909–14	—	301.8	13.3	205.4	—	—
1925–29	—	310.5	22.9	223.2	59.7	—
1935–39	93.4	298.2	27.6	196.4	74.2	46.1
1947–49	87.2	186.0	53.3	221.4	60.4	51.8
1955–59	93.6	149.1	81.9	171.4	71.1	76.6
1962–65	96.3	121.1	91.4	117.9	86.2	92.2

[1] Civilian consumption since 1941.
[2] Computed from unfounded data.
[3] Includes fats and oils used in cooking and salad oils, salad dressing, and mayonnaise, in bakery products, and in minor uses such as fish canning.
[4] Preliminary.
[5] Not available.

SOURCE: *Fats and Oils Situation.* U.S.D.A., E.R.S., FOS 212, March 1962 and FOS 237, April 1967.

industry. Acceptance of margarine has steadily improved with standardization and general quality improvement. Margarine manufacturers have also conducted a vigorous merchandising and promotional campaign, particularly since World War II. The increased consumption of margarine was made possible by the sharp growth in domestic output of edible vegetable oils in the last 20 years. The largest source of fats and oils for margarine—85 percent in 1959—was soybeans. Prior to the war cotton oil was the major constituent.

Total consumption of cooking fats (lard and shortening) has been relatively stable, averaging about 22 pounds per capita over the last 40 years. Increasing amounts of lard have been going into shortening manufacture—22 percent of total in 1959 compared to eight percent between 1949 and 1959, making lard the major cooking fat in the United States. Direct use of lard is tending downward. After reaching a postwar peak of 12.7 pounds in 1948 it fell to a record low of 5.6 pounds in 1966. Shortening consumption has shown an opposite trend, rising from 9.7 pounds in 1948 to 15.9 pounds in 1966 (Table 11-8).

Lard consumption is usually highest in low income groups, with shortening being substituted for lard as income level rises. Use of lard is also substantially heavier in rural areas, making the population shift from rural to urban areas a major factor in declining lard consumption. In the past decade there has been some replacement of solid shortenings by liquid oils both in home use and in the manufacture of mayonnaise, salad dressings, and related products.

Except during World War II, when use of all food fats declined, the "other edible" category (mostly cooking and salad oils) has shown a steady growth. Consumption per person rose from 3.5 pounds in 1921 to about 14 pounds in 1966. Of this total about 30 percent (3.3 pounds in 1959) is oil used in mayonnaise and salad dressing. Commercial use of oils in production of potato chips, frozen french fries, mellorine, and other prepared foods and food mixes has been rising. For example, frozen french fried potato production increased from an estimated 22 million to 360 million pounds in the ten-year period from 1949 to 1959. An even greater increase has occurred in potato chips, from 301 million to 725 million pounds in the same decade.

Rising incomes and a rise in the number of families using oils are the major reasons for the increases in consumption of cooking and salad oils. New deep fry products, and an increased number of restaurant meals has helped the consumption of food fats.[10]

Dairy products. The study of consumption trends for dairy products is one of sharp contrasts. The declining use of milk fat solids and the rising use of milk nonfat solids is immediately apparent. Fluid milk and cream consumption declined in the postwar period after reaching a high of 359 pounds per capita in 1947 to 1949. New low-fat and skim products have been introduced with increasing consumer acceptance. Sour cream is an example of a new lower fat cream product.

Use of cheese has more than doubled since 1930 and continues to increase steadily, although civilian use was cut sharply during the food rationing in World War II years. Postwar increases have averaged 40 percent for a number of varieties of whole and part whole milk cheeses, such as swiss, cream, brick, Münster, and Italian varieties. Use of cottage cheese doubled from 1947 to 1959, from 2.6 to 5.2 pounds per capita.

Ice cream consumption is over seven times larger than between 1909 and 1914, and almost twice what it was in the 1920's and 1930's. Increased consumer incomes, the widening of the distribution system at retail, and increased use of refrigerators and freezer appliances are primary factors

[10] Data in this section taken from *The Fats and Oils Situation,* U.S.D.A.

influencing ice cream consumption. A new product innovation, ice milk, with a low fat content has gained wide consumer acceptance. Ice milk consumption averaged 0.4 pounds per person in 1945 and rose to 3.9 pounds in 1959 (Table 11-9).

TABLE 11-9: Per Capita Consumption of Dairy Products for Selected Periods, Primary Distribution Weight with the Percentage Comparisons [1]

Period	Total Milk Fat Solids	Total Nonfat Milk Solids	Cheese [2]	Condensed and Evaporated Milk [3]	Fluid Milk and Cream [4]	Ice Cream [5]
				(Pounds)		
1909–14	29.2	35.8	4.0	6.9	330	2.5
1925–29	31.3	37.7	4.5	12.0	338	9.9
1935–39	31.7	36.7	5.6	16.8	330	9.9
1947–49	29.5	42.9	7.0	20.1	359	18.7
1955–59	26.4	47.4	8.0	15.3	346	18.1
1962–65	—	—	9.3	11.5	303	18.2
1966	26.4	47.4	—	—	—	—
1967 [6]	—	—	10.0	9.1	286	18.1
	Index (1962 = 100)			*Index (1967 = 100)*		
1909–14	122.7	83.6	40.0	75.8	115.4	13.8
1925–29	131.5	88.1	45.0	131.8	118.2	54.7
1935–39	133.2	85.7	56.0	184.6	115.4	54.7
1947–49	123.9	100.2	70.0	220.9	125.5	103.3
1955–59	110.9	110.7	80.0	168.1	121.0	100.0
1962–65	—	—	93.0	126.4	105.9	100.6

[1] Civilian consumption only since 1941. Data on calendar year basis.
[2] Whole and part whole milk, cheese; excludes full skim, cottage, pot and bakers.
[3] Case and bulk goods, unskimmed only.
[4] Includes cream in terms of whole milk equivalent.
[5] Product weight.
[6] Preliminary.

SOURCE: *Dairy Situation,* U.S.D.A., E.R.S., June and November 1962, July 1967.

The major influences affecting consumption of dairy products are growth of the total population, changes in consumer's tastes and preferences, and changes in supply and price of competing products. This list is little different than for any other food product.

Because young people use more fluid milk than older people, any shift toward a younger population would tend to increase milk consumption. While it would seem that this might be an important factor in the United States, there is the tempering effect of an increased proportion of people in the older age group.

In recent years new beliefs often in conflict with each other, concerning the effect of different foods on the human body, have come into vogue.

Some have undoubtedly had an effect on the consumption of dairy products. The fact that one out of three adults are overweight has made many people conscious of low fat diets for weight control. In addition, the controversy over the effect of cholesterol found in animal fats as related to the incidence of heart disease have tended to slow down milk products with high degrees of butter fat.

Rising per capita incomes have impeded the decline in dairy product consumption, as evaporated milk is the only product that does not increase in consumption with income. However, despite rising incomes and more families shifting to higher income brackets, the actual consumption of dairy products on a milk fat basis has declined. Adding further significance to the decline is the fact that retail prices for dairy products as a group have risen less than food products in general since 1949.

Institutional and technological changes in the dairy industry have also affected consumption. With increased specialization on dairy farms the number of farms keeping cows has dropped. Many of the people who formerly consumed milk and cream in large quantities from home production now purchase milk and other dairy products. Technological developments have resulted in dairy farmers being able to produce increased quantities of milk at the same relative prices. Developments in refrigeration, processing, and bulk handling methods have also made it advantageous for the farmer to sell a larger proportion of milk as whole milk. This has influenced available market supplies of milk solids.

For decades, the importance of milk in the diets of young people has been stressed. Two programs developed by the federal government have directly affected consumption of milk. Under the School Lunch Act of 1946, which endorsed the School Lunch Program, substantial quantities of milk, butter, cheese, and nonfat dry milk were distributed to schools. In addition, the Special Milk Program of 1954 was designed to stimulate consumption of fluid whole milk by school children. The government paid a major share of the cost. Milk distributed under these programs accounted for about two percent of total national consumption of fluid milk and cream in 1959. The government program of supplementing costs of milk and butter fat also influences consumption. While the first effect is to raise prices to producers and consumers, it encourages farmers to produce larger quantities of milk.

Current trends in consumption of dairy products are likely to continue. Solids-not-fat will continue to gain relative to milk fat solids as new products emerge and consumers remain conscious of weight control and health programs. The solids-not-fat parts of milk contain all of the valuable proteins as well as practically all the calcium and riboflavin. As a result, consumer preferences will be more permanently changed in favor of the nonfat solids parts of milk.

Fruit. Per capita consumption of fruit in the United States since 1910 is characterized by a rising trend in volume consumed, which has leveled off since 1950, and by a continuing shift in emphasis from fresh to processed fruit. Fresh and processed fruit, combined on a fresh equivalent basis, increased to a record level of 227.9 pounds per capita in 1946, 43 pounds higher than the 1910 to 1914 average. Recently, the total has been fluctuating around 200 pounds, some 40 to 45 percent of which is citrus fruits. About half of this total is fresh and half is processed.

Fresh fruit consumption has trended downward for 50 years and in 1966 was only 55 percent of the average for 1909 to 1914 (Table 11-10). However, citrus fruits, principally oranges and grapefruit, showed consistent increases into the 1940's but have since declined in favor of canned

TABLE 11-10: Per Capita Consumption of Fresh and Processed Fruits for Selected Periods, Primary Distribution Weight and Percentage Comparisons [1]

Item	1909– 14 [6]	1925– 29	1935– 39	1947– 49	1955– 59	1962– 65	1966 [7]
				(Pounds)			
Total fresh [2]	146.1	142.6	137.0	130.3	99.6	79.2	81.2
Citrus	18.6	31.9	48.5	53.9	36.4	26.7	29.1
Apples [3]	65.9	46.3	30.3	25.2	20.8	17.1	15.9
Others [4]	61.7	64.4	58.4	51.2	42.6	35.5	36.2
Canned Fruit	4.0	11.9	14.8	18.1	22.3	23.0	22.9
Canned Juices	0.3	0.2	3.9	15.9	12.1 [8]	11.7	11.6
Frozen [5]	—	0.3	0.8	3.2	8.7 [8]	8.4	8.1
Dried	4.0	6.0	5.8	3.9	3.4 [8]	2.9	3.1
				Index (1966 = 100)			
Total Fresh	179.9	175.6	168.7	160.5	122.7	97.5	100.0
Citrus	63.9	109.6	166.7	185.2	125.1	91.8	100.0
Apples	414.5	291.2	190.6	158.5	130.8	107.6	100.0
Other	170.4	177.9	161.3	141.4	117.7	98.1	100.0
Canned Fruit	17.5	52.0	64.6	79.0	97.4	100.4	100.0
Canned Juices	2.6	1.7	33.6	137.1	104.3	100.9	100.0
Frozen	—	3.7	9.9	39.5	107.4	103.7	100.0
Dried	129.0	193.5	187.1	125.8	109.7	93.5	100.0

[1] Civilian consumption only since 1941. Data on a calendar year basis except for dried fruits which are on a pack year basis; and canned fruits on pack year basis 1935-39.
[2] Farm weight.
[3] Commercial.
[4] Excluding melons.
[5] Including juices.
[6] Tangerines not included.
[7] Preliminary.
[8] 1956-59 average.

SOURCE: *Fruit Situation*, U.S.D.A., E.R.S., August 1962 and August 1967.

and frozen citrus fruits. The contrast is pointed up by the fact that in 1909 to 1914 only 13 percent of fresh fruit consumption was citrus, while in 1955 to 1959 the percentage was 35 percent citrus.

One of the most striking features of fruit consumption in the United States in the 1900's is the five-fold increase in per capita consumption of processed fruits, most of it in the last 25 years. These increases more than offset the decreases already discussed for fresh fruits. Processed fruits can be divided broadly into canned, dried, and frozen categories. In 1910 dried fruit comprised 78 percent of all processed fruits, while 22 percent was canned. Dried fruit increased from 1910 to 1920 and has decreased slowly since, mostly because of the decline in consumption of raisins and prunes.

Canned fruits and fruit juices trended slowly upward into the mid-1930's and then jumped sharply until the late 1940's, leveling off since then. Canned citrus juices accounted for most of the increase and also the postwar decrease. The postwar decrease in canned juices, however, was more than compensated for by the sharp increase in frozen fruits and frozen fruit juices, especially orange concentrate. Of the 100 pounds of processed fruit (fresh equivalent basis) consumed per person per year between 1956 and 1960, canned fruit and fruit juice accounted for 53 percent; frozen fruit and fruit juice, 35 percent; and dried, 12 percent. Of the total, about half was citrus.

The trends just discussed were the result of many factors. The increase in total fruit consumption was principally due to increased production of both citrus and noncitrus fruits. The shift in emphasis from fresh to processed fruits was largely due to new product and processing technologies which made canned and frozen products available throughout the year. The decline in dried fruit consumption in the last 25 years is due to consumers' preference for fruit in canned and frozen forms. Consumers now have a wide selection of fruits in all forms throughout the year.

Vegetables. Fresh vegetable consumption per capita reached a high of 120.4 pounds during 1947 to 1949, declining 20 percent to just under 100 pounds in 1966 (Table 11-11). The current level is just slightly less than 50 years ago. While the total per capita annual consumption on a fresh equivalent basis has remained quite stable at about 200 pounds, there have been important changes in the form in which these vegetables are sold. Frozen vegetable consumption has increased over five times since 1949, while fresh vegetables declined 20 percent (Table 11-11). Frozen vegetables retain many of the desirable characteristics of fresh vegetables, are easy to prepare, and are widely available throughout the year at relatively stable prices. Canned vegetable consumption increased 14 percent in the same period. Fresh salad items, such as lettuce and

TABLE 11-11: Per Capita Consumption of Vegetables for Selected Periods, Primary Distribution Weight with Percentage Comparisons [1]

Item	1909–1914	1925–1929	1935–1939	1947–1949	1955–1959	1962–1965	1966 [2]
				(Pounds)			
Fresh vegetables	(5)	104.9	113.2	120.4	103.3	99.6	98.2
Melons	(5)	32.4	27.0	27.4	26.4	23.6	21.7
Canned	17.0	24.2	30.1	39.2	44.4	47.4	48.6
Frozen	(5)	(5)	0.4 [6]	2.9	7.9	12.9	16.2
Potatoes [3]	175.0	144.5	130.0	114.0	101.8	109.0	113.0
Sweet potatoes [3]	24.0	24.1	21.6	12.6	7.3	6.3	5.9
Dry edible beans	6.4	7.9	8.8	6.7	7.6	7.3	6.5
Dry field peas [4]	(5)	(5)	0.6	0.6	0.6	0.7	0.3
				Index (1966 = 100)			
Fresh vegetables	—	106.8	115.3	122.6	105.2	101.4	100.0
Melons	—	149.3	124.4	126.3	121.7	108.9	100.0
Canned	35.0	49.8	61.9	80.7	91.4	97.5	100.0
Frozen	—	—	2.5	17.9	48.8	79.6	100.0
Potatoes	169.9	127.9	115.0	100.9	90.1	96.5	100.0
Sweet potatoes	406.8	408.5	366.1	213.6	123.7	106.8	100.0
Dry edible beans	98.5	121.5	135.4	103.1	116.9	112.3	100.0
Dry field peas	—	—	200.0	200.0	200.0	233.3	100.0

[1] Civilian consumption only since 1941. Excludes home garden production. Calendar year basis.
[2] Preliminary.
[3] Farm weight. Excludes quantities canned and frozen which are included with processed vegetables.
[4] Crop year basis.
[5] Not available.
[6] 1937-39 average.

SOURCE: *Vegetable Situation*, U.S.D.A., E.R.S., October 1962 and November 1967.

celery, have maintained their position, but for most other vegetables consumers now prefer frozen to fresh. Of the ten principal vegetables [11] used both in fresh and processed forms, only sweet corn and cucumbers escaped a decline.

Factors influencing the shift from fresh to processed forms are similar to those mentioned for fruit. The shift of the population from rural to urban areas which decreases production for home use, rising consumer incomes, the increasing production and availability of processed vegetables throughout the year at relatively stable prices, and the convenience to the housewife in using canned and frozen vegetables have all contributed to the changing pattern.

Sugar. Refined sugar consumption has been steady at just under 100 pounds for over 25 years (Table 11-12). Over the years there has been a slow but steady decline in the proportion of sugar delivered in consumer-size packages. This merely means that people are consuming an increasing proportion of sugar in processed food products.

Cereal Grains and Products. Per capita consumption of flour and cereal products has declined 20 percent since the end of World War II, a continuation of the decline registered for the past 50 years. Wheat is by far the most important grain, accounting for 80 percent of the flour and cereal products consumed as food. Corn contributes 10 percent, while oats, barley, rye, rice, and buckwheat make up the remaining 10 percent. In 1967 consumers used only 12 percent as much corn meal as between 1909 and 1914, 53 percent as much wheat flour, and 30 percent as much rye flour (Table 11-12). On the other hand, per capita consumption of corn syrup has nearly tripled and corn sugar is up 420 percent. Rice has maintained a per capita consumption of five to seven pounds since the 1920's.

One major cause of the decline in grain consumption is the increasing availability of meat, poultry, and vegetables at reasonable prices. Another factor is the decline in physical labor, bringing about a reduced need for such high energy foods as grains. Emphasis on weight control and dieting is frequently mentioned as a contributing factor.

In cereal products the decline of bread consumption has been in the homebaked form. Commercially baked bread has accounted for an ever increasing share of the total bread supply. In contrast to bread, other wheat products which include spaghetti, macaroni, vermicelli, and noodles have maintained a stable consumption level for many years.

Per capita consumption of prepared flour mixes increased 24 percent between 1947 and 1958. By type, cake mixes registered the largest increase, while pie crust mixes were the only item that declined.

---

[11] Asparagus, lima beans, snap beans, broccoli, cabbage, corn, cucumbers, green peas, spinach, and tomatoes.

TABLE 11-12: **Per Capita Consumption of Sugar, Grains, and Beverages for Selected Periods; Primary Distribution Weight with Percentage Comparisons** [1]

Item	1909–14	1925–29	1935–39	1947–49	1957–59	1962–65	1967 [2]
				(Pounds)			
Sugar, refined	76.4	101.0	97.4	95.1	96.1	96.9	96.9
Corn products:							
Corn meal	48.1	29.1	23.1	12.9	7.4	5.9	5.5
Corn syrup	5.1	7.7	7.7	9.9	9.4	12.8	14.3
Corn sugar	1.1	5.6	2.7	4.2	3.6	4.3	4.6
Oat food products [4]	3.2	5.4	3.9	3.3	3.6	3.7	3.7
Wheat: Flour [5]	209.0	177.0	160.0	137.0	120.0	113.8	112.0
Breakfast cereals	2.7 [3]	3.3 [3]	3.3	3.2	2.8	2.9	2.9
Rye flour	3.7	2.8	2.3	1.4	1.2	1.1	1.1
Rice, milled [6]	6.8	5.6	5.8	4.9	5.4	7.2	7.3
Coffee [7]	9.2	11.7	14.0	18.2	15.7	15.4	14.5
Tea	1.0	0.8	0.7	0.6	0.6	0.7	0.7
Cocoa beans [8]	1.5	3.3	4.4	4.1	3.5	3.9	4.2
Peanuts, shelled [9]	2.4	3.7	4.3	4.4	4.6	5.2	5.6
				Index (1967 = 100)			
Sugar, refined	78.8	104.2	100.5	98.1	99.2	100.0	100.0
Corn products:							
Corn meal	874.5	529.1	420.0	234.5	134.5	107.3	100.0
Corn syrup	35.7	53.8	53.8	69.2	65.7	89.5	100.0
Corn sugar	23.9	121.7	58.7	91.3	78.3	93.5	100.0

Oat food products	86.5	145.9	105.4	89.2	97.3	100.0	100.0
Wheat: Flour	186.6	158.0	142.9	122.3	107.1	101.6	100.0
Breakfast cereals	93.1	113.8	113.8	110.3	96.6	100.0	100.0
Rye flour	336.4	254.5	209.1	127.3	109.1	100.0	100.0
Rice, milled	93.2	76.7	79.5	67.1	74.0	98.6	100.0
Coffee	63.4	80.7	96.6	125.5	108.3	106.2	100.0
Tea	142.9	114.3	100.0	85.7	85.7	100.0	100.0
Cocoa beans	35.7	78.6	104.8	97.6	83.3	92.9	100.0
Peanuts, shelled	42.9	66.1	76.8	78.6	82.1	92.9	100.0

1 Quantity in pounds. Civilian consumption only since 1941.
2 Preliminary.
3 Approximations.
4 Principally oatmeal but includes an allowance for ready-to-eat cereals and infant foods in recent years.
5 Includes white, whole wheat, and semolina flour.
6 Rice year beginning August 1. Includes some table rice used by brewers prior to 1934.
7 Green bean equivalent.
8 Includes cocoa bean equivalent of cocoa products imported 1942 to date.
9 Crop year basis.

SOURCE: *National Food Situation*, U.S.D.A., E.R.S., May 1962 and February 1968.

part III

12

Production principles

The role of agriculture in economic growth has been discussed in the preceding chapters, as well as the relationships between farming and farm people, and the nonfarm economy. Part II included much data concerning production, marketing, and consumption of food products, and our concern now is with the tools necessary to analyze economic problems and manage businesses.

ELEMENTS OF THE PRODUCTION PROCESS

Production is the transformation of two or more inputs (resources) into one or more products. Transformation takes place by combining the inputs in various amounts for different needs and uses. When we say combine we necessarily imply that there must be more than one input to make a product. If nothing was added the original resource would simply remain whatever it was. Thus, nothing can be made with less than two inputs and some products take hundreds of different inputs for their creation. Think of the various products we use. Each product requires some sort of physical resource (metal, wood, cloth, chemicals, etc.), some labor, and some financial arrangement for the production process. Management is also necessary to conceive of the production idea, assume risks, make decisions about production, and solve problems related to the firm's production. Therefore resources can be classified under four general headings: land, labor, capital, and management.

Land may be thought of as providing the space for production.

Factory sites and farmsteads are both set upon land. However, land is not a resource whose quality is evenly distributed over the surface of the world. This uneven distribution gives rise to more production advantages in some areas than in others. Water is usually put in the land resource classification.

Labor is considered as the physical and mental effort spent in producing goods and services. Tractor drivers and harvest hands are examples of physical labor, while draftsmen and engineers use much mental labor in their work. It is important to distinguish between the effort and the agent of labor. The effort of labor is the particular physical or mental skill one can employ. An agent of labor is the human being possessing the skills. The effort can be likened to a *flow* of services; the agent of labor can be compared to a *stock* resource, i.e., a stock of human capital.

Capital also includes buildings, machinery, and livestock. The home you live in is a form of capital. Education is another form of capital. It enables a person to contribute to the production process (review Chapter 7).

Management is the final broadly defined resource. Here the individual or group makes choices and decisions concerning the use of land, labor, and capital. Management is the human element in the production process, the element that initiates, modifies, and maintains the production process through its never ending decisions regarding all the factors of production, including itself. Management is used synonymously with entrepreneurship in many economic writings.

Farmers producing crops and livestock use several different kinds of inputs. To begin with they use land as the factory to help in producing the crop. Through this manufacturing plant they pass machinery and labor to plant, cultivate, and harvest. Fertilizer is added at times decided upon by management. Water may be provided by rain or supplemental irrigation may be used. The crops in turn are fed to animals which produce meat, milk, eggs and many other livestock and poultry products through complex biological processes.

GENERAL DIFFERENCES BETWEEN FARMING AND INDUSTRIAL PRODUCTION

Perhaps the similarities between farming and industrial production should be stressed more than their differences. Generalizations concerning both similarities and differences between the two kinds of production do not always hold true. Goals of production and the need for management decisions concerning the allocation of inputs are strikingly similar between agricultural and industrial production. However, there are some differences that can be noted in general.

For example, *weather* affects farming much more than it affects manufacturing production. Production indoors goes on despite showers outside, but the farmer cannot get in his fields because of the rain and mud. (The construction industry is another industry also greatly affected by weather and the seasons.) *Production scheduling* is another factor that differs between most farms and factories. Many production schedules (except feeding, milking, etc.) on a farm can wait a day or two, whereas in a factory operating on strict production schedules, timing of production processes and operations is often more crucial. The farmer is ruled by physical *seasons* of the year in contrast to industrial production which is primarily governed by the seasonality of demand for its products.

Hired labor tends to be less specialized on farms than in industrial work. Farm help is generally capable of working at many different jobs, while production line processes, craft and trade unionization, and the emphasis on special skills (electronics, etc.) limit labor flexibility in industry. *Product perishability* is generally evident in farm products to a greater degree than industry. Spoilage of truck crops, bruising of livestock, and shrinkage are examples. Industry, in contrast, is faced with production line rejects.

There is more invested *capital* on the average per worker on the farm than that invested per worker in industry. However, the range in capital investment per worker is probably wider in industry than in farming. Agricultural products are produced by many relatively small production units, while the majority of industrial output is produced by large corporations composed of many divisions and plants. The large number of farm firms combined with their relatively small individual output places individual farmers in the position of having no effective influence on market quantities and prices. The opposite is frequently true in industry where few large firms can exert an influence on the prices of the products they sell and the resources they buy.

Lastly, farming for the majority of people in agriculture is a combination of home and business. On most farms production is conducted at the same place the family lives. Work and leisure time are both spent on the farm. This condition does not exist to the same extent in manufacturing.

CONCEPT OF A PRODUCTION FUNCTION

The concept of a production function is really quite simple: total yield, or output, varies with the quantities of inputs used in the production process. Management must decide the amount of production and the amount and kinds of inputs to be used because production does not vary evenly as inputs are fed uniformly into the production process. Thus, differences in production response to evenly applied inputs open the doors to economics as an aid to managerial decision making.

Let us discuss a production function using only one varying input of production which, in combination with the fixed inputs, produces only one product. Remember that we are investigating only the *physical* input-output relationships at this time, beginning with the notion that an input has productivity when combined with other resources.

There are three types of production response to an input or factor of production; increasing, constant, or decreasing returns to the variable factor. For example, *increasing marginal returns* (productivity) occurs when each unit of added input produces more product than the previous unit of input.[1]

Units of Input	Units of Output	Added Output or Marginal Physical Product (MPP)
1	1	1
2	3	2
3	6	3
4	10	4
5	15	5

In this case the second unit of input adds one more unit of product than the first input, the third input adds 3 units of output compared to only 2 units of output produced from the second unit of input, and so on.

Constant marginal returns occur when each additional unit of input always yields the same amount of additional product:

Units of Input	Units of Output	Added Output or Marginal Physical Product (MPP)
1	2	2
2	4	2
3	6	2
4	8	2
5	10	2

Each additional unit of input produces two additional units of output.

Decreasing marginal returns occurs when each additional unit of input yields a relatively smaller amount of additional products.

---

[1] Marginal product is defined as the change in units of total product (total output) divided by the associated change in units of input.

Units of Input	Units of Output	Added Output or Marginal Physical Product (MPP)
1	5	5
2	9	4
3	12	3
4	14	2
5	15	1

Less product is added to total product for each additional unit of input than was added by the previous unit of input.

A graphic presentation of these three relationships taken from the foregoing tables is shown in Figure 12-1.

The concept of constant returns to an input is the least important of the three. Such a condition is unusual in farming. However, the notions of increasing and decreasing returns are of utmost importance to the theory of production. These two ideas give rise to the laws of variable proportions discussed later.

Three methods to describe resource productivity were just presented: verbally, arithmetically in tabular form, and geometrically in the graph. A fourth way to describe resource productivity is by means of an algebraic equation. This fourth method enables us to set up a functional relationship between input and output which allows us to predict and analyze the consequences of varying the amounts of input used in the production process. The general equation for a production function which results in only one product using only one variable input is:

$$Y = f(X_1 \mid X_2, X_3 \ldots \ldots \ldots, X_n)$$

This equation states that output Y depends on (is a function of) the amount of the variable input (X_1) used in combination with a fixed quantity of other factors of production $X_2, X_3 \ldots \ldots, X_n$. In the equation, the bar between the inputs or factors of production separates those factors which vary from those which are fixed in the production process.

Limiting factors are those factors which are fixed in some way and finally slow down the production process, preventing the increase of total production. For example, the amount of land on any one farm used in crop production for any one crop year is generally fixed at a set amount of acres. Likewise the amount of labor may be fixed, for example, at two people, the owner-operator and his tenant; capital may be fixed by the amount of the operating bank loan.

Law of diminishing returns. In farm production processes, limiting factors tend to set in at some level of production before total output be-

comes very great, and thus decreasing returns are the most common type
of production response. The point at which increases in (additions to)
total output stop occurring at an increasing rate (the same point where
marginal physical product, MPP, begins to decline) is also the point
where diminishing marginal physical returns begin. The economic law
which says this point will always occur is called the "law of diminishing
returns." It states: when successive equal units of a variable resource are
added to a given quantity of a fixed resource, there will come a point
where the addition to total output will decline.

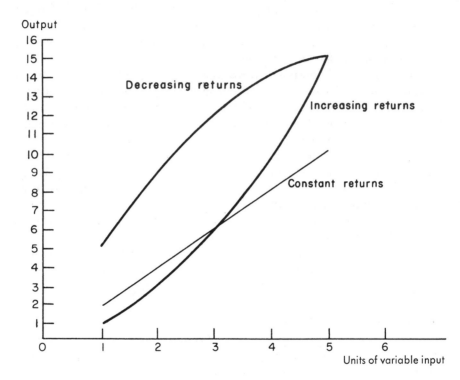

FIGURE 12-1:   Increasing, Constant, and Decreasing Returns.

       To test your understanding of the idea of diminishing physical re-
turns, think of what would happen if increasing or constant returns were
the case throughout all levels of possible output! It would be possible to
feed the whole world's consumption need for milk from the production
of one cow, by merely increasing her food intake. Or the world's needs
for corn could be satisfied from the production of one acre of land, by
simply adding more and more inputs to produce more from this single
acre of land.

Production functions. Combining the ideas of resource productivity and limiting factors we can now show the concept of a typical production function (Figure 12-2a).

The total amount of output produced as a result of the variable input and the fixed inputs is known as Total Physical Product (TPP). Its general shape is like that of a small hill. Increasing returns at an increasing rate are evident up to point A on Figure 12-2(a); from A to C returns are still increasing but the increase is slowing down (increasing

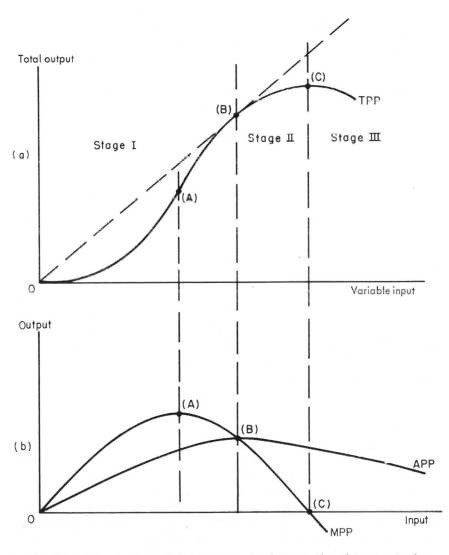

FIGURE 12-2: The Production Function: Total, Marginal, and Average Products.

at a decreasing rate); after C, TPP decreases because of the harmful effects that occur when the variable input increases.

Marginal and average physical product curves are shown in Figure 12-2(b). Let us consider the marginal physical product curve (MPP) first. Marginal production (extra production occurring by adding one more unit of input) is zero when total physical production is zero. As total production increases as indicated by the TPP curve, the marginal physical product curve rises. At A, the point on the TPP curve where returns to the variable input shift from increasing at an increasing rate to increasing at a decreasing rate (also called the inflection point), marginal physical product is at a maximum. When TPP begins to decrease at C, marginal physical product is zero again and any additional units of input produce a negative marginal physical product. Review the short tables just used to illustrate increasing, constant, and decreasing returns.

TABLE 12-1: Hypothetical Total, Average, and Marginal Products Related to Production Stages I, II, and III.

	Number of Units of Input	Total Product (TPP)	Average Product (APP)	Marginal Product (MPP)
	1	1	1	1
Stage I	2	5	2.5	4
	3	9	3	4
	4	11	2.75	2
Stage II	5	12	2.4	1
Stage III	6	11	1.8	-1

Average physical product (APP) is also zero when there is no production. Its maximum height occurs at B, the point at which the ratio of output to input is greatest. (This point can be found easily by drawing a line from the origin tangent to the TPP curve. This line has the greatest slope—the ratio of output to input—at the point of tangency to the TPP curve. Thus, the maximum height of the APP curve lies directly below the point of tangency.) Average physical product becomes zero again if and when TPP also becomes zero.

The production function (TPP) is divided into three stages. In stage I (up to point B), marginal physical product (MPP) is always greater than average physical product (APP). As long as it pays to produce at all, it will pay to add inputs and produce through stage I. In stage III (beyond point C), total production is decreasing and marginal physical product is less than zero, thus making it irrational for production because you simply get less and less product for increasing amounts of input. Stage II (from point B to point C) becomes the relevant part of the production function for profitable production to take place. However, physical conditions alone will not determine the profitability of production. One needs to know something about product prices and input (factor) costs. The points to remember from this discussion are that stage II is the only "rational" production stage, while stage I and III are "irrational" production stages, and that physical data alone do not decide the profitability of a production process.

In order to more clearly see the construction of a production function, hypothetical data (Table 12-1) were used to draw a simplified production curve (Figure 12-3). Although this example is highly simplified, all the essential elements are present.

Effect of new technology

Technology has the effect of raising the production function, that is, of producing more product per unit of input (Figure 12-4). Generally speaking, more output is produced for each unit of input. This means that more total output can be produced by or from the inputs that were used prior to the technological innovation, or the same amount of total output can be produced with fewer resources. These effects are quantitative. Sometimes qualitative changes are included in the new products.[2] However, qualitative changes are extremely difficult to measure and changes of this nature are usually resolved through the pricing system rather than solved through analysis of the production function.

In either the quantitative or qualitative case, technology changes the production function. Changes in total output per unit of input cause changes in the most profitable level of use of the factors used in production. The technological change may call for increased use of certain factors because of a more complex production technique (special fertilizer and feed mixtures for example); or they may call for decreased use of a factor (less labor is needed to produce a bushel of corn). Review Chapter 8 which dealt with technology in more detail.

Continuous and discontinuous factor and product relationships

A continuous input-output relationship may be thought of as a smooth curve with no breaks or bumps in it. Continuity implies that minute fractions of inputs may be used to produce minute fractions of output. Feed and fertilizer may sometimes be bought and used in fractions of pounds, and the resulting output measured.

[2] Some economists, notably T. W. Schultz, argue that the production function shifts simply because some input has not been identified. If all inputs could be identified the production function would not shift. The point is that conventional accounting of inputs does not include technological change.

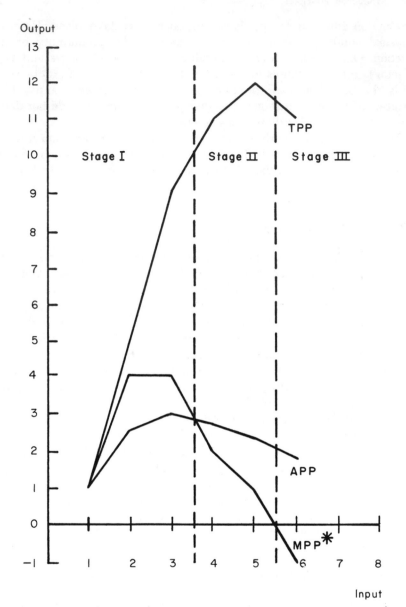

*Data from Table 12-1. Although MPP is correctly plotted arithmetically, the use of the calculus would show MPP = O when TPP is at a maximum.

FIGURE 12-3:   Hypothetical Production Function Illustrating Stages I, II, and III.

However, in agricultural production there are few opportunities for such factor and product continuity to exist. Many factors of production are not minutely divisible. A farmer cannot buy half a tractor, a third of a combine, or a fourth of a cow. He has to buy "lumps" of inputs. Even most fertilizer and feed inputs are bought in bulk units to save money. Discontinuous relationships look like steps, when graphed (Figure 12-3).

Input combinations. There are several types of input (factor) combinations: complements, substitutes, single, multiple, and fixed. Inputs are *complements* when they are combined in fairly definite proportions in the production process. An example is a one-man-one-tractor type of operation. Factors are *substitutes* when the production function allows one input to be substituted for another input. Livestock rations in the Midwest which use corn as a carbohydrate may utilize a barley substitute if the ration is used in the West or if corn prices become too high relative to barley. Silage and hay are sometimes used as substitutes by cattle feeders and dairymen. Production processes can be studied by changing one variable while holding others constant (single variable analysis), or by changing two or more inputs (multiple analysis). A *fixed* factor of production is one that remains constant in amount regardless of the production process with which it is concerned. For example, an acre of ground planted to corn remains an acre of ground regardless of how much corn is planted, how much fertilizer is applied, or how much labor is used to cultivate and harvest the corn crop.

There are three types of production management decisions directly related to the concept of a production function and input combination. These decisions may be classified as (a) factor-factor decisions, (b) fac-

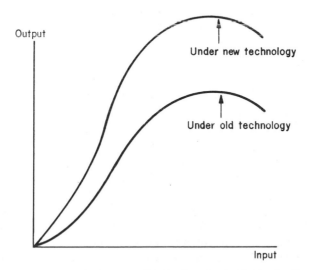

FIGURE 12-4:   The Impact of Technology on the Production Function.

tor-product decisions, and (c) product-product decisions. These help decide what products to produce, how to produce them, and how much to produce of any product.

Types of production decisions

Factor-factor decisions. In this type of decision the farmer must decide which inputs he will use in the production of a particular product and how the amounts of each used might vary in response to changes in their prices. For example, the dairy farm manager may vary the combination of grain and hay in his herd's ration, letting the cows have free choice silage. Criteria for changing the proportion of hay and grain will depend both on the amount of milk production desired and the relative prices of the two inputs. A factor-factor decision means a substitution of one factor of production for another. It does not necessarily mean, although it may by chance happen, that one factor will be substituted entirely for the other factor. It is more a process of varying input proportions within certain limits than it is using mutually exclusive (one or the other) inputs. The degree of substitution will depend upon the price of the two factors and how well they will substitute for one another.

Factor-product decisions. This is the general type of decision with which we began the discussion of a production function. Output is dependent upon the amount of a single variable input that was combined with certain fixed resources. Also included in the decision classification are multi-factor single product or multi-product decisions. For example, corn and protein supplement are multi-factors used in the production of pork. But corn and silage (multi-factor) may also produce mutton and wool (multi-products). A further example of multi-factor, multi-product relationships would be a farm on which fertilizer and water were used to produce a cover crop in addition to a seed crop later that same season.

Product-product decisions. In this decision category farm managers decide how many enterprises they will have on the farm and how much production each enterprise will attain. If a farmer has a feedlot operation and a group of sows, he must figure how many cattle and sows he can manage profitably with the resources at his disposal.

Some enterprises are *complementary;* by increasing the production of one enterprise you automatically produce more of another. An example of crop complementarity is grass and alfalfa; as alfalfa production is increased, up to a point, more grass is also produced. Crop rotations are also examples of complementary enterprises. The nitrogen-increased organic matter and improved soil structure left by producing legumes leads to increases in the next crop planted on the field.

Competition between enterprises occurs when the output of one can be increased only by reducing production of the other enterprise. Crop or livestock operations that require the same resources at the same time are competitive. For example, if two crops must be harvested immediately they are competitive for the resources of labor and capital (the combine) used in harvest. Competition between enterprises occurs only when all production resources are being used.

Enterprise *supplementarity* is evident in those operations which use the same resources at different times during the production season. For example, the first crop of hay is usually made before the winter grains are harvested and both of these are out of the way before the fall corn harvest. In this case hay, winter grains, and corn harvest supplement each other with respect to using available labor and machinery. Livestock and crops may also be supplementary enterprises with respect to labor resources over the years. Feeder stock may be bought to feed throughout the winter when the farmer is not working in the fields.

Specialization, diversification, intensive, and extensive farm management. As farmers make decisions concerning enterprise selection and resource combination, they necessarily make decisions about whether they will operate a diversified farm or a specialized one. A specialized farmer is usually one who receives a major portion of his farm income from one source (crops, livestock, dairy, poultry, etc.). Specialization offers a farmer the opportunity to engage in intensive management and production, i.e., he has the time and the motivation to dig deeply into the technology of a particular type of production and put it into effect. The result is to produce a relatively large amount of output from a proportionately small amount of input (often from a relatively small physical or geographic area).

Specialization offers farmers the chance to produce in volume and thus capitalize on the benefits of doing business on a big scale. Feed, fertilizer, and other resources may be bought in volume at lower costs for a large enterprise that would not be economic under small-scale management. Specialization also offers unique distribution and marketing contacts that might result in higher prices truly reflecting the quality of product produced.

Disadvantages of specialization are evident when the manager realizes that "all his eggs are in one basket." In many ways a specialized farmer is more vulnerable to market price fluctuation than a diversified farmer. He tends to cash in when the market price is up but he also is apt to lose relatively more when the market price declines. His enterprise inputs and management may not be flexible enough to shift over to another enterprise. For example, a milking parlor can effectively be used only to milk cows. It is not adapted to produce pigs or chickens. One way to eliminate much of the risk of being a specialized farmer and still remain specialized is to gain some control of the market channels. He may contract with a market agency to sell his output at some stipulated price (this practice is sometimes called prearranged selling), or he may organize and manage his own distribution outlets (a type of vertical integration). Examples of farmer groups organized to accomplish this goal include the citrus fruit growers, the walnut and filbert growers, and the cotton producers who organized a marketing cooperative to sell their product.

A diversified farm operation is one that has several production enterprises. The principal reasons that diversification appeals to many farmers, particularly smaller farm operators, are that (a) diversification tends to more fully utilize all the resources of the farm unit, and (b) diversification tends to reduce the risk of financial failure due to the failure of one or more crops or loss of animals through livestock diseases. Diversification is generally thought to spread the financial risks involved in farming. While prices of one enterprise may fall drastically it is unlikely that all farm prices will fall to the bottom together.

A diversified farming operation may be intensive or extensive in the same manner as a specialized farm. Intensive production means that full use is made of all fixed resources through application of all relevant technology.

Intensity of production leads to relatively large amounts of output from a relatively small resource base. Extensive production can also be specialized production but in this case a large quantity of fixed input is usually needed for production. An example of a specialized-intensive operation would be the "milk factories" in Los Angeles, in which cows are milked continuously 24 hours a day and all inputs are purchased and used on a small amount of land. An example of a specialized-extensive operation would be a cattle or sheep ranch where a great many acres of range land are needed to feed the livestock.

Whether or not a farm is diversified or specialized depends primarily upon the farm manager. His decision based on his interests, experience, qualifications, desires, and goals will determine the extent to which his farm is specialized or diversified.

The law of comparative advantage

Comparative advantage. At first glance it would seem that the advantage of any system of farming in an area would be determined by the physical yields possible, which are heavily influenced by climate and topography. However, economic aspects must be included to get a truer picture. For example, the Corn Belt region in the United States (from physical yield standpoint) produces more than other regions in many crop enterprises, including corn, wheat, potatoes, fruit. The Great Plains region specializes in wheat, while other areas specialize in fruit and other commodities. The answer to this phenomenon lies in the law of comparative advantage which says, "to maximize profits, one should produce those things, considering yields, costs, and returns, where the percentage return above cost is greatest."

Let us look at an example. To keep matters simple assume that there are only two producers and two consumers in the world who will be designated as farmers a and b. Their consumption needs are 60 bushels of corn and 60 bushels of wheat each. Farmer a is the more efficient producer in both corn and wheat, since with his inputs he can produce six bushels of corn in a day's work or four bushels of wheat, while farmer b's efforts will get him only one bushel of corn or two bushels of wheat. Farmer a has an *absolute advantage* in the production of both corn and wheat, or is in a position similar to that of the Corn Belt region in the production of corn and wheat.

Now if both farmers provide for their own corn consumption needs, farmer a will need to work 10 days to get his corn and 15 days to provide his wheat needs. Farmer b will work 60 days to get his corn and 30 days for his wheat. In other words, farmer a will work a total of 25 days and farmer b will have to work 90 days.

A logical question arises as to what benefits would be derived for each if they would specialize in the production of one crop and trade with each other. It seems clear that farmer b would gain from any such proposition, but it is not immediately apparent that a would gain. Let us check. Using the principle of comparative advantage, farmer a should specialize in corn where he has the *most* advantage (6 to 1) and farmer b should specialize in wheat where he has the least disadvantage (2 to 4). Quick arithmetic tells us that total expenditure by farmer a to produce corn for their combined consumption needs is 20 days. Farmer b needs to work 60 days to provide wheat for himself and farmer a. Farmer a has thus saved five days work.

Farmer b has saved 30 days. In total, 35 days have been saved. In this instance farmer a has a comparative advantage in the production of corn while farmer b has a comparative advantage in the production of wheat. It is this economic law that makes it profitable for both rich and poor nations of the world to trade with each other. Each country specializes where it has a comparative advantage, even though it may have an absolute advantage or disadvantage in all products. An important idea in comparative advantage is that just because an enterprise is profitable (a positive difference after subtracting costs from returns) it does not necessarily mean that the product should be produced. A manager looks for those enterprises which are most profitable relative to all his production choices and his trade possibilities.

The following Appendix can be studied to delve deeper into production relationships and principles. However, it is not essential, since the stage is now set to move from the physical aspects of the production process to considerations of dollars and cents as they relate to production.

Appendix

This section is designed for those who wish to study the principles of production more deeply than the previous material permitted. This appendix is technical and should be treated as supplementary to the prior presentation.

Optimum use of a single variable input used in a factor-product relationship

The rule in this situation is to use an input until the value of the last unit of output it creates just pays for the last unit of input used. Another way of saying this is that optimum use of an input occurs when the marginal value product (MVP) of the resource is equal to the price (P) of the resource. Algebraically the equation is:

$$(1) \quad MVP_{X_1} = P_{X_1}; \text{ when } MVP_{X_1} = MPP_{X_1} \cdot P_y$$

or

$$(2) \quad \frac{MVP_{X_1}}{P_{X_1}} = 1$$

When: MPP = marginal physical product produced by last unit of input X_1
P_{X_1} = price of a unit of input
P_y = the price of product Y
MVP_{X_1} = the marginal value product of input X_1

This equation indicates that the use of input X_1 should be increased if MVP_{X_1} is greater than P_{X_1}; that less of X_1 should be used if MVP_{X_1} is less than P_{X_1}; and that the optimum use of X_1 is attained when MVP_{X_1} just equals P_{X_1}. What this algebraic rule says is this: use a unit of X_1 to produce product Y if the value of product Y produced from a unit of X_1 is equal to, or greater than, the cost of X_1. Remember that although this is the general rule, changing factor and product prices and changing technology will change the answer to a specific problem.

Optimum combination of two or more variable inputs and one product (factor-factor relationships)

Equation (2) can easily be expanded to include the combining of two or of an infinite number of variable inputs. The form is:

$$(4) \quad \frac{MVP_{X_1}}{P_{X_1}} = \frac{MVP_{X_2}}{P_{X_2}} = ---- = \frac{MVP_{X_n}}{P_{X_n}} = 1$$

where $X_1, X_2, ----, X_n$ are all variable inputs.

If equation (4) is divided through by the price of the product, P_y, we have:

(5) $\dfrac{MPP_{x_1}}{P_{x_1}} = \dfrac{MPP_{x_2}}{P_{x_2}}$, or

(6) $\dfrac{MPP_{x_1}}{MPP_{x_2}} = \dfrac{P_{x_1}}{P_{x_2}}$

Equation (6) provides the formula for the optimum proportions of the use of inputs X_1 and X_2 at any set of prices in the production of a relevant product.

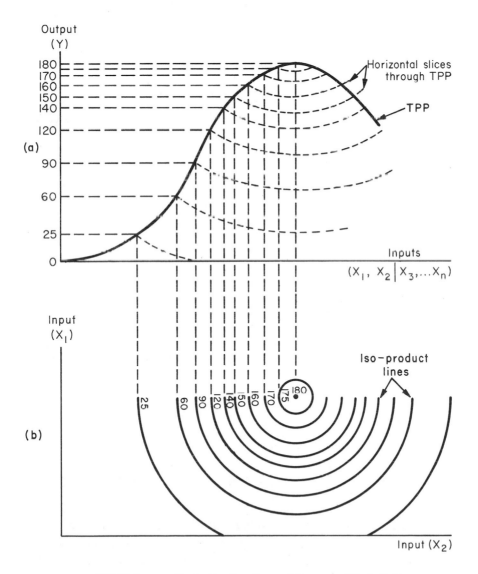

FIGURE 1:   Production Function and Iso-product Derivatives.

A graphic approach may serve to illustrate the algebra. We mentioned previously that the production function looked like a hill. Pretend that you have a huge knife and that as you walk up the hill you take horizontal slices out of the mountain. Then take these circular slices, lay them down in a stack and look down on them so that they look much like any topographic map you have seen. The resulting concentric rings (similar to topographic contour lines) are called iso-product (equal product) lines, each line being a certain fixed amount of production created by varying the amounts of each input. Figures 1(a) and 1(b) show this concept.

Note the change in the axes. In Figure 1(a) the axes are Output and Input; in Figure 1(b) the axes are both Inputs, X_1 and X_2, with output shown on the iso-product curves. The bunching together of the middle iso-product curves (90-150) shows that the production function hill begins to steepen beyond output of 90; the farther the rings are apart the more gentle the slope of the production function.

Let us take out just one of the iso-product contours and use it to illustrate the optimum point expressed by equation (6). Figure 2 shows this situation.

A given amount of money to be spent on inputs will buy either OB of X_2 or OD of X_1. It will also buy any combination of inputs possible along BD. BD is called the iso-cost (equal cost) line, that is, any combination of inputs X_1 and X_2 formed from this line cost the same amount. The slope of BD is $\dfrac{-P_{X_1}}{P_{X_2}}$. The slope of the iso-product curve is $\dfrac{-MPP_{X_1}}{MPP_{X_2}}$. Where BD is tangent to the iso-product contour, the two slopes are equal $\left(\dfrac{-P_{X_1}}{P_{X_2}} = \dfrac{-MPP_{X_1}}{MPP_{X_2}}\right)$. Hence, multiplying through by a minus one to get rid of the minus signs:

$$(6) \quad \frac{MPP_{X_1}}{MPP_{X_2}} = \frac{P_{X_1}}{P_{X_2}}$$

Under the example we have chosen, OA units of X_2 and OC units of X_1 would produce 140 units of product at the given amount of resource expenditures.

This procedure also provides the *least cost point of input combination* to produce a given amount of product. For example, no combination of resources other than OA units of X_2 and OC units of X_1 can produce 140 units of product at a lesser cost. This can be easily seen by examining the iso-cost line. The line runs straight from its extremes on the X_2 and X_1 axes to a point of tangency with the iso-product curve. At no point, under the assumed input expenditures, does the iso-product line intersect the iso-cost line. Thus, it can be concluded that E is the least cost point, using inputs X_1 and X_2, to produce 140 units of product.

Substitution of one input for another under changing factor prices

Let us take the situation described by Figure 2, in which the least cost combination on inputs was determined to produce a set amount of product (140 units), but let us change the prices of inputs to see what the new least cost combination and production points would look like. Let us assume as we did before that there is a certain set sum of money to spend on factors of production. However, let us say that the price of input X_2 increases; we can now buy less of it with a fixed amount of money than we could before. The new iso-cost line is shown in Figure 3 (BF), and the new and old input amounts are compared with the new iso-product lines.

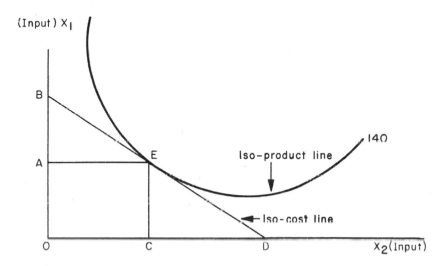

FIGURE 2: Diagram Showing the Different Amounts of Resources X_1 and X_2 Necessary to Produce 140 Units of Product.

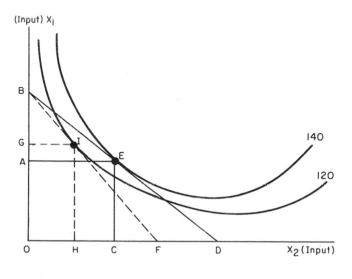

FIGURE 3: Factor Substitution Under Changing Factor Prices.

Under the assumptions of a constant outlay of input expenditures and a price increase in X_2, 140 units of output cannot be achieved. Some lesser amount must be produced because the amount of X_2 needed in the production of 140 units of output is not feasible under the new price structure. To determine the new lesser amount of production we proceed as before. The amount of X_1 we can buy at a constant cost outlay is the same as before. The amount of X_2 is lessened because its price has risen, and accordingly the point (F) is nearer the origin. BF is the new iso-cost line. It happens to be tangent to the 120 unit iso-product contour at I. This point then becomes the new least cost combination of X_1 and X_2 to produce 120 units with the original input expenditures. It is also the highest amount of production possible under the new prices, and accordingly OC and OH become the new amounts of X_1 and X_2, respectively, needed for production.

Optimum output combination with two or more enterprises (product-product relationship)

Combining enterprises is a difficult business, since preferences for various kinds of enterprises discount the economics of a situation. Despite these difficulties the theory of enterprise combination is straightforward. It answers the question "how can a maximum revenue be obtained from a given cost outlay?"

Figure 4(a) shows several types of production possibilities curves. Iso-cost line, or production possibilities curve, (1) shows a decline in one product as the other is increased, but the decline is greater than the increase. This situation would be encountered when a farmer took on a new hired hand and was faced with the prospect of training him. Total production generally decreases in a training situation and can be tolerated only if the trainee improves his knowledge and skill level to the point where total production increases. If it does not increase the farmer is most likely better off under the old system of management without the cost of the extra man. Production possibilities curve (2) shows a substitution of one product for another in some constant ratio. A situation like this often leads to specialization in one or the other product rather than continued production in both enterprises. Curve (3) shows the most common type of production possibilities situation. This curve is competitive throughout, but the curve permits substitution of one product for another for increased total production (not a straight line substitution). Production possibilities curve (4) combines complementary, supplementary, and competitive areas of production. Arc QM denotes an area of complementarity where the increase in production of one product leads to an increase in the production of the other product. The marginal rate of substitution ratio for this arc is greater than one. Arc MN is a supplementary situation where the marginal rate of substitution is equal to one. Arc NP illustrates the competitive relationship where the marginal rate of substitution is less than one.

Let us approach the product-product question in the same general manner as we did the factor-product and the factor-factor situations. Let us assume that we produce two products, Y_1 and Y_2, with certain variable and fixed inputs. We can trace an iso-production cost curve between the two outputs that shows the

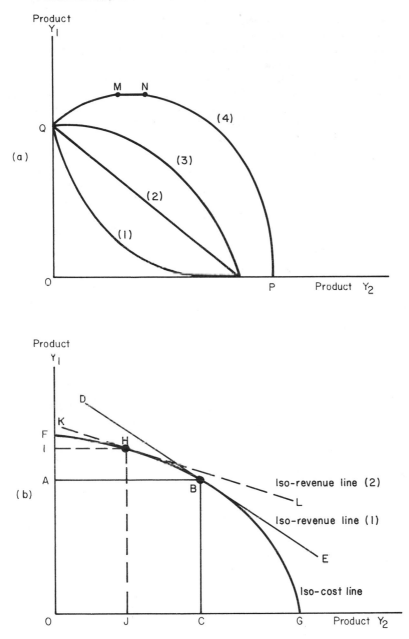

FIGURE 4: Iso-cost and Iso-revenue Lines Plotted to Determine the Optimum Combination of Two Enterprises Under a Given Total Cost Outlay and a Change in Product Prices.

relative amounts of Y_1 and Y_2 that can be produced for a given cost outlay. Figure 4(b) provides this diagram. The iso-cost line may also be thought of as a "production possibilities curve," indicating how much of each product it is possible to produce under a given cost condition.

The production possibility curve shown (FG) in Figure 4(a) is an example of a competitive relationship. The line DE is known as an iso-revenue (equal revenue) line and shows the amount of Y_1 and Y_2 necessary to obtain the same total revenue. Its slope is determined by the ratio of the prices of Y_1 and Y_2. Revenue received is constant throughout the length of DE for any combination of Y_1 and Y_2 that falls on DE. B is the point at which the greatest possible revenue (shown by DE) is equal to the given cost outlay. Our question is answered: we produce OA units of Y_1 and OC units of Y_2 to maximize profits from the given cost outlay. At point B the ratio of the marginal physical product of input X_1 in the production of Y_1 to the marginal physical product of input X_2 in the production of Y_2 is equal to the inverse price ratios of Y_2 and Y_1, equation (7):

$$(7) \qquad \frac{MPP_{(x_1)Y_1}}{MPP_{(x_2)Y_2}} = \frac{P_{Y_2}}{P_{Y_1}}$$

If we multiply through by the product and the factor prices we get:

$$\frac{P_{Y_1}}{P_{x_1}} MPP_{(x_1)Y_1} = \frac{P_{Y_2}}{P_{x_2}} MPP_{(x_1)Y_2}$$

Suppose now that a change in product prices was instituted and that the resulting iso-revenue line was KL, Figure 4(a). The new point of optimum product combination would be H. At this point maximum returns for a given cost outlay would be obtained by producing OI of Y_1 and OJ of Y_2.

13

Production costs, supply, and revenue

TYPES OF INPUT COSTS

The previous chapter developed the concept of the production function and the law of diminishing physical returns. The three major types of production decisions regarding the choice of level of output, combination of inputs, and combination of products were discussed. In this chapter analysis of the effect of varying the level of an input upon total costs and costs per unit of output is developed. These per unit costs will be used to derive the levels of production for an individual producer that would result in the most profit for him for different prices of the product. The individual producer supply schedule is related to the total market supply schedule for the product. Finally, the concept of supply elasticity and the difference between supply in the short and long run are discussed.

Fixed costs

Fixed costs are those costs which do not change as production changes. The notion of being fixed is a static concept, meant for a relatively short period of time. In the long run all costs become variable because more opportunity exists to change all the factors of production,

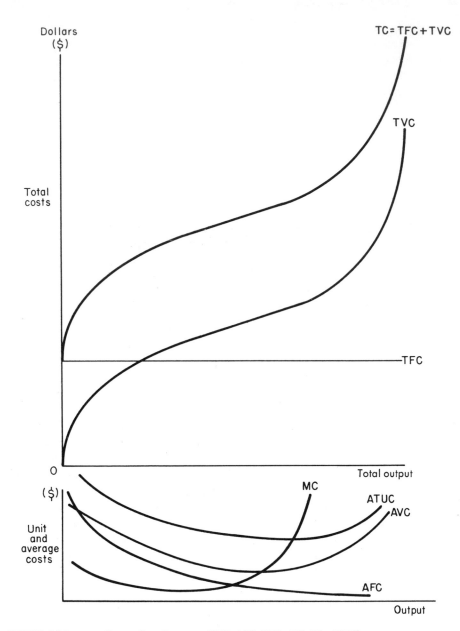

FIGURE 13-1:   Seven Cost Concepts (TFC, AFC, TVC, MC, TC, ATUC).

including plant and equipment. Taxes on property, for example, are a fixed cost of production. Farmers must have land on which to produce agricultural commodities, and consequently they are obligated to pay property taxes on the land they own. The amount of this tax does not vary with production; a farmer pays the same property tax if he raises 150 bushels of corn per acre or if he lets his land lie idle. However, over the years the amount of property taxes paid by the farmer may rise as more schools, roads, and other public facilities need to be built. The costs that are fixed include unpaid family labor, taxes, depreciation, insurance, interest, and some maintenance repairs.

TABLE 13-1: Hypothetical Cost Data Illustrating the Relationships Among The Various Cost Concepts.

Units of Output	Total Cost (TC) $	Total Fixed Cost (TFC) $	Total Variable Cost (TVC) $	Average Total Unit Cost (ATUC) $	Average Fixed Cost (AFC) $	Average Variable Cost (AVC) $	Marginal Cost (MC) $
0	50	50	0	Undefined Number		0	—
1	58	50	8	58.00	50.00	8.00	8.00
2	65	50	15	32.50	25.00	7.50	7.00
3	71	50	21	23.67	16.67	7.00	6.00
4	76	50	26	19.00	12.50	6.33	5.00
5	81	50	31	16.20	10.00	6.20	5.00
6	87	50	37	14.50	8.33	6.16	6.00
7	94	50	44	13.42	7.14	6.28	7.00
8	102	50	52	12.75	6.25	6.50	8.00
9	111	50	61	12.33	5.55	6.77	9.00
10	124	50	74	12.40	5.00	7.40	13.00

Variable costs

Variable costs are those costs directly related to production output. The level of these costs is dependent upon the level of output and is directly connected with the production function. Many examples of variable costs are evident on the farm. Total fertilizer costs rise as more plant food inputs are used to increase crop production; feed costs rise as higher rates of gain are attempted, or if increased numbers of livestock are fed. Hired labor is also a variable type cost.

Total costs

Total costs of production are found by adding total fixed costs and total variable costs of production together.

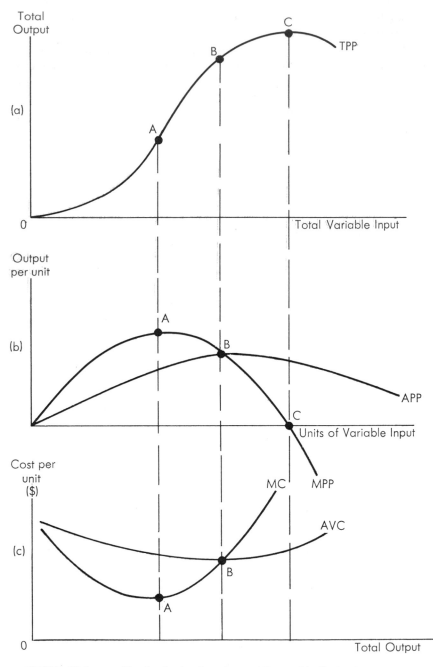

FIGURE 13-2:   The Production Function and Some of its Derivatives.

Note: It is recognized that the horizontal and vertical axes in each of the three figures above are not comparable on a quantitative basis. The importance is to show the relationship between various points on the physical product curves and the cost curves. Point A is the point of diminishing returns where MPP begins to decline and the TPP curve begins to increase at a decreasing rate (inflection point). Since MPP is at its highest point, the MC of producing that extra unit of output is at its lowest point. Where the APP and MPP curves intersect is also where the MC and AVC curves intersect (point V). This point on the TPP curve is the beginning of stage II or the beginning of the area of rational economic production. MPP reaches zero where TPP begins to decline. This is the beginning of stage III, an irrational area of production level.

Marginal cost

Marginal cost is the additional cost necessary to produce one more unit of output. Marginal costs depend entirely upon the nature of the production function and the unit costs of the variable inputs. Marginal cost is comprised entirely of variable type costs.

Summary of costs

[1] There are seven cost concepts derived from the production function that are used in economic analysis. They are:

1. Total Cost (TC)
2. Average Total Unit Cost (ATUC)
3. Total Fixed Cost (TFC)
4. Average Fixed Cost (AFC)
5. Total Variable Cost (TVC)
6. Average Variable Cost (AVC)
7. Marginal Cost (MC)

The computation of each and their relationship to each other are as follows:

1. $TC = TFC + TVC$
2. $ATUC = TC$: Number of output units
3. TFC = Simple sum of depreciation, taxes, maintenance repairs, interest, insurance, and unpaid family labor.
4. $AFC = TFC$: Number of output units.
5. TVC = Simple sum of all variable type costs.
6. $AVC = TVC \div$ Number of output units.
7. $MC = TC$ at any given output level minus TC for previous output level providing output increments are one unit. (Increase in TC associated with producing one additional unit of output.)

The above relationships are summarized in Table 13-1. Note that the total cost and the total variable cost functions increase continually as output increases. This would be expected from the definitions. Variable costs are one of the two components of total cost and by definition are associated directly with output level. Total fixed cost is constant over all levels of output. Again, fixed costs by definition have nothing to do with level of output and therefore are a constant dollar amount even at zero

[1] The student who attempts to gain an understanding of cost relationships merely by memorizing formulas or definitions will encounter difficulty in solving problems. For example, one must understand thoroughly why fixed cost is fixed, not merely some mechanical formula in its computation.

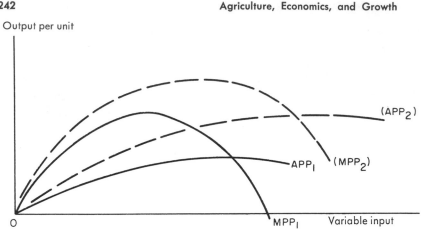

FIGURE 13-3:   The Effect of Technology on the Marginal and Average Production.

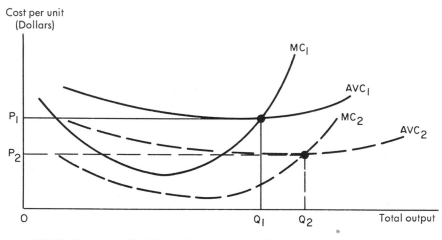

FIGURE 13-4:   The Effect of Technology on Marginal and Average Costs.

units of output. Average fixed cost is a continuously decreasing function since a constant dollar amount (TFC) is being divided by an ever increasing number of output units. The rest of the cost functions—average total unit cost, average variable cost, and marginal cost—are U-shaped; they first decrease at lower levels of output but then begin to increase once a certain output level is reached, although the output level at which each begins to rise is at different points.

Next, let us draw a picture of the seven cost concepts and see how each is related to the other (Figure 13-1). The difference between TC and TVC is always the constant TFC. Measure the vertical distance between the TC and TVC curves with your pencil or a ruler. It is the same anywhere on the graph. AFC is continually declining as output increases; a constant TFC is divided by a constantly enlarging number (increasing output). The MC curve crosses both the AVC and ATC curves at their minimum points. This is part of the symmetry of economics. The importance of cost structures and their relationship to output cannot be overemphasized. It is in these relationships that the symmetry of economics is found. An economist who fails to see these symmetries and relationships between output and cost is severely handicapped when he comes to solving applied economic problems.

The transition from the physical ideas discussed about the production function and the cost ideas is indicated in Figure 13-2, which illustrates the relationships graphically. The marginal and average cost curves are the mirror image of the marginal and average physical product curves. (Experiment with an actual diagram on a piece of paper and a mirror to see if you can get the mirror image.) Note the change in the labeling of the axes. In Figure 2 (a) and 2 (b) the vertical axes are labeled "Output" and the horizontal axes are labeled "Input." Measurements are in physical terms of output per unit of input. In Figure 2 (c) the vertical axis is "Dollars" and the horizontal axis is "Output." Measurements from this diagram are in economic terms of cost per unit of output. This is an important difference of notation and will be critical when we begin the discussion of profits.

Relationships between increasing and decreasing returns to marginal and average physical production and marginal and average costs may be summarized as follows: [2]

Physical	*Economic*
(input-output relationships)	(output-price relationships)
1. Where MPP is greater than APP, APP is *increasing*.	1. When MC is below AVC, AVC is *falling*.
2. When MPP is equal to APP (where the two curves cross), APP is at a *maximum*.	2. When MC is equal to AVC (where the two curves cross), AVC is at a *minimum*.
3. When MPP is less than APP, APP is *falling*.	3. Where MC is greater than AVC, AVC is *rising*.

EFFECT OF TECHNOLOGY ON COSTS

Technology and production costs are closely related. Remember that the effect of the adoption of new technologies was to raise the production

---

[2] These relationships assume the existence of perfect competition, which is discussed in Chapter 16.

function—to increase TPP with a given quantity of inputs and thus shift both marginal and average physical product curves upward (Figure 13-3). Under the old technology only production levels APP_1 and MPP_1 were attainable. Under the new technology average and marginal output levels of APP_2 and MPP_2, respectively, can be attained.

Remember, too, what we said about the symmetry between production and costs, and you will see that increased marginal and average production will cause decreased marginal and average costs of production. This is shown in Figure 13-4. Under the old technology the lowest costs possible were found at the intersection of the MC_1 and AVC_1 curves. Under the new technology, which permits increased output per unit of input, MC_2 and AVC_2 are attainable. The minimum cost per unit of output has declined from P_1 to P_2, and this lower cost is to be found at an increased volume of production, Q_2 instead of Q_1 (Figure 13-4).

The above effects were discussed under the assumption of constant factor, or input, prices. This assumption may not always be valid in applied problems, and care must be taken to include factor cost when considering the impact of technology. Often the individual farmer has too small an operating unit for his actions to influence factor prices. But volume purchases or inputs or the ability to handle inputs in a cheaper way through technological innovations (bulk fertilizer versus sacked fertilizer) do exert downward pressures on factor prices, a fact of which individuals may take advantage.

The principal purpose of adopting a new technology is to increase output or decrease costs per unit of output. Changes in output quality may also be affected, but differences of this nature are generally handled by changes in product prices rather than factor prices. New technology may increase total cost by increasing total fixed cost (buying a new self-propelled combine versus owning a small power-take-off six foot combine) or total costs may be increased through increased variable costs (buying and using a new fertilizer). The important thing to consider when making decisions about adopting a new technology is whether the innovation will lower per unit output costs and whether this total decrease will offset (or more than offset in order to make a profit under constant product prices) the increase in total costs accruing to the entire farm operation.

REVENUE CONSIDERATIONS

Revenue may be viewed from either input or output. That is, income to the producer may be measured either in terms of revenue per unit of input or per unit of output. Either way it can be measured in a total, average, or marginal sense.

Revenue per unit of input

Let us refer back to Figure 13-2, which is the first graph of a production function. The axes are in physical terms of output (vertical axis) and input (horizontal axis). If a third scale of dollars were added vertically the TPP, APP, and MPP curves look exactly the same but would measure revenue per unit of input instead of output per unit of input. Instead of TPP the curve would be TRP (total revenue product, or total revenue for total input); instead of APP the curve would be ARP (average revenue product, or average revenue per unit of input); instead of MPP the curve would be MRP (marginal revenue product, or marginal revenue per unit of input). All we have done to change the diagram so that it reads in terms of revenue instead of in physical terms is multiply the amount of product produced at each point of the production function by the price of the product.

Revenue per unit of output

Total revenue is determined by the amount of product sold multiplied by the product price. There are so many farmers that no one producer can influence the product prices appreciably. This means that the only way a farmer can increase his total revenue (TR) without changing quality of product is to increase his total production because total production multiplied by product price equals revenue. This revenue relationship is referred to as a linear one, a straight line relationship. Constant marginal dollar returns accrue from each additional unit of output. Average revenue (AR) under these conditions is the price received for the product. Marginal revenue (MR) is also equal to price. This follows since marginal revenue is the change in total revenue produced by selling one more unit of output (or the price of the product times one additional unit of product). Figure 13-5 illustrates these relationships. It should be noted that although these relationships hold generally for the majority of agricultural production, they do not hold for some commodities under production and market quotas, or for the majority of products sold in the rest of the general economy. This situation holds true only under the limiting assumptions of perfect competition, which are discussed later.

CONCEPT OF SUPPLY

The concept of *supply* involves price-quantity relationships. A farmer's supply of corn, for example, is defined as the different amounts of corn he is willing and able to put on a market at a given time within a relevant range of prices. The word *supply* as used in everyday language refers only to the variable of quantity offered to the market. Statements such as "the supply of corn last year was 100 thousand bushels in Jackson County" are misleading. Supply involves two variables, price and quantity.

Price⟶ SUPPLY ⟵Quantity

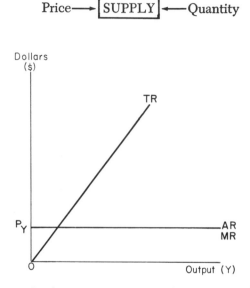

FIGURE 13-5:   Total, Average, and Marginal Revenue in Perfect Competition.

To make the statement correct we should say "farmers supplied 100 thousand bushels of corn in Jackson County at an average price of $1.15 a bushel." Since there are two dimensions to supply, price and quantity, the relationship can be easily illustrated (Figure 13-6). The graph tells us that if the price of the product were $1 producers would provide 40 units of product on the market, but if the price were $2 they would offer 90 units. Common sense would allow you to deduce the correct relationship between price and quantity with regard to supply. A higher price induces more production. A statement of the relationship between price and quantity constitutes the formal *Law of Supply*. The law says that the quantity of goods and/or services offered on a market varies *directly* with the price. The notion may be in an individual sense (individual producers) or in an aggregate sense (all producers in an industry).

The supply schedule

A *supply schedule* is a line (or a curve) showing the relationship between quantity of goods and/or services offered for a series of prices in a given market at a certain time. The supply schedule may actually be thought of as a boundary line beyond which no goods or services will be offered.

Determination of a supply curve. Economic supply is based on costs and revenues, but how does one determine an individual or an industry supply curve? Figure 13-7 illustrates these concepts. We have just noted that product prices (P_1 through P_7 in Figure 13-7) are also average revenue and marginal revenue for the farmer in perfect competition. In the previous chapter we saw that inputs are combined in a production process until the last unit of input just pays for itself, after which it costs more to produce a unit of output than the revenue received. Then the additional cost of production per unit of output (MC) must just equal the added revenue (MR) for inputs to be combined most profitably. (MC = MR is the rule for profit maximization discussed more fully in the next chapter.) Thus, the farmer will produce to the point where P_1 to P_7 (the marginal revenues) just equal the marginal costs (MC). At $P_1 = $ MC Figure 13-7 (left) even the variable costs of production are not covered so that it is not profitable to produce at all. However, at $P_2 = $ MC, AVC are covered, normal marginal profits are made, and the producer is willing to offer output quantity Q_1. This situation continues through $P_7 = $ MC. The price-quantity offered boundary relationship is the MC curve above AVC, from P_2 to P_7 and Q_1 to Q_6. These quantities (or up to these quantities) will be offered at the series of prices $P_2 = P_7$. This portion of the MC curve thus becomes the relevant supply curve for the producer.

The aggregate supply curve, or industry supply curve, can be determined by horizontally summing all the price-quantity offered relationships of all producers. The curve SS in Figure 13-7 (right) shows how this would be done, using Figure 13-7 (left) as an example. At every relevant price (P_2 to P_7 in this case) the quantities offered for sale are

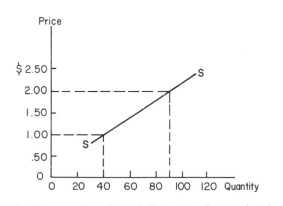

FIGURE 13-6:   Hypothetical Illustration of a Supply Schedule.

added up. The resulting total (Q_1 to Q_6 in this example) is then plotted against price and the resulting curve is the supply function for this particular commodity in the particular market at a certain time.

A change in supply occurs whenever more or less of the good and/or service is offered on the market for the same price or series of prices (Figure 13-8). A shift to the right is an increase in supply and a shift to the left is a decrease. A movement from A to B on SS in Figure 13-8, however, does not constitute a change in supply but merely a change in the quantity offered as a result of a price change.

Assume that SS is the original supply response curve: An increase in supply is denoted by a shift of the entire schedule to the right (S_1S_1), and a decrease in supply is shown by a shift to the left (S_2S_2). An increase means more (Q_1) will be offered for sale on the market at the same price; a decrease means less (Q_2) will be offered than before at the same price.

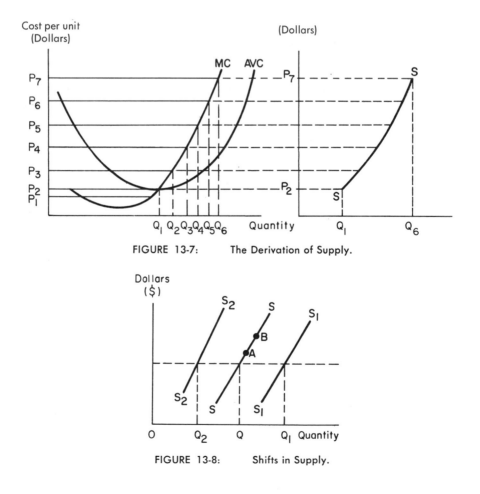

FIGURE 13-7:   The Derivation of Supply.

FIGURE 13-8:   Shifts in Supply.

A contraction of supply may be the result of increased costs of production (losses, rising factor costs, etc.). An increase in supply is usually the result of a new technology or of production areas.

Supply elasticity

Supply elasticity is a measure of the responsiveness of quantity offered to changes in price. More specifically, supply elasticity measures the percentage change in quantity offered in response to a proportionate change in price. The formula for calculating arc elasticity (an average elasticity between two known points of price and quantity) is:

$$E_s = \frac{\dfrac{Q_2 - Q_1}{Q_2 + Q_1}}{\dfrac{P_2 - P_1}{P_2 + P_1}}$$

There are three general types of supply elasticities—elastic, inelastic, or unitary elasticity. An elastic response is when the percentage change in quantity offered relative to price changes is greater than 1 ($E_s > 1$); an inelastic response occurs when the percentage change in amount offered relative to a price change is less than 1 ($E_s < 1$); and a response of unitary elasticity is when the percentage change in amount offered is equal to the relative price change ($E_s = 1$).

Instances of these three types of elasticity would be when a 10 percent change in price was associated with a 15 percent change in quantity offered (elastic); when a 10 percent change in price was associated with a 5 percent change in quantity offered (inelastic); and when a 10 percent change in price called forth a 10 percent change in quantity offered (unitary elasticity).[3]

Supply elasticity graphed. A curved supply function has all three phases of elasticity (Figure 13-9). Any straight line supply curve through the origin has a constant unitary elasticity throughout. Let us utilize this information to devise a general rule of thumb about supply elasticity. Given a curved supply function SS, how can we determine general areas associated with the three types of elasticity? If we draw a line tangent to SS at A through the origin, we know that at A the slope of SS equals the slope of the tangent and therefore SS at that point has an elasticity equal to one (point of unitary elasticity). We can then easily see that the arc of

[3] For the student with a mathematical background, the equation for point elasticity or that response taken at a specific point on the supply curve is shown at the right:

$$E_s = \frac{\dfrac{dQ}{Q}}{\dfrac{dP}{P}} = \frac{dQ}{dP} \cdot \frac{P}{Q}$$

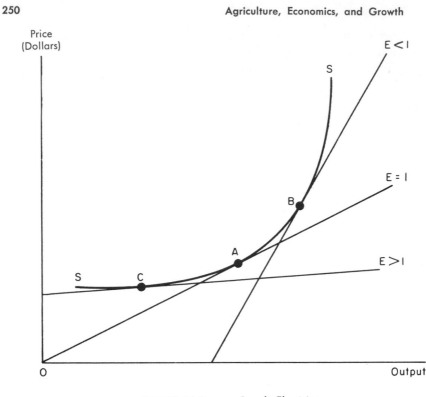

FIGURE 13-9:   Supply Elasticity.

SS to the left of A has an elasticity greater than one (see tangent at C) and the arc of SS to the right of A has an elasticity less than one (see tangent at B).

The elasticity concept in agriculture is of great importance when applied to questions of national agricultural policy. People estimating supply response in agriculture have recently been helped by rapid and far reaching mathematical and statistical advances. However, much work remains to be done in this field, as it is one of the least understood areas of agricultural economic research.

Supply in the short and long run

Supply response in farming in the short run is relatively inelastic because production is not easily changed in the short run. The reasons for this are that most commodity production periods are long, and few resources, if any, can be changed once the seed bed has been prepared and the crop planted, or once the feed has been harvested and stored and the feeder livestock purchased. The longer the time period involved the more opportunity exists for the farmer to respond to price (to change the quantity he produces with regard to farm commodity price changes). A longer time period permits a farmer to be more flexible in his choice of production enterprises and allows him to allocate his resources in adjustment with his more flexible enterprise selections. In effect then, elasticity of supply in agriculture depends more on the degree to which resources are fixed in their use than on time itself. Time allows for resources to lose their fixity and become variable. In the short run, supply response is relatively inelastic—in the long run it becomes fairly elastic.

Much depends then on the length of the production period. If a farmer raises several crops a year, as in the case of truck crops in some of the southern, eastern, and western states, resource fixity is much less than the situation faced by a Wisconsin dairy farmer who raises his own herd replacements.

The above comments pertain to the aggregate of farm production. However, there are differences between the response for individual commodities and the aggregate response. Response for meat products in general, for example, tends to be more inelastic than for any one meat source (beef, pork, etc.).

Factors influencing supply response. The two main factors responsible for shifts in supply are technology and changes in input prices. The discovery and adaptation of new technologies to farm production create lower costs per unit of output and act as an incentive for the individual farmer to increase production. Changes in the prices of factors concerned with agricultural production are often influenced by nonfarm factor markets. For example, jobs in manufacturing may bid labor away from the farm. Changing demands for fertilizer, insecticides, and capital are constantly causing dynamic changes in the prices of farm inputs.

Added to this dynamic economic situation are the individual managerial responses to supply pressures. Differences in the attitude, understanding, and response of managers can be attributed to one or more of the following three factors: differences in information available to individual managers, differences in individual interpretations of available information, and differences in the necessity to sell.

14

Principles of profit maximization

The purpose of this chapter is to show how the previous material covering input-output relationships, costs, and revenue may be combined into simple economic rules for profit maximization. First, however, we will briefly discuss management and its role in profit-making.

MANAGEMENT

Management is focused primarily on the decision-making process, on the intelligence of men to make "right" decisions. Management combines man's mental efforts to identify, organize and classify, analyze, decide, and act.

There are several functions of management. For example a good farm manager must be able to *observe* problems on his farm and to identify them precisely. By defining his problems (production or marketing) he shows his awareness of the situation confronting him. He displays his knowledge about it through his ability to devise ways to cope with the problems.

Problem analysis involves identifying that exact situation causing the problem as well as the formation of several different ways to solve it.

However, management is not content only with analysis; it must put the analysis into action. This is the decision-making focus given to management. The farm manager must choose which of several alternative plans of action offers him the "best" solution in view of his particular goals or desires and of the resources at his disposal. Once the manager makes the decision, *action* must be taken to implement the solution. Once the action is taken the manager becomes *responsible* for the outcome, good or bad. A further function of management is constant evaluation at each step of the decision-making process, both before and after the solution is put into action. Evaluation helps to insure management that the "right" decision was made and it also offers the manager the opportunity to insert new knowledge (technology, organization, prices, etc.) into his decision-making framework.

Managers are not limited only to profit decisions. Some decisions deal with operational-efficiency questions concerning how to do a job. Still other decisions are probably better classed as organizational decisions regarding "who should do what" questions. These last questions concern personnel and resource allocations. Answers to these questions are built on the answers to previous questions of "what" and "how." Decisions regarding time of production and marketing, decisions between slow or fast production and between selling or storing a product also involve management.

Management is constantly concerned with the step-by-step analysis of production, costs, revenues, and profits. This means that the manager is interested in technology as it affects both production and costs and as it is reflected in the demand (or revenue) for the product. He is also concerned with the problem of producing that volume of goods which will bring him greatest profits. Prices in both the factor (input) markets and in the product (output) markets affect how much profit the manager can look forward to. Often the manager does not know the particular price at which a commodity (for example, a load of steers) will sell, so that of necessity his decisions are based on expected prices. He must also be aware of the institutions whose facilities he uses, and of the possible changes in their operation that might affect him. And lastly, the manager must face problems of dealing with other people. This is because ultimately all his decisions must be communicated to others who will help put them into action.

This brief review of management may sound as though the manager would have to be a super-human person to handle all the areas of assembly, coordination and human relationships outlined. But all managers do not handle themselves equally well in each of the areas. This difference between managers, beginning with their initial goals and desires, is the reason that some managers are better than others. One man may do well producing a particular item, but he may overinvest to get his production and thereby raise his costs and lower his profits. Another manager may not overinvest, may get less production, but may realize more profit because his costs are lower.

Goals of management

Economists usually assume that managers want to make the most money they can from the resources they have. However, the assumption of profit maximization is not always consistent with the way managers work. For instance, although high risk enterprises, such as feeder livestock, are usually associated with relatively high profits, some managers simply do not want to assume the high risk of feeding. Instead they prefer to operate a relatively lower profit dairy enterprise that is not extremely risky but involves just as much management as a feeder operation.

Differences in goals of individual managers concerning choices of enterprises and willingness to assume risks are based on many factors. One factor is the age of the manager. Some younger men have not been farming long enough to have experienced severe economic hardship or to have been through a depression. Men who have lost farms and gone hungry are usually not as willing to risk the chance of another such loss as a man who has never had the experience. Another factor is education. This relates to the technical ability of the manager to handle the scientific innovations necessary for continued top management. The variable of time also influences the manager's goals as he plans for his family's future, sending his children to college, taking his wife on vacation, and for needed capital expenditures on the farm.

Although each farm manager views his situation as unique from other farms, and himself as different from other managers, there are pieces of common ground for all managers. Each manager performs all the functions of management and attempts to maximize profits within certain limits. One man may be interested in maximizing profits in the dairy business; another manager wants to make the most of his truck crops. In either case the following rules of thumb for profit maximization are relevant and can be easily applied.

MAXIMUM PROFIT IN TERMS OF OUTPUT

The concept of profit maximization is that profits are maximized when the revenue from the sale of the last unit of output just equals the costs necessary to produce it. At this point marginal costs equal marginal revenue ($MC = MR$). An example of this situation would be when the revenue from the last hundredweight of milk just paid for such factors as the feed, labor, and electricity necessary to produce it.

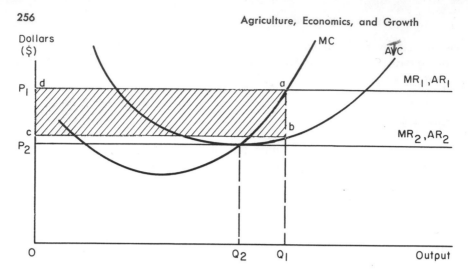

FIGURE 14-1:   Maximum Profits in Terms of Output.

The illustration (Figure 14-1) shows two marginal and average revenue curves. This is done simply to show that the least cost point of production is not necessarily the point of maximum profits.

At a price of P_1, maximum profits occur at $MC = MR_1$. The amount of output produced is Q_1. Total profit is shown by the amount of profit per unit of output (line ab) times all units of output (OQ_1), and is represented by the rectangle abcd. This profit is sometimes referred to as *pure profit* (in the short run) and means that the manager is making more than is needed to keep him in production.

At price P_2, maximum profits are made at $MC = MR_2$. Output production stops at Q_2. Note that at $MC = MR_2$ the low point on the AVC curve is reached. This is the least cost point of production. Yet much less profit is made here as compared to operating at a higher cost of production and at a different output price. At $MC = MR_2$, the profit per unit of output just pays for the costs of production. Managerial salary, labor wages, and other inputs have been paid their relative prices but no pure profit exists.

In each of the two cases maximum profits are made when $MC = MR$. But in one instance pure profits are made, while in the other instance only a "breakeven" profit is earned. Note the relationship between these cost curves, price received (average revenue AR), and profits.

Maximum profit in terms of total cost and total revenue

Net profit is determined by total revenue (TR) minus total costs (TC). Net profit is greatest when the difference between TR and TC is

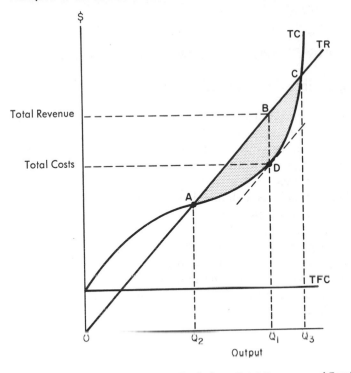

FIGURE 14-2:   Maximum Profit From Total Revenue and Total Cost.

greatest. Perhaps this case of profit maximization is easier to understand than the two marginal cases just discussed.

In Figure 14-2 total costs are less than total revenue only for the shaded area ABCD, which represents the area of profit. The "breakeven" point occurs at A with Q_2 amount of output production. At this point all fixed and variable costs of production are paid for, and for the first time revenue becomes greater than costs. To the right of point C, with production of Q_3, costs again become greater than revenue; hence the area of profitable production lies between Q_2 and Q_3. The task is to find the production point at which maximum profits are earned. This can be done in either of two ways. One method is simply to take a ruler and measure whether the greatest vertical distance between TR and TC is located. This distance is represented by the line BD. The other way is to draw a line tangent to the TC curve and parallel to the TR curve. At this point of tangency the rate of change along the TR curve is just equal to the rate of change of the TC curve. Because rates of change are the same as the marginal concept, we again have MR = MC and have discovered the point of maximum profits at an output of Q_1.

ILLUSTRATIONS OF PROFIT MAXIMIZING PRINCIPLES

Maximizing profits with unlimited inputs

Let us work through an example using simple arithmetic. Suppose Table 14-1 represents a production situation where feed is the only variable cost incurred in producing the output of milk. Our fixed resource is one dairy cow and feed is available in unlimited quantities at $60 per ton. Assume that total fixed cost is $50. The managerial decision facing the farmer is: "How much feed should I give the cow in order to maximize the profit from her milk production?" Milk is assumed to have a market value of $4 per hundredweight.

Maximum profit occurs where 1,300 pounds are fed to the cow or where 8,600 pounds of milk are produced. Note that up to this point marginal cost (MC) is less than marginal revenue (MR), but beyond this point MC is greater than MR. The correct answer can also be checked by looking at the total cost and total revenue figures. The greatest difference between total cost and total revenue is $255, and this occurs where 1,300 pounds of feed are being fed and 8,600 pounds of milk are being produced.

TABLE 14-1: Hypothetical Data Illustrating Profit Maximizing Principle When Inputs are Unlimited.

Feed Consumed (lbs.)	Total Milk Produced Per Year (lbs.)	Marginal Physical Product (lbs.)	Marginal Cost ($)	Marginal Revenue ($)	Total Cost ($)	Total Revenue ($)	Profit ($)
			Per Pound of Output				
500	5,000	—	—	—	65	200	135
600	5,800	800	.0038	.0400	68	232	164
700	6,500	700	.0042	.0400	71	260	189
800	7,100	600	.0050	.0400	74	284	210
900	7,600	500	.0060	.0400	77	304	227
1,000	8,000	400	.0075	.0400	80	320	240
1,100	8,300	300	.0100	.0400	83	332	249
1,200	8,500	200	.0150	.0400	86	340	254
1,300	8,600	100	.0300	.0400	89	344	255
1,400	8,650	50	.0600	.0400	92	346	254
1,500	8,675	25	.1200	.0400	95	347	252

At this point it would be well to check your understanding of many of the ideas that have been discussed since the beginning of Chapter 12. Let us review by asking some questions.

1. What kind of a production function is involved in the above ex-

ample? Since the marginal physical product declines throughout, it can be concluded that only decreasing returns exist over the range of output levels represented. Therefore, it is not possible to delineate the inflection point on the total physical product curve, which is the same as the point of diminishing returns. This reminds us that the point of diminishing returns has nothing to do with what level of output is most profitable.

2. Total physical product never declines. Does this mean that stage III of the production function does not occur in milk production? No, it does not mean that stage III does not exist for milk production processes, but it does indicate that stage III does not begin until the production level is beyond 8,675 pounds, the highest level of output given in the data. This also is a reminder that it is not economical to push for the highest possible milk production per cow. The same would be true for crop yields, weight per steer, or any other physical yields level.

3. Does the example prove that the level of total fixed costs has no influence on the most profitable level of production? Yes. Suppose fixed costs were increased to $100. Note that only two columns of data would be altered. Each total cost figure would be increased by $50 and each profit figure would decrease by $50. The maximum possible profit would then be $205 and it would still occur at 1,300 pounds of feed input and 8,600 pounds of milk output. The marginal cost figures are not changed because they are computed from variable costs only.

4. What is the effect of a change in the cost of feed or in the market price of milk? If the price of feed increased each of the marginal cost figures would increase. An increase to 85 dollars a ton would decrease the most profitable level of feed input to 1,200 pounds. Why? Because the marginal cost of producing each pound of milk between 8,500 and 8,600 would now be $.0425, which is greater than the marginal revenue of $.04. Therefore, this increase is not profitable. Now give yourself a test: how much would the price of milk have to change in order to change the most profitable level? The answer is below $3 or above $6 per hundredweight.

5. Would plotting the total physical product against the marginal costs trace out a supply schedule for the farmer with regard to this production process? Yes it would. As long as marginal cost is equal to or less than marginal revenue it pays to produce. Thus, the marginal costs trace out the output that would be produced at a set of milk prices per pound of the same amount. The supply curve has the expected positive slope. As milk price increases so does the amount the supplier is willing to offer, since the most profitable level of output increases in a similar fashion.

Maximizing profits with limited inputs and where several enterprises are profitable

The example just discussed assumed that feed was the only variable input used in the milk production process, that the feed was available in unlimited quantities, and that milk was the only profitable use of the dollars spent for feed. How realistic is this in a commercial farm operation? Not very. One of the input factors is usually available only in a limited amount. Since money will allow the manager to purchase added quantities of inputs, money capital is usually the most limiting factor.

The other assumption of having only one profitable enterprise is equally invalid for most farmers. Perhaps the wheat grower in western Kansas or the cranberry bog owner in Massachusetts has only one profitable enterprise alternative, but most others have several. A new problem emerges with regard to the production levels that are most profitable in this situation. It would go something like this: how can the limited amount of money capital be allocated among the profitable enterprises so that the total amount of profit is maximized from the total farm unit?

The opportunity cost idea. Before illustrating how this problem is solved let us gain understanding of a new idea. Every time one uses an input in a production process, potential income that could have been realized by using the resource in other uses is foregone or sacrificed. When one attends college, for example, he sacrifices or gives up income that could be earned by being employed somewhere. Opportunity cost, as it is called, is the amount of income you sacrifice to do what you are doing, or is the highest dollar return sacrificed by employing resources in some particular production process. You have probably already guessed that it is impossible to avoid opportunity costs.

Opportunity costs are not actual out-of-pocket costs, but they are real nevertheless. Perhaps some examples would help the understanding of this concept. What does a college education really cost? In addition to the approximate $1,500 or so of out-of-pocket costs per year, several thousand dollars of opportunity costs are involved. Certainly opportunity cost is not an out-of-pocket cost in this example of a college education, and it is a wise decision to incur these costs since a college graduate's earning power in later years will more than make up for the income foregone. Nonetheless, there can be no dispute that there is money income foregone while one is in college.

How does all this relate to the economic principle of maximizing profit with limited money capital when several enterprises are involved? It simply indicates that a smart manager will use his scarce inputs where the marginal return is greatest. Perhaps some profitable enterprises will not even be included in the "most profitable combination." The marginal idea is again put to use. The manager will maximize profits if he considers each unit of money capital as a marginal unit and employs it where it will return the greatest amount.

The equal marginal return principle. The guiding economic principle for the manager given this situation can now be stated: employ the scarce units of input until the marginal returns are equated in each enterprise. Assume that the data in Table 14-2 reflect a situation for a manager.

TABLE 14-2: Hypothetical Data Illustrating Equal Marginal Return Principle.

| Money Capital Used | | Addition to Net Income as a Result of Employing An Additional $1,000 of Money Capital In: | | | |
Total	Marginal	Corn	Wheat	Soybeans	Broilers
$ 1,000	$1,000	$1,800	$1,450	$1,600	$1,100 A
2,000	1,000	1,700	1,325	1,500	1,025 B
3,000	1,000	1,600	1,200	1,400	950
4,000	1,000	1,500	1,150	1,300	900
5,000	1,000	1,400	1,050	1,200	850
6,000	1,000	1,300	900	1,100	800
7,000	1,000 A	1,200	850	1,020	750
8,000	1,000	1,100	750	900	700
9,000	1,000 B	1,010	650	800	650
10,000	1,000	900	550	700	600

Given the data, the correct managerial decision can now be easily computed with any level of money capital available. If only $1,000 were available it is clear that the manager would employ it in corn production where the return ($1,800) is the highest possible. The next $1,000 would be employed again in corn, where a $1,700 return is possible, and so on. If $15,000 were available $7,000 should be employed in corn production, $3,000 in wheat production, and $5,000 in soybean production (line AA). Note also that the last $1,000 invested in *each* enterprise returns an equal marginal return—$1,200. This would fulfill perfectly the requirement stated for the equal marginal return principle. Check it. There is no other possible use of $15,000 that will return a larger amount of profit, $21,475. Note also that broilers, a profitable enterprise up to $2,000 input capital, do not enter into the most profitable combination.

To clarify the difference between this economic principle and the previous one, which assumed unlimited inputs, ask yourself how many dollars of money capital the manager should use if he had unlimited capital. The rule to follow is to push output until marginal cost is equal to marginal revenue. In this case the level in each enterprise would be indicated by line BB. The answer is $23,000—$9,000 in corn, $5,000 in wheat, $7,000 in soybeans, and $2,000 in broilers. Marginal cost can be thought of in terms of the $1,000 increments added, and the manager would continue to add them for each enterprise until less than $1,000 was returned.

Everyday uses for maximizing principles. The profit maximizing principles just discussed are very important. They can be applied to practically any situation involving a decision. The equal marginal return principle, for example, can be a guide for college students in allocating time. The restricted resource is 24 hours of time in a day. The problem for students is to allocate their limited time among their academic and nonacademic pursuits so as to maximize their scholastic achievement and personal satisfactions.

The housewife tries to allocate a limited amount of money in the food budget among the various foods to maximize the satisfactions of the family (to be discussed in detail in the next chapter). A person usually attends a movie only once because after seeing it the marginal return from a second viewing is below the price of admission; it is thus a poor decision to see the movie twice. In addition, considerably more satisfaction is realized by seeing a different movie where the satisfaction return (utility) is higher; hence, opportunity costs are held to a minimum. Numerous examples could be given. See how many you can think of and put into use.

15

Economic principles of consumption and demand

Economists are interested in people as receivers and spenders of money. In this chapter we are particularly concerned with the how and why of consumer decisions with regard to purchases of goods and services.

How can we explain the decision of the Smith family to buy a new green car with automatic shift? Was the purchase made because the Jones family had one? Or was it made because after checking all the various kinds of cars on the market, the Smiths found that the green model gave them the most for their money? Keeping up with the Joneses could be called a noneconomic reason; comparing the cost of different autos is an economic one. Most consumer decisions are based on a combination of economic and noneconomic factors. Both are determined by personal and social values.

CONCEPT OF UTILITY

Economists invented the concept of utility as a way to measure the personal satisfaction which people derive from owning and using goods

TABLE 15-1: Utility Received by Mr. John Doe from Ice Cream at a Stand at a Specific Time and Place.

Ice Cream Cones Consumed (number)	Total Utility Received (units)	Marginal Utility Or Disutility Received (units)
0	0	0
1	15	15
2	25	10
3	32	7
4	36	4
5	37	1
6	35	− 2

         Total Utility   Total Utility

and services. If eating ice cream satisfies a human want then we can say that the ice cream (a good) possesses utility. It is a little harder to think of services possessing utility, but the idea is the same. Getting one's hair cut and the daily mail are examples of services received which also satisfy needs and desires.

Let us use numerical units to signify different amounts of utility. A banana may yield 5 units of satisfaction or utility to Johnny. But if Billy does not like bananas he may get no units of utility at all. In fact, if Billy is allergic to bananas and gets sick, a banana will yield him a number of units of negative utility (disutility). The amount of utility obtained from any good or service may be different for each individual. How it differs depends on individual tastes and preferences.

A THEORY AND ILLUSTRATION OF CONSUMER BEHAVIOR

To formulate a theory or framework for studying and predicting consumer behavior, it is necessary to make several assumptions. To begin with, we assume man to be rational if he tries to maximize his satisfaction. When economists use the term *rational* they mean that people try to get the most income they can to use in reaching individual and family goals.

A second assumption is that man is aware of the relative amounts of utility or satisfaction which he gains from each of the many goods and services available to him. All of us can rank goods and services by comparing them in terms of more or less satisfaction. Given a dollar to spend at an amusement park, some people prefer to ride the merry-go-round while others choose the more daring roller coaster.

A third assumption is that man has limited income. The notion of limited resources forces man to make decisions based upon his satisfaction priorities.

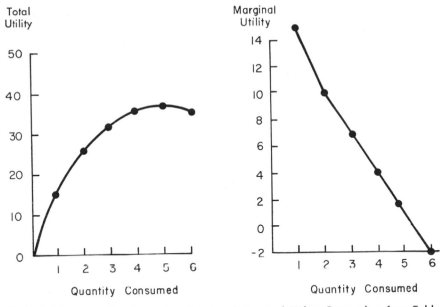

FIGURE 15-1:   Graph Showing Total and Marginal Utility. Data taken from Table 15-1.

Diminishing marginal utility

The utility of any one good or service varies depending upon how much of that good or service we have in our possession. For example, the satisfaction of an apple just received depends upon how many apples we already have. A formal statement of diminishing marginal utility is: as additional units of a good or service are consumed the utility derived from each successive unit declines. Marginal utility is the extra or additional utility derived from one more unit of product or service. When you decide to visit an ice cream stand the first cone tastes exceptionally good and gives you, let us say, 15 units of satisfaction. However, if you order a second one the extra satisfaction you gain may only be 10 units (Table 15-1 and Figure 15-1).

Note that in the title of Table 15-1, time and place is specified. This is important. A number of other variables could also be specified, such as health, sex, age, climate, and necessity of purchase.

Utility maximization principle

The economic principle states that one can maximize his total satisfaction by *allocating limited money income so that the last dollar spent on each good and service yields equal amounts of marginal utility.*[1] When the consumer equalizes his marginal utilities in accordance with this principle, we say his consumption pattern is in equilibrium and any change that he makes will decrease his total satisfaction.

To illustrate the utility maximization principle, let us assume there are only three goods available on the market, A, B, and C. Also, assume that we have a weekly income of $15 to spend and that we can exactly order our utility preferences from each of the three products. Product A costs $1 per unit, product B costs $3 per unit, and product C costs $5 per unit (Table 15-2). Note that diminishing marginal utility sets in immediately for each of the three products. Marginal utility information is described on a per dollar basis because a consumer's choices are influenced not only by the amount of additional utility which successive units give him but also by how many dollars he gives up to get them.

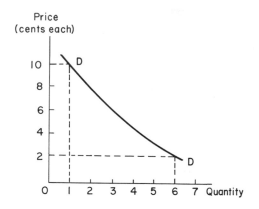

FIGURE 15-2:   A Hypothetical Demand Curve for Apples at Some Specified Place and Time.

Let us consider one dollar of expenditures at a time. Looking at the marginal utility per dollar columns in Table 15-2, we see that a dollar spent on product A provides the most satisfaction. On neither B nor C is the marginal utility return as high as A's 14 units. A dollar would buy only 1/3 unit of B which yields 9 units of increase satisfaction per dollar spent on B. A dollar spent on C would buy 1/5 unit of C which gives only 6 units of added utility for that dollar. Continuing our expenditures, if the second dollar is spent on A it again buys the most marginal utility. However, when spending a third dollar, a switch to product B returns 9 units of added satisfaction as opposed to 8 if the dollar is spent on A. Continuing in this fashion and considering each dollar of expenditure in marginal terms, the best combination we can purchase with $15 would be

[1] This idea has also been called the equal-marginal principle (see Chapter 14).

4 units of A, 2 units of B, and 1 unit of C. Total utility generated would be 113 units. Four dollars spent on A gives 38 units of satisfaction; 6 dollars spent on B gives 45 units; and 5 dollars spent on C yields 30 for a total of 113. No other combination will result in a total this high with an expenditure of $15.

If you have remembered the formal statement of the principle you will note that the example worked out perfectly. The last dollar that was spent for each of the products yielded an equal amount of marginal utility —6 units. "Balancing" our marginal utility per dollar spent is the best we can do. In real life we seldom get such a neat solution. Nevertheless, if we operate our lives using this principle we will gain greater satisfactions.

DEMAND

The theory of consumer behavior will help us understand the concept of demand. The word *demand* as commonly used in everyday language refers only to the variable of quantity consumed. Statements such as "consumers demanded 12 billion pounds of pork last year" are common, but this reference to demand is misleading. Demand really involves two variables—price and quantity.

Price⟶ DEMAND ⟵Quantity

To make the statement above correct we should say "consumers de manded 12 billion pounds of pork last year at an average price of $.50 per pound." Now the idea is complete.

The concept of demand involves price-quantity relationships. Your demand for apples is defined as the different amount of apples that you

TABLE 15-2: Price and Utility Information for Products A, B, and C.[1]

Unit of Product	Product A (Price $1)		Product B (Price $3)		Product C (Price $5)	
	Marginal Utility (units)	Marginal Utility Per $1	Marginal Utility (units)	Marginal Utility Per $1	Marginal Utility (units)	Marginal Utility Per $1
First	14	14	27	9	30	6
Second	10	10	18	6	25	5
Third	8	8	9	3	20	4
Fourth	6	6	6	2	15	3
Fifth	4	4	3	1	10	2

[1] It is necessary to assume that the amount of marginal utility received from extra units of each of the three products is independent of the quantity of the other product.

would be willing and able to buy within a reasonable range of prices. Since there are two dimensions to demand we can easily illustrate the relationship between the two variables (Figure 15-2).

The graph tells us you would buy one apple if the price were 10 cents, but should the price drop to 2 cents you would be willing to purchase 6 apples. This is just good common sense and anyone would have been able to tell us that people tend to buy larger quantities if the price is low. Be sure to remember that the concept of demand encompasses the entire curve labeled DD. It is a line (schedule) that shows the quantities you would buy at various prices. Remember that although demand is an abstract notion it is also operational in the real world. There need be no apples present in order for us to conceptualize the demand for apples and predict what might happen under various price and quantity changes.

The negative relationship between price and quantity [2]

The common sense statement that "consumers will buy a larger quantity as price is reduced" states the relationship between the two variables of price and quantity and is usually referred to as the "law of demand." Other terms to describe the relationship are *negative* and *inverse*. We will increase our understanding of demand by investigating the various reasons why this relationship exists.

First, as noted before, not all people have equal desires for the same commodity. Let us take fresh strawberries. Some people desire strawberries enough to pay 70 cents a quart for them. However, the number of people with this intense desire for strawberries is small relative to the number of people with more usual desires, who will buy at 40 cents a quart. Figure 15-3 helps us understand the idea. While only 20 percent of the population desires to purchase berries at 70 cents (a high level of desire intensity), virtually 100 percent would purchase them at 10 cents (a low level of desire intensity). This, then, is one reason that there is an inverse relationship between price and quantity.

Second, there is wide variation in the income of individuals and in their ability to buy goods and services. Although a millionaire oilman and a poor ditchdigger may have the same size stomachs and an equal desire for strawberries, it is not hard to understand that the millionaire can afford to pay 70 cents a quart while the ditchdigger may not. As the price of berries is lowered a greater quantity can be sold because more and more people can afford them. This is the second reason why a demand curve slopes downward to the right.

Third, price varies inversely with quantity because of diminishing

---

[2] This relationship has often been explained in terms of an "income-substitution effect."

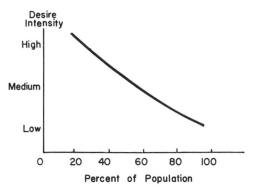

FIGURE 15-3:   Hypothetical Illustration of Consumer Desires for Strawberries.

marginal utility discussed earlier in this chapter. As an individual consumes additional units of a commodity, the added or marginal utility which he gains diminishes. With regard to food, this is basically because our stomachs cannot expand indefinitely.

Building market demand from Individual demands

Until now we have discussed only an individual's demand for a commodity. In order to study the total market for a commodity it is necessary to think of the total or aggregate demand for commodities. As might be expected, the market demand for apples is derived by summing up the amounts of apples that are demanded at each price by each consumer. Taking an unrealistic situation of 10 million consumers with identical individual demands and assuming these people made up the entire market, we could then think of the market demand as a 10 million-fold enlargement of the individual demand curve (Figure 15-4).

A change in demand

A change in demand is not the same thing as a change in the quantity demanded. For example, using the data in Figure 15-2, when price is lowered from 8 to 6 cents for apples the quantity demanded increases from 2 to 3. This is not a change in demand but merely a movement from one point to another on the demand schedule. What has happened is merely a reflection of the law of demand working; the two variables of price and quantity have moved in opposite directions.

To have a change in demand it is necessary for one of the variables (price or quantity) to remain constant while the other variable changes. A change in demand also occurs if both variables move up or down together. For example, if consumers purchase 5 million tons of oranges this

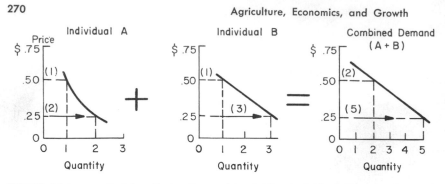

FIGURE 15-4: Deriving Market Demand by Adding Individual Consumer Demands.

year at an average price of 50 cents a dozen and next year they buy 5½ million at 50 cents a dozen, then demand has changed. At the same set of prices, consumers will purchase greater quantities all along the line. Thus, a change in demand constitutes a shift in an entire demand schedule (Figure 15-5). A movement from A to B would be a change in quantity demanded. A move from B to C is a change in demand. The concept of a change in demand for an entire demand schedule is shown by going from DD to D′D′.

Price elasticity of demand

The law of demand is applicable to virtually all products. However, while demand curves slope downward to the right, there is considerable difference in the steepness of the slope for individual commodity curves. Price elasticity of demand indicates whether the demand curve slopes steeply or whether it lies flat. The word elasticity brings to mind something that can be stretched. Price elasticity of demand refers to the "stretchiness" or the extent to which quantity changes in response to some given price change.

We know that when price is increased less will be bought. The concept of elasticity is concerned with the question of how much less. When the percent change in quantity taken is greater than the percent change in price, we say that the demand is elastic. If the price of T-bone steak is reduced from $1.20 a pound to $.60 (a 50 percent decline) it is quite likely that consumers would buy more than a 50 percent greater quantity.

In a situation where demand is elastic the total expenditures by consumers will increase as you go down the demand curve (Figure 15-6). As price falls from $.70 to $.40, the quantity taken increases from 2 to 14 units. As a result of the relatively larger change in the quantity taken than in price total, expenditure (revenue to sellers) increases from $1.40 ($.70 × 2 units) to $5.60 ($.40 × 14 units). If total expenditures increase as one moves down the demand curve, that portion of the demand curve

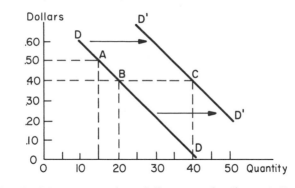

FIGURE 15-5:   Hypothetical Illustration of a Change in Demand.

examined is elastic. The demand for most luxury type items or those not considered necessities is elastic.

Total revenue can decrease as you sell a larger quantity. This may be surprising, but the classic example of salt will quickly prove this point. Most people consume about the same quantity of salt regardless of its price. With salt at 10 cents a box and with a 50 percent reduction in price, one certainly would not expect consumers to buy much more salt. Figure 15-6 (YZ portion) illustrates this inelastic type of demand. In this situation, where price is falling but quantity taken is not increasing at as fast a rate, total consumer expenditure will fall. This is exactly what happens as we move from point Y to point Z in Figure 15-6. Total expenditures decrease from $5.60 ($35 × 16 units) to $3.60 ($15 × 24 units). It is not difficult to think of a number of items which have an inelastic demand. For the most part, items in this group would include necessities. If you smoke it should not be hard to understand this idea.

There is a third type of price elasticity called unitary elasticity. A commodity has unitary price elasticity of demand if relatively equal changes occur in both price and quantity. Since the change in both of the variables is identical, total expenditure remains constant. Looking at Figure 15-6, note that as price falls from $.40 to $.35 the quantity taken increases from 14 to 16. As a result, the total revenue is $5.60 at both points.

A quantitative measurement. In addition to applying the test of total revenue to indicate whether a demand curve is elastic, inelastic, or shows unitary elasticity, we can also derive a precise coefficient of elasticity of demand. The formula for measuring price elasticity of demand is:

$$E_d = \frac{\dfrac{Q_2 - Q_1}{Q_2 + Q_1}}{\dfrac{P_2 - P_1}{P_2 + P_1}} \qquad \text{(see computations in Figure 15-6)}$$

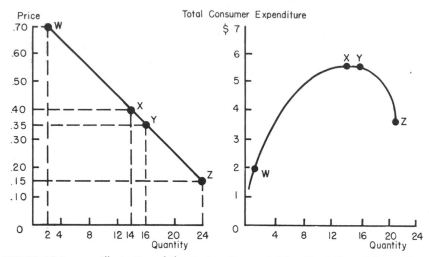

FIGURE 15-6:   Illustration of the Various Types of Price Elasticities of Demand and
Corresponding Total Revenue Functions.

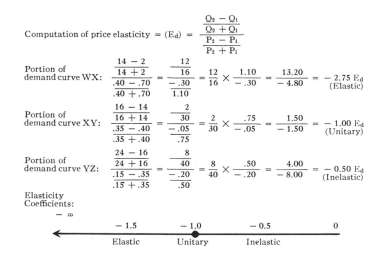

P_1 and Q_1, and P_2 and Q_2 refer to two points on a demand curve. The
formula describes the way to measure the elasticity between these two
points. While this appears to be a rather complicated formula, it is quite
easy to manipulate. The price elasticity coefficient will always have a
minus sign in front of it because there is a negative (inverse) relationship
between the variables of price and quantity in demand. A price elasticity
of demand coefficient between zero and minus 1.0 is inelastic. A coefficient
of minus 1.0 is unitary elasticity, and a coefficient of less than minus 1.0
is elastic (Figure 15-6).

Factors affecting the level of demand

The term "level of demand" refers to the horizontal distance of the demand curve from the price axis. As the demand level increases the curve will shift farther and farther to the right. Conversely, if the demand curve shifts to the left there is a decrease in the level of demand.

The general factors affecting the level of demand are categorized as follows:

Consumer disposable income. Disposable income means that income left for spending on goods and services or for saving after taxes have been paid. This is probably the most important factor affecting the level of demand. For "superior" food products such as T-bone steak and ice cream, there is a direct or positive relationship between income level and demand level. For "inferior" food products such as potatoes and corn meal, there is a negative or inverse relationship between income level and demand level. The positive effect that an increase in income level has on the total demand for goods and services is not difficult to understand. Let us assume that a man's limited income of $100 a week is so arranged that it will purchase an amount of goods and services that will maximize his satisfactions. Now let us assume that he gets a raise of $20 per week. The increased income allows him to rearrange his purchases of goods and services so that he will be able to derive a greater amount of satisfaction. He may want to save some of his increased income but he will probably spend a high percentage of the increase. As incomes increase the proportion spent on food diminishes even though the total dollars spent is greater.

Population. Many people believe that a rapidly expanding population will directly increase demand, contributing to general economic prosperity. However, we need only compare the per capita consumption levels of various products in the United States and India to see that this is not altogether true. An increase in population will definitely have a positive effect on demand level, providing per capita income levels are maintained or increased. Whether or not this is possible depends upon the total productivity of the country. In the United States the rate of real per capita incomes has more than kept pace with the rate of population increases. To date this has not been true in India, for example. The population elasticity of demand for food in the United States is thought to be about 1.0. This means that a one percent increase in population is accompanied by a one percent increase in food consumption.

Changing consumer tastes and preferences. A change in consumer tastes and preferences affects the demand for individual commodities more than it affects the total or aggregate demand. For example, as a result of the emphasis on weight consciousness, supplemented by the health authorities warning people about the intake of large amounts of animal fats, the demand for lard has decreased while the demand for vegetable oils has increased. At the same time the demand for all fats and oils has remained fairly constant.

The introduction of completely new products also tends to shift demand levels among commodities. When the motor car was introduced demand for buggy whips and carriages declined.

Substitute products. Oleomargarine is a substitute for butter and its low price makes it attractive. Other examples could be mentioned. The demand for oranges is directly conditioned by the possible substitution of grapefruit. If there were no synthetic fiber available, consumers would have to use more cotton and wool even if prices were higher.

Other factors. Environmental and cultural factors also affect demand levels. More ice cream is consumed in the summer than in the winter (at equal prices). Holidays alter the demand for turkeys and flowers. National customs and religious beliefs are other factors which also influence demand.

THE DEMAND FOR FOOD PRODUCTS

The generalization already made that necessities have inelastic demands would lead to the correct conclusion that the demand for food is highly inelastic. However, as one would suspect, the demand for individual food items varies widely.

Demand for food items can be measured at two levels in the marketing channel: the retail level and the farm level. The demand for commodities at any point prior to the retail level is called a derived demand —derived from retail prices. For example, the demand for live beef animals as they are ready to leave the farm is derived from the demand for beef in retail stores. In order to derive the demand curve for live animals at the farm level it is necessary to subtract the costs of slaughtering, processing, transporting, and packaging from the retail demand curve. The costs are all necessary to transform a live steer to edible beef. The demand curve D'D' was derived from the demand curve DD in Figure 15-7 by subtracting (vertically) a constant 20 cents for marketing charges. Of red meats, veal, lamb, and mutton show quite elastic demands at retail, beef shows about unitary elasticity, and pork is the least elastic (Table 15-3). Turkey is more elastic than chicken. If retail prices of each red or poultry meat would increase or decrease one percent, which might occur if overall livestock supplies would generally decrease or increase, changes in consumption would be smaller because there would be no incentive to substitute one meat for another. Brandow estimates the expected changes in consumption to be .67 percent for beef, .47 percent for pork, .54 percent for chicken, .70 percent for turkey, and .60 percent for all red and poultry meats collectively.[3] This illustrates the principle that since there are less substitutes for meat than there are for beef the price elasticity for meat as a category of competing products is less elastic than the weighted average for beef. There exists greater substitutability within a class of meats (beef, pork, and mutton) than between groups of meat (red meats, poultry, fish). The greater degree to which the consumer can substitute, the more elastic is the demand.

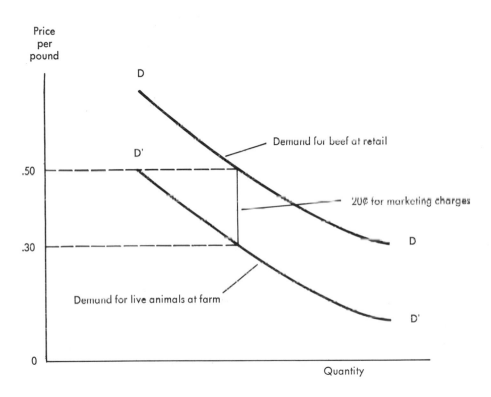

FIGURE 15-7:   Hypothetical Illustration of the Derived Demand for Beef.

This principle helps explain the low price elasticity of demand for all foods and why a relatively small increase in the total quantity of food will drive farm prices down substantially if "dumped" on the market.

In our discussion of marketing we learned that farm prices are lower than retail prices in accordance with the amount of the costs of marketing (marketing margin). In Figure 15-7 the derived demand at the farm was

[3] George E. Brandow, "Interrelations Among Demand For Farm Products and Implications for Control of Market Supply," Bulletin 680, Pennsylvania Agricultural Experiment Station, August 1961, p. 4. These elasticities assume that prices of all red meats and poultry change simultaneously.

illustrated by subtracting the marketing margin. Demands derived from farm level for domestic food use is less elastic than retail demand for foods—much less elastic when marketing margins are large. For example, the price elasticity of eggs, for which the marketing margin is relatively low, changes only from .30 to .23 from retail to farm, while evaporated milk, a more highly processed product with a relatively high marketing margin, changes from .30 to .15. The difference in elasticity at retail and farm levels is another reason why small changes in total farm output cause considerably larger changes in farm prices. The application is equally valid for individual products. At the farm level only calves and sheep appear with elastic demands.

TABLE 15-3: Price Elasticities of Demand for Various Food Products.[1]

Item	Elasticity Retail Level	Farm Level[3]	Item	Elasticity Retail Level	Farm Level
Beef	− .95	− .64	Fluid milk and cream	− .29	− .15
Veal	−1.60	−1.08	Evaporated milk[4]	− .30	− .15
Pork	− .75	− .45	Cheese	− .70	− .38
Lamb and mutton	−2.35	−1.78	Ice Cream	− .55	− .11
Chicken	−1.16	− .74	Fruit	− .60	− .20
Turkey	−1.40	− .92	Vegetables	− .30	− .10
Fish	− .65		Cereals, baking products	− .15	− .03
Butter	− .85	− .66	Sugar and syrups	− .30	− .18
Shortening	− .80		Beverages	− .36	
Margarine	− .80		Potatoes, sweet potatoes	− .20	− .08
Other edible oils	− .46		Dry beans, peas, nuts	− .25	− .08
Lard, direct[2]	− .40	− .40	All foods	− .34	− .23
Eggs	− .30	− .23	Nonfoods	−1.02	
			All goods and services	−1.00	

[1] Assumes that prices of all substitutes remain constant.
[2] Does not include lard contained in shortening and margarine.
[3] Raw product at farm (cattle for beef, hogs for pork, etc.).
[4] Includes condensed milk.
SOURCE: George E. Brandow, "Interrelations Among Demands for Farm Products and Implications for Control of Market Supply," Bulletin 680, Pennsylvania Agricultural Experiment Station, August 1961, data in Tables 1 and 10, pp. 17 and 50.

The grain and livestock economies are highly interrelated because grains and other concentrates are the major input in meat production. Demand for corn, wheat, and other feed grains can also be thought of as derived demands. Brandow's results indicate that:

> . . . with no changes in rates of feeding and apart from the upward trend in total feed requirements, an increase of one percent in the tonnage of concentrates fed increase hog production 1.3 percent, broiler production 1.8 percent, egg production .66 percent; and milk production .33 percent. . . . Weight added in cattle-feeding operations rises 1.9 percent and, with the same number of head slaughtered, the total liveweight cattle slaughter

increases .23 percent. Farm prices of hogs decline 3.5 percent, chickens 3.4 percent, turkeys and eggs 3.2 percent, and beef cattle 1.0 percent. Increased production of lard and butter fat reduces prices of soybean and cottonseed oils about 1.5 percent if their production remains the same. Concentrate prices decline 4.4 percent. . . . Thus the elasticity of demand for feeding purposes is low, only about −.23. Livestock is the principal means by which a large share of total crop production is or might be utilized, but this low elasticity shows how difficult it is to expand utilization through livestock by reducing feed prices . . .[4]

Cross elasticities of demand

It is possible to compute a coefficient to show the effect that a price decrease or increase for one food has on the consumption of another food. This notion is called the cross elasticity of demand between the two commodities. The formula for calculating cross-elasticity coefficients is:

$$\frac{\dfrac{Q_2 - Q_1}{Q_2 + Q_1}}{\dfrac{P_2 - P_1}{P_2 + P_1}} = \text{Cross elasticity coefficient}$$

(where Q is the quantity of one food and P is the price of another)

If two products are easily substitutable for each other (beef and pork) the cross elasticity coefficient will be much greater (more elastic) than for two products which are not good substitutes (beef and coffee). Cross elasticities are also lower at the farm than at retail. For example, Brandow estimates the total cross elasticity of the quantity of cattle demanded on prices of other livestock and poultry to be .18, and the corresponding figure for beef .28.[5] The effect of the price of one farm product on purchases of another is reduced if the first product has a high marketing margin.

Another general relationship is that when all prices of a group of competing products advance, the consumption of the highest ranked luxury item within the group will be affected most. Again, using Brandow's estimates, a one percent advance in *all* fat and oil prices at retail decreases butter consumption by .52 percent but margarine consumption by only .08 percent. Coupled with this is the fact, already mentioned, that the marketing margin is lower for butter than for vegetable oil products.

The tools needed to study how prices are determined in markets will now be considered. The next chapter uses the concept of supply from Chapter 13 and the concept of demand just discussed to study market price determination.

[4] George E. Brandow, *op. cit.*, p. 7.
[5] *Ibid.*, p. 51.

16

Principles of market price determination

One of the major characteristics of capitalistic economies is their heavy reliance upon a price system as a means for allocating society's scarce resources. The importance of resource allocation has been emphasized as being at the very heart of the study of economics. It should be no surprise then that considerable time in the study of economics must be devoted to an understanding of the price system which embodies an understanding of individual market prices.

Even the most casual observer of the American business scene will observe that there are many different kinds of market arrangements in the purchase and sale of goods and services. There is no such thing as a "typical" industry, yet all industries use some form of a price system which, except in a few instances, is not directly regulated by a central governmental authority. For example, at one extreme we may find only a few firms producing aluminum, while at the other extreme there are several million farmers who produce corn. In between is a myriad of situations which are far too numerous to study individually.

A more reasonable approach is to look for certain similar characteristics in industries and classify them. Traditionally, economists have envisioned four relatively distinct market situations. These are pure competition, monopolistic competition, oligopoly, and monopoly. While some business firms do not fall neatly into one of the classifications, the framework is very useful in understanding markets and prices. Furthermore, this classification of economists is not that typically employed by business-men or laymen. These classifications are also necessarily abstractions and do not purport to present a clear picture of the operation of any single business or industry.

MARKET MODELS

Pure competition

The most distinguishing feature of pure competition which sets it apart from all the others is that the individual firm in the industry faces a perfectly elastic demand function (Figure 16-1). As a result, individual

FIGURE 16-1:   An Illustration of the Demand Situation Faced by an Individual Firm in Pure Competition.

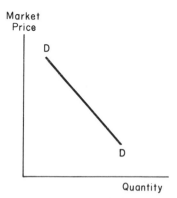

FIGURE 16-2:   Hypothetical Demand Situation Facing the Industry Group in Pure Competition.

firms exert no influence over market price by themselves. They are price-takers and therefore at the mercy of the market.[1]

The reason the individual firm is in this situation stems from two other characteristics of pure competition. The first is the presence of a large number of independent sellers acting individually. The second is that firms in pure competition produce a virtually standardized or homogeneous product. This means that the buyer or consumer of the product is indifferent as to the seller from whom he purchases, since the products are, for all practical purposes, perfectly substitutable for each other. It is fruitless for any particular firm to attempt to extract a price higher than the going market price from the consumer since the purchaser can buy the same product from many other firms at the going market price. Because of the large number of firms the output of each producer makes up a negligible part of the total industry's output. If there were two million corn producers each producing 1,000 bushels, market supply would be two billion bushels. If one producer increased or decreased his output 50 percent, total supply would change by only 500 bushels or .00025 percent. It is apparent that this small change in total supply will not affect market price noticeably. The individual producer, then, sells all he can at the going price. He must adjust to market price since he has no influence on it.[2]

All firms in an industry can, *as a group*, cause market price to vary and the demand situation facing the industry may be highly elastic or inelastic. (Figure 16-2.) For example, using the same illustration, if *all* firms producing corn would change production by 50 percent the total industry supply would change by a similar amount. This would have a very large effect on the going price for corn. Thus, even though price to an individual producer is fixed the market price is free to move up and down in accordance with changing conditions in total demand or total supply.

For pure competition to exist it is necessary that new producers be

---

[1] A distinction is often made between pure and perfect competition. Perfect competition does not exist in any market and is an abstract model helpful to the theoretician. In addition to the requirements for pure competition, perfect competition is typically thought to mean that buyers and sellers have perfect market knowledge and that no other frictions exist; therefore all sales would take place at equilibrium and the price discovery process would be nonexistent.

[2] However, even though the farmer may sell all his wheat at the going price, variation likely exists in the prices at various elevators which are not the result of transportation cost differentials. Farris has shown that a band of prices exist on both sides of the average market price and that the width of the band (magnitude of price differences) varies by commodity and the amount of market information possessed by the buyer and seller. Farris further points out that if either the buyer or seller were more skillful than the other it would be expected that he would influence the location of price transactions within the band of his advantage. See Paul L. Farris, "The Pricing Structure for Wheat," *Journal of Farm Economics* (Volume 40, August 1958, Number 3), p. 622.

free to enter production and that existing firms be free to discontinue production.

When purely competitive firms produce nearly identical products, they have no reason to try to compete with one another on a nonprice basis. If there are virtually no differences in product quality, buyers will recognize the products as the same and advertising efforts by individual farm producers will be of little avail.

These characteristics of pure competition are quite restrictive. However, farming is the one industry which in many instances could be classified as purely competitive. Using wheat as an example, there are a large number of producers. Farmer Brown's wheat may not be identical to Farmer Smith's wheat but through our systems of grading and standardization each market grade of wheat is made to be identical. Similarly, for corn, eggs, and many other commodities, the same situation exists. Even though the eggs produced on several farms are in many ways different, by the time they are graded into quality classes and size classes each market grade class becomes identical and thus meets the criterion of homogeneity necessary in pure competition. Each producer grows a negligible part of the total industry's supply and has no effect on price. The homogeneity of farm products is also reflected by the fact that little advertising is carried on by individual farmers. There is free entry into and exit from the industry with minor exceptions. It is difficult to find other examples in American industry other than farming which meet the requirements of pure competition so well.

Monopoly

At the opposite pole from pure competition is monopoly. Instead of an extremely large number of firms there is only one firm. This single firm's output is thus also the industry's output. The demand situation facing the monopolist firm is likely to be inelastic.

While in a broad sense all goods and services compete for the consumer's dollar and are substitutable for each other, a television set is not a good substitute for an automobile. Buying taxi service is a better substitute for a family-owned automobile but is still an inferior service to most people. Following from the definition of a monopolist as a one-firm industry and applying the idea of substitution in a narrower sense, the monopolist produces a product for which there are no close substitutes. This means that a buyer has no alternative but to purchase from the firm or do without the product.

In direct contrast to the firm in pure competition which has no control over price, the monopolist could exert direct influence (if allowed) on price by manipulating the quantity of product put on the market. It is immediately apparent that the producer or seller could take unfair advantage of the consumer or buyer by charging very high prices. Thus, monopolies are illegal unless franchised and regulated. Examples are the U.S. Post Office and the utility companies. It is also apparent that these type industries, because of the nature of the production process, lend themselves to a monopolistic structure. Imagine the cost if 10 or 20 electric power or telephone companies each strung wires down our highways. To utilize just one set of wires for all is certainly most economical. But to make sure that the electric company does not exploit the public, the rates charged are reviewed and approved by a public utilities commission. The rates set are determined to yield a fair return to the input factors of the electric power company. Typically, after expenses for labor's wages, management's salaries, and other operating costs are substracted from gross profits the utility company is allowed to earn some "fair" percent on capital invested.

Why is there lack of competition for monopolists? The case of industries in which the production process lends itself to monopoly has already been mentioned. To perpetuate a monopoly barriers of an economic, legal, or some other nature must exist to prevent other concerns from entering the field. For example, it would be extremely difficult for a private firm to compete in the mail delivery business.

The extent of advertising by monopolists varies with the product or service offered. It would hardly seem necessary for a water company to advertise since everyone uses water, wants to continue to use water, and will probably not use more water as the result of advertising. It is common, however, to find advertisements by utility companies in local papers, television, and other media. The advertising is mostly of a public relations or "good will" type rather than the advertising of the attributes of water or electricity. The monopolist wants the public to feel well about his company so that consumers do not feel they are being hurt by too high rates or charges. The monopolist is usually quick to point out his firm's technological progress or their contribution to civic projects in the community.

To summarize, in monopoly there is a single firm in the industry producing a product for which there are no good or close substitutes. There are barriers of some nature preventing entry of other firms. Advertising is designed to promote good will toward the public and to explain their service to the community. Private industry monopolies are illegal except those which exist under regulation. Examples are the public utility companies: water, gas, and electricity.

Monopolistic competition

As the name implies, monopolistic competition has some aspects of both pure monopoly and pure competition. It is somewhat closer to pure competition in that a large number of sellers are involved, each of whom produces a fairly small share of the total industry output and thus has a very limited amount of control over market price. However, products of these industries are not homogeneous or standardized as in pure competition. Differences among products are usually slight and may be real or imagined. Many times the only difference is in brand name. Differences in workmanship and the imaginary differences implanted in the consumer's mind by effective advertising and attractive packaging are difficult to separate.

Product differentiation is important in two respects. First, to the extent that consumers have preferences for the products of a particular firm, they will be willing to pay a higher price than for competing products. This allows the seller some small degree of price control and acts as an incentive for him to win the consumer to his slightly differentiated product. Second, in order to win the consumer the seller will probably also engage in nonprice competition, adding a complicating factor to the analysis. The primary emphasis in competing is to win a larger share of the market by offering such things as better services, by extending credit, and by having a more attractive looking store, prettier salesclerks, or giving away trading stamps.

Another important characteristic of monopolistic competition is that no one firm recognizes its rival or feels any mutual interdependence with any other firm. This would seem reasonable in a market of many sellers. Any form of collusion would be ineffective unless a fairly large number of firms were involved. And any gain an individual firm might make by lowering its price would be spread so thinly over its many rivals that their sales loss is negligible and hence brings no retaliation.

Strict adherence to this latter characteristic of no mutual interdependence among firms would seem to rule out practically all real life situations. However, some which are typically listed as firms in monopolistic competition include the apparel and furniture industries.

Entry into monopolistically competitive industries tends to be easy from the standpoint of capital requirements, since individual firms are small. However, if existing firms hold patents and have been successful in building consumer allegiance via advertising, costs of entry and operating may be higher for rivals, making survival difficult.

To summarize, monopolistic competition is a situation where a fairly large number of firms produce slightly differentiated products. No firm recognizes his rival in deciding on price policy. Nonprice competition is emphasized as each producer strives to win a consumer to his particular product which will afford him a small degree of price control. Price competition is still important, however, since entry of new producers is relatively easy.

Oligopoly

Where a few firms dominate an industry and where sellers think of their rival's reaction before setting a price policy, the industry is labeled oligopoly. A moment's reflection brings convincing evidence that oligopoly is the dominant form in American capitalism, not in terms of numbers, but in the total volume of commerce and business.

To the extent that oligopolists produce identical products they are called pure oligopolists. Basic steel and aluminum are examples. However, most oligopolists are differentiated in that they produce differentiated products. Examples of differentiated oligopolists are numerous and would include firms manufacturing automobiles and electrical appliances.

The prime feature of oligopolies, namely, a few firms with each controlling a significant share of the market, necessarily brings about mutual interdependence. One cannot lower its price without considering what its rival will do. If firm a cuts its price and increases its share of the market, firms b and c may note a sizeable loss in sales and in retaliation may also lower price to recapture its previous market share. The net result is that everyone is worse off, with the consumers the only benefactors. It is not long before price competition of this nature is recognized by the sellers as futile. Price wars or competing on a price basis most often hurts every seller.

The reason that oligopolists most often choose to compete on a nonprice basis is clear. The oligopolist, being rather powerful, is usually in a better financial position to compete on a nonprice basis. More funds are available for advertising and product development and he must not only advertise in an attempt to expand his market share but merely to hold steady his market share.

The paucity of firms in oligopoly suggests some barriers to entry; otherwise firm numbers would increase considerably. In some of the manufacturing industries, such as automobiles, there are considerable economies in large scale production. As as result, huge amounts of capital would be required to enter the industry and produce at an efficient size. Also, any new competitor would need to have large amounts of operating capital to carve out a niche in the market, as existing firms already have a large number of consumers convinced that their product is best. In the past half century, where economies of size do exist, the trend has been for firm numbers to decrease because some firms have not been able to produce efficiently or to gain a large enough share of the market due to ineffective advertising or lack of funds for advertising and product development. Other barriers to entry may include such factors as ownership of strategic patents or control of raw material sources. In terms of advertising outlays creating an effective barrier by themselves, the cigarette industry is the classic example.

Some industries must be classified as oligopolies even though firm numbers are large and entry is easy. These include the gas stations, barber shops, and restaurants where, within a given locality, the reaction of rivals must be considered in setting price policies. Some of the most vicious price wars have occurred in retailing gasoline. Here again the most common form is for all to charge the same price and compete for share of the market solely on a nonprice and service basis. Entry and exit occur continuously in these industries and they are often referred to as the "sick" or "overcrowded" industries. The rigid price charged by all is usually excessively high, since fixed resources are highly underutilized. Total returns and profits to owners are usually low because a large number of firms force market shares to be quite small for each seller. For firms in these industries to succeed, they need a particular desirable location or a unique ability to compete successfully on a nonprice basis.

In summary, the two primary factors of oligopolies are fewness of firms and recognition of rivals' existence in establishing pricing policies. Nonprice competition is prevalent and advertising expenditures may be heavy to assure consumer loyalty in holding a share of the market. There is often a going industry price maintained by tacit collusion. Entry is difficult in those oligopolies where capital investment is high and large economies of size exist. Some oligopolies, such as gas stations, afford easy entry, but excessive numbers of firms make financial success difficult because market shares are low in most instances. Oligopoly is the predominant market form in American industry.

MARKETS IN AGRICULTURAL AND NONAGRICULTURAL INDUSTRIES

The only industry which approaches the conditions of pure competition is farming. The farmers producing corn, wheat, cotton, feed grains, soybeans, hogs, cattle, sheep, broilers, eggs, etc. have no control over market price. However, for some raw food products, such as cranberries or walnuts, the number of producers is relatively small and they may be able to exercise some control over prices through joint action. Often the group of producers exercises control through a marketing cooperative association. Also in the case of milk, for example, producers may exercise control via bargaining associations. These latter situations are encouraged where the production of the commodity is geographically concentrated or where the perishability of the products keeps it from moving long distances before consumption. The tendency for a greater amount of collective action on the part of farmers is stimulated by the lack of price control by the individual.

In the agribusiness complex, including both the farm supply industries and the processing and food distribution industries, one finds many degrees of imperfect competition. The poultry breeding, farm machinery, and meat-packing industries are examples of a few large firms dominating the industry and therefore meeting an important criterion of oligopoly. A common situation can be noted in the food retailing and feed processing industries, where there are several large firms and many small ones. In these cases, small independents seem to be surviving and competing successfully. The relative use and importance of price versus nonprice competition varies widely. Food retailers compete heavily in both kinds while bankers loaning money to farmers compete virtually entirely on a service or nonprice basis. Thus, there is no general rule. Again the delineation of the four market models is just an analytical aid in helping to understand the real world. Businesses cannot be classified neatly into any of these categories except in a few instances. The four-model framework does allow us to understand and perhaps predict the policies that will be followed in particular cases.

AN ALTERNATIVE APPROACH [3]

Another framework for explaining how markets behave and the differences among them has recently been outlined by Bain. Bain is concerned with the environmental setting within which similar enterprises operate and perform as an industry. Elements of market structure and conduct are outlined and discussed with reference to their effect on market performance crucial in an enterprise economy.

Market structure refers to how a market is organized, with particular emphasis on the characteristics which determine the relationship among the various sellers in the market, among the various buyers, and among the buyers and sellers in a market. In other words, market structure deals with the organization of a market as it influences the nature of competition and pricing within a market. Bain discusses four strategic elements:

1. *The degree of seller concentration.* How many sellers are there in the industry? How large and how important are they? Are there a few large ones, several large ones and many small ones, or only many small ones?

2. *The degree of buyer concentration.* How many buyers are there for the product? How much do they buy?

[3] For a discussion, see Joe S. Bain, *Industrial Organization* (New York: John Wiley and Sons, Inc., 1959). Italicized portions that follow appear on pages 8-12.

3. *The degree of product differentiation.* Product differentiation has the same meaning here as in the previous discussion of market models.

4. *The condition of entry to the market.* Is the market open to new producers or are there barriers to entry? How much influence can existing farms exercise in keeping new competitors out? Do existing firms own strategic patents or raw material sources that make entry difficult?

Market conduct refers to the ways firms adjust to the markets in which they are engaged as sellers or buyers. Generally, market conduct is concerned with the pricing policies of a firm as a seller and with its recognition of other firms in decisions regarding product development, advertising, and so on. Specifically, Bain outlines five dimensions of market conduct:

1. *The principle and the method employed by the firm or group of firms in calculating or determining price and output.* Is the objective to maximize profits to an individual firm or a to a group of firms, or is the concept of a "fair" profit used in setting prices? Are all buyers charged the same price?

2. *The product policy of the firm or group of firms.* Are efforts made to improve the product's quality through individual efforts or group efforts? What orientation does product change take?

3. *The sales promotion policy of the firm or group.* How much advertising is done by individual firms and by group action? What determines the volume of advertising expenditures?

4. *Means of coordination and cross-adaptation of price, product, and sales-promotion policies of competing sellers.* Are there any collusive agreements with regard to prices, products, or sales promotion expenditure? Is there tacit collusion in the form of price leadership by one major firm in the industry? Are collusive agreements abrogated by secret price-cutting, leading to imperfect collusion? How closely are rivals' prices analyzed when changing prices?

5. *Presence or absence of, and extent of, predatory or exclusionary tactics.* Is there price-cutting with the objective of wiping out competitors? Are there attempts by individual firms to monopolize strategic raw materials? Are there binding contracts with buyers so that other competitors cannot sell to them? Are there restrictive uses of patent licensing?

Market performance refers to the end results which are essentially brought about by the nature of the market structure and the way firms conduct themselves.

Market performance includes:

1. *The price relative to the average cost of production, and thus the size of profits.* From society's viewpoint a price which just covers cost of production is ideal. This price assumes a fair return to the inputs used in production but allows no excess profits. This ideal would be reached under conditions of pure competition.

2. *The relative efficiency of production so far as this is influenced by the scale or size of plants and firms relative to the most efficient, and by the extent, if any, of excess capacity.* Are firms operating with a plant of sufficient size to avoid excess capacity resulting in higher costs? If excess capacity exists is it because there are too many firms trying to operate in the industry or because of a temporary lack of demand?

3. *The size of sales-promotion costs relative to the costs of production.* Are promotion costs excessively high? What percent are advertising costs of the total costs of production?

4. *The character of the product, including choice of design, level of quality, and variety of product within any market.* Is the quality of the products of the industry high? Is there any variety available to the consumer? Are products excessively improved to the point where buyers would prefer lower quality at a lower cost?

5. *The rate of progress of the firm and industry in developing both products and techniques of production.* Are firms attempting to find cost-reducing techniques? One indication might be the scope of their research activity. Do firms try to discover what the consumer wants? Does the firm have a good public image?

Bain's approach to looking at the various kinds of markets is not in any way contradictory to the previous discussion or to the four market models of pure competition, monopoly, monopolistic competition, and oligopoly. The approach is different. Understanding each should be helpful about the markets for goods and services where buyers and sellers meet.

PRICE DISCOVERY AND DETERMINATION

The concepts of supply and demand have been explained in detail in Chapters 13 and 15 respectively. We will now study the interactions of supply and demand in price determinations. Since we have discussed two kinds of markets (purely competitive and imperfectly competitive) it will be necessary to talk about price determination for both.

Purely competitive market pricing

While it is correct to say that market price is determined by the forces of supply and demand, let us delve a bit deeper. Why is this so? Consider the situation depicted in Figure 16-3, where the market price settles at $1.00 per unit and 500 units are sold. How and why did this come about?

As you remember, demand represents what buyers are willing to take from a market at a given price, while supply represents what pro-

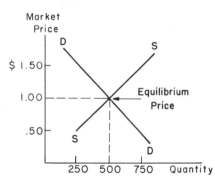

FIGURE 16-3:   A Graphical Portrayal of Equilibrium Price Determined by Intersection of Supply and Demand.

ducers or sellers are willing to offer. Because the relationship between
price and quantity is negative for demand but positive for the supply
relationship, the two functions must intersect each other at some point.
This point of intersection traces out the equilibrium price and quantity in
a purely competitive market. This is not to say that the sale of each unit
of the commodity will move at exactly the equilibrium price, although
theoretically if all buyers and sellers had perfect and complete market
information all sales would take place at this one price.

In a sense, then, buyers and sellers are trying to discover the equilibrium price. And as sales are made in a market the market price of any
one transaction adds to and makes more complete and valid the actual
supply and demand situation in the market. In the hypothetical case
posed in Figure 16-3, as soon as a buyer who paid $1.25 noted others
paying less he would probably tell himself that he paid too high a price
and would not do so again. On the other hand, the seller who received the
$1.25 probably feels quite fortunate and would not expect to do that well
again. The opposite situation with regard to feeling of a buyer and
seller would exist after a sale transaction at a price of $.75. Thus, in a
competitive market with a large number of transactions taking place the
price will tend to settle closer and closer to $1.00, the true equilibrium
price. Markets approximating this situation would be grain, fruit, and
livestock auction markets. The prices quoted in the newspapers for these
and other commodities can be thought of as approximating or equalling
the true equilibrium prices. Of course each new day brings a changed
set of supply and demand conditions which result in price fluctuations.

It should also be remembered that the elasticity of the supply function depends upon the time period involved. It is often said that market
price is demand determined in a very short time period—perhaps one
market day (Figure 16-4). In a time period short enough that sellers

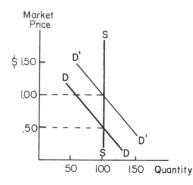

FIGURE 16-4:   Equilibrium Price Determination in a Very Short Time Period at Two
                    Demand Levels.

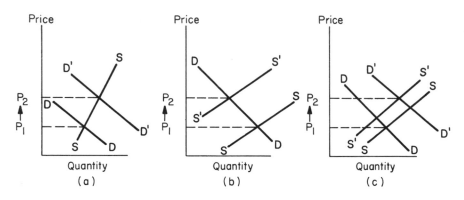

FIGURE 16-5:   Price Increases Resulting From Changes in Supply and Demand.

cannot offer more to the market than the amount on hand, as indicated
by the perfectly inelastic supply function in Figure 16-4, a very high level
of demand would push the price to $1.00. In this sense, price is deter-
mined virtually by demand alone. We shall see later, however, that
whether one of these prices persists or not is considerably dependent on
supply, which is in turn determined by the producer's cost of production
and profit potential at the particular price. The situation depicted in
Figure 16-3 would tend to represent more of a long-run situation, as indicated by a greater elasticity in the supply curve.

Effect on equilibrium price of changes in supply and demand. Price
will tend to rise in response to the following: (a) demand increases with
no change in supply, and (b) supply decreases with no change in demand
(Figures 16-5a and 16-5b). A relatively larger price will occur when
supply decreases and demand increases simultaneously (Figure 16-5c).

Price will tend to fall in response to the following: (a) demand decreases with no change in supply, and (b) supply increases with no change in demand (Figure 16-6a and 16-6b). A relatively large decline in price will occur if supply increases and demand decreases simultaneously (Figure 16-6c).

If supply and demand change in the same directions in equal magnitudes the equilibrium price will tend to remain unchanged (Figure 16-7a and 16-7b).

Price determination in imperfectly competitive markets

Monopoly. In single firm industries the seller will attempt to set a price which will maximize his profit. This price would be determined without regulation from the demand curve, corresponding to the quantity where marginal cost is equated with marginal revenue (Figure 16-8). Under regulation, the monopolist would probably be forced to reduce his price to P_2 in Figure 16-8, a price where he is just able to recover full costs. Full costs would include a fair return to factor inputs. Most often regulatory commissions allow monopolies such as the utility company to earn a return of 6 percent above explicit costs on the capital invested. The utility company is then allowed to set a price which will yield this return.

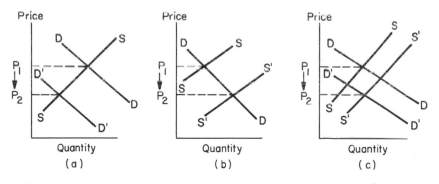

FIGURE 16-6:   Price Decreases Resulting From Changes in Supply and Demand.

Oligopoly and monopolistic competition. Pricing in oligopoly and monopolistically competitive markets is complicated by many factors. As a result, no attempt will be made here to translate pricing by one firm into terms of equilibrium prices similar to pure competition. The rigidity of price, particularly in oligopolies, has already been discussed. But how the price is established at the level used by each and all firms is another matter. Details of profit maximizing by firms is discussed in Chapter 14.

Often in oligopolistic industries a price leader will emerge whose price policies will be followed by other firms in the industry. U.S. Steel is an example for the 25 years prior to 1962. In service industries such as morticians and barbers, price may be more or less tacitly agreed upon and controlled through their professional associations.

Cartels or written agreements among producers to share markets and price stipulation are illegal. So are other *sub rosa* or written forms of collusion where it can be proved that the public is hurt from market price agreements. Therefore, a form of tacit collusion emerges in manufacturing oligopolies, a "live and let live" policy where nonprice competition largely determines the share of the market each firm has. Firms strive to increase their profits via advertising to get a larger market share and to reduce unit costs through more efficient methods. The price charged for products changes rarely and is at a level allowing the major firms to continue production.

THE ALLOCATIVE ROLE OF PRICES

Now that price determination has been discussed, what role do prices play in an economy? The price received times the number of units sold determines the total gross revenue or return for any business. After the firm subtracts all of its operating costs the amount left over is available to pay dividends to stockholders or owners of the business. If price persists at a low level and the firm cannot reduce its cost of production, it will necessarily be forced to cut production and probably go out of business. On the other hand, if price is at a high level, returns above costs that are often called profits will be high and will encourage the firm to continue and perhaps expand production.

Prices dictate then, to a considerable extent, the production or output level of any good or service over time. And since resources are required to produce goods and services, it follows that prices provide the allocative mechanism in the economy which directs resources into use. Take the example of buggy whips. With the advent of the automobile which replaced the horse-drawn buggy for transportation, consumers stopped voting for buggy whips, the price fell, buggy whip manufacturers went broke, and resources were no longer channeled into buggy whip production.

The price mechanism in its allocative role is a basic ingredient in a free private enterprise system. It is a system where no one individual, no level of government, and no other planning authority has to be conscious of effecting the "proper" resource allocation in society's interest. In our economy, profits or returns above cost provide the incentive for individual initiative. Profits are the "carrot before the donkey" that has allowed our economy to achieve a high level of production and thus

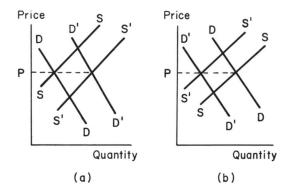

FIGURE 16-7: Price Stability With Changes in Supply and Demand.

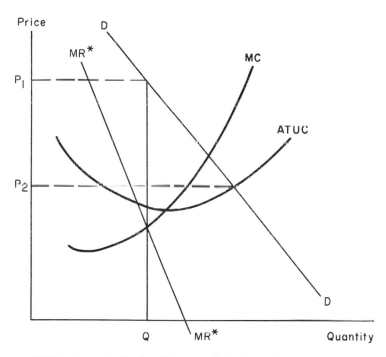

*MR is not equal to D when D is not perfectly elastic. MR will always be at points midway between the Y axis and the D curve.

FIGURE 16-8: Pricing by Single Firm Monopolist.

achieve a high standard of living for the American people. However, modifications of the price system, particularly in imperfectly competitive industries, was noted. In part VI further modifications of the price system by government action will be discussed in policy context.

THE TIME ELEMENTS IN PRICES

Relationship of price to cost of production (Pure Competition)

Day-to-day fluctuations in prices occur primarily for three reasons: (a) fluctuations in demand, (b) fluctuations in supply, and (c) experimentation in the price discovery process. Price changes occurring for these reasons in time periods of less than one production cycle bear practically no relationship to the cost of production.

However, over a longer period of time price tends to move toward and become equal to cost of production.[4] Why is this so? Let us assume that in any particular year the majority of producers in a competitive industry were able to earn an excess profit—returns above what would be considered fair return for the input factors used. Such a situation is depicted in Figure 16-9(a). The individual producer is selling 10 units at a price of $.80 for a total revenue of $8.00. His costs are $.65 per unit, or $6.50, yielding him an excess profit of $1.50. This excess profit will attract new producers to the industry the following year, generating the situation in Figure 16-9(d). The increased supply will drive price downward (toward cost of production) until the individual producer has his excess profits squeezed away from him (Figure 16-9b) and until the industry equilibrium of supply and demand conditions exists as shown in Figure 16-9(e).

Beginning with the opposite situation where the individual producer is experiencing short-run losses as in Figure 16-9(c), what will happen? Again conditions will evolve to push the individual to the situation illustrated in Figure 16-9(b) and the industry to the situation shown in Figure 16-9(e). Why? When producers experience losses, at least some will cut back or discontinue production entirely in the following year. A decrease in supply in the industry will drive price upward the following year, as indicated in Figure 16-9(f). Thus, regardless of whether excess profits or losses are being incurred in the short-run time period, forces will be put

---

[4] This does not necessarily mean that price will eventually become equal to the cost of production with the passage of time. The tendency is always present for price to move towards the cost of production but imperfect elements in the market may prevent it from doing so; the rigid price in oligopoly is an example. Thus, a type of "permanent disequilibrium" may occur or new and changing market elements may continually cause 'new' disequilibriums.

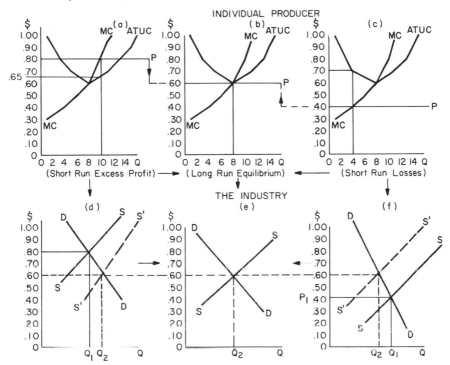

FIGURE 16-9:   Movement of Price Toward Cost of Production in a Purely Competitive
Industry.

in motion which will tend to generate long-run equilibrium for the individual producer and the industry, as depicted in Figures 16-9(b) and 16-9(c) respectively.

Seasonal price variation

Commodities where production and marketings vary within the year experience seasonal price variation. Virtually all agricultural commodity prices fit this pattern. Seasonality in crop production arises from the weather cycle. Livestock production is influenced by the reproduction period and seasonal changes in weather that affect pasture and other feed supplies. The magnitude of seasonal price variation is lessening as both crop production and particularly animal production increasingly occur under partially or completely controlled environmental conditions.

The seasonal nature of production affects prices in two ways. First, perishable or semiperishable commodities which are difficult to store must move into consumption at harvest time. The increased quantity is moved to consumers only at lower prices. Then when market receipts diminish as the commodity becomes out of season, higher prices can be obtained. Examples of foods that fit this pattern well are lettuce, broccoli, oranges, strawberries, and pork and beef to a lesser extent.

Second, nonperishable commodities which can be stored tend to have their lowest price at harvest time. Then price generally tends to rise during the remainder of the year by an amount approximately sufficient to cover storage costs. The year's production is channeled into consumption in rather evenly distributed amounts over the year.

Prices during the year are affected not only by day-to-day supply and demand conditions but also by anticipated or future supply and demand conditions. These latter fluctuations should not be considered as part of seasonal price variation. Another influencing factor for some commodities is government-owned stocks and the expected way in which these supplies will be fed into market channels.

Some commodities, such as hogs, cattle, and milk can be used for more than one purpose. When cattle receipts increase, the quantity of fresh beef sold increases and the price falls. However, part of a steer can be processed into canned meats which can be stored for a considerable length of time. Milk can be sold fresh or manufactured into cheese, butter and other products which are not nearly as perishable. In these instances the seasonal price fluctuation is less than it would be if the commodity's form could not be changed to a less perishable one.

In Table 16-1 the seasonal price variation in Indiana farm prices is exhibited. Note the low corn, wheat, and potato prices at harvest time. Whole milk prices are lowest in June when pasture conditions are good and when cows move into peak production after the more common spring

TABLE 16-1: Seasonal Price Index Variation for Selected Commodities in Indiana (1956-60 = 100).

Month	Hogs	Choice Steers[1]	Whole Milk	Eggs	Corn	Soybeans	Wheat	Potatoes
				(Price Index)				
January	96	97	107	98	94	101	104	97
February	95	96	104	100	95	100	103	100
March	100	102	101	103	97	101	105	108
April	102	104	95	100	104	103	105	116
May	105	103	90	92	106	103	102	117
June	108	100	88	88	107	103	93	117
July	108	100	90	94	108	103	94	111
August	106	102	95	99	110	102	94	98
September	100	103	101	104	106	94	96	84
October	94	100	107	109	91	94	98	79
November	91	98	111	108	88	97	102	85
December	95	95	111	105	94	99	104	88

[1] Chicago terminal prices.

SOURCE: J. H. Armstrong and R. L. Kohls, "Seasonal Variation in Indiana Farm Prices," Research Bulletin 766 (Lafayette, Indiana, Purdue University Agricultural Experiment Station, September, 1963).

calving period. For eggs the low price month is June (88) and the high is October (109)—a fluctuation from low to high of only 21 points. However, in 1943 the average egg price for the United States ranged from a low index of 82 in March, April, and May to a high of 138 in November. This is a range of 56 points. This example of less seasonal price variation over time fits for most agricultural commodities.

Annual price variations

While the general proposition that price tends to move toward cost of production has been discussed, annual price changes deserve more of our attention. Annual price fluctuations are most characteristic of crops where year-to-year changes in production occur as acreage and yields change. Fluctuations in demand are less important in influencing annual price changes.

There seems to be little regularity in the annual variation in crop prices. Severe fluctuations in weather may result in several successive or alternating periods of large and small quantity crops. Disregarding the influence of government programs, evidence suggests that several years of high or low prices are necessary to markedly influence crop acreages. As a result, it is variations in yields influenced by the weather and technology which account for most of the change in annual production.

The resulting year-to-year price variations for individual commodities is widely varied. Year-to-year percentage variations in prices for the long period between 1920 and 1955 are as follows: [5]

Whole milk	6.1
Beef cattle	9.7
Wheat	13.7
Corn	17.8
Hogs	15.3
Soybeans	19.2
Potatoes	48.7

Individual commodity prices also fluctuate around the general farm price level in divergent patterns. Whole milk prices, for example, tend to move in close harmony with the farm price level, while others, such as potatoes and hogs fluctuate around the overall farm price level in an uncertain fashion.

When the pattern of annual price changes is superimposed onto the farm price level, which revolves widely around the general price level, the study of prices and their movements become very complex. The importance of price fluctuations as it influences the farmer and agricultural policy formulation will be discussed in more detail later.

[5] Wilcox and Cochrane, op. cit., p. 263.

part IV

17

Managing the farm business

The history of farm management goes far back. One of the earliest known works concerning farm management was written by Cato over 2000 years ago. Although much of the original work in farm management was based on trial and error plus farmer experience, in recent years great strides have been made in combining scientific analysis with the aspects of the farming arts.

WHAT IS FARM MANAGEMENT?

Farm management is the combination of science and art applied to maximize the economic profitability from a given set of resources. Farm management is concerned primarily with the individual farm unit and is therefore a form of business management. The farm manager is concerned with knowing what factors affect farm profit. He attempts to control these factors so that the economic returns to the farm unit will be high.

It is important to distinguish between the farmer and farm management. Farm management is devoted to profitability; the farmer is concerned with maximizing his and his family's total satisfaction, both economic and noneconomic. The final farm plan will be determined not only by the farm manager, the farm's resources, and the farmer's economic commitments (loans, etc.) but also by the farmer's and his family's goals and preferences as they reflect their ultimate desires and values.

ROLE OF THE FARM MANAGER

The managerial functions have been described in Chapter 14. Each manager repeats these functions as he conducts his farm business. They cannot be eliminated, although the extent to which any one function is emphasized will vary among managers and the kind of problem situation encountered. Throughout the process of decision making the manager should leave time for evaluation of his progress. The time spent on reflection and consideration of the items included in the managerial functions will allow continual modification of previous management decisions. These changes will, in turn, permit a greater degree of managerial efficiency in future management decisions.

Farm management decisions

Types. Farm managers consider two main types of planning decisions. One is *organizational* planning, which involves such things as farm layout, mapping soil productivity, drainage, and building layout. This area also involves calculating the farm's resources of land, labor, and capital both from a physical count aspect (425 acres, 46 cows, 3 tractors, etc.), and from a quality aspect as well (425 acres—100 acres flat, extremely fertile; 125 acres gently rolling, fertile but subject to slight erosion, some gullies; 100 acres, rolling pasture, sodded, no erosion; 100 acres rough woodland). Organizational decisions involve most questions beginning with *what:* what enterprises to have, what buildings and machinery are needed, and so on.

The second type of planning is sometimes called *operational* planning. It involves questions beginning with *how:* how to combine the various factors of production on the farm, how to do the work associated with each enterprise (family labor or hired labor), how to use the land, how to harvest the crops, and how to handle the livestock.

Importance. While the farm manager is almost constantly involved in the decision-making process, not all of his decisions are of the same importance. The frequency with which certain decisions have to be made is one aspect of their relative importance. The most frequent decisions are concerned with the day-to-day operation of the farm. Although the daily pattern of feeding livestock, for example, may become routine, constant decisions regarding levels of feeding are required since feed input must be altered at various stages of animal growth.

Other decisions a farm manager makes may occur only once during a production cycle. Deciding which variety of corn to plant, how many calves to save for breeding purposes, and how many acres of soybeans to plant this crop year are some examples. In most cases, these decisions are relatively more important than day-to-day decisions since a decision one year may have residual effects that carry over to the next production cycle. Use of a herbicide for weed control this year might restrict what could be planted on the same plot of ground the next year. Some of the most far-reaching decisions are those relative to livestock breeding programs where over a long period, type, conformity, and feeding efficiency are all affected.

Decisions regarding the acquisition of new land, the construction of new farm buildings, and the purchase of farm machinery are examples of decisions that are of large relative importance but made less frequently. The long-run success of a farmer is highly dependent upon these types of decisions and they are very difficult to make because the manager has incomplete information about the future.

The importance of farm management decisions are also influenced by the size of dollar outlay involved. The decision to purchase another 100 acres of land is of considerably greater importance than the decision to buy a new set of spark plugs for the tractor. An irrevocable decision is of more importance than one that can be retracted at a later date. There are additional factors that affect the importance of a decision such as the effect it may have on the goals of the farm family as well as its effect on the profitability of the farm business.

Factors increasing the difficulty of decision-making. There are a number of factors which increase the difficulty of management decision-making. First, the manager must continually cope with a *lack of current information* on all aspects of farming. He must keep up to date on all prices that are relevant to his farm business. The changing costs of inputs must be weighed and evaluated to see whether one factor might profitably be substituted for another in the production process (see Figure 3, Chapter 12, Appendix). New markets may open up and old ones disappear. Competition from other food products may change the price structure for the farm commodities the farmer produces. Quality requirements of products can change. The farm manager must keep his technical ability current in all the production methods that apply to his farm enterprises. He must be constantly on the lookout for new ideas and innovations he might adopt if he is to maximize income.

A second broad area of problems is concerned with the manager's ability to adjust profitably to market *price changes, institutional changes,* and *political changes.* Changes in local market structure, such as the introduction of a new marketing and supply cooperative in the area, may offer the manager a chance to possibly improve his profits. He must weigh the ability of these changes to affect his profit and must adjust his farming and marketing operations so that he may take advantage of them if they offer him increased economic opportunity. Perhaps the most visible change in this category has been a marketing organization which allows payment for efforts to improve quality of product and limit the amount offered on the market. Shopping for the best credit sources, such as those with low rates of interest combined with managerial help to their borrowers, is another adjustment with which many farmers are confronted. Choosing whether or not to participate in government price and production programs is another area of adjustment. The large response of farmers to the Wheat Referendum of 1963 is an example of the nationwide farmer expression of interest and concern with government policies. Other institutional adjustments include decisions about urban sprawl and planning and zoning as metropolitan centers and population satellites expand into rural farm areas.

A third area is *risk*. Risk is reflected partially in income fluctuations and can be insured against formally and informally. Crop insurance, title insurance, fire insurance, and livestock insurance are examples of formal insurance. Premiums are paid to shift the risk from the farmer to a company which specializes in handling large numbers of similar farm risks. The company is able to calculate the probabilities of damage for the individual manager, and offers to assume his potential loss for an insurance premium. Informal insurance includes methods in which the individual farmer attempts to minimize production losses or fluctuations in income. Traditional examples of informal insurance are the extent to which a farmer engages in specialized or diversified production. Specialization helps to increase production efficiency because the manager's knowledge and technical ability is concentrated upon only one or a few enterprises rather than many, because there is a greater opportunity for increased volume of production because of this concentrated technical ability, and because the capital resources of the farm unit are concentrated in the production of one item rather than many. Specialization gives rise to economizing of size both in purchasing inputs and in selling output. The Los Angeles milkshed dairies operating within the city limits are excellent examples. Here the cows are milked in a continuous rotation 24 hours a day. All feed, stock, and labor are bought. The job revolves around feeding and milking cows, scheduling the necessary labor to milk the cows, and seeing that the milk is sold according to the distribution agreement. Diversification means that several independent enterprises are engaged in within roughly the same annual income period. A farm may be diversified with many different enterprises (horizontal diversification), or may engage in many steps in the production of a single product (vertical diversification). Choosing the size of enterprise and choosing the kind of enterprise (dairy produces steady income, as opposed to a livestock feeding operation which may produce high profits or severe losses) are also ways in which the farm manager may informally insure against risk.

A fourth problem area involves the *fixity of farm resources*, their utilization, their salvage value if any, and how best to combine them with the variable resources at hand in order to maximize farm income. Increased volume of production lowers per unit costs of production and helps explain why farmers buy more machinery and equipment (applied technology) when faced with declining farm prices.

So far this discussion has only touched on the broad areas of managerial functions, and problem areas that continually confront the farm manager. However, the farm manager must successfully apply his decision-making abilities in three areas in order to run his farm business profitably: in the area of production, in the marketing area, and in the area of financing. Each of these areas will be discussed in more detail later in this chapter. Let us first look at the principal tools which the farm manager can employ in decision making.

TOOLS FOR MANAGERIAL ANALYSIS AND DECISION MAKING

To make good decisions a manager must continually collect information and learn about his business. He needs to have the relevant facts and an understanding of economic principles so that his decisions will be economically sound. Some of the facts needed are economic facts, such as price information. Other kinds of facts are technical in nature, such as the rate of gain that can be expected by feeding a steer a particular ration under given conditions. Records are a way to record both kinds of facts needed by the farm manager.

Farm and business records

Although there are many types of farm records, most are kept for income tax purposes and/or analysis and farm planning. As with other businesses, accurate accounting of financial transactions for income tax purposes is an important consideration. The minimum needs include listing of cash receipts and expenses, preparing a depreciation schedule, and recording capital gains or losses that are applicable to the current business year. Other reasons for keeping records include: to record financial growth, to aid in borrowing money, to make partnership and tenant-landlord relations more explicit, and to make farming more businesslike and intellectually rewarding.

Farmers may keep tax records on either the cash or accrual basis. On a cash basis, receipts and expenses are recorded when the actual payment is made or received by the farmer. Under the accrual system, receipts and expenses are recorded when earned or incurred without reference to the time when the money changes hands. Most farmers find the cash system easier and simpler than the accrual method. It avoids the problems of recording changes in inventory and allows for a more even distribution of income and expenses from year to year.

While records are an important source of information, there are other ways a farm manager can learn which are often overlooked. The United States Department of Agriculture publishes many reports on all aspects of agriculture. There are monthly situation reports with titles such as: The National Food Situation, The Marketing and Transportation Situation, The Livestock and Meat Situation, The Feed Situation, The Wheat Situation, The Fruit Situation, The Vegetable Situation, The Fats and Oils Situation, The Cotton Situation, The Dairy Situation, and The Farm Income Situation. There are crop and livestock reports and a flow of research bulletins on most any topic in which a farm manager needs help. There are the many farm magazines, the reports from the state and district offices of the Agricultural Extension Service and the information disseminated from the state university. Manufacturers of farm inputs hire technical sales representatives who often have valuable technical information to give farmers in their efforts to stimulate sales. Trade associations such as the American Meat Institute provide information of use by livestock producers. Agricultural colleges and universities host field days and organize farm tours giving further opportunities to learn. And, of course, radio, television, and newspapers are other media a farmer can use to increase his learning. A good manager will learn how to take advantage of these and other ways to improve his managerial capacity.

Financial records. Some of the financial records that may be kept by the farmer include: an inventory and balance sheet, a ledger of cash receipts and expenses, and a depreciation schedule. From these records a summary can be prepared of the several measures of overall farm success, including farm income, labor income, and percent return on capital investment.

The balance sheet or net worth statement is a record of financial growth, often referred to as a net worth statement. A balance sheet is prepared by listing assets and liabilities. The listing of assets is an inventory and involves recording everything that is owned (whether or not it be free of debt). Farm real estate, livestock, equipment, feed and supplies on hand, cash in the bank, accounts receivable, growing crops, and anything else to which one has title is included. Usually, personal assets which have nothing to do with the farm operation are also included, such as the family car, household furniture and equipment, stocks and bonds. Assets may be divided into two categories: current and fixed. The differentiation is determined by how readily convertible to cash the asset is. Asset values are imputed and putting a "correct" dollar value on them is difficult. Usually a conservative market value is the best policy for stored crops. Possible ways to evaluate longer life capital assets are (a) replacement cost, (b) original cost minus depreciation, and (c) value if the income stream resulting from the asset can be capitalized (see Chapter 7).

Liabilities include items which are owed to others. Common items include unpaid bills for feed, fertilizer, electricity, notes due at the bank, and mortgages on real estate. A differentiation may also be made between current and fixed liabilities, the criterion for classification depending on time of repayment. A mortgage payment due ten years from now is a fixed liability. A feed bill due next week would be current.

Net worth is the difference between total assets and total liabilities, and can be a negative figure. It is the amount of money you would have left should you sell off all of your assets and then pay off all of your liabilities. When net worth is added to total liabilities the balance sheet is made to "balance."

The balance sheet is the financial record which your banker wants to see when you approach him to borrow money. He will probably want personal assets and liabilities included in addition to those pertinent in operating the farm business.

A depreciation schedule is prepared for capital items which have a useful life of more than one year, and hence their initial cost cannot be written off as a business expense in the year that they are purchased. Farm buildings, farm machinery and equipment, breeding and dairy live stock, fences and tile, orchards and vineyards, and wells are the common items for which a depreciation schedule is prepared. The discussion of costs in Chapter 12 listed depreciation as one of the fixed type costs which have no bearing on determining the most profitable level of production.

The difficult question with regard to depreciation is how much of the initial cost of a capital item such as a tractor should be charged against each year's business operation over its expected life. An easy method is to charge equal dollar amounts against each year of expected life. This is called the "straight line method." For example, if a new tractor were purchased in January for $4,000 and its expected life was eight years, $500 of depreciation expense would be charged against the farm operation in each of the succeeding eight years. This method is more commonly used on buildings and livestock.

Since 1954 other methods which allow a more "rapid write-off" or greater depreciation expense in the early life of the item have been legal. These methods, used principally for machinery and equipment, allow the book value (original cost minus any depreciation expense taken) to more nearly approximate the market value over the life of the item. A common method is called the "declining balance method." With this method a constant percentage of the book value is taken in arriving at any year's depreciation expense. The percentage allowed for new items is two times the straight line rate. If used equipment is bought, only 1½ times the straight line rate is allowed. For example, using the tractor just mentioned the straight line rate is 12½ percent (100 divided by 8). Therefore, the allowable percentage would be 25 percent since it was purchased new. Depreciation allowed in 1962 would be $1,000 (25% × $4,000); the second year, $750 (25% × $3,000); the third year, $562.50 (25% × $2,250); and so on. This method of faster write-off allows more depreciation expense to be taken in the early years, which tends to reduce tax liability. To encourage the purchase of capital equipment various laws have been passed which allow for extra depreciation the first year, liberalization of the estimate of expected life, and several other considerations.

A cash record or ledger for cash receipts and expenses is a necessity in any business. This may be a very simple ledger with receipts and expenses listed in separate columns or on separate pages. Others may desire more detail or grouping of expenditures to assist in management. In this case, the ledger becomes a sheet with columns and pages for various types of receipts and expenditures. A simple calendar with entries on each day's sheet would be one type of simple cash account. More complex ledgers can be made for each type of farm cost or return.

Measures of return for farm businesses. If a farm is to be a financial success, it must: (a) pay all farm expenses incurred, (b) pay a return on capital invested commensurate with best alternative use, (c) pay the operator a fair wage for his labor input and a fair wage for his management input, and (d) leave the farm as physically productive at the end of the year as it was at the beginning. Let us suppose that a farmer operated the following hog-crop farm in the Corn Belt of the United States: a 375-acre farm with 325 acres tillable, of which 260 acres are in row crops; 26 sows on a two litter system, 25 feeder cattle, employing operator plus some part-time and family help. His financial success may be summarized in the following way:

Capital Investment:	Jan. 1	Dec. 31
Real estate	$ 95,000	$ 95,000
Machinery and equipment	9,700	10,000
Livestock	11,800	12,400
Feed, grain, and supplies	12,800	13,300
Total	$129,300	$130,700

Average investment for year: $129,300 + 130,700 divided by 2 = $130,000

Cash Receipts			Cash Expenses	
Hogs	15,800		Feed	5,800
Crops	14,500		Livestock purchased	4,600
Cattle	6,200		Fertilizer and lime	3,300
Misc.	3,700		Equipment purchased	6,000
Total	$40,200		Seed	1,100
			Building repair expenses	1,100
			Hired labor	2,000
			Taxes, insurance, rent	2,200
			Livestock expenses	500
			All other expenses	800
				$27,400

Cash Receipts	40,200	Net farm income		$14,000
Cash Expenses	27,400	Imputed value to		
Net cash income	12,800	operator's labor		
Inventory change	1,400	and management		6,200
	14,200	Return to capital		7,800
Unpaid family labor	200	% earned on investment		6%
Net farm income	14,000			
Interest on capital @ 5%	6,500			
Labor income	7,500			

Net cash income is the difference between cash receipts and cash expenses, including cash expenses deferred from other years. Payments of interest and principal on borrowed capital are not included. Net cash income is not a particularly good measure of farm profits for analytical purposes since a high net cash income could result from decreasing inventory of cattle and grain. In this case, the net cash income is $12,800 after $27,400 of expenses were subtracted from $40,200 income.

Farm income is the return to all factors of production. It is net cash income adjusted for changes in inventory and a charge for unpaid family labor. In this instance the inventory valuation of assets was $1,400 higher at the end of the year than at the beginning and the family contributed $200 worth of labor. This is a net addition of $1,200 to cash income, producing a $14,000 farm income for the year. Although this is a better measure of farm profit than cash income, it gives an advantage to the farmers with large capital investments.

Labor income is probably the most common measure of farm profits. It is calculated by subtracting an imputed charge for the capital investment from farm income. Labor income represents, then, a return to the operator for his labor and management. The capital charge is often calculated at a 5 percent rate (to reflect opportunity cost of capital) and is made against all assets. With an average of $130,000 invested in this business over the year, a 5 percent capital charge amounts to $6,500. Deducting the capital charge from a farm income of $14,000 leaves a labor income or return to operator's labor and management of $7,500. It is now possible to compare the success of various farm operators, since all charges that might vary with size and type of farm have been accounted for and a residual has been calculated that is the same for all.

The most desirable measure of farm income that might be used would include the value of home and environment privileges of farmers. This sort of measure is particularly needed if any income comparisons are made between farm and nonfarm people. Labor earnings is another measure. The value of farm produce consumed in the household and a year's rent value of the house is added to labor income. If rent value of the house is $60 a month and meat, garden, and other produce are valued at $480, the labor earnings are $7,500 labor income plus $1,200 of privileges, or $8,700. This measure of profits is not often used because accurate information on amount and value of farm products is difficult to obtain.

With regard to the balance sheet, if debts were $36,800 on January 1 net worth would be $129,300 less $36,800, or $92,500. If the indebtedness were reduced by $3,600 during the year the net worth at the end of the year would be $130,700 less $33,200 indebtedness, or $97,500. This amounts to a gain of $5,000 in net worth, $3,500 from reduced liability and $1,400 from an increase in net worth.

Profit before income tax is also a measure of farm profit. This, however, has both the problems of being manipulated by inventory sales and biased in favor of larger farms. Income differences could also occur as a result of depreciation methods in effect.

Net returns per acre or return per dollar cost are measures of farm profits, particularly if farms of similar size and type are compared. Without supplementary information to this effect, these measures would have little meaning since two farms could have the same results with different incomes due to volume of business.

Production records. Production records are kept to aid in management analysis and are not required for tax purposes. They help the farm manager in the computation of physical efficiency ratios and may improve the accuracy of the financial measures just discussed.

Livestock records assist greatly in effective animal management. Health, breeding, feeding efficiency, and production records provide a basis by which a farmer can cull, select prime breeding stock, or determine the most profitable feeding level. They also provide a basis whereby a farmer can determine if he has the capacity to effectively manage a livestock enterprise.

Crop records are easy to keep on a map of the farm fields. Each year the farmer can list the crops grown, variety planted, fertilizer applied, tillage practices used, and production received. Such information will aid in decisions of continuing practices that appear profitable and will help eliminate those that are not. In time, it will help in finding the crops best adapted to the whole farm and to various fields within its boundaries. Weather plays a dominant role in crop production and its influence often exceeds that of man. Recording of the weather helps the manager base future plans on more complete information, including both the factors under and beyond the farmer's control.

Marketing records would include: prices received for products sold, quality of products sold, place and type of market agency where products were sold, and the market expense involved (advertising, transportation, telephone, etc.).

Some of these records, such as product prices received and market expense, are kept simultaneously with the cash records. A simple extension (additional columns in the cash receipt record) can easily facilitate the others.

Efficiency factors. Most farmers want rules of thumb to use in evaluating their own progress and efficiency of production. These factors are often based on individual and area experience in production. Rates of gain for livestock, transportation costs, product prices, labor loads, and production per acre or per man are typical examples of the kinds of things which farmers wish to compare with their neighbors and with other parts of the country.

Physical and economic efficiency factors can be calculated from farm records. These factors can serve as a rough guide for comparability between neighboring farms or between farms in different farming regions. Caution should be exercised concerning the use of efficiency factors, especially when they are taken from incomplete records or from records which cover a short time period. These factors often contain nothing about net income, but only refer to gross measures like bushels or tons per acre, gross returns per cow, and so on. Cost data necessary for a *net* figure are often glossed over.

Physical technical production efficiency factors can be obtained by dividing the total product from an enterprise by the resources involved in that enterprise. For example, divide the total number of eggs obtained per year by the average number of layers kept on the farm to arrive at a number of eggs per hen. The same process can be done for crop yields per acre, for pounds of milk per cow, for pigs raised per sow, for percentage calf crop, or for average daily gain on fed cattle.

Feed efficiency factors are arrived at through the same process described above. For example, divide the total cash receipts from livestock by the value of all feed necessary to get the livestock receipts per $1 of feed fed. Other feed efficiency factors include amount of gain from a particular livestock enterprise, such as hogs or cattle per pound of feed.

Labor, machinery, and equipment efficiency factors are computed in a like manner. The number of acres tilled is divided by the number of tractors involved to get the machinery factors. Divide the total machinery costs for field operations of a particular kind by the machinery involved to get a machinery cost per acre. In each case, the farm manager must consider the time involved in the operation. For example, a farmer may have an efficiency factor of 200 tilled acres with one tractor in three weeks, as compared with only 150 acres tilled per tractor in ten days for another farmer. Standards for comparing these efficiency ratios are available at most state universities. Specific efficiency ratios often help to spot weak points which can go unnoticed when only overall measures of return are computed.

Budgeting as a tool for decision making

Budgets put information to use. Budgets aid in projecting future farm costs based on past records and experience and help identify which costs are most likely to increase. They also help to predict expected revenue from farm production and aid in scheduling and timing crop and livestock enterprises. Budgets help guide the farmer to choose between those farm enterprises most likely to fulfill his family's needs, and his own personal goals of income and satisfaction.

Budgeting is the principal working tool at the disposal of a farm manager. It is the mechanical vehicle for calculating maximum profit points and for looking at the probable results of many alternative actions. The concept of marginality discussed in Chapter 12 says that farmers should think in terms of additional costs and the additional returns resulting from a change in organization or production practice. It is logical, then, that there are two general sets of data that are basic to any useful budget. First, the changed physical input (with accompanying costs) associated with a particular action; and second, the changed physical production (with its value) that results from the action. In any adjustment to a going farm business, one may add to or reduce existing income. A typical budgeting form would follow this outline.

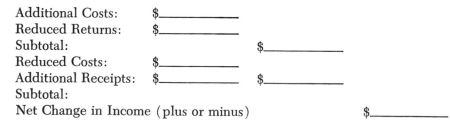

The job of identifying the changes in costs and returns resulting from a change in the farm business will vary with the complexity of the change. Farmers will recognize that with some changes in their farm business certain costs will remain unchanged while others will vary proportionately with the size of the change. Adding two sows to a large-sized hog business would probably not necessitate additional costs for taxes or building insurance or perhaps even equipment (fixed type costs), but it would require additional costs for feed (variable type cost) in direct proportion to the number of sows added.

On the other hand, the additional costs and returns resulting from adding a secondary enterprise, such as growing heifers for sale, may be more difficult to identify since the additional enterprise may involve joint use of resources and entail changes in every aspect of the going farm business. The identification of the costs that will not change, that is, of those that are *fixed* as a result of a particular action, and of those that will change—the *variable* costs, constitutes a major problem in the budgeting procedure.

The key point to remember in the mechanics of testing alternatives through the budget process is that only variable or additional costs should enter the calculations (Chapter 13). Fixed costs by definition are those costs that do not change with the adjustment. Adjustments may be measured in terms of additions to and subtractions from existing total costs and returns. It is not necessary to deal with the totals themselves.

The budgeting process is rapidly becoming more sophisticated with the advent of new mathematical techniques such as linear programming and the use of computers. These new developments allow more variables to be considered at one time in budgeting problems because of the speed at which computers can do arithmetic.

Economic principles

While economic principles useful to any manager have already been discussed in detail in Part III, let us review some of the more important ones. The overall objective of farm management is to maximize dollar returns given the constraints of the limited factor inputs. Since money capital will buy any input, the manager's limiting resource is often capital. If this is the case he will employ the equal marginal return principle which will guide him into using inputs in enterprises until the marginal returns from the last input unit used in each enterprise is equal (review Chapter 14, particularly explanation of Table 14-2).

To accomplish this end he will utilize the overall law of comparative advantage (Chapter 12) in selecting enterprises for initial consideration. He will employ product-product analysis (Chapter 12) to help in finding enterprise combinations that yield the greatest amount of total output, and factor-factor analysis (Chapter 12) to find he least cost way of producing the optimum level of output (Chapter 12, Appendix).

We will now apply economic principles in making decisions in the areas of production, marketing, and financial management.

PRODUCTION MANAGEMENT

The rule of comparative advantage in farm production holds equally true whether the comparison is made within a single farming region or between farming regions. The Corn Belt, the Tobacco States, the Citrus States, and the Dairy Lake States (review Figure 9-1) offer explicit evidence that certain areas of the country have, and try to maintain, an advantage either in the production or marketing, or both, of a particular product. Location of urban centers, technology adoption, and transportation costs have much to do with influencing the location of farm production.

Selection of enterprises

The first production consideration with which most farm managers must deal is determining the cropping system; the second is the livestock program. In each case selection of enterprise combination within crops and livestock and between crops and livestock are important decisions. The choice of enterprise(s) depends in part on the farmer's personal preferences and family goals, in part upon the farm manager's ability to apply his technical ability and economic reasoning, and in part upon the resources with which the manager must work. The profitability of alternative enterprises is influenced by the law of comparative advantage. In a majority of cases the product-product relationships and the equal marginal return principle are most important. After a decision has been made as to what enterprises are to be used, the factor-factor relationships help the manager find the least cost combination for producing any particular level of output. The determination of the most profitable size of each

TABLE 17-1: Illustration of Enterprise Relationships on Two Different Soil Types for Crop Rotations, Including Corn, Oats, and Hay.

		Soil Type: Drummer Silt Loam, Illinois					
				Per Acre Yields		Production	
				Small			
		Acres Planted		Corn	grain	Hay	Grain	Hay
	Rotation[1]	Grain	Hay	(Bushels)		(Tons)	(Pounds)	
(A)	C	100	0	24.3	—	—	136,248	0
	C – O/SCl	100	0	33.6	34.5	—	149,212	0
	C – O – Cl	67	33	51.1	49.8	0.82	149,891	54,200
		Soil Type: Clarion-Webster Silt Loam, Iowa					
(B)	C	100	0	40.0	—	—	224,000	—
	C – C – O – Cl	75	25	59.9	56.5	1.79	212,920	89,600
	C – O – Cl	67	33	59.5	50.1	1.46	166,194	96,400

[1] Rotation Abbreviations: C – Corn   O – Oats   SCl – Sweet Clover   Cl – Clover.
Source: Earl O. Heady, and others, "How to Choose the Most Profitable Crop Rotation for Your Farm," *Iowa Farm Science*, June, 1952.

enterprise is aided by studying the factor-product relationships and by employing marginal analysis to find at what level the marginal input unit for each enterprise is returning the same value of production (equal marginal return principle).

Developing the cropping system. After an inventory of the physical characteristics of the farm such as the kind of soils, topography, etc., the manager first considers the cropping system. The physical factors of soil type, rainfall, length of growing season, topography, and temperature will in most cases eliminate a large number of crop enterprise possibilities. A general guide is to attempt to grow the highest profit crops which are adapted to the natural conditions of the area.

But there are other pertinent questions. Is a crop rotation necessary to maintain fertility and/or prevent soil erosion? How much will a crop rotation reduce risk by diversifying production? What are the relationships among enterprises when put together in various crop rotations? Each of these merits consideration.

Let us review our understanding of enterprise relationships (discussed in Chapter 12) by using the data from Table 17-1. In part A of the table, when grain acreage was reduced by ⅓ and clover hay was introduced, production of grain was slightly increased. Over 27 tons of hay were also harvested. This illustrates a *complementary* relationship between grain and forage. It always pays a farm manager to take advantage of any complementarity that he can find among his enterprises. In part B of the table, however, introducing hay into the rotation reduced the amount of grain that could be produced, illustrating a *competitive* relationship. All enterprises (both crop and livestock) become competitive with each other at some point. The manager must search for the combination that will return the highest total reurn to his limiting resources; in the case just illustrated, only 100 acres of land were available.

To determine the most profitable rotation the price of each product and the production costs per acre for each crop are needed. Assuming that production costs are equal (to make calculations easier) and the prices of corn, oats, and hay are at $1.10 a bushel, $.80 a bushel, and $20 a ton respectively, the most profitable rotation (part B of table 17-1) would be C-C-O-Cl—the four-year one. Check it: [1]

Rotation	Corn		Oats		Hay		Total Value
	Bushels	Value	Bushels	Value	Tons	Value	
C	4000	$4400	—	—	—	—	$4400
C-C-O-Cl	2995	3295	1413	$1130	44.75	$895	5320
C-O-Cl	1983	2181	1670	1336	48.66	973	4490

[1] The optimum (most profitable) combination for two competitive enterprises is where the marginal rate of substitution is equal to the inverse price ratio. See Appendix, Chapter 12.

Developing the livestock system. The kind of livestock kept will be determined partially by the kind of feed produced from the cropping system. In general, the *minimum* amount of livestock kept on most farms should not be less than enough to utilize profitably the roughage and pasture produced. The *optimum* amount of livestock for a farm depends upon many factors.

Management is highly important to the successful operation of livestock enterprises. Livestock efficiency (the principal source of variation in income on livestock farms) is directly influenced by many livestock husbandry factors. The manager must have knowledge of good, economical feeding practices, be able to control disease, be familiar with, and have a knowledge of, breeding, have ability to judge feeding efficiency, know what the basic requirements are in shelter and equipment, know when to buy and sell, and have the ability to organize work and get it done well and on time.

The amount, cost, quality, and distribution of available labor will influence livestock enterprise selection. Expansion of livestock enterprises is often justified on certain farms because of the relatively large amounts of family labor (a fixed cost). On small farms where the problem is to profitably utilize labor, livestock with high labor requirements and with a yield of high returns for feed (dairy cattle and poultry) are usually better adapted. But on farms where labor is scarce, livestock which yield lower returns for feed but higher returns for labor (hogs and feeder

TABLE 17-2: Grain-Forage Combinations for Various Outputs of Milk by Good Cows.[1]

8000 Lbs. Milk			9000 Lbs. Milk		
Pounds of Hay[2]	*Pounds of Grain*	*Total Cost*[3]	*Pounds of Hay*[2]	*Pounds of Grain*	*Total Cost*[3]
4500	3875	$122.50	4500	5000	$145.00
5000	3450	119.00	5000	4500	140.00
5500	3050	116.00	5500	4050	136.00
6000	2700	114.00	6000	3625	132.50
6500	2365	112.30	6500	3275	130.50
7000	2075	111.50	7000	2950	129.00
7500	1820	111.40	7500	2650	128.00
8000	1565	111.30	8000	2375	127.50
8500	1330	111.60	8500	2125	127.50
9000	1115	112.30	9000	1890	127.80
9500	900	113.00	9500	1690	128.80

[1] A 1200 pound cow capable of giving 10000 pounds of 3.5 percent fat content milk when fed a grain milk ration of 1:4.

[2] Includes silage and pasture converted to hay equivalent consumed. This does not include the portion of hay fed but not consumed, which is normally about 8 percent.

[3] Assumes a hay cost of one cent per pound and a grain cost of two cents per pound.

SOURCE: Station Bulletin 648, Kentucky Agricultural Experiment Station, Lexington, July, 1956.

cattle) are often better choices. Most farms with above average management should keep enough livestock to utilize labor not required for the cropping system.

Returns per hour of labor and returns for dollars worth of feed vary widely. But in general *dairy and poultry* enterprises pay high returns for feed but comparatively low returns for labor. Capital requirements per man are relatively low. They fit best on farms where labor utilization is a problem and where capital and feed are limited. *Hogs* pay high returns for labor and medium returns for feed. They require moderate capital investment per man. *Beef and lamb feeding* enterprises pay high returns for labor over the long run, but are highly speculative in any one year. They pay relatively low returns on feed. Their financial requirements are moderate. They fit best where it is necessary to utilize roughage with little or no grain or where available grain is fed to higher yielding classes of livestock. *Poultry (eggs)* returns are average to feed and require little labor. Often a poultry enterprise is supplementary to other crop and livestock enterprises.

After a given level of output for enterprises has been selected, factor-factor analysis aids in finding the least cost combination of inputs which will produce the desired product. Look at the data in Table 17-2. The least cost combination for cows producing 8000 pounds of milk is $111.30, where 8000 pounds of hay are fed in combination with 1565 pounds of grain. For 9000 pounds of milk production the least cost is $127.50 at two different combinations—either 8000 pounds of hay and 2375 pounds of grain or 8500 pounds of hay and 2125 pounds of grain.[2]

Size of enterprises and income

If resources were unlimited the manager would push the production of each enterprise where there was a return above cost until marginal cost was equated with marginal revenue (Chapter 14). Limited resources, however, do not allow the manager to push production this far for all enterprises. He must therefore employ the equal return principle. A summary of principles guiding decision making where the objective is profit maximization would be as follows: (a) Produce products in such a combination that the last unit of resource used in the production of any product will result in an equal value of production. (b) Use such a combination of resources for the production of any product that the last dollar invested in each resource (input) will result in the additional production of the same amount of product. (c) Add inputs to the busi-

---

[2] The least cost combination is where the marginal rate of substitution between grain and hay is equal to the inverse price ratio. At the least cost combination the marginal rate of substitution and the inverse price ratio are both 2.0 in this case.

TABLE 17-3: Size of Farm Related to Labor Income Per Farm and Rate Earned
on Investment, Farm Account Cooperators, Indiana, 1957-60 and
1961.

Productive Man Work Units Per Farm[3]	Labor Income Per Farm[1]		Rate Earned on Investment[2]	
	1957-60	1961	1957-60	1961
	(dollars)		(percent)	
Less than 200	1482	3002	0.3	2.5
200 - 399	3217	4632	3.6	5.1
400 - 599	4181	6009	4.6	6.1
600 - 799	5434	7370	5.0	6.1
800 - 999	7252	9094	5.7	6.9
1000 - 1199	9498	18209	6.1	9.4
1200 and over	10472	22817	5.1	8.7

[1] Return for labor and management supplied by operator; it is "net farm income" minus an imputed
charge to capital of five percent on average capital invested — both equity and debt capital.
[2] Rate earned on investment; it is "net farm income" minus imputed charges of $232 a month for
the operator's wages (labor) and eight percent of the value of farm production for management.
[3] Not less than 10 farms in any category.
SOURCE: *Farm Business Summaries*, Purdue University Cooperative Extension Services, Lafayette,
Indiana. Published annually.

ness until the last unit of input produces just enough to cover marginal
cost or until capital is exhausted.

Size is one of the most widely discussed principles of farm management. In nearly every instance the advice has been to expand rather than
contract the farm business because increased volume of production is the
best way a farm manager can increase his gross revenue. Although the
capacity of the farm manager is largely responsible for the success of such
a venture, there are other reasons for expansion.

In nearly every instance high fixed costs are alluded to as reason for
expansion. Once such capital items as equipment and buildings have
been obtained, costs such as depreciation, taxes, and interest do not
increase when larger units are farmed. Spreading such costs over increasing volumes therefore tends to reduce average total costs per unit of
output.

The experience of farmers indicates that returns increase as farm
size increases (Table 17-3). In both the 1957 to 1960 period and in 1961,
labor income and rate earned on investment rose as size of farm increased.
The farm income of the largest operation was nearly seven times as great
as that produced on units with less than 200 productive man work units.

Relating size to profit is applicable on farms throughout the entire
country. It is well to remember, however, that not all operators are capable of handling larger businesses. Most farmers whose businesses grow
steadily from year to year are able to cope with problems more easily
than in those situations where changes in size are abrupt.

The intensity of operation of a farm business is a more difficult question to answer. Intensity is increased by employing a greater amount of resources on a given acreage or size of unit (Chapter 12). Most farmers find that a more intensive operation involves adding or changing either the livestock or crop enterprises. Often substantial inputs in capital for buildings and equipment is required to handle the additional enterprise. On farms with small acreages this may mean introduction of enterprise below the optimum level with respect to size. Increase in livestock numbers often leads to a faster increase in problems of breeding and disease control, for example, that are crucial to the operation.

Gains in labor efficiency are generally evident as intensity increases up to a certain point. However, intensity that improves labor efficiency without increases in income would indicate that the success of such a business change is largely dependent upon the operator.

Physical efficiency and income

Under many observable farm conditions the higher the physical rates of production, the higher the profit per unit. Increasing yield per acre and pounds of milk per cow are all worthwhile objectives for a farm operator. In most cases, such increases come about as a result of a slightly increased amount of inputs, such as fertilizers, feed, or improved production methods. Job timeliness, use of proper equipment, and adaptable crop varieties can all increase production. Although experimental results from colleges indicate that a level is reached beyond which it is not profitable to produce, there are very few farmers who have reached this point.

Production costs and prices of farm commodities are the most popular topics discussed relative to farm profits. However, it is the combination of the two, not each by itself, which is worthy of the farm operator's attention. The relevant point is the net amount left after production costs are deducted from cash receipts. Since farmers have more control over their costs than over the prices of the things they sell, the essence of farm management involves producing any given level of output at as low a cost as possible. In this way the farmer may increase the margin between price and cost, thereby raising his income.

MARKETING MANAGEMENT

Marketing problems are becoming of greater relative importance as the volume sold per farm unit increases. As a result, a slight variation in the sales price at which farm products are sold can make a large difference in net income.

The marketing problems facing a farm manager involve when,

where, and how to sell the farm's products. *When* to sell involves deciding at what stage of maturity of the product it should be sold. This is particularly important for fruit and vegetables, where degree of ripeness affects quality of product to a very large degree. When to sell is also influenced by the day-to-day and week-to-week variation in product prices (for review, see Chapter 16).

A farmer may decide to store his corn and sell it the following spring. *Where* to sell involves the selection of a buyer. Should it be sold to a market agency at a terminal or local market? Or might it be sold directly to a processor or retailer? *Where* also involves physical location. Suppose there are two grain elevators equally distant from the farm. At which one should the grain be sold? *How* to sell concerns whether the product should be graded before sale. It also involves whether the farmer should transport the product to the buying agency or have it picked up. Another related decision for selling corn might be: Should I take a moisture discount and sell the corn with 20 percent moisture or dry it to 15 percent and receive a higher price? In some cases *how* may also involve a decision regarding whether to advertise.

To function as a good marketing manager requires being knowledgeable about how prices are determined, why price variation occurs in the same market over time, and why there are price differences among markets at any given time. Also necessary is technical information, such as determining when a product has the correct amount of ripeness which maximizes its quality and judging the quality of various products (such as looking at a live steer and assessing its carcass quality); the institutional facets of markets which may explain price variability; and the marketing regulations pertinent to products sold.

Seasonal price variations

Seasonal price variations for most farm commodities are becoming less and less extreme as time passes. Improved production scheduling and more environmental control over livestock production, in particular, have evened out the flow of livestock and livestock products into the marketing channel throughout the year, which has promoted less fluctuation in prices (Chapter 16). For nonperishable products, such as wheat and corn, seasonal price fluctuations occur largely in relation to the cost of storage. If it costs two cents a bushel per month to store corn the price rise between November and April will probably be about 10 cents, assuming that overall demand factors remain constant. (Check the verification of this by looking again at the data in Table 16-1.)

The manager should strive to sell his products at the highest price possible, and marketing considerations will influence the production decision as to when to plant a crop, breed an animal, or buy a feeder steer. Nature prohibits most farmers from harvesting their corn crop in August, but a broiler producer can time his production cycles for any time of the year. The following general guidelines are valid: Gear production to hit high-priced markets provided added expense of doing so does not exceed the extra returns realized from higher prices. (This is using the marginal cost-marginal return principle discussed in Chapter 14.) Store nonperishable products only if additional returns exceed the cost of storage plus the cost of having capital tied up in grain. (A further use of the marginal principle plus the idea of opportunity cost of capital, Chapters 14 and 15.) Do not wait for a high-priced market if quality of product deteriorates so that returns are lowered because of price discounts for low quality unless the anticipated prices more than offset the deterioration discounts. (Again, this is a use of the marginal principle.)

Selecting a market

Location principles of economics tell us that prices will be lowest at the point of highest production concentration and will increase in magnitude by the extent of transportation cost as one moves away from the center of production. However, there is virtually no product for which there is one center of production. Asparagus, cranberries, and rice come the closest for products in the United States. It is clear, however, that fluid milk prices are higher in New Mexico than in Wisconsin; oranges are cheaper in Florida and California than in Kansas; corn is cheaper in the Midwest than in Utah; and raw tobacco is cheaper in North Carolina than in North Dakota. Similarly, in marketing livestock, prices for medium steers may vary between a local market two miles from your farm and a terminal market 300 miles from your farm by the cost of transporting a steer 300 miles. Imperfections in markets where prices are in disequilibrium occur all the time due to factors discussed in detail in Chapter 16.

The alert manager will be well informed about price variations among kinds of markets and market locations so that he can strive to increase returns. The United States Department of Agriculture, the state universities, trade associations, farmer organizations, radio and television media, and newspapers all are sources of help to enable the farmer to improve his marketing strategy. Selling through a marketing cooperative may be another alternative.

The general guideline for market selection is to get the best price. The manager's knowledge of how markets function and his ability to recognize a relatively higher-priced market is important. It is to be remembered that most farm products are sold in a purely competitive market (Chapter 16). Since the individual farmer rarely can influence price, he strives to try to find the best price among the possible market outlets from which he has to choose.[3]

Product merchandising

Because of the homogeneity of a large number of raw farm products and the cost of grading products, it does not pay the individual farmer to advertise or promote his product unless there is some special situation involved. For producers who choose to specialize or for those in close proximity to a consuming area, such as a sweet corn producer near a suburban housing development, there may be gains to revenue by incurring variable promotional costs. The marginal rule can again apply. If extra returns exceed extra costs, it pays to spend money for advertising.

In those situations where the farmer can perform grading, processing, or other market functions efficiently, it pays to do so as long as a higher enough price is received to pay a fair return on the extra factors of production required. It should be remembered (Chapter 10) that marketing functions cannot be eliminated. If a farmer markets at a roadside stand, all eight marketing functions are still performed, although some, such as storage and standardization, may be simplified.

FINANCIAL MANAGEMENT

The large amounts of capital involved in operating a farm were vividly portrayed in Chapter 7. Acquiring the necessary capital to begin a farm business is a major roadblock to many desirous of getting into the farming business. It follows logically that acquiring and managing capital is of prime importance—indeed acquiring capital after the business is "going" may be the major financial management problem facing the farm manager.

The financial responsibilities of the farm manager include financing the organization and operation of the business, recording business transactions, and safeguarding the financial position of the business as a going concern over a long period of time. Financial management for a farm operator differs from many nonfarm businesses in that cash income is received more sporadically over time. A dairy farmer receives a milk check every two or four weeks; a cash grain farmer may receive payment for grain once a year; hogs may be sold only twice a year, while a broiler grower may sell his product every six to eight weeks. This variation necessitates much advance planning so that there is always sufficient cash to

---

[3] For storable products, futures markets exist to allow any commodity owner the shifting of price risk to someone else (see Chapter 10).

meet current liabilities. Nonfarm financial management personnel have the same obligation but usually products are sold more continuously, although seasonal demands are evident for most any product.

The financial manager needs several kinds of knowledge. He should have at his command a knowledge of elementary bookkeeping and of how to keep financial records. He should know what capital sources are available, how to compute capital costs, and how to decide what proportion of debt or equity capital to use in making a new investment. It is surprising how few people can compute an interest rate when borrowing. He should understand the economic and business management principles that deal with capital-replacement decisions, whether to buy or lease, whether to rent land or own it, whether to substitute capital for labor, and whether to adopt a capital-using technology. He should stay reasonably up-to-date on changes in tax laws and should understand the rudiments of business law so that he can communicate effectively with a lawyer or tax accountant. And finally, he must be a keen analyst of financial statements which he or his accountant may prepare. If the manager does not know how to interpret a balance sheet or income statement and use it to guide future decisions, there is little use in keeping the record.

Capital-replacement decision

A major financial decision is when to replace capital equipment. How old should a tractor be before it pays to buy a new one? How many times should the livestock "escape" before a new fence is built, or how many times should a fence be repaired? These types of problems constantly face any manager. Let us take one example. You have a two-year-old tractor. Its original cost was $3600 and you have been depreciating it under the declining balance method, taking the maximum write-off. Therefore it now has a book value of $1600. This assumes an original expected life of six years and no salvage value (Check your understanding of depreciation earlier in this chapter by proving that this is correct.) Your equipment dealer will sell you a comparable new model for your old tractor plus $2400. The list price of the new tractor is $3800, since prices have gone up. It appears that the dealer figures your old tractor to be worth $1400. Should you trade? How do you decide? Let us assume that it is your practice to analyze your tractor situation every two years.

The trade would involve an immediate capital outlay of $2400. If you had enough money in your savings and loan account you would have to sacrifice $120 a year interest to move the money capital into the form of the new tractor if the rate of interest was 5 percent. Another consideration which is difficult to calculate is whether depleting your cash would jeopardize any other aspect of the business, as the risk of failure because of finances may be increased. This is offset partially by the fact that you could probably sell the tractor and recover cash, but then this would hurt farm production and farm receipts since a tractor is necessary to operate the business. To finance the tractor from debt capital from a bank loan, assuming your credit rating would allow a loan of $2400 over a two-year period, you would incur an interest cost of $144 a year at an interest rate of 6 percent.

You then figure that the new tractor will have a maintenance and repair cost of $50 for the next two years, $50 lower than if the old one were kept. Your state levies a personal property tax and the cost of the new tractor will increase by $40 the first year and $25 the second year. You estimate that as a result of using a new tractor the variable costs of the machine can be reduced by $30 the first year and by $20 the second.

Depreciation expense compared for the old and new tractors for the next two years would be as follows:

Old tractor: Year 3 (in terms of age): depreciation would be ⅓ of $1600, or $533. Year 4 it would be ⅓ of $1067, or $355.

New tractor: Year 1 (in terms of age): depreciation would be ⅓ of $4000 (cost basis equals book value of old tractor plus cash outlay under 1962 tax laws), or $1333. Year 2 depreciation would be ⅓ of $2667, or $889.

The difference would be that depreciation expense would be $800 higher with the new tractor the first year and $534 the second. If the farmer fell in the 20 percent bracket for income tax, he would save $160 of income tax the first year and $107 the second. Remember that depreciation is a fixed cost but that this is a legitimate deductible expense in figuring income tax or farm income. These computations of added costs and savings utilize budgeting for analysis. Summarizing then (assuming you finance purchase with equity capital):

Item	Added costs from buying new tractor		Adding savings from buying new tractor	
	1st year	2nd year	1st year	2nd year
Opportunity costs of money	$120	$120	$	$
Additional property taxes	40	25		
Lowered maintenance costs			50	50
Lowered tractor variable costs			30	20
Tax savings			160	107
Total	$160	$145	$240	$177
Total (both years)		$305		$417

From a farm management viewpoint alone it appears that it is a wise decision to trade the old tractor in and get the new one. However, when the farm operator considers total family needs and goals he may decide not to trade. Perhaps son John needs the $2400 to go to college or his wife needs new kitchen appliances.

The other types of financial decisions could be approached in a like manner, utilizing the budgeting method.

The present value concept

When making financial decisions that involve a long period of time, there is an additional idea that becomes important. It is the *present value concept.*

If one were asked whether he preferred to have a dollar now or a year from now, he would likely take it now. If one were offered a dollar now or $10 a year from now, he would probably wait and pick up the $10. What about a dollar now or a $1.10 a year from now? This is more difficult. Essentially, present income is worth more than future income. In other words, one tends to discount the future. It is this discounting that generates interest rates [4]

What is the present value of a dollar income a year from now? It depends on what value you impute to the use of your money. If it is 10 percent the present value of one dollar is 90.9 cents. The proof is that should you invest 90.9 cents for a year at 10 percent interest, it will grow to a dollar. So this idea also helps us understand rate earned on investment. The return is the discount rate which, when applied to earnings, equates the present value of the earnings to the investment.[5]

Let us take one example. Suppose you are making a financial decision with regard to whether to buy or lease a particular piece of equipment. Assume you are considering a five-year period. The machine costs $1000, has no salvage value, and will return you annual net earnings of $250 each year for the five-year period. You can rent the machine for $17 a month which is $204 a year or a total of $1020 for the five-year period, which is about the same dollar outlay as buying it new. What should you do?

First, let us compute the present value of the net earnings which the purchase of the machine will give you.

[4] Except for administrative costs and the risk costs in loaning money.

[5] The formula for computing the discount rate is $\frac{1}{1+r}$ where r is the rate of interest. In the example, then, the discount factor is $\frac{1}{1+.10}$ or $\frac{1}{1.10}$ or .909. The discount rate for the second year is $\frac{1}{(1+r)^2}$, for the third year $\frac{1}{(1+r)^3}$, and so on.

Year	Net Earnings	Discount Factor at 8%	Present Value of Future Earnings
1	$250	.926	$232
2	250	.857	214
3	250	.794	198
4	250	.735	184
5	250	.684	171
		Total	$999

It is now clear that making the investment in buying the machine will surely return 8 percent, since the present value of the net earnings for the five years, using an 8 percent discount factor, totals about $1000. Note that someone who did not utilize the present value concept might conclude that buying the machine would return 25 percent a year ($250-$1000).

But back to the decision of whether to buy or lease. You would buy the machine if the next best alternative investment for a $1000 of equity capital returned less than 8 percent. If your $1000 of capital were already earning you more than 8 percent it would be the best decision to rent the machine.

Note that the present value concept also helps you to decide whether to purchase the machine in the first place. If there was an alternative investment in some other venture for the $1000 return, you might not even buy the machine.

18

Managing the
agribusiness firm[1]

Agribusiness, a relatively new addition to the vocabulary of many persons, was first used publicly by John H. Davis in 1955. The concept of agribusiness evolved from the realization that the food and fiber segment of our economy is closely related to large segments of our industrial economy.[2] In fact, a great deal of interdependency is found between agriculture and the industrial sector. Agribusiness is defined as the sum total of all economic activity involved in supplying farmers with farm inputs, in the production of farm crops and livestock, and in the processing and distribution of farm output.

Although not formally recognized, the concept of agribusiness was appropriate even during the early 1800's, when most farming units were self-contained enterprises. A typical farmer during this period produced most of the supplies used in farming, raised crops and livestock, and processed and distributed any excess above family needs.

As farms became commercial business operations and as specialization increased, many of the operations formerly performed on the farm were transferred to businesses outside farming. New industries, such as

---

[1] This chapter was contributed by Dr. W. D. Gorman and Dr. R. J. Williams, Department of Agricultural Economics, Purdue University.

[2] See John H. Davis and Ray A. Goldberg, *A Concept of Agribusiness* (Boston: Graduate School of Business Administration, Harvard University, 1957).

farm implement companies, meat-packers, fertilizer firms, and food processors were developed to serve modern agriculture. These off-farm firms became an integral part of agriculture, with farmers depending on them for materials and service and, in turn, with business firms depending on farmers as a source of supply of agricultural commodities and as a market for nonfarm products. This close interrelationship led to the development of the concept called agribusiness.

Since agribusiness has been more clearly enunciated and recognized by educators and businessmen, the training of college students in agriculture and business management principles has received greater emphasis. Furthermore, research and extension activities carried on by land grant institutions and by the U.S. Department of Agriculture also gave more emphasis to the management problems of business firms serving agriculture. A few examples of the problems currently being studied are: improving supermarket operations, measuring the effectiveness of promotional programs for agricultural products, labor efficiency in food processing firms, farmers' purchasing behavior, consumers' attitudes toward broilers, cost control methods for food wholesalers and retailers, and the important factors in choosing a milk plant location. The purpose of this chapter is to outline the various functional areas of business management and see how they relate to decision making in agribusiness firms.

FUNCTIONAL ORGANIZATION OF AGRIBUSINESS FIRMS

Farm businesses are generally of a size enabling the farm operator to handle all of the necessary management tasks. The operator generally decides when, what, and how much to plant; how much fertilizer to apply; and which, if any, livestock enterprises to engage in. These decisions can be grouped under the general heading of production decisions. The farm operator also decides when and where to sell his products and arranges for financing. These decisions can be grouped under the general headings of marketing and financial control.

Agricultural business firms are frequently of such a large size that the management function cannot be adequately handled by an individual operator. This phenomenon gives rise to the need for delegation of many management functions.

A simple organizational structure, similar to organizational structures found in many agriculturally related businesses, is presented in Figure 18-1. The general manager in this type of organization does not supervise work directly or make all management decisions directly. However, he is responsible for making decisions that are basic to the entire organization. He depends upon his departmental managers to implement his decisions in their respective specialties.

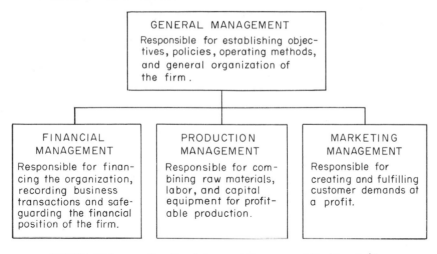

FIGURE 18-1:   Functional Areas of Management Decision Making.

Production, marketing, and financing (Figure 18-1) are the three basic functional areas involved in the total management of business firms. Each of these three areas will be discussed in detail in an attempt to explain the nature and role of these functions in the management of agricultural business firms.

Marketing management

Scope of marketing. Marketing occupies an important place in the organizational structure of most firms. Directing the marketing functions will be an individual who may have the title of Vice President for Marketing. The marketing executive is responsible for the performance of business activities that direct the flow of goods and services from the firm to consumers in order to best satisfy consumers and accomplish the firm's objectives. One of the firm's prime objectives would be maximization of profits. In addition, the firm may have nonprofit-maximizing goals, such as a desired rate of growth, increasing market share, or developing a corporate image.

The marketing executive position has been elevated in recent years. This occurred because the top executive of the firm came to realize the importance of the marketing functions. During and following World War II major emphasis was on production and sales. The philosophy at that time was, "This is what we can produce, now let's sell it." However, as more and more of the consumers' heavy demands from the war years were satisfied, this philosophy began to change.

During the mid-1950's a new philosophy of marketing developed.

FIGURE 18-2:   Typical Organizational Chart for the Marketing Functions.

This philosophy was, "This is what the consumers want, can we produce it at a profit?" As this philosophy became accepted the former sales executive either took on additional responsibilities or was replaced by a marketing executive.

For the marketing manager to carry out his responsibilities he has the assistance of several departments. The organization of the marketing functions is illustrated in Figure 18-2.

Marketing strategy. To successfully perform the responsibilities delegated to him, the marketing manager develops a "marketing strategy," or plan. Marketing is primarily concerned with implementing that strategy.

A marketing strategy consists of two elements: (a) The market target, which is the selection of the market segment (the particular group of consumers) that the firm wishes to satisfy. (b) The marketing mix, which is the choice of the tools (product, price, place, and promotion) which the firm intends to combine in order to satisfy the selected market target.

The market target is defined by a detailed analysis of potential consumers in light of the firm's abilities and objectives. Moreover, the market for a particular product is likely to consist of submarkets. The market for farm machinery would consist of tractors, tillage implements, planters, and harvesters. These submarkets could be further divided by size of tractor and amount of auxiliary equipment. The particular abilities of a firm are important. For example, if the firm was highly specialized in farm machinery it is not likely that the firm would be interested in marketing beefsteak, because steak would not make good use of the firm's production facilities, engineering talent, and present distribution channels.

Marketing mix. The consumer is the key to the selection of a marketing strategy. Once the target consumers have been chosen the marketing manager combines all the resources at his command in an effort to make a direct hit on the target, and in turn, to accomplish the firm's goals. The four variables which the marketing manager commands are: product, price, place, and promotion. These are called elements of the marketing mix.

First the marketing manager must decide what product he is going to offer the consumers. Often the marketing manager will conduct a market research study of the consumers within the market area so that he can learn of their product or service needs. An example of how this can be accomplished for a supermarket will be discussed later in this chapter. Following the decision on the type of product, the marketing manager must decide on packaging, branding, and other items needed to fill out the line.

Next the marketing manager must decide on a pricing policy. If he has a patent on the product he may try to capitalize on his monopoly position by charging a high price so that he can recoup his development costs quickly. This pricing policy is called skimming the market. Or there might possibly be some real cost advantages to building up a large volume of sales. In this case the marketing manager may charge a low price to obtain volume sales. This is called penetration pricing. Depending on the objectives of the firm and the market target, the marketing manager will establish a pricing policy. This will, of course, need to be established in light of competition (for review, see Chapter 16).

Another variable to be considered is place strategy. How should the product be distributed to the target consumers? Here the marketing manager would consider whether to sell directly to the consumers, to sell through wholesalers and retailers, to use brokers, or to employ some other combination of channels of distribution. A point that is often overlooked is the fact that if a firm plans to use the independent middlemen they must be first committed to the merits of the products. If this is not the case, the consumer may never see it.

Last, the promotion variable must be considered. This broad category consists of advertising and personal selling. The function of promotion is to communicate the merits of your product to the target consumer. The consumer needs to be made aware of the product, aware of its satisfying benefits, and persuaded to purchase it not once but a number of times. To some extent advertising and personal selling are substitutes. However, considering the many possible ad themes, media, frequency of appearance, and types of personal selling methods, this is an area that raises many problems for the marketing manager because the number of possible promotional mixes available is infinite. Promotional costs are variable except for fixed dues to trade associations or groups.

In addition to the four variables making up the marketing mix, the marketing manager must be aware of the other variables, over which he has little control, that make up the marketing situation or marketing environment. The main uncontrollable factors are: resources of the firm, business conditions, cultural and social environment, and legal environment. These factors all have an impact on the decisions made by the marketing manager.

Production management: its functions and role

Production, as defined in Chapter 12, is the process by which goods and services are created. Production processes are found in offices, factories, supermarkets, and so on. Production management deals with de-

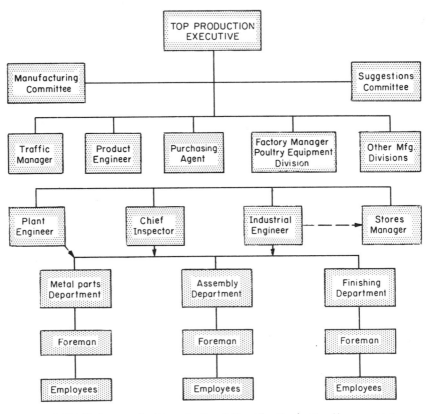

FIGURE 18-3:   An Organizational Chart for Production Management.

cision making related to production processes, so that the resulting good or service is produced according to specifications in amounts and time allotted, and a minimum cost. In accomplishing these functions production management is concerned with two broad areas of activity: the design and the control of production systems.

Production management is probably most frequently associated with factory management rather than with the broader definition just given. This is probably because production management as a field of knowledge developed largely in the factory system. It was in the factory where production problems were first studied and solved on a systematic, scientific basis. However, the principles and procedures first developed in the factory in relation to layout, product design, labor relations, supervision, materials, handling and moving, job evaluation, inspection, and purchasing and inventory control are just as appropriate for nonfactory type businesses such as a supermarket.

For the production manager to carry out responsibilities he frequently has the assistance of several operating departments, depending upon the size of the firm. An organizational chart for a typical production management and control department in a manufacturing plant of average size is presented in Figure 18-3. Formal organization is simply a tool used by management for accomplishing the objectives of an enterprise. Consequently, the details of organization will vary greatly with ultimate objective, type and size of business, and historical development.

Let us examine closely how the size of business influences production management and controls department organization in a retail food store. Figure 18-4 shows the organizational structure for a retail food store doing a volume of business of about $8,000 weekly. An organization chart for a supermarket doing about $30,000 weekly sales is presented in Figure 18-5. In addition to the meat, produce, and grocery departments, op-

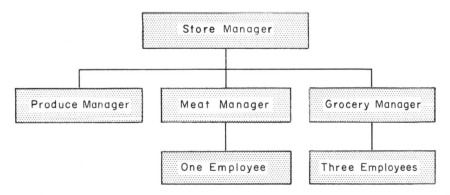

FIGURE 18-4:   Typical Organizational Chart for a Retail Food Store Doing a Volume of Business of $8,000 Weekly.

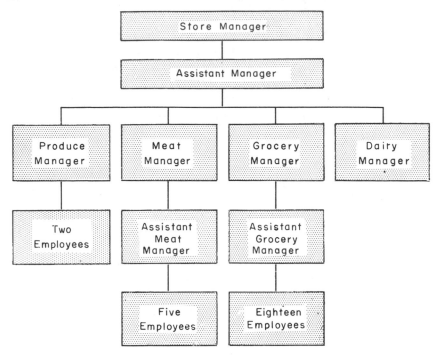

FIGURE 18-5:   Typical Organizational Chart for a Supermarket Doing a Volume of
Business of $30,000 Weekly.

erations of this size generally separate the dairy department from the
grocery department and place it under separate control. One also notices
that as the number of employees increases the need for assistant managers
develops.

   Production management problems. Problems faced by production
management require two major types of decisions; one relates to the design of the system and one relates to the control and operation of the
system. This involves both long-run and short-run decisions. A brief outline of the production problems to be solved by management follows:

A. Long-run System Design Problems
    1. *Selection of Equipment and Processes.*
       Usually alternative equipment and processes are available for
       a given need. Management must make decisions that commit
       capital of the enterprise and its basic approach to production.
    2. *Design of Products Processed.*
       Production cost is closely associated with product design. De-
       sign decisions often set the limiting characteristics of cost and
       processing for the system.

    3. *Location of the System.*
    Location decisions can, in most cases, be important in determining market potential and production costs.

B. Short-run Operation and Control System Decisions
    1. *Inventory and Production Control.*
    Schedules must be worked out; the load on men and machines and the flow of production must be controlled. Decisions on how to allocate productive capacity consistent with demand and inventory policy must be made.
    2. *Labor Control.*
    In most companies labor is the single largest expense item and hence must be controlled carefully.
    3. *Quality Control.*
    For effective quality control, inspection costs must be balanced against the probable loss due to passing defective material or services.
    4. *Maintenance and System Reliability.*
    The degree of maintenance consistent with cost and loss of sales due to down-time must be determined.

The relative importance of these problems of production management varies considerably, depending on the nature and type of the system and product. Nevertheless, every system has these problems in some degree.

Financial management

Role of the financial manager. The financial manager's general responsibility is to keep the financial records of the firm so that he and others can stay informed about its financial condition. He must be able to interpret records and use them as guideposts for the future development of the firm. He has the task of arranging for the funds needed by the firm on the most favorable terms that are compatible with the objectives of the business. He must see to it that the business has the funds available to pay its current bills and to meet long-term obligations.

Basic financial statements

The two most important and widely used financial statements are the balance sheet and the income statement. Learning to interpret the information summarized in these two statements allows one to do a considerable amount of financial analysis.

The balance sheet. The items on the balance sheet were discussed in the last chapter. The balance sheet equation is:

ASSETS = LIABILITIES + OWNERSHIP EQUITIES

Excluding all personal items, every asset that the business has is either owed to someone (liabilities) or is owed to the owner(s) of the business (ownership equity often called net worth). Equity is an accounting term describing ownership of assets. For the balance sheet depicted in Table 18-1, the owner(s) have 48.4 percent equity in the business (net worth divided by total assets expressed in percentage). Or, on the average, for each dollar's worth of assets about 48 cents is debt free. A balance sheet is like a still camera picture of a business. It is recorded as of a particular day and may be prepared as often as is deemed necessary in order to study the financial growth of the business.

The income statement. The income statement is prepared for a period of time and is often called a profit and loss statement (P and L). The income statement records the revenue generated for a period of time and expenses incurred for the same period of time. The income statement is kept on an accrual basis and it is important to distinguish between cash receipts and revenue, and expenditure and expense. As mentioned in the last chapter, income tax records are usually kept on a cash basis and are concerned with cash receipts and expenditures.

A brief example will help explain. Suppose you were a feed salesman who sold $200 worth of feed to farmer Smith on June 20 and sent him a bill. On the following July 5 farmer Smith sent you a check for $200 in payment for the feed. To which month should you credit the feed sale, June or July ? On a cash basis a *cash receipt* of $200 would be credited to July, but on an accrual basis sales revenue of $200 would be credited to June.

Again suppose that on January 5 you paid the annual premium for

TABLE 18-1: Hypothetical Balance Sheet as of January 1, 1960.

	Balance Sheet		
Assets		*Liabilities*	
Cash	$ 18,195	Accounts Payable	$ 52,960
Accounts Receivable	43,802	Accrued Taxes Payable	8,266
Inventory	19,200	Notes Payable	15,786
Total Current Assets	$ 81,197	Total Current Liabilities	$ 77,012
Machinery	36,257	Net Worth	72,153
Trucks, Autos, Trailers	29,139	Total Liabilities and Net Worth	$149,165
Furniture and Equipment	2,572		
Total Fixed Assets	$ 67,968		
Total Assets	$149,165		

	Balance Sheet Ratios
Current Ratio	1.05
Quick Ratio	.236
Return on Total Investment	12.5
Return on Owner's Equity	21.9%

fire insurance on your office building for the coming year of $300. On a cash basis you incurred an *expenditure* of $300 in the month of January. However, on an accrual basis, provided that you prepare an income statement monthly, fire insurance *expense* for January would be only $25 ($\frac{1}{12}$ of $300 since there are 12 months in the year). This distinction is an important one. Cash records are not very useful for management analysis. Therefore, it is the important task of the financial manager to match revenue with expense, which has little importance when cash is received or paid out. Only when accounts are kept on an accrual basis can management make valid comparisons of income statements for similar periods in each year.

Table 18-2 illustrates how an income statement is constructed. Sales revenue minus cost of goods sold give the gross margin. Cost of goods sold is equal to beginning inventory plus purchases minus ending inventory. From the gross margin, all expenses are subtracted leaving net profit for the period. In Table 18-2 interest expense is separated from the other expense. Note that the category of expenses includes items which do not require cash outlays, such as depreciation. This reminds us once again that the income statement matches revenue with expenses and is not concerned with when cash is actually exchanged.

Relationship of income statement to balance sheet. The net profit of $15,791 which appears on the income statement for January 1 to June 30, 1960 would show up on the balance sheet of June 30, 1960 as an increase to owner's equity or net worth. Net worth on June 30 would thus be $87,944 ($72,153 + $15,791). Revenues tend to increase owner's equity while expenses tend to diminish it.

TABLE 18-2: Hypothetical Income Statement for Period January 1 to June 30, 1960.

Sales	$1,252,341
Cost of Goods Sold	997,201
Gross Margin	$ 255,140
Expenses:	
Labor	73,846
Manager's Salary	11,775
Supplies	92,339
Repairs	11,406
Taxes	14,000
Utilities	12,851
Federal Grading Inspector	6,674
Depreciation	7,701
Legal and Auditing	1,096
Miscellaneous	4,767
Total Expenses	$ 236,455
Net Operating Profit	18,685
Interest Expense	2,894
Net Profit	$ 15,791

Financial *ratios* are computed to aid management in analyzing problems and implementing changes in the business. The current ratio and the quick ratio are commonly used to test how able the business is to meet its short-term obligations. The current ratio is computed by dividing current assets by current liabilities. From Table 18-1 the current ratio would be 1.05 ($81,197 divided by $77,012). In other words, for each dollar of obligations due in the near future the firm has $1.05 ready to meet it. Because accounts receivable and inventory may not be readily convertible to cash (this depends on the nature of the business; inventory in grocery stores converts to cash much quicker than the implement dealer's inventory of tractors), a quick ratio is often computed which is cash divided by current liabilities. The quick ratio from the data in Table 18-1 is .236 ($18,195 divided by $77,012). Or, for each dollar of current obligations there is about 24 cents of cash in the bank to meet them. For some industries, standards of what are good and bad current and quick ratios have been developed. The banker looks at these ratios when more credit is requested from the business.

Two tests of the profitability of the firm are return on total investment and return on owner's equity. From Tables 18-1 and 18-2, return on total investment would be 12.5 percent ($18,685 divided by $149,165 x 100). Whether these rates of return are high or low depends on whether the capital could have earned a greater amount if invested elsewhere. It can also be compared to the rate that similar firms are earning in the industry.

Various tests of efficiency can be computed from information on the income statement. Profit as a percent of total sales and profit as a percent of gross margin are two of them. Each item of expense can be expressed as a percent of total expense and comparisons with other periods can be made to see whether expenses are increasing or decreasing. For example, if labor expense is increasing as a percent of the total it is a signal that the efficiency with which employees are working may be slipping. A corrective measure may be to more closely supervise their work.

Depending on the records kept, many physical operating ratios may be computed which give indications of trouble spots in the business. For supermarkets, sales per square feet of display case and sales per hour of labor are two examples. Individual business managers must decide what is appropriate and most useful to them.

CASE PROBLEM IN BUSINESS MANAGEMENT

The following case history problem is presented to illustrate how the three functional management areas (marketing, production, and finance) interrelate with one another, arriving at a solution to a problem. The first functional area treated is marketing. If there is not an adequate market for the given product there is no reason to expand or build new facilities. The second area considered is production—arrangement, layout, and size of plant. Third, the financial area is considered; what are the costs involved, sources of financing, and the economic feasibility of operating at these costs?

The Shop-Rite Supermarket is located in Happy Hollow, U.S.A. Happy Hollow, a small industrial city of 8,250 inhabitants, is located in Centerline County. Happy Hollow is the principal trading center of the area.

Mr. B. J. Brown, manager of the Shop-Rite Supermarket, was considering remodeling his old store and building an addition to the store. The supermarket was doing approximately $12,500 in gross sales per week. This volume of business had been achieved with relatively little effort. However, to carry out the total expansion program B. J. would need to get a loan to finance the additional capital investment required.

Just recently, B. J. had explained his plan to Mr. Thorn of Centerline County Bank. Mr. Thorn thought it was an excellent idea, especially since the Shop-Rite Supermarket had not been remodeled since 1949. B. J. also told Mr. Thorn that he would need a sizable loan to carry out the expansion program and that he was counting on the Centerline County Bank as a source of funds. Mr. Thorn said this might be possible; however, he would need a detailed plan of the projected earnings to present to the bank's board of directors. This startled B. J. He had never considered the idea that the bank would require information in addition to his credit rating. However, B. J. told Mr. Thorn that he would have a projected financial statement within 30 days.

That evening B. J. spent some time looking over some of the bulletins from his trade association on projecting financial statements. As he read the reports it became very clear to him that in order to project his financial statements he would need to make a sales projection for the new store. But how? This was an area that was completely foreign to him. However, as he pondered the problem he remembered that Jim Johnson at the state college had presented a paper on market analysis at one of the trade association's meetings. B. J. decided to give Jim a call.

Two days later Jim Johnson paid a visit to Shop-Rite Supermarket. B. J. explained to Jim that he needed help in making a market analysis of Happy Hollow so that he could develop a projected sales forecast. He realized too that the study would probably be valuable in deciding on the type of store image desired and on the store size, and he studied the following report carefully.

Market Analysis of Happy Hollow Trading Area
by Jim Johnson

1. Population, 1968:

	Total Population	Farm Households	Households
Centerline County	20,500	5,350	1,000
Happy Hollow	8,250	2,010	—

2. Projected Population, 1972:

Centerline County	22,750	5,600	850
Happy Hollow	9,400	2,310	—

3. Income Distribution, 1961-67:

	Centerline County	
	1961	1967
$0 - $5,999	49%	46%
$6 - $8,999	34%	36%
$9,000 and over	17%	18%

4. Location of Food Stores Within City:

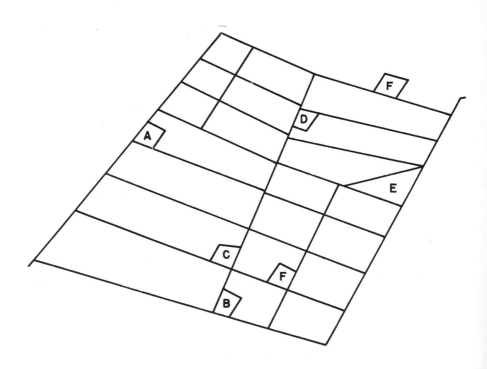

	Name of Store	Estimated Weekly Sales
A.	Shop Rite	$12,500
B.	McHenry's	4,500
C.	Blue Boy	6,000
D.	Karl's Market	12,000
E.	Big Value	8,000
F.	Others (2 small stores)	4,000

5. Expansion Plans of Competition:

McHenry's: not likely, owner getting old

Karl's Market: quite possible but current management relatively poor

Blue Boy: not likely, basically an overgrown meat market

Big Value: recently remodeled, poor job

6. Social Characteristics:

1. Highly intergrated society where almost everyone knows everyone else on a somewhat personal basis.
2. People tend to be somewhat reserved in their attitude toward change.
3. Some industry moving into this area, but not rapidly.
4. Basically a low income area.

7. Sales Projections:

Projected weekly grocery sales within the market area based on (a) $5.00 per capita per week consumption of food products, and (b) growth estimates from city planning commission.

	Total Weekly Food Sales	
	1963	1967
Centerline County	$82,000	$91,000
Happy Hollow	33,000	37,600
Rural Area	49,000	53,400

8. Sales projection of remodeled and enlarged store:

Weekly Sales by Firms, 1968		Percent of Sales Likely to be Lost	Potential Sales for Remodeled Store
Shop-Rite*	$12,500	100	$12,500
McHenry's	4,500	10	450
Blue Boy	6,000	15	900
Karl's Market	12,000	25	3,000
Big Value	8,000	10	800
Others	4,000	10	400
Total			$18,050

* The old store loses 100 percent of sales to the new store.

Estimated weekly sales volume for a remodeled and enlarged store is $18,050 weekly. If B. J. is able to obtain and hold this increased share of the market, projected sales by 1965 would be $23,000.

Store Image

1. Product line: quality at reasonable prices.
2. Price policy: low price image.
3. Promotion: low prices with personal service. Use local newspaper to a large extent.

After reading Jim's report B. J. felt that he had the basis for projecting his financial statements. He had also learned a lot about the community which would be valuable in the selection of decor for the store so as to project an image which involved appeal to the people of Happy Hollow.

Production management—design of facilities

Based on the market analysis report, B. J. knew that he must build a store capable of handling $18,000 to $23,000 of weekly sales. After studying available reports and the recommendations of Jim Johnson, B. J. decided that sales of $2.50 per square foot would be a reasonable figure on which to plan. He was aware that most stores are capable of doing more than $2.50 of weekly sales per square foot; however, he wanted to be careful not to lose many customers due to overcrowding during peak weekend periods. A store slightly larger than necessary would also provide a hedge against potential competition and future growth of the city.

B. J.'s next step was to decide on the building dimensions and layout of the floor plan. He decided that he would visit several new or recently remodeled stores to gain information for his decision. B. J. first visited Luther's Market in a neighboring city. Luther's situation was somewhat similar to B. J.'s in that his business had increased to a point where enlarging the store seemed desirable. Figure 18-6 shows a floor plan of Luther's enlarged market.

From visiting the store, B. J. found out that Luther was not entirely satisfied with his remodeled layout. Luther pointed out the following facts: (a) His produce labor expense had gone up more than anticipated and customers frequently complained of items not in display case, (b) customer traffic was very light (less than 30 percent) in parts of the store, and (c) customers were frequently going in opposite directions within the same aisle, giving rise to considerable confusion.

What was wrong with Luther's remodeled layout? First of all, he started with an almost impossible situation. He was unable to obtain the property where the apartments were located. This resulted in an irregular

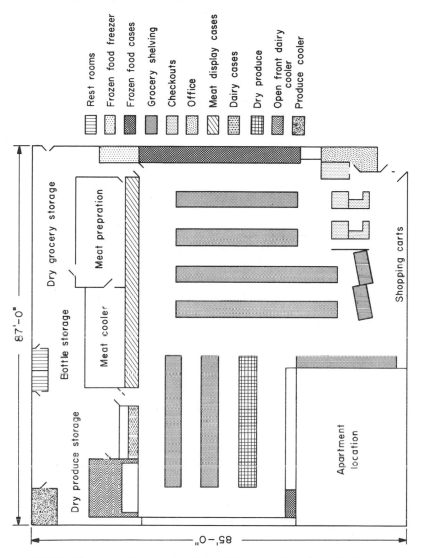

FIGURE 18-6:   Supermarket Layout Showing a Poor Shopping Pattern.

shopping area. Because he wanted the new shelving to be at least 32 feet in length, he was forced to turn it in the opposite direction from the existing shelving. This offered customers too many alternative choices of directions to shop, resulting in a poor shopping pattern. Luther also made a poor selection in the location of the produce department. The produce display area was much too far from the produce work room, necessitating additional time in stocking the produce shelves. It would have been well

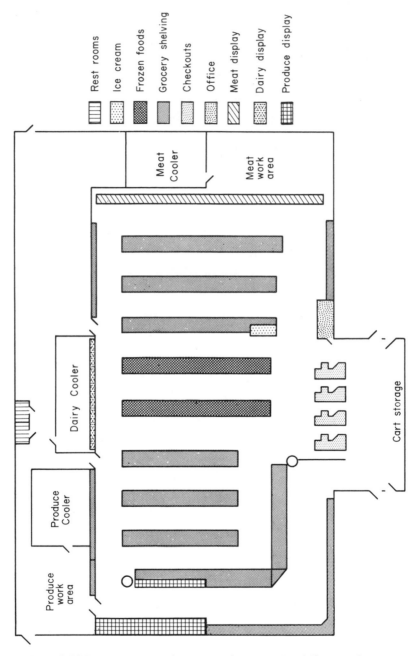

Rest rooms
Ice cream
Frozen foods
Grocery shelving
Checkouts
Office
Meat display
Dairy display
Produce display

Meat Cooler

Meat work area

Dairy Cooler

Produce Cooler

Produce work area

Cart storage

FIGURE 18-7:   Supermarket Layout Showing a Good Shopping Pattern.

if the produce display area were visible from the produce work area, enabling the produce employees to guard more easily against emptied display cases.

From his visit to Luther's Market B. J. realized that there was a great need for careful planning in his layout. B J. decided that he would again consult Jim Johnson. Jim sent him the floor plan outlined in Figure 18-7. B. J. examined the proposed layout and found that it contained none of the limitations of the layout shown in Figure 18-6. The meat, produce, and dairy storage and work areas were located close to the display area and it appeared that the customers would file through the store evenly. This floor plan was designed for a building 100 feet wide and 80 feet long, thus yielding the necessary 8,000 square foot floor space. B. J. decided he would utilize this floor plan. The next question to answer was could he afford to build it?

Financial management

B. J. had to consider how he was going to obtain the money necessary to build, equip, and stock the new store. With the help of Jim Johnson he budgeted his estimated expense.

B. J. decided he would like to have a concrete block building with a glass and brick front and no interior supports. Inquiries to a local contractor placed the cost of the building at $8.00 per square foot or about $64,000 for an 8,000 square foot building. Since B. J. was short of capital he decided to let a local investment corporation construct the building and lease it to him for 20 years. The two parties agreed to a lease with one percent of gross sales payable as rent. Based on projected sales of $18,000 to $20,000, the investment company anticipated a return of 13 percent to 17 percent on their investment.

Having made arrangements to finance the building, B. J. then turned to financing the fixtures, equipment, and additional stock for the new store.

B. J. called for bids on the fixtures and equipment contract and accepted a low bid of $75,000. This figure was in line with what Jim Johnson estimated using his floor plan.

B. J. had 3,000 square feet in his old store and it required about $21,000 in inventory to stock it. This amounted to $7.00 per square foot. Since his new store would contain 5,000 additional square feet, B. J. estimated that it would require $35,000 more to stock the new store.

	New Capital Requirements	Capital Source
Building	$64,000	Investment Corp.
Fixtures and Equipment	75,000	?
Inventory	35,000	?

B. J. had accumulated $50,000 in savings from his food business in recent years. This left $60,000 that he would need to borrow from the bank. With the help of his accountant he prepared the following projected income statement and balance sheet to use as evidence of his ability to pay.

Department Sales Mix Projection

	% of Sales	Gross Profit	Contribution to Expenses and Profit
Grocery	69	14.00%	$ 9.66
Meat	23	20.00%	4.60
Produce	8	27.00%	2.16
	100		$16.42

From his past records B. J. estimated that from every $100 of sales $16.42 would be available to pay operating expenses and profit.

Projected Income Statement
(Per Week)

Sales	$18,000	100.0%
Cost of Goods Sold	15,048	83.6
Gross Margin	$ 2,952	16.4%
Expenses		
Wages	$ 1,080	6.0%
Manager's Salary	198	1.1
Advertising	270	1.5
Rent	180	1.0
Supplies	144	.8
Taxes	144	.8
Insurance	36	.2
Repairs and Maintenance	54	.3
Depreciation	198	1.1
Utilities	126	.7
Accounting and Legal	18	.1
Other Expense	72	.4
Total Expense	$ 2,520	14.0%
Net Operating Profit	$ 432	2.4%
Interest Expense	70	.4
Net Profit	$ 362	2.0%
Other Income	54	.3
Income, Before Taxes	$ 416	2.3%

PROJECTED BALANCE SHEET
December 31, 1968

Assets		*Percent of* *Total Assets*
Current Assets		
Cash	$ 12,967	8.46%
Accounts Receivable	2,344	1.53
Inventory	56,523	36.88
Total Current Assets	$ 71,834	46.87%
Fixed Assets		
Fixtures and Equipment	$ 75,271	49.12%
Truck and Auto	1,172	.76
Leasehold	806	.53
Other Fixed Assets	1,172	.76
Total Fixed Assets	$ 78,421	51.17%
Other Assets	3,003	1.96
Total Assets	$153,258	100.0 %

Liabilities		
Current Liabilities		
Accounts Payable	$ 2,699	1.76%
Other Current Liabilities	10,403*	6.78
Total Current Liabilities	$ 13,102	8.54%
Total Fixed Liabilities	65,156	42.52
Total Liabilities	$ 78,258	51.06%
Net Worth	75,000	48.94
Total Liabilities and Net Worth	$153,258	100.0 %

Balance Sheet Ratios

Current Ratio	5.48
Quick Ratio	.989
Sales to Total Assets	6.11
Sales to Current Assets	13.03
Sales to Fixed Assets	11.94
Average Inventory Turnover	13.84
Percent Return on Total Investment	14.66
Percent Return on Owner's Equity (Net Worth)	25.09

* Includes $10,000 due on proposed bank note during the next year.

Break-even analysis

Another way to calculate whether the remodeling and expansion of the store is a good management decision for B. J. is to calculate the weekly sales volume which he needs in order to break even. Break-even analysis is used instead of marginal analysis (as in Chapter 14) when considering output levels and profits, since for a multiproduct business such as B. J.'s supermarket, computing marginal costs and marginal revenues is exceedingly difficult.

In businesses where variable costs remain constant per unit of sale over a relatively large range of outputs and where prices are administered, break-even analysis can be quite helpful. The break-even equation is:

Fixed Costs + Variable Costs Per Unit Sale × Units Sold = Administered Price × Units Sold.

Units sold is the unknown in the equation.

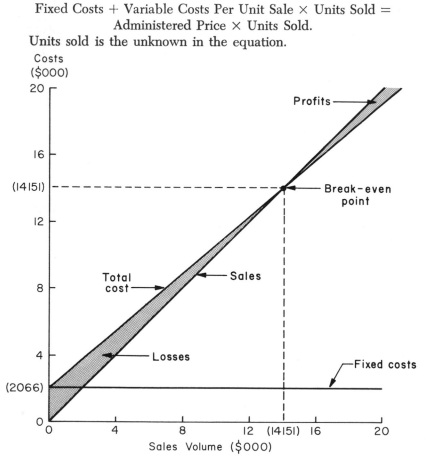

FIGURE 18-8:   Illustration of Break-even Point Calculation.

B. J. has to determine what would be the lowest weekly sales volume that would enable him to break even, or to have his revenue equal expenses. B. J. has to decide which of his expense items would vary with his sales volume and which are fixed or do not decrease as sales volume decreases.

In examining his wage expense B. J. decides that if sales were to fall 5 to 25 percent he could cut his labor by one checkout, one carryout boy, one part-time employee in the meat department, and one part-time stock boy. This would result in a weekly labor savings of $130. B. J.'s labor expenses do not decrease substantially with a decrease in sales because he is forced to keep his higher-paid key employees.

Manager's salary, advertising, taxes, insurance, repairs and mainte- nance, depreciation, utilities, accounting, legal, and other expenses would remain basically unchanged if sales volume fell. However, rent and sup- plies would decrease as sales fell. These expenses vary directly with sales within wide ranges.

From the information on his projected income statement B. J. knows that for every dollar of sales he gets 16.4 cents gross profit. His fixed weekly expenses would be as follows:

Wages	$ 950
Manager's Salary	198
Advertising	270
Taxes	144
Insurance	36
Repairs and Maintenance	54
Depreciation	198
Utilities	126
Accounting and Legal	18
Other	72
Total Fixed Expenses	$2,066
Variable expenses:	
Rent	1.0 percent of sales
Supplies	.8 percent of sales

B. J. can figure his break-even sales volume by putting the above information together in the following form:

Fixed expenses + variable expenses = revenue from sales, or:

$$\$ 2,066 + .010\,X + .008\,X = .164\,X$$
$$2,066 = .164\,X - .010\,X - .008\,X$$
$$2,066 = .146\,X$$
$$\$14,151 = X$$

It would require about $14,151 of weekly sales for B. J. to break even on his investment. See Figure 18-8 for a graphic presentation.

If you were the banker would you lend the money to B. J.? B. J. should have the ability to pay installments of about $2,500 per month, or $30,000 per year, without undue strain on the business.

This is an example of a case problem which illustrates how the functional areas in business management are considered in solving a problem.

part

19

The world agricultural situation

The world agricultural situation can be viewed in several ways. "Prophets of doom" look at the rapid rate of increase in the world's population and compare it to the slower rate of increase in food production. Admittedly, if one looks at these two rates over the past 25 years for many of the countries of the world, it is a dismal outlook. Looking at the situation in another way, however, considerable optimism can be generated. The productive potential of the vast unopened lands in Africa and South America, the strides forward in discovering new biological and mechanical technologies which can be applied for more intensive cultivation of existing farm lands, the improvements in communication and transportation facilities, the ability of man to influence and often control the biological environment in which agricultural production takes place—all of these and more constitute legitimate reasons to be hopeful.

THE OVERALL VIEW

The world food problem arises from the uneven distribution of what food is currently produced among the countries of the world, within countries, and among families whose level of income differs. World-wide surveys in the 1960's indicate no food shortages based on total food produced per person in the world. But two thirds of the world's population live in the "developing countries" where evidence indicates that 20 percent suffer from too few calories and 60 percent suffer from too little protein. There are families with nutritionally deficient diets in every country of the world.

In the "developed economies," the major causes are not a lack of availability of food but rather an inadequate purchasing power to buy the right foods and ignorance about what constitutes a good diet. These would still remain serious problems even if the current world food supply could be distributed properly in a physical sense. Individual government efforts to subsidize food purchasing power or institute education programs can help the situation, but the difficulty experienced in getting many of the low income families in the United States to purchase more, better-quality food under existing programs points to no easy answer.

Dietary variations within countries varies perhaps as widely as between countries. Using minimum diet standards developed by the Food and Agricultural Organization of the United Nations (FAO), surveys in South Asian and Latin American countries show that the poorest 25 percent of the people consume diets with caloric and protein contents that are only about three-fourths of the country average and fall far below minimum nutritional requirements. Within these low income groups, preschool children, pregnant women, and nursing mothers are particularly susceptible to malnutrition.

World food needs [1]

World population was about 3.5 billion in 1965. It is expected to grow to about five billion by 1985 and reach six to seven billion by the turn of the century. If the world population continues to increase at 1965 rates (1.8 percent), about half again more food calories will be required in 1985 than were needed in 1965. Even with a progressive reduction to 30 percent in fertility rates there will be need for a 43 percent increase.

These projections of world requirements, however, mask the needs of heavily populated countries within the underdeveloped world. For example, India and Brazil at their present rate of population increase will need over 100 percent more calories in 1985 than in 1965, and Pakistan will need nearly 150 percent more.

These quantity estimates portray two crucial aspects of the relationship between population growth and food needs. First, population and food problems are centered in the already poor, diet-deficient countries where food production is low and population growth rates are high. Sec-

[1] Estimates taken from *The World Food Problem,* A Report of the President's Science Advisory Committee, Report of the Panel on the World Food Supply, The White House, May 1967, Volume 2.

ond, the disproportionate need for food in the developing countries cannot be solved during the next 20 years by successful programs of family planning.[2]

The protein dimension is of equal or greater importance than the caloric dimension. There are 22 amino acids of which ten are known to be essential for proper growth and development. Amounts of protein vary among foods while the protein quality is based on the degree to which all the amino acids are present. Wheat, rice, and corn, which constitute a staple in the diet of nearly all peoples in the underdeveloped countries, are all incomplete protein sources since two or three of the essential amino acids are either missing or present in very small amounts. Protein requirements also vary with a person's age, weight, and rate of metabolism. FAO has estimated that world protein requirements will be 50 percent higher in 1985 as compared to 1965. Again, as in the case of calories, protein needs in developing countries such as India and Brazil run two to three times higher than the 50 percent world need estimate.

Regional needs

The Foreign Regional Analysis Division of the Economic Research Service, USDA prepared *The World Food Budget, 1970* which summarizes the supply and utilization of food commodities for the countries of the world, assesses world food needs, and evaluates the problems and possibilities of closing the food gap.[3] Food balances were prepared for 92 countries for two 3-year periods, 1956-58 and 1959-61 with projections for 1970.

The world was divided into two groups: diet-adequate[4] and diet-deficit[5] countries. The diet-deficit countries are usually poor and food deficiencies merely reflect the low level of living in general. A diet deficit was defined to exist when food availabilities per capita per day (calories, protein, and fat) yield a nutritional level below that representing minimum physiological requirements for normal activity and health, plus a 10-12 percent loss allowance between the retail level and consumption.

The diet-adequate countries are typically higher in total calories

---

[2] Assuming 1965 rates of population increase, the world population would be 5.03 and 7.15 billion respectively for 1985 and 2000. A 30 percent reduction in fertility would reduce these figures to 4.65 and 6.00 billion. Note that the difference in the two estimates is only 385 million for 1985 but widens to 1.15 billion by the year 2000.

[3] *The World Food Budget 1970,* Foreign Agricultural Economic Report No. 19, E.R.S., U.S.D.A., October 1964.

[4] U.S., Canada; Mexico; Brazil; Argentina; Uruguay; Northern, Southern, and Eastern Europe; USSR; Southern Africa; Japan; and Oceania.

[5] Central America and Caribbean; Bolivia; Chile; Colombia; Ecuador; Paraguay; Peru; Venezuela; Northern, West Central, and East Africa; West Asia; India; Pakistan, and Ceylon; East Asia; Mainland China.

consumed per capita, lower in the percentage of calories ingested from high carbohydrate foods, and higher in the percentage of calories obtained from meat, fish, eggs, fats and oils, and milk products. (Table 19-1.) Diet-deficit populations get most of their calories from cereal grains, high carbohydrate foods, and other starchy crops.

RESOURCE AVAILABILITY FOR WORLD FOOD PRODUCTION [6]

The agricultural potential of any land area is influenced by (a) the physical, chemical, and biological properties of the soil, (b) the annual range and seasonality of temperature, (c) the annual amount and seasonal distribution of precipitation relative to evapotranspiration, and (d) man's ability to make available additional moisture through irrigation.

Soil and water

Recent estimates indicate that the area of potentially arable land is about 7.86 billion acres or 24 percent of the ice-free area in the world. Less than half of the potentially arable land is now cultivated, and it is more than three times the world acreage actually harvested in the 1960's. Another 9 billion acres (28 percent of total) has potential for grazing; the rest (48 percent of total) has no agricultural potential.

In Asia and Europe, over 80 percent of the potentially arable land is cultivated, but in Africa and South America there are many acres of land to be opened to cultivation. (Table 19-2.) More than half of the potentially arable land lies in the tropics. Most of the presently cultivated land is in the cool temperate zones.

About 11 percent of the potentially arable land in the world needs irrigation water to grow even one crop. In the remaining seven billion acres, at least one crop could be grown without irrigation, and multiple cropping is possible over much of it. Without irrigation, multiple cropping could increase the gross cropped area (cultivated area times number of crops) to 9.8 billion acres annually. This is about three times the presently "cultivated" land and about two billion acres more than the total potentially arable land. If irrigation water were made available for double or triple cropping, the gross cropped area on the earth would amount to over 16 billion acres.

The rate of increase in harvested acreage has averaged nearly four percent since 1960 in South America but only 1.4 percent in Asia and even less in Africa. If rates of population increase in developing areas are to be matched by increases in food production, expenditures on water and

---

[6] Data in this part taken from *The World Food Problem, op. cit.*, 407-469. Human resource availability is omitted as it is discussed elsewhere in the text.

TABLE 19-1: Per Capita Calorie Levels by Food Groups and Geographic Regions, Average 1959-61
(Ranked According to High Carbohydrate Foods Consumed)

	Calorie level (Number)	High carbohydrate foods[1]	Wheat	Rice	Other grains[2]	Other starchy crops[3]	Pulses and nuts[4]	Sugar	Vegetables and Fruit	Fats and oils[5]	Meat, fish, and eggs	Milk products[6]
								(Percent)				
United States	3190	40	17.4	0.9	2.5	3.1	3.3	15.7	6.2	20.5	16.9	13.5
Canada	3100	42	18.8	0.6	1.9	4.5	1.9	16.3	4.8	15.1	22.0	14.1
Oceania	3260	43	25.2	0.6	1.3	2.7	1.3	13.4	4.7	14.3	24.8	11.7
Northern Europe	3060	48	23.4	0.6	4.0	3.9	1.7	13.4	4.5	17.8	16.4	11.3
Argentina, Uruguay	3200	56	33.2	1.7	2.3	3.0	1.0	12.4	3.3	12.5	21.0	6.6
Southern Europe	2720	60	40.1	2.4	3.8	3.0	4.4	7.3	7.4	15.6	6.9	5.8
Eastern Europe	3000	66	32.1	1.0	16.5	7.8	1.3	8.5	2.9	11.4	11.9	6.6
Central America and Carribean	2240	69	8.8	9.4	23.0	12.7	5.9	15.0	4.2	8.6	7.4	5.0
Mexico	2580	70	11.1	1.6	42.2	1.8	8.0	13.0	2.8	8.1	6.1	5.3
Other South America	2260	70	16.9	5.9	16.0	15.5	3.9	15.9	3.9	7.5	9.0	5.5
Brazil	2710	71	8.6	14.5	11.2	20.9	8.9	15.4	2.3	5.9	8.4	3.9
Southern Africa	2670	72	14.0	1.1	41.6	1.1	1.7	14.0	2.4	5.3	12.4	6.4
West Asia	2350	72	48.0	4.2	8.8	1.6	4.1	9.4	7.6	8.1	4.0	4.2
U.S.S.R.	3040	73	35.7	0.8	16.9	3.9	1.4	9.3	1.9	8.9	8.1	6.6
North Africa	2210	73	26.4	3.1	36.2	1.3	5.7	6.1	6.1	6.0	4.3	4.8
India	2060	74	11.3	33.1	19.0	2.6	13.2	8.2	2.0	4.2	0.9	5.5
Japan	2360	78	11.7	46.9	4.6	7.7	5.9	6.7	4.2	5.0	5.9	1.4
Other East Asia	2150	78	1.8	50.1	7.7	12.7	6.6	5.2	5.4	5.7	4.1	0.7
Other South Asia	2120	79	19.4	47.1	4.9	1.0	5.9	6.7	3.6	4.0	3.0	4.4
West Central Africa	2460	81	1.2	5.7	27.2	45.3	6.5	1.5	1.0	9.0	2.0	0.6
East Africa	2390	83	2.3	8.4	55.9	12.4	6.5	4.3	0.8	3.4	3.6	2.4
Communist Asia	1790	87	12.2	44.3	18.1	11.1	5.9	1.2	1.7	3.1	2.3	0.1

[1] Grains, sugar, roots, tubers, and plantains.
[2] Corn, barley, oats, rye, millet, sorghum, buckwheat, quinoa, spelt, and teff.
[3] Potatoes, sweetpotatoes, yams, cassava, and similar root crops.
[4] Beans, peas, lentils, chickpeas, and similar dry leguminous seeds.
[5] Butter (fat content), edible animal fats, marine oils, and vegetable oils used for food.
[6] Except butter.

SOURCE: *The World Food Budget 1970*, Foreign Agricultural Economic Report No. 19, U.S.D.A., E.R.S., October 1964, Table 1, p. 4.

357

TABLE 19-2: Present Population and Cultivated Land on Each Continent Compared with Potentially Arable Land

Region	1965 population (millions)	Total	Area potentially arable (billions of acres)	Cultivated [1]	Cultivated land per person (acres)	Ratio of cultivated land to potentially arable land (percent)
Africa	310	7.46	1.81	.39	1.3	22
Asia	1855	6.76	1.55	1.28	.7	83
Australia and New Zealand	14	2.03	.38	.04	2.9	2
Europe	445	1.18	.43	.38	.9	88
North America	255	5.21	1.15	.59	2.3	51
South America	197	4.33	1.68	.19	1.0	11
U.S.S.R.	234	5.52	.88	.56	2.4	64
Total	3310	32.49	7.88	3.43	1.0 (ave.)	44 (ave.)

[1] Same as FAO "Arable land and land under permanent crops." It includes land under crops, temporary fallow, temporary meadows for mowing or pasture, market and kitchen gardens, fruit trees, vines, shrubs, and rubber plantations.

SOURCE: *The World Food Problem*, Report of the Panel on the World Food Supply, President's Science Advisory Committee, The White House, May 1967, Volume II, Table 7-9, p. 434.

land development must be increased more than four times present levels. The cost of developing new land for agricultural use varies widely and is influenced by political and social conditions as well as physical and economic factors. Development costs per acre range from only a few dollars per acre to over $1000 per acre.

About 11 percent of the world's cultivated land was irrigated by the mid-1960's. This relatively low percentage suggests that irrigated farming plays only a small role in the world food situation. But this is not the case. When the irrigated acreage is related to the distribution of world population, it becomes apparent that a large fraction of the earth's people, mainly in diet-deficit countries, depends heavily upon irrigation for food. Diet-deficit countries with two-thirds of the world's people have less than half the arable land, but three-fourths of the irrigated land. Estimates place the total irrigated land at 500 million acres by 1975 and 750 million acres by the turn of this century.

Fertilizer, seed, pesticides, and machinery

Four kinds of capital inputs of major importance to increasing agricultural production are fertilizers, seeds, pesticides, and machinery.

Fertilizer. Only six (15 percent) of the 44 million metric tons of commercial fertilizers [7] used in 1965-66 was applied to crops growing in the developing countries. To keep food production growing at an equal pace to population, it is estimated that fertilizer usage should increase to 34 million metric tons by 1985 and 67 million metric tons by 2000.

To achieve the needed increase in fertilizer by 1985 will require a $17 billion investment plus an additional annual cost to farmers of $9 billion. There will be large increases in international trade in fertilizer and fertilizer raw materials. Because efficient potash and phosphate mining operations are large and complex, they are usually located at the source of raw materials. The suggested cost estimates do not include costs associated with facilities, roads, and railroads which might be required. Additionally, it is estimated that three skilled and five unskilled people are required for each thousand tons of plant nutrients that are provided and distributed per year, which suggests that 50,000 college graduates could be needed by 1985 in the fertilizer and associated agri-industries.

Seeds. Improved seeds must be available and used by farmers if significant gains are to be made in crop yields. FAO has given a "seed rating" to characterize nations on their development, production, distribution, and proper use of better seeds. Using corn, rice, and wheat as indicators, the highest rating (1) was given to such countries as Japan, Taiwan, and the Netherlands. The lowest rating (4) was given, for ex-

[7] Neither human nor animal wastes used for fertilizer are considered.

ample, to Pakistan, Iran, and Jordan. Yields for nations with a "1" rating averaged 2.3 times higher than those in the "4" category, and the top group had almost all of their grain crop land planted with improved seed as compared to less than 10 percent for the bottom group.

It has been estimated that if 50 percent of any cultivated area is planted with improved seeds instead of traditional varieties, yields can be expected to double. Even in developing areas the private commercial firms could supply a good portion of the new seed. These estimates assume that other improved practices such as use of fertilizers, pesticides, machinery, etc. will also be used. If commercial firms only supplied 25 percent of the seed requirements of the developing free world areas implying a doubling of food production by the year 2000, an investment of about $305 million in seed plants will be required (70 percent in Asia and 15 percent each in Latin America and Africa), and the annual operating costs to farmers would approximate $1.6 billion.

Pesticides. Large increases in pesticides will be necessary to increase food production. Minimum losses of food from pests range from 20-30 percent on a world wide basis. Viruses, bacteria, fungi, protozoa, nematodes, insects, birds, and rodents compete directly with man in consuming food, and while weeds do not consume food directly, they compete with plants for water and soil nutrients thus reducing crop yields.

Pests can be controlled by biological or chemical methods. The development of rust-resistant wheat varieties has also had a major impact on yields in the United States although constant research effort is necessary since the rust organism changes rapidly. Elimination of certain insect varieties has been accomplished by sex sterilization techniques. However, chemical agents remain as the chief control weapons, and their use increases rapidly as plant production is intensified. The amount of pesticides applied in Africa or India amount to only about one percent of the quantities used in Japan with its intensive agriculture and high yields. Increased use of pesticides for insect control calls for increased use of fertilizer, fungicides, herbicides, and fumigants.

In the United States, the use of herbicides is regarded as a labor-saving measure, but recent studies in the Philippines on rice indicated that when propanil (a modern selective herbicide) was applied as a weed control, a 43 percent increase in yield resulted over conventional hand weeding. If these favorable results can be duplicated in other areas, selective herbicides are likely to be widely adopted for rice production, even in areas having large labor supplies and low wages.

By the mid-1960's only 120,000 metric tons of pesticides were used annually by the developing world (excluding China). To double food production, usage is expected to increase five fold which will require $1.2 billion in manufacturing plant investment plus $670 million for formulation and distribution facilities.

Machinery. In the United States, the rapid mechanization of agriculture has been construed as an attempt to make more efficient use of labor rather than to increase yields. However, recent studies have shown that the use of mechanized power influences yields favorably for several reasons: better seedbed preparation, more timely seedbed preparations, it may allow double or triple cropping, seed placement is more accurate, machines allow for a uniform application of pesticides, and, finally, more timely harvesting is possible.

The basic machinery units needed include tractors, plows, disc harrows, peg harrows, gain drills, planters, distributors, cultivators, sprayers, and threshing equipment. Improved animal drawn seeders, harrows, and cultivators would also help.

The number of tractors used in the developing world increased from about 400,000 in 1955 to 900,000 in 1965, an average compound growth rate of eight percent per year.[8] It is estimated that the addition of horsepower per unit of land in developing countries has a significant effect on increasing yields up to at least 0.5 horsepower per hectare (2.5 acres). The United States has about one horsepower available per hectare while Latin America has .19 and Africa only .05 horsepower per hectare.

The cost of agricultural machinery is surprisingly low relative to the costs of other inputs. To provide manufacturing plants to produce tractors, power tillers, power sprayers, power harvesting and threshing requirements up to a half horsepower per hectare in Asia, Latin America, and Africa would require about $1.8 billion. A more difficult problem would be developing the manpower to develop, produce, distribute the machinery and train people in its use.

Livestock [9]

Total livestock in the world numbers over three billion animals plus an equal number of domesticated fowl. While about two out of three animals are located in the developing countries, they produce only 20-30 percent of the world's meat, milk, and eggs. This low productivity can be attributed to a failure to utilize scientific principles of breeding sanitation and disease control. The quantity of animal food products produced in the developing world are sufficient to supply an average of only nine grams of animal protein per person per day. In contrast, there are 44 grams available per person per day in the developed countries.

Infrastructure

Agricultural production is aided and encouraged directly by the amount of infrastructure or social overhead capital available. Roads, com-

[8] Wheel and crawler tractors, estimated average of 30 horsepower each.
[9] *The World Food Problem, op. cit.,* pp. 243-292.

munication systems, power, and educational institutions are examples. Without roads, inputs of seed and fertilizer may not be moved to farmers, and similarly, they allow farmers to move their product to market. Generally, the more infrastructure a country has, the lower the relative cost of its food production is likely to be. There is more economic incentive to produce food. With this brief sketch of resource availability in the world, let's look at the recent record of world food production.

THE RECENT RECORD OF FOOD PRODUCTION [10]

The year 1967 was one of record output for world agriculture and more significantly, a record for the developing countries. Excluding Communist Asia, per capita food production increased 5-6 percent, and heavily populated countries like Pakistan, Brazil, and India made substantial gains in grain production. India registered a 20 percent gain, although there was no measurable improvement in some countries such as Indonesia (Table 19-3).

Per capita food supplies in the developing world were static during the 1960's at two to four percent above 1957-59 levels. India's per capita food supplies slipped below 1957-59 levels in 1965 and 1966, but bounced back dramatically with the 1967 record harvest. In the developed countries, per capita supplies have climbed rapidly, standing 13 percent higher in 1967 than 1957-59 levels.

Grains

Wheat. World wheat production in 1967 was 277 million metric tons 25 percent higher than in 1960 (Table 19-4). The world's leading producers are U.S.S.R., United States, Canada, China, France, India, Italy, Turkey, Australia, and Argentina. It is grown mostly in the temperate climate zones, and provides one of the staple foods for several developing countries including Northern China and India. The United States and Canada account for over half of total world exports of wheat. Western Europe and Asia are major importers.

Rice. Rice rivals wheat as a food grain being the staple food of the populous Far East. World rice production reached a new high in 1967 of 262 million metric tons with most of the increase occurring in importing countries. Mainland China produces one-third of the world's total production followed by India (23 percent), Pakistan and Japan (7 percent

---

[10] Data in this section taken from *The World Agricultural Situation*, Foreign Agricultural Economic Report #38, E.R.S. U.S.D.A., February 1968 and *A Graphic Summary of World Agriculture*, Misc. Publication #705, E.R.S. U.S.D.A, revised 1964.

TABLE 19-3: Indices of Total and Per Capita Agricultural Production for the World and Selected Areas, 1960-67 (1957-59 = 100)

Area	Total for year							
	1960	1961	1962	1963	1964	1965	1966	1967[4]
World [1]	106	108	111	114	117	118	122	127
Developed countries [2]	106	107	111	112	116	117	123	126
Less developed countries [3]	107	111	112	117	119	121	120	130
India	110	115	110	117	120	109	107	128
Other less developed countries	106	109	113	117	119	126	125	130
	Per capita							
World [1]	102	102	103	103	104	103	104	107
Developed countries [2]	103	103	106	105	108	107	112	113
Less developed countries [3]	102	103	102	103	103	102	98	104
India	105	108	101	104	105	93	89	104
Other less developed countries	101	101	102	103	102	105	102	103

[1] Excluding Communist Asia.
[2] North America, Europe, U.S.S.R., Japan, South Africa, Australia and New Zealand.
[3] Latin America, Asia (excluding Japan and communist Asia) and Africa (except South Africa).
[4] Preliminary.

SOURCE: *The World Agricultural Situation,* Foreign Agricultural Economic Report No. 38, E.R.S., U.S.D.A., February 1968, Table 1, p. 6.

each), Indonesia (5 percent), Thailand (4 percent), Burma and Brazil (3 percent each), Philippines and the United States (1.5 percent each). Leading exporters, however, are the United States, Thailand, and Burma.

Gains in rice yields have been disappointing in the rice bowl countries of Asia except for Japan. After extensive research in breeding desirable characteristics selected from several thousand rice varieties, the International Rice Research Institute completed the development in 1968 of a new variety which has hopes of significantly boosting yields.

Corn. Corn is classified as a feed grain but some varieties are also an important food source for many people in the underdeveloped world. The United States accounts for over one-half of world corn production which totaled 227 million metric tons in 1967. Other important producers are U.S.S.R., Brazil, Argentina, Yugoslavia, Mexico, Romania, and South America. Western Europe is the major importing region. The United States, Argentina, South Africa, and Romania are principal exporters. In recent years, Japan has become an important importer of corn to supply

TABLE 19-4: World Production of Food and Feed Grains, 1960-67

Commodity	Year							
	1960	1961	1962	1963	1964	1965	1966	1967
				(million metric tons)				
Food grains:								
Wheat	222	211	237	226	255	247	280	277
Rice, rough	229	233	233	242	253	243	241	262
Rye	34	34	32	30	32	34	30	32
Total	485	478	502	498	540	524	551	571
Annual change		− 7	+24	− 4	+42	−16	+27	+20
Feed grains: [1]								
Corn	180	177	179	193	182	193	206	227
Barley	71	69	78	82	87	86	94	98
Oats	56	49	48	45	41	43	44	43
Sorghum and millet [2]	35	31	34	35	34	35	40	43
Total	342	326	339	355	344	357	384	411
Annual change		−16	+13	+16	−11	+13	+27	+27

[1] Excludes communist Asia.

[2] U.S.A., India, Argentina, Mexico, U.A.R., Pakistan, South Africa, Turkey, Australia and Japan.

SOURCE: *The World Agricultural Situation,* Foreign Agricultural Economic Report No. 38, E.R.S., U.S.D.A., February 1968, Tables 2 and 6, pp. 7 and 16.

her rapidly growing livestock industry. A large part of Japan's corn imports come from Thailand where production has grown rapidly—doubling since 1960.

Other Grains. Barley production was 98 million metric tons in 1967, up a third over 1960. Barley is the world's second most important feed grain, and like corn is used as a food grain throughout Asia and Africa. Principal producers are the U.S.S.R., United States, Mainland China, France, Canada, and the United Kingdom.

Millet and sorghum are widely grown and used as feed grains except in Asia and Africa. World output which was stable at 34-35 million metric tons, 1960 to 1965, rose to 43 million metric tons in 1967. Mainland China, India, and the United States are leading producers with the United States as the only significant exporting country.

Oat production at 43 million metric tons in 1967 was nearly 25 percent lower than in 1960. Production is limited to temperate North America, Europe, and the U.S.S.R. Rye production at 34 million metric tons in 1967 is some four percent lower than 1950-54 and is produced principally in Soviet-bloc countries. The decline in oats partly reflects replacement of animal power by mechanical power and its consequent lower economic value compared to other grains.

Oilseeds

Oilseeds (including oil bearing tree fruits) are the source of more than half of the world's supply of fats and oils. In terms of quantity harvested, soybeans, cottonseeds, and peanuts are the leading oilseeds. There were record world crops of soybeans, peanuts, and sunflowerseed in 1967. The United States accounts for about three-fourths of total world production of soybeans.

India is the world's leading peanut producer with about one-third of the total. Nigeria, Senegal, United States, Indonesia, and Brazil account for another fourth. African countries are the major exporters and European countries are large importers. About two thirds of the peanut production is crushed for oil. Peanut oil comprises one fifth of total world trade of edible oils and oil beanery materials.

The economic components of cotton are lint and cottonseed. As a source of human food protein, cottonseeds are limited because a toxic agent gossypol is present. A new variety has been developed without the toxin. However, a great virtue of cottonseed is that it is indigenous to protein-poor tropical areas of Africa, Asia, and Latin America, and can readily be used as a feed for ruminant animals.

Other important oil-beanery crops include sunflower seed, produced mainly in the U.S.S.R.; rapeseed produced principally in India and Mainland China; flaxseed, largely produced in Argentina and North America; olives, the traditional source of oil in the Mediterranean area; tropical palm products-coconuts, obtained mostly from the Far East in the form of copra; and oil palm fruit coming mostly from Africa as palm oil and palm kernels.

Livestock

The world has about one billion each of cattle and sheep, over a half billion pigs, about one-third billion goats, 100 million buffalo, and more than 130 million horses, mules, asses, and camels. World meat production increased 57 percent in the ten-year period 1952-54 to 1962-64 (Table 19-5). Beef and veal constituted about 47 percent of the total, pork about 44 percent, and mutton and lamb the remaining 9 percent. Gains in North and South America and Africa were substantially below that in other nations.

Milk production in the world (excluding U.S.S.R. and Mainland China) gained 18 percent in a similar period. Cow milk accounts for 90 percent of the total; buffalo milk is an important food source to people in the Far East (Table 19-6). Egg production increased 21 percent in

1962-64 over 10 years earlier showing wide gains in Europe, Latin America, and Africa. The Near East, Far East, and United States actually declined (Table 19-6).

TABLE 19-5: Indices of Average Meat Production from Indigenous Animals by Geographic Regions, 1962-64 [1] (1952-54 = 100)

Region	Beef and Veal	Pork	Mutton and Lamb	Total meat increase
World	151.0	166.3	149.3	157.2
World [2]	133.6	137.4	128.8	134.6
Europe	145.2	153.5	120.7	147.8
North America	134.7	115.5	108.1	125.6
Latin America	121.5	119.3	105.0	120.1
Near East	162.7	—	169.2	165.8
Far East	125.9	203.3	110.5	145.9
Africa	117.2	111.9	132.4	120.0
Oceania	144.3	125.4	150.6	145.5
United States [3]	134.8	116.6	108.8	126.1

[1] Data were obtained from FAO Production Yearbooks from 1953 through 1965. Some data were incomplete and some averages involved approximations.
[2] Totals given are the sum of the regions and exclude the U.S.S.R. and Mainland China.
[3] Included in North America.

SOURCE: *The World Food Problem,* A Report of the Panel on the World Food Supply, President's Science Advisory Committee, White House, May 1967, Volume II, Table 4-4, p. 256.

TABLE 19-6: Indices of Average Milk Production and Egg Weight by Geographic Regions, 1962-64 [1] (1952-54 = 100)

Region	Cow	Goat	Sheep	Buffalo	Total milk	Total egg weight
World [2]	120.2	94.2	104.2	129.1	118.1	121.3
Europe	125.4	67.8	117.8	83.5	120.8	153.1
North America	106.1	—	—	—	106.1	101.3
Latin America	134.3	142.8	—	—	134.6	145.6
Near East	135.4	87.9	97.7	123.6	115.9	91.4
Far East	121.1	113.6	—	130.4	125.1	98.2
Africa	120.0	111.1	95.5	—	116.8	158.5
Oceania	119.2	—	—	—	119.2	125.9
United States [3]	104.7	—	—	—	104.7	96.6

[1] Data were obtained from FAO Production Yearbooks from 1953-1965. Some data were incomplete and some averages involved approximations.
[2] Totals given are the sum of the regions and exclude the U.S.S.R. and Mainland China.
[3] Included in North America.

SOURCE: *The World Food Problem,* A Report of the Panel on the World Food Supply, President's Science Advisory Committee, White House, May 1967, Volume II, Table 4-5, 6, pp. 257-259.

SUMMARY

Growth in per capita food supplies must be accelerated above the recent record in developing countries if the problems of hunger and malnutrition are to be alleviated. Population reduction through programs to reduce fertility will help but will not have any major impact before 1985. There is no shortage of land resources in Africa and South America. In Asia, however, the emphasis will probably be on increasing yields on existing cultivated land from the introduction of improved seeds, fertilizer, and pesticides. Water development projects and the introduction of mechanical power should give added impetus to the possibility of more double and triple cropping.

Despite their lack of several essential amino acids, wheat, rice, and corn will continue to be the principal food sources for most of the world's people. However, oilseeds are increasing rapidly (particularly soybeans). Present cereal grain production levels indicate a potential to supply as much protein as that supplied from animal sources. Animal meat supplies have great potential in places like East Africa and South America, provided certain animal health hazards are effectively controlled such as ticks and tsetse flies.

Trained and educated manpower may be as much a limiting factor to realizing gains in world food production as any physical or biological input. For example, the estimate of technical manpower needed to produce and distribute the inputs of seeds, fertilizer, pesticides, and machinery in the developing free world is 75,000 university graduates or their equivalent by 1985. Additional specially trained people will be required for research and extension education programs.

20

Increasing world food supplies

While increasing world food supplies might be considered a matter of organizing the land and water resources, adding necessary capital resources and man's labor, and teaching managers to efficiently coordinate the production processes involved, its initiation and coordination is enormously complex. A review of important ideas would perhaps be helpful. In Chapters 2 and 3 the efficiencies gained in production processes by specialization were emphasized as a key to man's early economic development. This notion has not lost its significance. In Chapters 4 through 8, natural resources, people, capital, and technology were discussed regarding their role in agricultural development. In Chapter 10, the importance of an effective marketing system was portrayed, and Chapter 11 on food consumption pointed out that money purchasing power was the prime determinant of the economic demand level for food by that part of the population not growing their own. In Part III, the economic principles which managers can use to guide their decisions as to what, how, and how much to produce were explained. In the chapter preceding this one, world resources that contribute to food production were surveyed. In addition, the favorable effect of a country's social overhead capital (infrastructure) was pointed out. A continuing awareness of these broad based ideas will be helpful.

THE "PACKAGE OF TECHNOLOGY" CONCEPT

How often do people commenting about the world food situation make statements like: "What's so complicated about increasing the food supply abroad? Fertilizer on those rice paddies in Asia is what's needed. In South America, straighten out the land reform problem and the rest will be easy. In the arid areas like Egypt, it's just a matter of getting irrigation water to the land." All of these statements and others of a similar nature certainly contain some truth and sound quite plausible to the uninformed layman. But these people miss one extremely important idea which should never be forgotten. While the use of one improved technology will probably have some positive influence on yields, it will also generate a need for other technologies to be introduced simultaneously if yields are to continue to be significantly increased. The process continues as new technologies are introduced. Higher levels of management input are also required. Hence, it is nearly always desirable to introduce several new technologies at the same time because of the interaction effect on yields. Adding fertilizer to the rice paddy on a Thailand farm might well cause the plant to grow much taller and add more rice kernels. But, if a strong stemmed rice variety is not used when the larger seed head forms at the top of the longer stem, it is likely to fall over and be lost resulting in a yield below that received from an unfertilized plot.

In the village of Tegalega in West Java, Indonesia, 57 farmers increased corn yields 600 percent by (1) using a new variety, (2) using recommended amounts and kinds of fertilizer, (3) changing the depth of planting the seeds, and (4) controlling insect pests. In most cases, only a package of new techniques can achieve such results.[1] Because of risk and uncertainty factors, a farmer in most developing countries needs promise of a substantial gain in yields (perhaps 40 percent or more) before he will be convinced to adopt a farming change. A cautionary factor in all countries is that sometimes a farmer's managerial capacity may be too low to effectively "put the package together."

METHODS OF ATTACKING THE WORLD FOOD PROBLEM [2]

Intensification of plant production

A comparison of crop yields between developing and developed countries indicates that food supplies can certainly be increased through

[1] A. T. Mosher, *"Getting Agriculture Moving."* New York: Frederick A. Praeger Publishers, October 1965, p. 78.

[2] "The World Food Problem," A Report of the President's Science Advisory Committee, Report of the Panel on the World Food Supply, The White House, May 1967, Volume 2.

intensification of plant production. For example, rice yields in Japan and the United States are over three times larger than in India (Table 20-1).

TABLE 20-1: Indices of Comparative Yields of Major Food Crops in Brazil, India, and Japan, 1964-65 (United States = 100)

	Brazil	India	Japan
Crop:			
Wheat	50	41	138
Corn	30	25	60
Rice	33	35	112
Potatoes	29	40	86
Sweet potatoes	107	68	206
Dry beans	46	21	57
Peanuts	82	49	118

SOURCE: Production Yearbook, FAO, 1965.

Corn yields within the United States were nearly three times higher in 1961-63 than in 1931-35; soybean yields were up 60 percent in the same period.

Developing Higher Yielding Varieties. The development of new grain germ plasm and varieties by conventional plant breeding techniques is one approach. The practice of hybridizing crop varieties has played a major role in increasing the quality and quantity of crops in the United States.

Adaptation of plants to specific environmental conditions, i.e., tolerance to drought, heat, light, soil salinity, and poor drainage, has received considerable effort. Plant environments are also continually changed by the introduction of other new technologies such as increased levels of fertilizer use and better use of irrigation water. Developing new varieties capable of absorbing improved practices is required.

Genetic resistance to pests, a form of biological control, is often the most economical control measure. Control of many damaging species of rust that attack cereal grains is an outstanding example although such control measures are not usually permanent since rust organisms rotate and attack previously resistant varieties. Genetic resistance to attacks from insects, such as the Hessian fly in winter wheat varieties, is relatively newer and good progress is being made. Other examples include building a resistance to aphids in alfalfa, the European corn borer in corn, and nematodes in lespedeza and soybeans. The breeding out or lowering of toxic agents like gossypol in cotton seeds and prussic acid in Sudangrass and forage sorghum are additional improvements.

Dwarf plants can be used to increase production since more plants can be planted per acre utilizing sunlight more efficiently. They respond to high fertilization rates without the resultant tall growth that stimulates lodging and reduces the efficiency of mechanical harvesting. Grain sorghums, wheat, corn, and rice have received primary attention.

Grain quality improvements have been sought in wheat where good milling and baking properties are essential, and also in barley where malting quality is important. Gas chromatography has expedited analyses of the fatty acids in vegetable oils. The improvement of the quality of protein will be discussed later in this chapter.

Utilization of Hybrid Vigor. Few programs to increase yields by hybrid vigor have been as dramatic as hybrid corn. Corn is one of the few plants that produce male and female flowers separately and the relative ease of removing the male flowers (tassels) makes it easy to hybridize. Few plants exhibit the necessary degree of self-sterility which allows cross-pollination by interplanting. Male sterility, which is transmitted from one generation to the next in the cytoplasm of the female sex cells, was discovered in onions in the 1920's and used in the production of commercial hybrids. It was later found in corn. But because commercial corn breeding depends on seed production, fertility must be restored when the hybrid is grown, or seed of nonsterile types must be blended with the hybrid seed. This difficulty has been overcome by incorporating fertility restoring genes in the male lines which overcome the sterilizing effect of the female cytoplasm. This method of hybridization eliminates the need for costly detasseling. More recently, cytoplasmic male-sterility and genetic restorer genes were found in grain sorghum and Sudangrass.

There is hope for hybrid wheat varieties by 1970. Germ plasm for wheat hybridization was found in the early 1960's and intensive research efforts are underway. In plants where cytoplasmic male sterility has not been found, attempts to introduce male sterility by genetic means is being pursued. Limited success has been achieved in castor beans, spinach, and barley.

Broadening the Germ Plasm Base. Improvements in crops through plant breeding are limited by the available genetic diversity. When certain desired characteristics do not appear within the germ plasm of a crop, the plant breeder must look to other sources. Alteration of germ plasm by irradiation is one source. X rays and ultraviolet rays were used earlier and, with the advent of nuclear energy, gamma rays and neutrons have brought new possibilities. Mutation can also be introduced by chemical means.

Single gene changes are sought which offer resistance to pests. Oats resistant to blight and rust resistant bluegrass have been isolated. The most spectacular results, however, have been obtained by breaking the chromosomes and rearranging their fragments. Wild progenitors of domestic crops often retain desirable characteristics which are no longer present in the germ plasm of domestic species. As a result, wide crosses are sometimes helpful although they pose other serious problems. Leaf rust resistance was transferred to wheat from a weedy wild relative. When close linkage of the new rust resistant gene to other undesirable characteristics posed a barrier, irradiation broke the chromosome freeing the resistant gene from the undesirable gene.

Plant Nutrition and Fertilizer. Plant nutrition and soil fertility research coupled with rapid advances in fertilizer production technology have resulted in huge increases in fertilizer use. Sound fertilization practices are the result of plant nutrition and soil fertility research. When combined with other good practices of soil management and crop protection there have been phenomenal increases in yields. In the early 1940's corn yields in the Southeastern United States were not markedly different from yields in many of the developing countries in the late 1960's. However, between 1945 and 1965, average corn yields in North Carolina increased from 21 to 70 bushels per acre. Most of the fertilizer research has centered on nitrogen, phosphorus, and potash. However, more attention is being given to the micronutrients and trace-minerals such as boron, zinc, and iron.

Plant Protection. Losses to insects, diseases, and weeds take a huge toll each year all over the world. Use of agricultural chemicals for pest control has been a significant factor contributing to the "take-off" in crop yields in the United States. Empirical evidence shows that increasing the intensity of plant production is associated with the need for increased use of pesticides. Pesticide usage is also closely positively correlated with fertilizer usage. The average return measured as yield increase per dollar invested for pesticides is usually considered to be about 5 to 1. While these advances have brought about many additional problems from undesirable side effects, pest control of some kind is an integral part of modern farm management.

Intensification of animal production

The potential for increasing animal production is huge. While it is indisputable that human food cannot be produced as efficiently when one turns to animal production compared to grains, livestock thrive on many feeds, forages, wastes, by-products, and even chemicals that are not suitable for human food. Whether or not grains which man can eat are fed to animals is a matter of economics confined largely to the developed countries where most consumers have enough purchasing power to choose to eat more of their food in animal product form than as cereals.

The hen and the dairy cow are the most efficient in converting protein in feed to human food products. They are followed by the broiler, the pig, and finally the beef animal. The ruminant animal can utilize feed that cannot be used directly by man, and is indeed salvaging materials otherwise lost and making them available to humans. Also, the animal proteins which they provide humans are also of much higher quality than the plant proteins.

Use of World Grazing Lands. Nine billion acres (27.8 percent) of the earth's surface is suitable only for potential grazing by livestock. The productivity of these lands could be improved greatly if modern forage and range management techniques were used. Even some of the arable land produces a more valuable human food resource through the production of high yielding forages, alfalfa or Sudangrass for conversion by livestock than when it is used to produce cereal grains for consumption by people.

Use of Wastes and By-Products. Almost every food crop or product has some useable wastes or by-product associated with it. Unfortunately, most of these valuable products are lost in developing countries where animal proteins are badly needed. Corn, wheat, rice, sorghum, sugar beets and oats have large plant residues and mill wastes that are extremely valuable sources of energy and protein. The animal industry generates a number of salvageable products as animal feeds including meat scraps, tankage, bone and blood meal, animal fats and even animal manures. Oilseed by-products in meal form are also valuable animal feedstuffs.

Production of Animal Protein by Urea. Cattle, sheep, and goats can use nonprotein nitrogen in the form of urea as a source of dietary nitrogen because microorganisms in their rumens convert these substances to proteins. Dairy cows fed urea, ammonium salts, potato starch, cellulose, and sucrose have produced up to 9515 pounds of milk containing 361 pounds of protein without any other source of protein.[3] A beef calf weighing 290 pounds gained an average of one pound per day until it weighed 930 pounds and produced a calf with urea as the only protein source.[4] Where a shortage of protein feedstuffs exists in developing countries, urea may be able to make a significant contribution.

Improved Animal Nutrition. Inadequate nutrition is an important cause of low livestock productivity in the developing countries. Animals, like man, have nutritional requirements that vary with age, sex, and rate of growth. Livestock needs are also determined by its production of meat, milk and eggs, diseases, climate, and other stresses. Animals are highly adaptive and can survive in nearly any environment but their usefulness to man as a food source is dependent upon their having proper nutrition.

Feed Preservation and Storage. Few areas of the world are endowed with the climate, soil, and rainfall to support year-round high quality plant growth. Animal production can be intensified where improved systems of harvesting, preserving, and storing plant materials offers food for

[3] A. I. Viramen, "Milk Production of Cows on Protein Free Feed," *Science* 153 (3744), Sept. 30, 1966, pp. 1603-1614.
[4] L. A. Moore, *et. al.*, Unpublished data, Animal Husbandry Division, U.S.D.A., Beltsville, Maryland.

animals the year round. In the developed countries, extensive use is made of hay, silage, crop residues, and root crops which have been preserved and stored.

Animal Breeding. Livestock developed in temperate climates cannot thrive under adverse tropical and subtropical conditions prevalent in most developing countries. Thus, importing highly productive animals from the temperate zone will not suffice as a means to increase production in these areas of the world. The indigenous breeds in Asia and Africa have evolved an ability to survive the heat, parasites, exotic diseases, and the low level of nutrition available to them from native vegetation although their ability to produce meat, milk, and eggs is relatively low. Through careful selection animal breeders can develop new strains and breeds. Some of the more successful new breeds of cattle developed in the tropics are the Santa Gertrudis, Brahman, Boran, and Nandi. While indigenous breeds can be upgraded such as the Sindi dairy cow, the process is painfully slow and yields poorer results than crossbreeding programs.

For swine and poultry, relatively more attention is being given to transplanting the whole "production package" into the developing country as a means of reinforcing animal production rather than crossbreeding existing stock. This involves introducing the improved breed or strain along with a complete balanced diet and husbandry practices which provide protection from the adverse environmental factors, including disease. For example, commercial egg and broiler operations in the United States control the environment in which the animal lives to such an extent it approaches a manufacturing industry. In such a situation, the total "system" can be transplanted into another part of the world providing inputs are available and management is capable.

Animal Reproduction. Reproductive efficiency is a key item in the success of intensifying animal production. In the United States, expectations are that 70 to 80 percent of healthy range cows will become pregnant when inseminated with high quality semen or mated with a fertile bull. In many areas of the world, however, reproductive rates of 40 calves per 100 cows are common. Calf mortality is also higher. The same situation exists for swine and sheep. The difference is largely due to a lack of understanding of basic principles of reproduction. Estimates are that the use of fertile sires, improvements in the management of females of breeding age in relation to the reproductive characteristics of the species, and an understanding of normal reproductive processes could double or triple present reproductive rates in some countries.

Animal Disease Control. In 1962, FAO estimated that losses caused by animal diseases were 15-20 percent of total annual production in those countries having reasonably adequate veterinary services and 30-40 percent in countries having less intensive services. Based on these conservative estimates, a 50 percent reduction in losses from animal diseases would increase the supplies of animal protein in areas of greatest need by 25 percent.[5]

Epizootic diseases capable of killing or debilitating large populations of animals are largely uncontrolled in developing countries. These include rinderpest, contagious bovine pleuropneumonia, hemorrhagic septicemia, foot and mouth disease, hog cholera, fowl plague, trypanosomiasis, African swine fever, and Newcastle disease. But the greatest total loss results from the many parasitic infections, nutritional, toxic, metabolic, and organic diseases that affect livestock particularly in the developing countries. Some of the more important are brucellosis, tuberculosis, mastitis, vibrosis, lumpy skin disease, bluetongue, parasite infestations and localized diseases such as Nairobi sheep disease. To gain control of these diseases will probably require a worldwide control plan sponsored by some worldwide association such as the International Veterinary Congress.

With regard to priorities, foot and mouth disease is estimated to reduce South American cattle production 25 percent annually. Rabies kills another million head annually, and the reproductive disease of brucellosis has been recorded up to a 40 percent prevalence. In Africa, rinderpest has decimated cattle populations on several occasions. Contagious bovine pleuropneumonia is probably as widespread as rinderpest once was. Trypanosomiasis is endemic in nearly five million square miles of Africa infested with the tsetse fly. Eradication of the fly would enable Africa to stock another 125 million head of cattle, and significant progress in this direction is underway. In Asia, hemorrhagic septicemia of cattle and water buffalo destroys a million animals in some years. Hog cholera is enzootic in many parts of Asia and its control depends on the successful distribution of vaccine. Sheep pox occurs commonly in the arid pastoral regions of Asia causing death losses up to 50 percent.

Increasing high quality protein

So far this chapter has dwelled primarily on increasing the quantity of food produced per unit of land area per unit of time. Remembering from earlier discussions that there is a quality dimension to the world food problem, the following will survey ways of increasing the quality of food as an end to alleviating malnutrition problems. Diets of the world's peoples can be classified into: (1) those high in protein calories of animal origin, (2) those high in grain calories, and (3) those low in grain calories and high in fats, sugars or tubers. In the first group characterized by North America, Oceania, and most of Europe, there is no acute malnu-

[5] W. R. Pritchard, "Increasing Protein Foods through Improving Animal Health," National Academy Science Proceedings 56 (2): August 1966, pp. 360-369.

trition problem. In the second group, the protein quality problem becomes increasingly worse as the staple food changes from wheat to rice to corn. Sensitive groups within the population, such as preschool children, suffer most. Kwashiorkor, a childhood disease caused by protein deficiency, often occurs in the rice staple diet and is also prevalent in the corn staple diet. People in the third group suffer most and Kwashiorkor is widespread since the protein intake is inadequate. It has been shown that about 90 percent of a person's brain development takes place by age four and a protein deficient diet which occurs immediately upon weaning may cause irreparable damage to one's mental capacity.

Improving Protein Quality by Genetic Means. It has already been pointed out that cereal grains provide incomplete proteins. An exciting research area is the improvement of protein quality of cereal grains by genetic means. This is a long-range effort, but some scientific breakthroughs have already been made. A superior variety of corn containing about 65 percent more lysine, more tryptophan, and a better amino acid balance than ordinary hybrid corn has been developed.[6] Young children fed this high lysine corn at the rate of two grams of protein per kilogram per day, retain similar amounts of nitrogen as children who are fed skim milk.[7] This finding illustrates the feasibility of attacking the protein problem in cereals by germ plasm manipulation.

Fortification of Cereal Grains. Fortification of cereal grains is simply the addition of the limiting amino acid(s) or protein concentrate(s) to the grain in order to increase its nutritive value. A pertinent question is whether such a practice is really nutritionally sound. Many experiments have been conducted and others are continuing. Pioneering work at the Institute of Nutrition of Central America and Panama since 1952 has demonstrated the potential efficacy of cereal fortification with amino acids or protein concentrates, or both.[8] They conclude that fortification will not cure protein malnutrition in children but is effective in alleviating much of the problem. In diets where calories are derived mainly from sugar or tubers such as cassava or plantains, the problem is extremely difficult since these diets need more protein as well as protein of a higher quality.

The exact technique of fortification depends on the grain, on the

[6] E. T. Mertz, *et. al.,* "Mutant Gene that Changes Protein Composition and Increases Lysine Content of Maize Endosperm," *Science* 145 (3629), July 1964, pp. 279-280.

[7] E. T. Mertz, *et. al.,* "Growth of Rats Fed on Opaque-2 Maize," *Science* 148 (3678), June 25, 1965, pp. 1741-1742.

[8] N. S. Scrimshaw, *et al.,* "Supplementation of Cereal Proteins with Amino Acids. 1. Effect of Amino Acid Supplementation of Corn-masa at High Levels of Protein Intake on the Nitrogen Retention of Young Children," *Journal of Nutrition* 66 (4), Dec. 10, 1958, pp. 485-499.

     R. Bressani, "Improvement of Nutritional Status in Developing Countries by Improved Food Production: Cereals." International Congress on Nutrition Proceedings, 1966.

form in which it passes through central facilities (whole or in flour), and on the cost. For flours, it is possible to improve the quality of the protein by adding amino acids or protein concentrates, such as oilseed meals or fish protein concentrate. Fortified flours must not be priced too high compared to unfortified products if low income consumers are to purchase them.

Fish Protein Potential. Only a few dozen of the 20-25 thousand species of fish are used directly or indirectly as food by man, and the 56 million ton harvest in 1964 is a small part of the potential. Fish protein is a high quality protein and is important to improving the quality of the rice staple diet of people in the Far East. Fish are efficient converters of feed into meat, and fish farming is gaining momentum. Fish protein concentrate with a protein content of 80 percent by weight is an important means of fortifying foods.

Single Cell Protein. Single cell protein produced by the culture of yeasts or bacteria is being given added attention as a new source of protein. It can be produced independently of existing agricultural techniques or climate. However, little impact is expected before the 1970's.

Fungi appear less desirable than bacteria or yeasts as sources of single cell proteins because their protein content is lower and they grow no more quickly. While amino acids of single cell proteins seem to be comparable to other proteins, little information is available on the digestability of such proteins, their taste, and their salability.

Leaf Protein. A protein-containing material can be isolated [9] by extraction techniques from leaves of plants and grasses. Its composition approximates other plant proteins.[10] Frequently leaf materials are wasted or at best fed to animals. Some leaf protein is used directly by humans in the case of leafy green vegetables, a significant factor in high sugar and tuber diets.

Algae. Although the composition of algae protein is comparable to other plant proteins, the major barriers are economics and palatability. Its major contribution to human nutrition is more likely through its serving as an animal feedstuff.

PRODUCTION INCENTIVES FOR FARMERS

Even if large quantities of fertile land, fertilizer, water, seeds, pesticides, machinery, and so on were available, no commercial food produc-

[9] M. G. Davys and N. W. Pirie, "Protein from Leaves by Bulk Extraction," *Engineering* 90 (4923), August 1960, pp. 274-275; I. H. Chayen, *et. al.*, "The Isolation of Leaf Components," Science Food Agriculture 12(7), July 1961, pp. 502-512.
[10] R. F. Wilson and J. M. A. Tilley, "Amino Acid Composition of Lucerne and of Lucerne and Grass Protein Preparations," *Journal of Science Food Agriculture,* 16(4), April 1965, pp. 173-178.

tion will take place unless a farmer decides to use them. What gives a farmer the incentive to produce? Mostly, economic profit, a desire to provide for his family, and the basic drive to survive. Fundamentally, the input-output ratio or cost-return ratio has to be favorable. Initially, the farmer is interested in producing food for his family but as additional goods and services become available in his community for purchase, he wants to upgrade his family's level of living. To get the necessary purchasing power to educate his children, buy a radio or bicycle and obtain medical services, the farmer must sell products worth more in the market than they cost to produce. The difference or margin between cost and return represents the farmer's *net income* for his labor and management.[11] In order to achieve a rising standard of living his net income must rise.

An increasing amount of evidence that farmers do respond to favorable prices is mounting. The response to favorable price includes both increased acreage planted and an attempt to increase yields per unit of land.[12] In making the "how to produce" decision, farm prices directly influence the amount of inputs used. Farmers can afford to use new inputs of fertilizer or pesticides if the value of the extra yield exceeds the cost of the extra input. In the 1960's a Thai farmer, for example, had to produce five times as much rice to pay for a bag of fertilizer as the Japanese farmer, so it is not surprising that the Japanese use much more fertilizer than the Thai's. The principal reason is that the Japanese farmer can sell his rice at a much higher price than the Thai farmer can because in Japan, the price is subsidized by the government (held higher than equilibrium), while in Thailand, the government's policy of extracting taxes from exports of rice artificially holds the farm price at a low level. This suggests that price policies and taxation methods by central governments are mechanisms to thwart free market prices in either direction. Thus, government policies can and do influence production incentives through farm product prices.[13] In addition, governments can and often do influence the price of inputs to the farmer.

Another factor affecting incentive is the share of the harvest going to the landlord if the farmer leases the land he farms. Generally, the larger the share of the harvest going to the landlord, the less incentive the tenant has to use a new technology to increase production. This accounts for part of the efforts to encourage ownership of farms and/or change share rentals to cash rentals.

---

[11] Also it is a return to the fixed costs associated with his long term capital investments like buildings and machinery.

[12] Hopefully, readers will be able to become more sophisticated students of economics by using new elasticity ideas, such as "elasticity" of acreage planted, "elasticity" of total supply, of market supply, etc.

[13] A compelling example in the United States was the effect of the Steagall Amendment to the Agricultural Act of 1941 which finally became effective in 1949—see Chapter 22.

INFRASTRUCTURE AND AGRICULTURAL PRODUCTION

Infrastructure or social overhead capital has been mentioned briefly as influencing food production. Its relevance is discussed more fully below.

Transportation

Transportation along with production incentives, markets, constantly changing technology, and local availability of supplies and equipment is listed as an essential ingredient by Mosher for agricultural development to take place.[14] Without low cost and efficient transportation, the other farm essentials cannot be effectively provided.[15] The essentials of a transport system are shown in Figure 20-1.

Agricultural production is necessarily widely dispersed over large areas of land since food production depends ultimately on capturing solar energy. If farming is to rise above a subsistence level and become commercial, road networks are necessary to get "inputs in" to the farm and "outputs out" to commercial markets. The relationship between transportation and the ability to grow and market food can be vividly pointed out by two examples. When Friendship Highway was built in Thailand, partially used jungle land was transformed into highly productive farms along a 100 mile course. Average travel time to market was reduced from eleven hours to three. The production of sugar cane, vegetables, bananas, and other fruits more than tripled in three years, and Thailand began to export corn produced in the area to Japan.[16] In Costa Rica, before the Inter-American Highway was constructed, driving beef cattle from grazing lands to San Jose customarily resulted in a 40 percent weight loss, and the country had to import beef to satisfy domestic demand. With an all weather highway, it became possible to deliver cattle by truck-trailer overnight and Costa Rica has become self-sufficient in meat.[17]

A transportation network complete with main highways and feeder roads besides reducing the cost of inputs, potentially increases the farmer's income by lowering marketing costs. A Philippine study indicated local village price increases of 25 percent for corn one year after feeder roads were built. In addition to bringing in inputs for purchases by farmers, roads bring in manufactured goods from the city. Additionally, new serv-

[14] A. T. Mosher, op. cit., pp. 111-120.
[15] Loc. cit.
[16] Wisit Kasiraksa, "Economic Effects of Friendship Highway," SEATO Graduate School of Engineering, Bangkok, 1963.
[17] U.S. Department of Commerce, "Motor Transport in Middle America," World Trade Information Service, 4, No. 55-13.

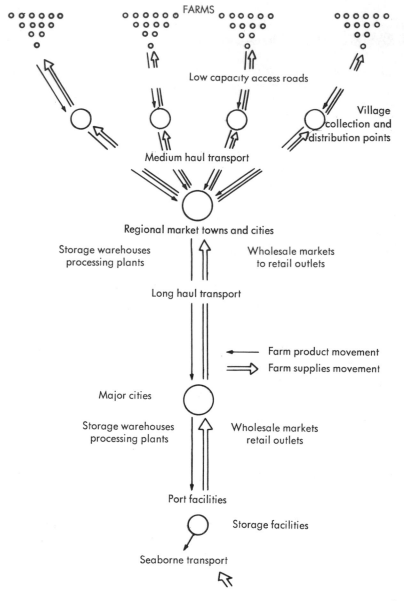

FIGURE 20-1: Essential Elements in Transportation System Serving Agriculture.

Source: "The World Food Problem," A Report of the Panel on the World Food Supply, President's Science Advisory Committee, White House, May 1967, Volume II, Figure 11-1, p. 577.

ices become available. The Philippine study also indicated that visits to the locality by educational and service officials increased dramatically. Rural health doctor visits increased 580 percent; social workers' visits were up 1000 percent, agricultural credit representatives up 267 percent, for only a few illustrations.[18]

Marketing processing and distribution

Commercial agriculture and urbanization of the population necessitates the establishment of markets and a marketing system. Storage facilities to allow the creation of time utility; processing plans to produce form utility; and a communications system to permit rapid dissemination of market information were all discussed in Chapter 10. Both private and public investment are likely to be involved. The functions of standardization and market information are government controlled, and the systems evolved are part of social overhead capital. Although the evolution of a complex market system is necessary for agricultural development, the rate of increase in per capita income is the primary factor in influencing market development. A farmer must have a market to sell his produce or else there is no incentive to produce. Rapid growth of the urban population in many of the developing countries complicates the task of providing efficient marketing machinery to move food. For example, between 1941 and 1961, the total population of the area which is now Pakistan grew by nearly 30 percent while the population of the cities increased by 250 percent.[19]

Research and educational institutions

A form of infrastructure affecting agricultural development is the country's educational institutions. They are directly responsible for upgrading the quality of the management input. They also improve the literacy rate of rural populations. When farmers learn to read, they can learn about new farm practices through newspapers, pamphlets, and books as well as obtain market news and information of nonfarm job opportunities. The more formal education a person has, the more complete and informed his thought processes can be contributing to management decision making.

Extension Education. Informal noncompulsory education programs for adult farmers can have a significant impact on agricultural production. Continuous learning is essential for all managers as new technologies are constantly discovered. Extension education may take the form of group

[18] A. T. Mosher, *op. cit.,* p. 117.
[19] *The World Food Budget 1970,* U.S.D.A., E.R.S., Foreign Agricultural Economic Report No. 19, October 1964, p. 17.

farmer meetings, method and result demonstrations, presentation of analyses for management purposes, farm tours, exhibits, and fairs. A good extension worker is one who makes the farmer aware of new ways to do things on the farm as well as relating the nonfarm economy to the farm economy.

Experiment Stations. A constantly changing technology is considered necessary for agricultural development.[20] No country has achieved a high level of agricultural development without the establishment of objective experiment stations for agricultural research.[21] Although good farmers do some experimenting on their own, the need for research stations with scattered field trials in various parts of the country and access to technical experts is necessary. To be effective, research stations need to be adequately financed, organized to attack the correct problems, and equipped to continually train new personnel.

Financial institutions

Farmers must buy improved inputs to produce more food which increases their cash expenses prior to any returns from sale of the crop. These expenditures must be financed either out of previous saving or by borrowing. In many developing countries, money is available from local moneylenders but interest rates tend to be so high they become restrictive. The purpose of production credit is to allow farmers to purchase improved inputs. Thus it follows that while production credit is one input, it is secondary to the actual availability of other inputs. This is the reason some economists list input availability in local areas as an essential ingredient for agricultural development and classify production credit as a development accelerator.[22] The value of production credit in the development of U.S. agriculture is well accepted (see Chapter 7).

Other considerations

The above list is by no means complete with regard to indirect factors and institutions which can affect food production. Social clubs and farmer organizations can have an impact. Formal or informal group action by farmers to help each other in times of emergency, to build community facilities, to build local feeder roads, to build a market facility, to meet and exchange ideas on farming, these and many other considerations might be cited as necessary or accelerating development factors.

The concepts of national planning are gaining strength in nearly all developing countries and planning for agriculture is an integral part of

[20] *Ibid.,* p. 75.
[21] *Ibid.,* p. 81.
[22] *Ibid.,* p. 141.

the total planning effort. Comprehensive planning can be helpful by providing certain incentives to food production. For example, government efforts to open and settle new lands, to improve land tenure systems, to finance water development projects all can contribute significantly to increased food production.

The challenge facing mankind to increase food supplies and eliminate hunger and malnutrition is real. It cannot be shrugged aside. Almost all nations are attacking the problem with numerous solutions, some more effectively than others depending on the gravity of the domestic situation, the culture, and the national political responsibility.

part VI

21

The problem-solving approach and policy formulation

POLICY DEFINED

A policy can be defined as a specific plan of action to attain a specified goal within a designated span of time. The plan of action may be quite vague and loosely defined, or it may be a rigid, step-by-step program procedure. The time for which the policy is operative may be an extremely short period, as in time of flood or fire emergency, or it may last many years like the Old Age and Survivors Insurance Program (Social Security). Our national Bill of Rights has been a policy of this country from the beginning. In any case, policy determination and application implies a degree of control over the means necessary to achieve the specific goal.

GOALS OF POLICY MAKERS

The broad goals for which most policy is created and initiated are relatively few. These goals include peace, economic growth, stability, security, justice, and freedom. All societies in the world today wish to have each of these goals to a certain degree. Some of the goals are contradictory. Some are compatible. Let us look at them.

Peace is a national goal of our country today. But as a nation we have not interpreted that goal to mean peace at any price. We maintain armed services to fight at designated times in a state of national emergency when our peace is in jeopardy. Perhaps peace cannot be maintained without sacrificing time, effort, money, and sometimes even lives.

The goal of *stability* poses many questions. Economic stability refers to the avoidance of inflation and depression or wild fluctuations in the nation's output and purchasing power of the dollar. How much stability should we have in this country? We certainly want as much economic stability as possible. Run-away inflation is disastrous because a predictable and stable purchasing power of the dollar (or any currency) is necessary for trade within the country and between countries. But how much stability can we have if we have economic growth?

In many ways *economic growth* promotes instability and uncertainty. Growth refers to increasing the national product per capita which gives us a higher standard of living. It is disturbing to many people to see familiar landmarks torn down and uprooted in the name of progress. Almost everyone wants to have more than he now has—more money, a better job, more time to enjoy the social and cultural advantages available in our society. But hardly anyone wants the maximum economic growth possible from our society, since it would probably entail restrictions on personal freedom in the form of increased hours of labor and reduced leisure time.

We are a country that prides itself on *freedom* of the individual. However, there are many restrictions which we voluntarily impose on ourselves that curb this individual freedom. Stop signs and speed limits deny an individual the freedom of driving as fast as he chooses. However, most of the social and legal restrictions we impose on our individual freedom give more freedom to individuals and groups than they take away. For example, many families can send their children to school with little worry about fast drivers because they realize that speed limits will help protect their youngsters. At the same time that we cherish the notion of individual freedom we are also constantly creating laws and regulations that limit individual freedom, business entrepreneurship, and certain types of social activities. Economic freedom refers to the freedom to produce and consume whatever goods and services the individual desires in the economy.

Personal *security* is a high priority goal with most people. Fear and uncertainty of what will happen after death to one's family is a major reason why we have life insurance. Sickness, unemployment, and old age are all factors influencing security. Some people would feel secure if the status quo were kept indefinitely; others would feel more secure if there were a change of some kind. Policies designed to increase personal and family security are in evidence everywhere. Retirement programs, unemployment insurance, health insurance, and church programs are evident in almost every community.

Everyone wants some degree of *justice:* economic justice (equal pay for equal work); social justice (no discrimination of minority groups); legal justice (trial with due process of law for everyone, regardless of the accusation); and political justice (everyone who is qualified to vote can vote). Throughout this country we have a complicated legal system dedicated to providing this justice. In fact, the founders of the nation set up the judicial branch (the Supreme Court) to act as a check and balance on the rest of government in insuring equal opportunity for justice. Economic justice also raises the question of what is the income distribution among people that will maximize satisfactions. How much poverty can, or should, exist in a society? How much luxurious living?

Each of the above goals is essentially a statement of personal or group values. Some people want one goal more than another; some people would substitute one goal completely for another; many people have never thought about the goals at all. Since certain of the goals are contradictory it is impossible to have an unlimited amount of all of them. The attainment of these goals is of varying degree throughout our country and between the nations of the world. Recognition of the varying attainment of these goals which are activated by varying degrees of personal conviction, knowledge, and values, is an essential first step in the problem-solving approach to policy issue and questions.

SOME CRITERIA OF POLICY FORMULATION

Awareness and general understanding of the pertinent issues and conflicts of interest involved in a policy question is fundamental to its solution. This awareness and understanding is relative, varying from group to group and from person to person. We have earlier pointed out that education is essential to this understanding and awareness, but we have also pointed out that experience and a broad acquaintance with many people of different points of view and background is also essential. The number of years of formal schooling which someone has is no substitute for inherent shrewdness and reasoning ability. Formal education is merely a complement and tool to bring out the natural characteristics with which a person is born.

The process of policy formulation is one which must be meaningful in terms of people's particular needs, their goals, and their resources. An effective policy must also be politically acceptable, administratively feasible, economically sound and socially acceptable, and capable of modification as conditions change. For example, in this nation few people will vote for a new policy if its aim is to destroy the things for which this country stands. If a policy cannot be administered it cannot even be tested by action; if a policy is not economically sound or socially acceptable it will soon fail of its own accord or be voted down. Furthermore, if a policy is not capable of modification a dynamic society will soon outgrow it (our Constitution is a perfect example of a political and social policy that allows change through amendment). To meet these criteria the area for policy decisions is severely restricted (see Figure 21-1, where policy decisions may take place only in the blacked out area), and compromise is necessary.

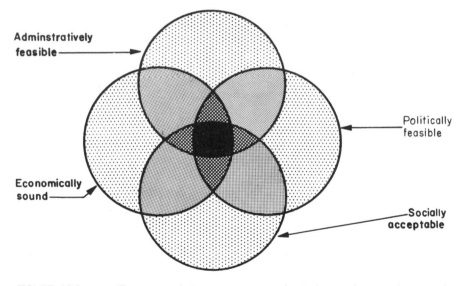

FIGURE 21-1:   Illustration of Compromise Area for Policy Making Within Social, Economic, Political, and Administrative Constraints.

THE PROBLEM-SOLVING ENVIRONMENT

Problems arise from individuals and groups for personal or collective reasons. Usually these reasons revolve around conflicts of interest. Such conflicts originate from the basic questions of what should be produced, when it should be produced, how it should be done, and who shall benefit from the production and distribution. Underlying these questions are the individual and group goals which we have just discussed. One can easily see how there can be a great many answers to each of the above questions when the variety of opinions concerning the desirability and extent of a nation's goals is considered.

A problem-solving orientation to policy problems is really the application of the scientific method. This approach to policy provides a basis for selecting facts which will help in problem analysis. The approach also reduces random effort and focuses analysis on a specific problem area. For example, when a community does an economic study there are certain defined steps through which the study proceeds, based upon the desires of the community. First, the goals of the community are defined so that everyone starts from a common ground. Second, there is an inventory of the resources available in the community, followed by an identification of the obstacles in the way of attaining the specific community goals. Finally, the study will finish by outlining plans to overcome the obstacles identified.

When one begins to use the problem-solving approach he immediately realizes that awareness of problems and of their causes is a relative situation depending upon his level of knowledge and training, his experience, and his intuitive analytical ability. This recognition applies equally well to groups and to nations. A student will soon find that there is no end to the problems to be solved, but that he can improve in his ability to solve them.

Decision making about policy would be much easier if one could work in a static framework where everything is held constant and no changes are allowed. But the world does not operate that way. Decisions have to be made periodically despite the lack of certain information. This condition is simply the result of a dynamic economy. Time, money, and labor shortage put limitations upon the amount of knowledge one can gain and the depth of analysis that can be done before a decision must be made. However, despite the pressure of time the value of the method by which problems are approached should not be overlooked. The method itself provides savings in time because it is a logical procedure that helps to eliminate waste of time and effort.

When one deals in the area of policy there is a good chance that there will be controversy and differences of opinion that must be reconciled before a solution can be formulated and put into action. In order to create meaningful policy and in order to stay out of meaningful arguments that waste the time of the policymakers before a decision can be made, it is helpful to remember the following: People make decisions primarily on the basis of three categories of knowledge. The first is facts. Facts are provable statements or data that can be collected, analyzed, and duplicated by anyone. The second category includes statements or propositions which are taken as fact although it is not absolutely sure whether or not they are fact. In either case the statements are treated as facts in the decision-making process. When relevant facts are generalized upon, guiding principles are evolved. The third category encompasses all one's personal values which determine his attitude toward any person or subject, such as friends, religion, business, government, or politics. One must formulate policy on meaningful facts and principles and must be aware of the values of the people who will be affected. If these considerations are ignored the forthcoming policy will be quite limited in its duration and effectiveness.

Factors which influence the decision in one way or another include the simple economics of the solution. Does the policy pay or does it not? Often the sheer size of the problem approached outweighs the economic considerations. For example, during a wartime emergency troops and citizens are treated in a particular manner with little or no mention of the cost involved. Traditions of individuals or groups within the society may also have a bearing on how certain decisions are reached. The relative strength of pressure groups and the lobbyists they employ to provide data and analysis will undoubtedly influence some people who have to choose between two or more alternative solutions. There are many other types of influences directly related to the knowledge, experience, and values of the problem solver, whether it be an indivdual or group responsible for the solution, whether the problem occurs in private or public life, or whether the problem is big or small.

At the national level

The creation of policy at the national, and sometimes state, level is often extremely difficult to pinpoint at the start. The "felt needs" stemming from grass roots opinion, and the sometimes vague phrasing of issues and subjects upon which there is no majority of agreement, create an extremely loose problem-solving framework for legislators. For example, questions with which policymakers begin a study are usually those that start, "*What* shall we do about . . . ?", or "*What* shoud be done about . . . ?". Asking the question this way permits all alternatives to be considered, including the choice of doing nothing. Once the question is asked, the issue is framed and the alternative courses of action and their consequences can be discussed and studied. After a specific course of action has been chosen the principal problem for national policymakers involves how to state the particular policy choice in legislative language and get it voted into law.

At the state and local level

In contrast to the above, policymakers working on some state issues and on almost all county or community development issues are mostly concerned with questions that begin with the words *how* or *which* or *ought*. These words imply that the basic issue has already been analyzed, that many of the *what* questions have been answered, and that a specific course of action has been decided upon. Analytic effort has been focused, and the question of "what ought to be done" is no longer relevant. The problem thus resolves itself into the community, and some method must be found by which that particular policy can be implemented if the community desires it.

Examples of national issues include the following: What should be done about the poverty problem in agriculture? What ought to be done about controlling floods on the Mississippi River? What ought to be done about medical aid to people over 65? Examples of state issues include: How can the property tax best be administered? Which of our highways should be developed first? Examples of local issues include: How can we make our municipal power plant more efficient? How can we make our schools better? What should be the level of our local tax rate?

To summarize: public policy formulation usually deals with a particular issue about which no general agreement has been reached. Local policy formulation deals primarily with how to activate more broadly defined policies at the state, county, or community level. A public policy issue can arise from the "grass roots" if enough people become concerned about a particular subject. Or a public policy issue can arise separately from local concerns.

THE PROBLEM-SOLVING APPROACH

The problem-solving approach consists of the following general steps: defining the current and historical situation from which the problem comes, defining the goal(s) to be attained, stating the problem, outlining the alternative means by which the problem could be solved and tracing the consequences of each, choosing one of these solutions and implementing it, and then, after a time, evaluating the policy to see if it needs to be modified in any way. Wise policy formulation, therefore, builds on both descriptive economics (gathering and organizing relevant facts) and on principles of economics (generalizations about economic behavior).

Throughout the problem-solving approach the analytic frame of reference provided by tested generalizations or principles, the use of logic, experience, and intuition offer the main criteria for determining which facts are relevant to the problem at hand. As man's knowledge of the world around him increases and as he becomes more aware of the physical, social, political, and institutional relationships around him, his ability to correctly diagnose troublesome situations increases through the application of scientific methodology. Continually refined tools of analysis, more internally consistent and expanding disciplines of theory, and previous trial-and-error attempts at analysis all indicate more clearly which factors or relationships are relevant for use in analyzing a particular problem.

The situation

When people begin to solve problems or resolve issues they often neglect getting any facts on the subject which they want to discuss. Sometimes the assumption is made that everyone already knows the facts and that there is no need to repeat them. Only a very small percentage of the time is this assumption valid. Most of the time it is necessary to establish a firm footing of fact that describes the historical situation. For instance, if the problem involves employment, data showing trends in the number and kinds of jobs in the area and in wages, population, and training facilities are highly important. While some people might know the facts about one of these areas, it is highly unlikely that everyone will know the facts about all the items.

Goal identification

The next step is to identify the goals to be attained. These may be individual goals or they may be goals some group or nation wants to achieve. The goals of national policymakers generally tend to be those discussed earlier (peace, stability, growth, freedom, security, and justice), and are generally either known or intuitively agreed upon. However, the goals of local policymakers will usually be very specific. For example, the town board of City x may state a goal of creating 500 new jobs in the town within the next year. If a group is involved in determining the goals there will most likely not be unanimous agreement on them, but there will be a consensus of opinion instead. The explicit goals will likely include such items as increased income, increased employment, a better library, more health facilities, increased efficiency in government administration, and so on.

Problem formulation

It is important to recognize that without a goal and without carefully defining the situation to be used as a point of departure, it is impossible to identify and solve a problem. The problem emerges when one tries to decide how to move from the present situation to the desired position or goal.

It has been said that the problem of problems is to determine the problem. Identifying the problem explicitly is an extremely difficult thing to do. What are the obstacles to formulating the problem? The biggest block is one's own value system. Sometimes our minds are made up without the facts, and often we honestly do not want to know the facts. Differences in opinion concerning the general underlying goals of peace, freedom, security, growth, stability, and justice also cloud the issue. Our own lack of knowledge about an area further limits us in our ability to formulate problems in that area.

It is perhaps easiest to view problem formulation in terms of asking a question. For example:

> Situation: Five hundred people are unemployed in city x. There are four old industrial plants whose managers are not anxious to hire new employees. City x is gaining population but the county is losing rural population.
> Goal: To create new employment in city x.

Problem: How can employment be created in city x for those who want jobs? When a question is asked an answer is demanded. That answer is the solution to the problem. Questions focus directly on some issue about which there may be controversy and about which some policy might be formulated. By asking the question, analytical effort is brought to bear immediately on the subject at hand. Only relevant data need then be gathered, and the minds of the policymakers can be put to work

Outlining alternative solutions and their consequences

It is a general maxim that if there is one way to solve a problem there are usually several other ways to solve it. These alternative solutions should be outlined and the consequences of each should be noted before a final choice is made, since the best solution might perhaps be overlooked. Although each of the various alternatives suggested may well attain the desired goal, there might be severe economic hardships imposed on a particular sector of the economy by one solution, a shortrun hardship by another solution, and an economic gain from a third solution. One alternative may necessitate relatively large political or social changes, while another may work within the existing political and social framework. A final alternative may speak for the creation of a whole new set of institutions, whereas none of the other suggested alternatives contemplated institutional change.

Some type of compromise solution will be forthcoming when people having different social, cultural, economic, and political values meet to decide an issue. There will likely be some give and take on all sides in order for an agreement to be reached. In most policy solutions involving the problem-solving approach it is rare that anyone is completely happy with the final decision.

It should be understood that compromise does not mean compromise of principle. Far from it. What it does suggest is that, through the democratic process and given the limitations of time, knowledge, and analytical effort, the best possible solution to a problem is reached, consistent with the total values of the people who made the decision.

Solution implementation and evaluation

The final steps are simply to implement the policy decision and evaluate it. Policy implementation is more an administrative task and a technical one than it is a function of legislation. Yet policy must be implemented in order for the policymakers to see whether or not it should be modified; and if it should be changed, they must decide in what manner the changes should be effected.

In each of the following sections dealing with farm price and income policy, the low income problem in agriculture, international trade, and other selected problem areas, the problem-solving approach will be applied. Using this approach is not easy for the student. But once the method is learned it will be most helpful in solving many problems usually encountered at some time by most people.

22

Farm price and income problems

THE BACKGROUND

Farm price and income policy issues have undergone considerable changes since the first farm price legislation was introduced into Congress. The first support price laws were based on a concept of parity between the farm and nonfarm sectors of the economy. Later, farm price legislation was aimed at stimulating food production for the World War II effort. During the 1950's the main emphasis was on maintaining farm incomes and helping to ease the adjustment of the human resource out of farming. In the 1960's the main policy thrusts were an attempt to apply voluntary supply management through acreage limitations, continued rural development program formulation, and expanded programs of foreign trade.

Previous legislative attempts helped policymakers in the 1950's and 1960's to realize that the "farm problem(s)" was not just the farmer's problem(s) but was an integral part of the economic growth process of a country and concerned the entire society. During this time Congress explicitly recognized that a majority of the farmers do not benefit from commodity price supports, since less than half of the commercial farmers produce 90 percent of the volume of products and by 1968 only about 15 percent of the farmers produced 85 percent of our food and fiber. Price supports are geared to the farmer who has a significant volume of production because supports are offered on a per unit of output basis; a man with few tillable acres and little output will get a correspondingly lower income from supports than a farmer with a large acreage and large volume of output. The fact that supports are offered on only part of the agricultural commodities further emphasized the concern that support prices were not solving the farmer's income problems.

Many people have suggested that there is no one farm problem, and that instead the farm problem is composed of many relatively small problems that occur simultaneously, each in its own turn being both a cause and an effect. In any case, farm problems are interrelated and connected to the rest of the economy. And the magnitude of the farm problem is large, affecting all of the farmers and most of the rest of society.

Policymakers have recently concentrated their legislative efforts on three major problem areas: (1) Returns to the labor of some farmers and their workers are low, particularly on small farms. (2) Price fluctuations can be severe as a result of weather, livestock production cycles, and international developments. (3) And price instability is compounded by excess capacity and a consequent chronic tendency to produce more of certain major crops than the market can readily absorb at reasonable prices. Other problems related to these three primary ones include concern about the equitable distribution of farm income within the farm sector, the misallocation of resources in farming with resulting inefficiencies of production and loss of benefit to all of society, a lack of rapid enough adjustment of the farm population to nonfarm progress, particularly with respect to education and training, and the disposal of our stored surpluses.

The complexity of the situation confronting policymakers is better understood when one considers how the economic growth process binds the farm and nonfarm sectors together. The diversity of human attitudes, purposes, and values from both sectors creates a continuing conflict of interest. These conflicts are seen not only between the two sectors but within agriculture as well. Combined with the complexity of the problem is the declining political importance of the farm vote. What might happen to farmers as a result of the decline is not yet fully understood or appreciated. A majority of people now live in urban centers and their problems, on the surface at least, are urban problems, not rural ones.

The criteria for any farm legislation will vary depending upon who is doing the evaluating. Urban people will consider certain criteria more important than will rural people, and both of these viewpoints may be in conflict with that of the highly specialized commercial farmers who produce the majority of our food and fiber. Even though the relative importance of the following criteria will vary, most of them will be considered. The fact that some sort of compromise can be worked out from the conflicts of interest is the essence of a political system that permits any legislation to be created.

One criterion considered is the effect of the policy on farming and on those in farming. Will the proposed legislation improve the income situation, increase efficiency in resource use and production techniques, aid in reducing risk and uncertainty, and not distort price relationships within the agricultural sector? Another criterion is the effect of the policy on the same items in the agribusiness sector. Other criteria include the effect on government (the cost of the program and how it relates to other domestic policies), the effect on consumers (quantity, quality, and price of food), and the effect on foreign policy and world trade. An overall consideration is whether the proposed laws will be consistent with the broad policy goals discussed in Chapter 21, including the goal of freedom for farmers.

THE FARMER'S DILEMMA [1]

Since World War II there have been significant changes in our farm economy. Technology has been adopted by farmers at an unprecedented rate. Agricultural output has increased at the rate of about 2 percent annually since 1950. Domestic demand for food, based primarily on population growth and consumer disposable income levels, has increased at slightly less than that rate, and has been insufficient to match our agricultural output potential. In fact, the combined demand increases for farm commodities for domestic food, foreign demands, and industrial uses have still left the United States with an agricultural plant geared to produce and process 5 to 8 percent more farm products than could be taken off the market at reasonable prices.

Overall demand for food products is highly inelastic. Although the derived demand for farm products at the farm level tends also to be inelastic, the demand curve facing each individual farmer is almost perfectly elastic. No matter how much of a commodity any one individual farm sells, the same price will be received for the item. Furthermore, the only way that an individual farmer can increase his income in this situation (inelastic industry demand, elastic farm demand) is to increase his production. Thus, despite the fact that an inelastic demand for the industry (at both retail and farm levels) means less total revenue for the industry if supplies are increased, the response of individual farms to lower prices was to search for further cost-reducing technologies which were generally available. With a high proportion of committed resources, total farm output was maintained and even increased in the face of lower

[1] This section draws heavily on an understanding of the historical development of farming and resource use (Part I) and on the tools of economic analysis (Part III). Policy is the medium in which historical knowledge, experience, and reasoning ability are blended.

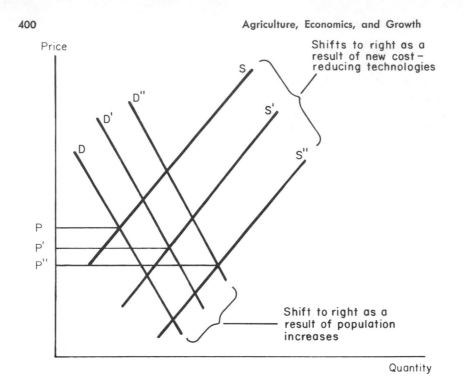

FIGURE 22-1:   Illustration of General Supply-Demand Relations in the Farming In-
                    dustry.

prices. Increased production continued to depress price and the seemingly
paradoxical situation of lower prices and increased output continued.

Because farm income is affected both by prices of farm products and
the return to resources, i.e., costs of production, labor moved out of farming to higher paying nonfarm jobs. Capital in the form of new technology
was substituted for labor. Technology was also adopted partly because it
helped an individual farmer increase his production and partly because
it tended to lower per unit costs of output. By adopting technology,
marginal costs of production could be lowered and the most profitable
level of output for farmers was a larger amount at a lower price. As a
result, many farmers, particularly those without any alternative place to
"sell" their labor, found themselves on a treadmill running faster and
faster. They had to adopt new technologies in order to hold costs down,
but this also meant increasing output. Industry or total farm output increased faster than demand, bringing lower and lower farm prices
(Figure 22-1). The farm cost-price squeeze was on.

Two other facets of farming aggravated the situation. Many of the
farmer's resources are fixed, and when he adds more land, buildings, and
equipment to his existing resources it makes his total resource base even
more fixed. It is therefore harder for him to move off the farm profitably.

Also, the substitutability of resources among enterprises within the farm sector is relatively easy compared with moving resources outside the farm sector. Therefore, a reduction of output of one commodity because of continued low prices or some production control program most often results in resources being transferred to the production of other food commodities. An attempt to solve the farm income problems on a partial basis, then, is not likely to succeed. The farm price and income problem is an aggregate problem.

Although migration of people out of farming has continued at a rapid rate since the 1940's, a rate of movement fast enough to equalize incomes between the farm and nonfarm sectors was hampered by the lack of nonfarm job opportunities available to farmers. In general, the skills that the farm population had to transfer to nonfarm employment were inadequate. This situation was particularly noticeable among the young high school dropouts, among those men and women who chose not to go to college or could not afford to take some form of technical training, and among many of the elderly farmers who felt compelled to give up operating small unproductive tracts of land.

All the farm resource adjustments to declining farm income were taking place during a rapid rate of economic growth in the rest of the economy. Even the recessions experienced by the whole economy were not as deeply felt in the nonfarm sector as in the farm sector. Real nonfarm income levels were rising faster than farm incomes, nonfarm population was increasing while farm population was falling, educational levels were rising more rapidly in nonfarm areas than in farming areas, and the number of nonfarm jobs were also increasing while farm job opportunities actually declined.

At the heart of the farm problem lies the fact that the rapid adoption of new farm technology permitted output gains never before anticipated. Besides more efficient use of resources, new technologies forced changes in farm organization, in managerial techniques, in marketing structures, and in techniques of wholesale and retail food distribution. At the beginning of the 1950's rates of increase in yields of crops per acre began to exceed the rate of increase in the population. Average crop yields increased by about one-third during this time, while the demand for food from our population only increased about one-fifth. It took less land, less labor, but more capital per farm unit to feed the population in 1970 than it did in 1950.

The farm problem of the commercial farmer can be summarized in the following way. Gross farm income depends on farm prices and on the quantity produced and sold. Farm output has continued to expand in the face of lower prices, since the individual farmer must adopt new technologies in an attempt to lower costs. Lower costs increase the level of output which is most profitable. At the same time a higher output level will more fully utilize his fixed resources. These resources cannot easily be transferred out of farming. Farm prices fluctuate more than farm production costs. The result is that net farm income fluctuates to a much greater extent than gross farm income. Look at the following hypothetical example:

	One Year (Bils.)	Following Year (Bils.)	% Change
Gross income	$30	$27	− 10
Production expenses	17	17	0
Net income	$13	$10	− 23

A 10 percent reduction in gross income coming from lower prices can reduce net income by 23 percent if production expenses remain unchanged. The commercial farmer is vitally interested in stabilizing his income situation from year to year. However, this may or may not come about by stabilizing commodity prices.[2]

FARM POLICY GOALS

The goals for farm policy have been the same for many years. First, there is the need to have the farm sector operate at such a level of production efficiency and profitability that our nation need never fear for lack of food and fiber and consumers can buy food at reasonable prices. Second, there is a sincere desire on the part of legislators to have the economy operate in such a way that all the people in farming may contribute the use of all their talents and total productive powers to the benefit of all society. Third, there is the explicit desire to create legislation that will remove the instability and price risks which have traditionally characterized farm income, and at the same time raise farm incomes up to reasonable levels of comparison with the rest of the economy. These three goals, again, must complement the broad goals previously discussed, within which all of policy is constructed. In addition there may be specific budgetary, foreign trade, and foreign food aid goals which need to be considered.

WHAT ARE THE POLICY ALTERNATIVES?

Because our country is now fortunate enough to have an oversupply of food and fiber, the key question confronting farm policymakers is,

---

[2] A stable price could actually unstabilize gross income, particularly if a farmer specializes in the production of one commodity where output varies considerably from year to year.

"What should be done about farm incomes and resource adjustment within farming and between farming and other sectors in the economy?" Many proposals have been advanced over the years to cure the various ills of the farmers. Essentially, there have been variations on three main policy approaches offered: (a) to expand the demand for farm products both domestically and through foreign outlets, (b) to establish programs of price supports and farm product storage programs, and (c) to adjust farm production to demand through some type of resource or quota controls. Each of the three approaches would solve the farm problem as defined. However, the relative weight attached to each of the methods has varied over the years. The criteria mentioned previously have been applied to the formulation of farm price and income policy and certain proposals have been found lacking in one or more respects.

Before the principal policy alternatives are discussed a word should be said about the permissiveness of policy alternatives. There is a constant battle about how much the farmer should be allowed to do on a voluntary basis for himself as opposed to how much should be imposed as mandatory controls. Congress has not explicitly answered this question for all the farm products for all time. Some programs are mandatory, some are voluntary. For example, federal milk marketing orders are under quite strict control, but participation in the Soil Bank land retirement program was completely voluntary. Some of the most rigidly controlled programs affecting farm commodities have been instituted by private industry. The citrus and walnut crop associations are perhaps the best examples of commodity production and marketing control by private industry.

One of the real policy issues, derived from the question of whether or not farm policy should be mandatory or should allow for voluntary participation, is to what extent the farm production or resource adjustment is actually desired. The extent of voluntary participation in any program is difficult to predict and the program can be inefficient for this reason. On the other hand, policymakers know that if the proposal is accepted voluntarily by the farm public it is evidently palatable to the majority of farmers from a value standpoint. Policymakers can see that mandatory controls remove the uncertainty of not knowing how much farmer participation there will be to speed its implementation. However, they can also see that proposals of this type run the risk of not being well accepted by the farmers and by the rest of society and may have dire political implications. There have been examples of each kind of control in the past. No conclusive answer on which kind of proposal is best has been found, since it is up to the values of the individual or group evaluating alternative proposals to determine which proposal is best. For instance, during wartime emergencies the strict controls established in order to stimulate production may not be deemed desirable when peace has been won. Generally, a compromise position is found in most farm price and income legislation that is passed, implemented, and found effective and acceptable by the majority of farmers, farm groups, and by the rest of society. Let us now examine some of the proposals advanced in each of the three categories: demand adjustments, price support and farm product storage programs, and supply adjustments.[3]

Expanding the demand for farm products

Expansion of domestic demand. The main reasons given for trying to solve the farm problem by expanding domestic demand (consuming more farm products at any given price levels) are that the nutritional level of our people will be improved, surpluses will be reduced, and more farm products will be sold in the long run. All these consumption effects will act to raise farm income at the same time that the whole of society is also benefited.

Annual per capita consumption of food in the United States has been about 1,500 pounds for almost the last 50 years. People in this country generally get enough to eat, but there are many people who might improve their nutritional level with a proper diet. With a relatively inelastic demand for food in general, and with everyone getting most of the food energy they need from their food, the opportunity for expanding domestic demand lies in three areas: population growth, income growth, and a change in diet from a low value food diet to one of higher value.

Population growth provides the agricultural sector with more stomachs to fill. An inelastic demand for food products and a fairly full and satisfied population probably mean that there is not likely to be much future expansion of demand except in terms of the addition of more people (population elasticity for food is thought to be about unitary). Income elasticity of demand for food is quite low and tends to be reduced towards zero as levels of income rise. However, as incomes go up and as more total money is spent for food there tends to be more waste and a substitution of high value foods for low value foods. As consumers change their eating habits toward higher quality foods, more farm resources are used. For example, the consumption of livestock products requires from five to ten times as many farm resources as the consumption of basic cereal products.

Effecting a change in diet most likely offers the greatest hope for significant expansion of domestic consumption of farm products. This change can be helped by promotion and advertising and through various food distribution programs. In 1966, advertising by processors ($1,215

---

[3] Data in the following section are taken from "The Farm Problem . . . What Are the Choices?", a series of 13 pamphlets prepared by the National Committee on Agricultural Policy, sponsored by the Farm Foundation and the Center for Agricultural Economic Adjustment, Ames, Iowa, undated but published 1962.

million), wholesalers ($88 million), and retailers, including restaurants ($641 million) totaled almost $2 billion, an 81 percent increase over the 1957-59 average expenditure. Some promotion campaigns (such as trading stamps) by commodity group or retail food stores would be added to this total. The merits of advertising food and food products is a subject of much controversy. Results from advertising campaigns are hard to evaluate, especially over the long run. Some people evaluate promotion programs by asking the question, "What would happen if we didn't advertise?"

Government-sponsored food distribution programs have taken many turns. Federal assistance for feeding school children first became available in the early 1930's. A School Milk Program was authorized in the Agricultural Act of 1954. During the school year 1967-68 about 18.8 million children were included in the School Lunch Program, and 17 million children participated in the milk programs. Other programs include distribution of food to needy people in designated communities. A food stamp program, attempted during the 1930's, has recently been revitalized. This program attempts to provide people with low incomes and low levels of nutrition with an adequate diet. Such a program is justified on the basis that these people are then in a better position to contribute their talents and productivity to society.

In general, programs to expand domestic demand only offer a partial solution to the farm price-income problem. The total volume of goods affected is a minor share of the total farm output.

Expansion of foreign demand. There are several reasons for trying to expand demand for our food products overseas. One is the simple humanitarian desire to share our farm abundance with the hungry peoples of the world. Other reasons are to promote economic development and thus stimulate international trade for our other products as well as our food.

Competing on world markets with other countries of the world presents problems. Some countries depend almost wholly on agricultural exports for their income, and competition by the United States in these markets can cause severe internal economic disturbances in these countries. Another facet of competition which also has political and economic ramifications arises with the producers of commodities within the foreign countries who raise either the same crop we are trying to export or a crop which acts as a close substitute. These farmers and their merchants are not at all happy if the United States crowds the world market with her products, which ultimately may force down the price they receive for their output.

As a result of this situation our policymakers have tried to dispose of some of our agricultural surpluses through such programs as Food for Peace (Public Law 480 and others), which are discussed in greater detail in Chapter 24. Although some farm production may be sent overseas, many problems are encountered which often depend for their solutions on the policies and attitudes of people within the countries to which we are trying to send our food.

Expanding demand through new food and nonfood uses. New uses are primarily aimed at developing new products for consumption on overseas markets. Such programs confront the challenges of foreign competition and policy convergences just discussed.

Nonfood use of farm products took between $3.5 and $4.5 billion worth of the gross value of production annually. Optimistic reports indicate that perhaps an additional $1.5 billion worth of products could be diverted into industrial uses if research were first stepped up accordingly. Farm products are facing severe competition with other commodities which can be substituted for them in industrial uses. For example, nearly half the market for natural fibers of cotton, wool, flax, and silk has been absorbed by synthetic fibers; about two-thirds of the shoes made today utilize leather substitutes; about two-thirds of the soap market now use detergents instead of agricultural fats; and paint and varnish are being made with continually lessening proportions of vegetable oils.

There is little evidence to indicate that new uses for farm products will even approach solving the farm problem by themselves. Although they contribute partially to the solution, their overall contribution is not large and many problems are encountered, especially in developing new uses for overseas markets.

Summary. Evaluation of the principal policy suggestions for getting rid of our farm surplus production through expanding demand shows that demand expansion is a slow process geared primarily to the natural increase of population.[4] Stomachs are limited in their capacity to absorb food, increasing incomes have little impact on food consumption, foreign trade and development and the increased use of farm products in nonfood uses offer limited hope. A policy to improve the diets of our existing population perhaps offers the most immediate favorable prospect of solution.

Farm product storage and price support programs

Crop storage. Experience with crop storage programs has shown that they can be effective in supporting farm incomes if the storage program is big enough. However, such a program in no way removes or reduces the cause for overproduction and hence for low farm incomes. In certain

---

[4] The notion that effective demand expansion cannot be implemented by only one solution is also supported by J. M. Wetmore, and others, "Policies for Expanding the Demand for Farm Food Products," Part I, Technical Bulletin 231, University of Minnesota Agricultural Experiment Station, April 1959, p. 101.

cases, crop storage programs have stimulated crop production when the support prices and storage payments combine to offer higher profits than might be expected with immediate sale after harvest.

Storage programs were initially set up in 1929 and later modified in 1933 to stabilize farm income. The objective was to smooth out price variations caused by production variations resulting from weather influences. However, within a very few years the objective changed from merely stabilizing prices to "stabilizing them upward." When the storage programs were used as price-raising programs they became less relevant to the problems of reducing an already existing overproduction which was the cause of low farm prices and income.

One of the equity problems associated with programs having storage and nonrecourse commodity loan provisions is that they reward the large producer proportionately more than the little producer, and are thereby somewhat self-defeating in terms of really being of much economic help to the small or low income farmer. In the mid-1960's, for example, farmers grossing less than $5,000 farm income had realized net farm incomes of around $1,200 of which only about $200 came from agricultural programs. This same group averaged almost five times as much income from off-farm sources as from farm sources. Such information has caused many people to question the reasons behind keeping price support programs on the basis of helping raise the level of income for our low income farmers.

Storage programs act as a temporary price and income support for farmers by withholding crop stocks from the market. However, studies indicate that if and when these stocks are released they will depress farm prices about as much as they raised prices when they were taken off the market. In addition, the costs of storage must be paid.

Direct payments to farmers. Direct payments support farm income by supplementing farm product prices rather than by raising income through price supports. This type of program has been in effect in this country for sugar cane, mohair, and wool. This type of payment has sometimes been called a compensatory, transfer, deficiency, equalization, income, stabilization, or production payment.

Direct payments work in the following manner. Growers sell their product in regular commercial markets at free market prices. An "intended price" is calculated on a national or "large area" average. If the commercial market price received is less than the price intended under the program, growers then receive a direct payment from the federal government equal to the difference between the market and the intended price for each unit of the product that is sold.

Direct payments that raise prices above long-run free market prices do not offer a solution to the problem of overproduction. In fact, if the price were raised above current support rates, production would be further encouraged. Direct payments will also not encourage an inefficient farmer to manage his resources more efficiently. However, they do have the potential of stabilizing and increasing farm income.

Multiple pricing. Multiple pricing means setting two or more prices for the same commodity. Marketing orders are sometimes an example of multiple pricing. Markets, to which the different prices apply, may be separated on the basis of location, time, utilization, or quality. Domestic and foreign markets illustrate separation by location; fluid milk markets utilize milk in a different manner than do milk manufacturing plants; potatoes for human consumption are separated by a quality differential from potatoes for livestock consumption; and holiday consumption of certain foods illustrates time division.

The effectiveness of multiple pricing depends upon the ability of the market to maintain its price differences, to clearly identify all products, to sell most of the product in the higher priced market, and to institute an adequate and fair method of making the payments. The principal objective of multiple pricing is to reduce the incentive for farmers to expand their production. Multiple pricing programs require the use of the product bases, and farmers are paid higher prices for base production than for excess or overbase production. The administration of such a program is quite involved, and experience with programs of this type is too limited to determine exactly how effective they might be in curtailing increased production.

Free market prices. Free market prices provide perhaps the most automatic resource allocator and guide to production and consumption. However, the total social costs may be too high to institute such a policy since they may also emphasize price and income fluctuations, and lead to drastically reduced farm incomes, at least in an unspecified "short run" period. Free market prices for farm products means the removal of all production controls and price supports and the offering of products for sale on both domestic and foreign markets. No restrictions on the freedom of the individual farmers or of commodity groups would be imposed. Any overall increases in production would occur in response to actual or anticipated increases in commodity prices; decreases in production would occur in response to actual or anticipated declines in prices.

The effect of free prices on farmers would likely lower net farm income by between 25 and 30 percent in the short run. How long this short run would last is not known. Undoubtedly, there would be considerable adjustment within the farm sector of people who would have to seek nonfarm employment. The magnitude of this transition has been theoretically likened to the kind of farm depression that existed during the 1930's.

The immediate effect of a free price policy would be to intensify the price-cost squeeze in agriculture. Exactly how steep the price decline would be depends partially upon what policy might be adopted with regard to the large storage stocks of farm production now held by the government. Long-run adjustments might mean fewer farmers more closely organized, so that consumers might end up paying more for their food products than they now do. In the short run, however, consumers would benefit by paying less for their food. Undoubtedly a return to free prices would solve the problem of overproduction in the farm economy. However, it is of considerable doubt that the cost of such a move would be worth the gain.

Production quota and resource controls

Marketing quotas. The objective of a policy which establishes a marketing quota is to limit the marketing of farm products. In effect, this reduces supply (shifts the supply curve to the left or temporarily slows the advance to the right so that it is in balance with increases in demand).

This is the way marketing quotas might work. Congress would set what it considers to be a price which would return a fair income to farmers for their food production efforts. With these goals of price and income in mind it would then become the task of the Department of Agriculture to establish national sales quotas designed to call forth the desired food production. Each farmer could receive his share of the national quota. His share could be determined from an historical record of production on his farm. One or more certificates would be issued to the farmer indicating how much the farmer's share of the local market might be. Production and marketing regulations would be rigidly enforced, with many penalties on both the producer and the buyer for nonconformity. Farmers would be free to buy or sell their certificates in an effort to expand their farm business or to get out of farming altogether. Regardless of the movement or transfer of certificates within the farm sector, the limits on production would be set. Production (denoted by certificates) would tend to move to those farm managers who have the greatest efficiency of production, and into those areas which have the greatest comparative production advantage. The program would be protected from undue imports by foreign countries.

A program of this kind would probably succeed in holding farm incomes high. However, there might be some resource misallocation. Either part of the resources now used in farm production would become unemployed, or if all available agricultural resources were used it would be in a less efficient manner. The use of historical bases in establishing quotas would mean that the most efficient farmers would probably get the bulk of the quotas. Thus, there would likely be a mass migration out of farm production into the nonfarm sector. However, since the people who moved out under these circumstances would probably not be highly trained, the net impact on the whole economy could be more unemployment. Consumers might have to pay more for their food items, but this situation would depend ultimately upon the price levels which Congress set.

The certificates of production and marketing ability would most likely be capitalized into the farm sector quite rapidly. For this reason the government would hesitate to withdraw its support from farming because of the high losses which might accrue to certificate owners. This argument is similar in many respects to the reasoning that a return to free farm prices would be so painful. Further, if quotas were not imposed on all commodities resources within farming would shift to nondesignated commodities. This would likely result in continued overproduction and would necessitate further extension of quotas.

Land retirement programs. The objective under both a voluntary and a compulsory land retirement program is to limit the amount of land on which farmers can raise crops or livestock. Under a mandatory program a national acreage allotment would be determined from a national "need" estimate, or national marketing quota. This acreage allotment would then be allocated to individual farmers in much the same manner as a marketing quota. The program would control the land resource while it permitted the farmer to apply freely all the capital, technology, labor, and management he could and wanted to. Penalties would help enforce the law. Production rights under this program would be salable. Land withdrawn from production would be put into a compulsory conservation reserve. Federal assistance would be provided to plant this acreage to trees, grass, and so on. The effect on farm incomes from this program would be to push them upward, but eventually the acreage allotments would be capitalized into the farm units and the then current owners would fall heir to windfall gains in much the same manner that they would under a marketing quota system. The total amount of land under cultivation would be reduced as would the number of farmers needed.

Under a voluntary system of land retirement much the same total effects will take place. One of the major problems would be to make payments high enough to induce voluntary retirement of the 60 to 70 million acres which will have to be withdrawn in order to reduce farm production significantly. Land could be retired voluntarily on a per farm basis, on a per region basis, or on a quality of productive land basis. On a national basis, payments to withdraw the necessary land would probably average $25 to $30 per acre, and require total payments, administrative costs, and conservation payments of between $1.75 and $2 billion annually.

If enough land is taken out of cultivation farm production can be reduced and farm incomes increased. Land can be taken out on a compulsory basis or enough land may be withdrawn voluntarily providing the payments offered are high enough to induce withdrawal.

Restricting capital and technology. Throughout Part I we have discussed the increased use of almost all capital items and the rapid adoption of technology. We have also noted that the use of new technologies are at the heart of the overproduction problems of farm income. It is a natural conclusion now to consider policies that restrict the use of capital and technology.

Farm production could be cut back by restricting the use of farm credit, fertilizer, hybrid seeds, improved strains of livestock, and the investment in the technical research of farm production and education. Little public support of such a program would be likely, as food prices would rise and inefficiencies of production and distribution would be the result of a restriction of research inquiry and legislated obstacles to adoption of the resulting technology.

Programs to help farmers move out of farming. The idea of a program to help those farmers who choose to move out of farming is not a new idea. It has been suggested time and again over the last 25 years. However, how to make such a program palatable to the people involved is another question. A program to reduce the number of farmers would eventually mean that the farm income would be divided among a smaller number of people, presumably small enough so that each farm family left in farming would have an adequate income.

The difficulty with such a program comes when one considers the people after they move off the farm. Training programs have been suggested for farmers who migrate to nonfarm jobs. However, training that is available will not provide jobs for all the people who move off the farm. In addition, what if increasing unemployment is evident in the nonfarm economy, brought about by many of the same reasons (increasing technology adds to structural unemployment). It becomes a difficult question to determine whether or not a low paid farmer is better off on the farm or risk unemployment in the town or city. In terms of total cost to the nation, which combination of farm income support programs and welfare programs to support the possibly unemployable, recently removed farmer, is best? Personal values cannot be overlooked in such a determination.

Summary. Of all the policies considered under this section the two dealing with marketing quotas and land retirement (under a program of modified supports) have received the most support from Congress and the farmers throughout the country. The adoption of the Soil Bank Program is explicit recognition of the ability of a land retirement program to eventually solve the farm problem. On the other hand, increasing adoption of federal market orders for milk is explicit recognition that quotas also have a significant part to play.

A vital and responsive agriculture and a dynamic nonfarm economy present our country's policymakers with a continual challenge. The goals of increasing economic growth, freedom for the individual, and security for the farmer and his family present conflicts of interest that must be resolved. The task is not an easy one. But it is imperative that it be attempted and continually modified to fit the changing conditions of our times.

Appendix[1]

1920-1930

The quarter century prior to 1920 was a relatively prosperous period for United States farmers, and often is referred to as the Golden Era of Agriculture. Industrial activity was high and both domestic and foreign demand for food products was strong.

This period of optimism continued until 1920, when agricultural prices broke. The farm price drop came before the drop in industrial prices. Farmers were caught with drastically reduced incomes as a result of the high costs of the 1920 crops and the low income it produced. Many were under heavy debt for land and machinery and their cash reserves were low. The sudden disparity between farm income and cost created ferment in farm groups and coincided with an election year for president.

Early in 1921 the new Congress created a Joint Commission of Agricultural Inquiry which was directed within 90 days to investigate:

1. Causes of present condition in agriculture.
2. Causes of the high farm-to-retail cost margin.
3. Comparative conditions of industries other than agriculture.
4. Relation of prices of commodities other than agriculture.
5. Banking and financial resources of the country.
6. Marketing and transportation facilities of the United States.
7. Legislative recommendations concerning agriculture.

This commission attributed the farm distress to a general business decline, particularly aggravated by the failure of export demand. Overproduction was not adjudged to be an important cause of the price decline.

A National Agricultural Conference was called by Secretary of Agriculture Wallace in January 1922. Some 400 agricultural leaders met in Washington to discuss the farm problem of low prices which had pushed net farm incomes

[1] Data sources include "Farmers in a Changing World," *Yearbook of Agriculture, 1940*, U.S.D.A., Washington, 1940; M. R. Benedict, *Can We Solve the Farm Problem?* (New York: Twentieth Century Fund, 1955); "Can the Feed Grain Programs Help You?" Mimeo EC-216 with revisions (Lafayette, Indiana, Purdue University Agriculture Extension Service). For an excellent summary of farm commodity programs and agricultural legislation, see the following: "Farm Commodity and Related Programs," Agriculture Handbook No. 345, ASCS, USDA, and "Compilation of Statutes Relating to . . . ", January 1, 1967, Agriculture Handbook No. 327, ASCS, USDA. For additional insights and theoretical presentations, see: *Government and Agriculture: Public Policy in a Democratic Society*, Dale E. Hathaway, Macmillan Company, New York, 1963, and *Readings in Agricultural Policy*, R. J. Hildreth, University of Nebraska Press, 1968.

lower yet. The group was split into 12 sections, each of which was to wrestle with the same problem of what to do about low farm incomes.

One group was led by George Peek (Moline Plow Company). His group came up with the slogan *Equality For Agriculture* which has resounded throughout every subsequent political campaign. It set prominently before the country the objective for which organized agriculture was to strive in the turbulent farm fights of succeeding decades. The conference recommended:

1. Higher tariffs.
2. More foreign credits to facilitate exports.
3. An intermediate credit system for farmers.
4. Recognition of cooperative marketing associations and price stabilization through their operation.
5. For study, a system of crop insurance and the whole question of government guaranty of prices.

In the meantime Peek and his business associate Johnson had filed a brief with the American Farm Bureau Federation in which he outlined a plan of operation which was in general incorporated into the surplus control bills. This was known as the McNary-Haugen Proposals. The more common name given to the proposals is the "two price plan"—the maintenance of a domestic price above the world market price and the disposal of any surplus production on the world market at the lower price. It was expected to work as follows:

Suppose the U.S. wheat crop were 800 million bushels, of which the domestic demand would take 600 million bushels at a price of $1.42 (equal to world price of $1.00 plus tariff of $.42). The result would be a 200 million-bushel surplus to be disposed of abroad at a loss. Since the surplus would be bought from U.S. farmers at $1.42 and sold abroad for $1.00, the loss incurred would be $84 million. To make up the loss the $84 million would be distributed back as a cost to U.S. farmers for each bushel ($84 million ÷ 800 million bushels). Thus, the net price per bushel to U.S. farmers would be $1.315 ($1.42 − $.105), or a gain of 31½ cents over the world price. Total gain would be $252 million (800 million bushels × 31½ cents per bushel).

President Coolidge's objections to the two price plans were that they: (a) attempt price fixing, (b) promote bureaucracy, (c) encourage profiteering and wasteful distribution by marketing middlemen, (d) stimulate overproduction, (e) would not work unless product is exportable, (f) require a high cost of administration, (g) invite retaliation by foreign countries, and (h) assume an inelastic demand at home and an elastic demand abroad.

The 1920's were characterized by a period of general agricultural disinterest. No legislation was passed pertinent to price supports until 1929, although the McNary-Haugen proposals went through Congress twice and were vetoed by President Coolidge. The Capper-Volstead Act, passed in 1922, gave legal status to agricultural cooperatives and exempted them from antitrust legislation. Tariffs were continually raised during the 1920's and few seemed to realize that promoting more trade and increasing tariffs were somewhat incompatible. Two changes of importance during this period were (a) the U.S. was now a creditor nation rather than a debtor nation, and (b) most of the free good land was taken up so there was no frontier to act as a shock absorber for dispossessed farmers and for the unemployed from industrial centers. All the farm groups were for some kind of legislation but differed as to the best plan, as is the case today. The Farm Bureau was pushing the two-price plan, the Grange wanted an export debenture plan, and the Farmers Union favored a plan to insure coverage of costs of production. The South was rather indifferent, as rice, tobacco, and cotton were faring rather well under cooperative marketing. The East and other industrial centers were generally opposed to any farm legislation, as were most government officials except for a group close to the Secretary of Agriculture.

The first act of federal legislation aimed to alleviate the price-income problem was the Agricultural Marketing Act of 1929, commonly referred to as the Federal Farm Board. It undertook to encourage cooperatives and stabilization corporations (owned by cooperatives), to unify the process of agricultural marketing with support of loans, and was given $500 million to be used as a revolving fund. At the beginning of its operation the board viewed its principal function as the fostering of a system of cooperative marketing associations. However, the drastic decline of agriculture prices in the latter part of 1929 caused the board to become increasingly concerned with stabilization of prices. Unfortunately the period selected for this first legislative venture in supporting prices coincided with a worldwide depression of unprecedented scope and severity.

1930 to 1940

The difficulty experienced by the Federal Farm Board in supporting prices convinced many policymakers that gains in withholding supplies from the market could be realized only if production were held in line with actual market demand at home and abroad. The foreign demand situation worsened as tariffs reached an all time high with the passage of the Smoot-Hawley Bill. With mounting surpluses and stagnant markets, the argument for production control gained momentum.

Agricultural Adjustment Act of 1933 (AAA)

The AAA of 1933 was based on the domestic allotment plan as a means to limit production. Essentially, a farmer's acreage allotment was determined by looking at his historical production. For example, a farmer who had planted a larger acreage than his neighbor for the previous five years would get a larger allotment.

Millions of farmers entered contracts to reduce acreage in return for benefit payments. The payments were financed chiefly by taxes levied on agricultural processors of commodities concerned. In order to assure success of the plan, cotton farmers were soon asking for marketing quotas with a penalty tax to force noncooperators into line. The program was brought to a sharp halt in 1936 when, in the Hoosac Mills Case, the Supreme Court ruled the program unconstitutional because the processing tax was an inseparable part of the scheme to control production.

Soil Conservation and Domestic Allotment Act of 1936

With the establishment of the Soil Conservation Service (SCS) in 1935, interest turned to issues of soil conservation and erosion control. Under the 1936 conservation act an open offer on the part of the Secretary of Agriculture replaced the contracts under the original adjustment program, conditional payments replaced benefit payments, direct appropriations replaced processing taxes, and the emphasis was shifted from acreage control to conservation. This act did not solve the price-income problems of farmers.

Agricultural Adjustment Act of 1938

The AAA of 1938 represented a synthesis and culmination of earlier efforts. It was the first piece of legislation with lasting results. The major objective was stated as the maintenance of soil resources. The Act encompassed five general areas.

Soil Conservation, Good Farm Management, and Balanced Output. This provision permitted payments to farmers to conserve and build up their soil. The supplemental income received for cooperating in the program enabled farmers to check the inroads of soil erosion, which is an important step in good farm management.

Loans, Marketing Quotas, and Parity Payments. This was a measure to enable producers of corn, wheat, cotton, tobacco, and rice to obtain storage loans to put a floor under prices when these were threatened by a slump and to finance the holding of surplus supplies until they were needed. Further, marketing quotas could be employed if two-thirds of a commodity's producers approved buttressing the price-supporting influence of the loans. Finally, if loans and quotas resulted in prices still too low in view of the goals of parity prices and income, the Secretary was authorized, insofar as funds were available, to make payments to the producers of the five commodities; these, together with the income from the sale of their crops, were to bring the farm producer a return equal to parity price on their normal production. Support levels would have been 50 to 75 percent of parity under this provision, using the old parity formula.

Marketing Agreements. This part provided for farmers and distributors to establish permanent and rational marketing quotas for entire crops and groups of crops. This would permit groups to exercise centralized control over the marketing of a product (see Chapter 10).

Surplus Diversion and New Uses. This provision authorized the establishment of four regional laboratories to conduct research into, and develop new uses for, agricultural products. The objective was to expand the demand for farm products, to alleviate surpluses, and to improve prices.

Crop Insurance. This act authorized the establishment of the Federal Crop Insurance Corporation (FCIC) to write crop insurance against loss in wheat yields, beginning with the 1939 crop. The new agency was given a capital stock of $100 million.

1940 to 1950

Even though the 1938 Act was a major piece of legislation, the nation found itself gearing for the demands of World War II soon after its passage. The war rather quickly solved the farm problems of low prices and overproduction. Prices began to rise rapidly in 1941 and controversy shifted to the levels of price ceilings that should be imposed rather than the level of supports. The first general price control legislation of the war period (Emergency Price Control Act of 1942) prohibited the application of price ceilings on farm products at less than 110 percent of parity. This did nothing to stabilize the farm situation in the early years of the war. The prices-received index increased from 95 in 1939 to 123, 158, and 196 in 1941, 1942, and 1945, respectively (this figure was 100 from 1900 to 1914). Output increased 30 percent in 1945 over the 1935 to 1939 levels.

The Steagall Amendment

Probably the most important legislative act passed in World War II affecting prices and income for farm products was the Steagall Amendment. This legislation was attached as a rider to the Act of 1941, and was passed in 1942. Its objective was to stimulate farm production for the war effort and it called for rigid price supports at a high level. It required that 90 percent of parity supports be applied to the basic crops (corn, wheat, cotton, tobacco, rice, and peanuts) until two years after January 1 following the close of the war. The latter feature was to avoid the losses sustained by farmers should prices fall precipitously after World War II as they did after World War I in 1920. In addition, the Act authorized payments of not less than 90 percent of parity on a number of other commodities (nonbasics or, as they were often called, Steagall commodities) which were deemed vital to the war effort. In 1945 the price support on Steagall commodities ranged from 90 percent of parity on eggs to 130 percent of parity on milk and butterfat. The end of the war was declared on December 30, 1946; thus, the Steagall Amendment was in effect until January 1, 1949.

Agricultural Act of 1948

The struggle between those wanting to return to the policies under the 1938 legislation and those wanting to retain the high rigid price supports under the Steagall Amendment resulted in a compromise in 1948. Title I of the Act extended wartime support levels on basics until January 1, 1950 and provided for some relaxation of support levels on the Steagall commodities.

The major feature, however, was the introduction of the "flexible price support" feature to go into effect in 1950, which allowed the support level on basic commodities to vary depending on the amount of the commodity that was produced. If the crop was large the support level would be lower. The range of flexibility was set at 60 to 90 percent. If the crop were 70 percent or more below normal, the support level would be the maximum 90 percent of parity. For every two percent increase in the percent of normal supply produced, the support level would be reduced by one percent. Therefore, a normal supply (100 percent) would receive 75 percent support level. The support level would be 60 percent for supplies 130 percent or more of normal. For nonbasics, price supports were authorized at the discretion of the Secretary up to 90 percent of parity. The 1948 act also introduced the new parity formula designed to eliminate the distortions in parity prices computed under the old formula due to changes in the cost of production.

Agricultural Act of 1949

In 1949 the 81st Congress proceeded to extend the rigid wartime price support levels on the basic crops through 1950. Though the Act of 1949 basically retained the idea of a new or modernized parity formula, the prices-paid index was made to include hired farm labor. This tended to increase parity prices. Also, for any basic commodity the parity price would be calculated by both formulas and the higher parity price would be used until 1954. The range in the flexible price supports was reduced to 75 to 90 percent rather than 60 to 90 percent. Some changes were also made in the support of nonbasics.

The Brannan Proposals

Secretary of Agriculture Brannan made proposals of an income support program which never became law but which were widely discussed. The Brannan Plan would have provided for parity incomes to farmers based on the profitable years 1938 to 1947, with the mechanism to be price supports that would yield these parity incomes; this would have required a very high level of price supports. For perishable products the Brannan Plan would have allowed direct payments to producers to make up the difference between market prices received and the support price established. Another clause would have restricted total payments to any one farm.

1950 to 1960

Large stock accumulations in 1949 and 1950 were somewhat relieved by the Korean conflict and there were no major changes in price-income farm policy through 1953.

Agricultural Act of 1954

The Act of 1954 did not drastically change the main features of the farm program, and essentially called for a return to the more flexible provisions originally introduced under the 1948 Act. The price support range was to be 82½ to 90 percent of parity for the 1955 crop and 75 to 90 percent of parity thereafter.

Soil Bank Program

Large crops and low livestock prices prompted further attempts to control production while prices were supported, which ended in a two-part Soil Bank Program enacted in 1956. The program allowed for voluntary farmer participation. This was an effort to limit the land resource in farming, which in turn was an attempt to reduce production.

Acreage Reserve. Under the acreage reserve program for 1956, 1957, and 1958, farmers could receive payments for renting their land to the governmnt. If they were complying with other programs farmers could put up to half of their allotted acreage in basic crops in the reserve but were not allowed to use the land for any other crop, including hay and pasture. Producers were paid on the basis of their normal yields multiplied by some payment per bushel. Average rates paid were $.90 a bushel for corn and $1.20 for wheat. The essential and important difference from previous programs was that the land put into the reserve could not be diverted to any other use

Conservation Reserve. This part of the program was to help producers shift poorer cropland into permanent long-range conservation uses. Payments averaged $10 to $15 per acre, and by 1960 about 28 million acres of low productivity land were put into the conservation reserve

1960 to 1970

Despite the efforts to hold production in line with population and overall demand increases, the total output of farm commodities for other than the basic crops increased 23 percent from 1952 to 1958 (basics increased three percent); population rose 11 percent. Thus, the farm income situation at the end of the 1950's had not materially improved in spite of efforts to reduce production, get rid of excess stocks, and support prices. There was wide disagreement among farm groups in the formulation of congressional policy alternatives for the price-income problem.

Legislation in the 1960's was by no means limited to the basic commodities. Efforts were begun early in 1961 to expand the existing program authorizing food distribution to needy persons. A pilot food stamp program was begun. Expansion of the School Lunch and Special Milk programs was undertaken. Rural development efforts were stepped up (see Chapter 23). More efforts were made to use constructively our food abundance and food producing technology abroad.

The Feed Grain Act (approved March 22, 1961) and the Agricultural Act of 1961 (approved August 8, 1961) provided the basic framework for legislation in the following decade. Specific programs for wheat and feed grains with provisions for crop acreage diversion to soil conserving crops and practices, authorization of marketing orders for specific crops, and extensions of the National Wool Act of 1954 and Public Law 480 laid the initial foundation.

Feed grain programs of 1961, 1962, 1963, and 1964

In the early 1960's legislation was passed applying in particular to the feed grain sector of farm production. The program was voluntary and utilized the idea of the conservation reserve of the Soil Bank Program. It offered direct payments for the voluntary reduction of cropland acres of feed grains. By 1963 corn, grain sorghum, and barley were under the program.

For 1961 and 1962 the support price and loan rate on corn was $1.20 a bushel. If a farmer took 20 percent of his allotted acres out of corn production he was entitled to payments based on normal yields of 50 percent of the support price. For diversion of acreage between 20 and 40 percent of a farmer's allotment, the land retirement payment would be 60 percent of the support price. The minimum participation would be at the 20 percent level. But on small farms where the allotted acreage is 25 acres or less, 100 percent could be diverted into the program. Participants were not allowed to harvest anything from the diverted acres, nor could the land be used for grazing between May 1 and November 1. For each acre diverted from feed grain production it was required that an additional acre be added to soil conservation acreage. On these acres farmers would receive a flat payment of $10 per acre plus another $3 per acre if seeded to cover crops.

The 1963 program included several variations. A farmer's feed grain base in 1963 was taken from the historical average acreages of corn, grain sorghum, and barley produced on the farm between 1959 and 1960. Within the total permitted acreage any combination of the three crops could be planted. The loan rate was set at $1.07 (national average) for corn and a supplemental price support payment of 18 cents a bushel was added which would be paid on total acres planted rather than just on allotted acreage. The support price would thus be $1.25, with a 20 percent of support price payment for the first percent of allotted acreage diverted. Fifty percent of the support price was paid on additional acres up to 40 percent. For example, assume that a farmer had a corn base of 100 acres with normal yields appraised at 70 bushels per acre and actual yields at 80 bushels per acre. For complying, he would receive the following:

Supplemental price support payment: 18¢/bushel x 70 bushels x 80 acres planted = $1,008 if 20 percent is diverted, or 18¢/bushel x 70 bushels x 60 acres planted = $756 if 40 percent is diverted.

Land retirement payment: for the first 20% diverted, (20% x $1.25) x 70 bushels x 20 acres = $350. If the 20% diverted is added, (50% x $1.25) x 70 bushels x 20 acres = $875.

CCC Loan: (if 20% is diverted) 80 acres x 80 bushels x $1.07 = $6,848.
            (if 40% is diverted) 60 acres x 80 bushels x $1.07 = $5,136.

Alternative values would depend on market price if sold or on value if fed to livestock.

Conservation value on retired acres with seeding and maintenance costs subtracted:

(if 20% is diverted) 20 acres x $10 = $200.

(if 40% is diverted) 40 acres x $10 = $400.

Under the 1963 program supplemental price support payments were 14¢ per bushel for barley and 16¢ per bushel for grain sorghum. National average loan rates were $.82 for barley and $.96 for grain sorghum.

In May 1963 the Nation's wheat farmers overwhelmingly voted down the Administration's proposal for stronger supply management tools in Federal hands. The Wheat Referendum price support alternatives were two: (1) severe payment penalties to farmers who overplanted their acreage allotments, issuance of marketing certificates based on estimates of domestic and foreign demand, support for those certificates at 65-90 percent of parity, with any surplus wheat supported at feed prices, or (2) no overplanting penalties, but wheat grown on allotted acres would be supported at only 50 percent parity— essentially a "free price" market system. In voting down the first alternative the farmers were stuck with the second, but in reality the farmers had added a third unwritten alternative to the ballot: that Congress would come up with something more acceptable to them. It did—the Cotton-Wheat Act was approved April 11, 1964. Under this Act there was a voluntary wheat-marketing certificate program for 1964 and 1965 permitting acreage allotment and diversion compliers to receive price supports, marketing certificates, and land diversion payments. Noncompliers received no benefits. Wheat food processors and exporters were required to buy certificates for all the wheat they handled.

Cotton was also well treated. The Secretary of Agriculture was authorized to make subsidy payments to domestic cotton handlers or textile mills which, in effect, made up the difference between the support price (totaling about 33.5 cents per pound in 1964) and the export or world price of cotton.

1965 through 1970

The Food and Agriculture Act of 1965 (effective for calendar years 1966-1969) broke the tradition of annual Congressional battles and set out legislation covering a four year period. This innovation allowed farmers, their suppliers, processors, indeed all of agribusiness, a firmer base on which to plan their business operations. However, it carried an inherent disadvantage, too: farmers and farm groups might not use this time to consolidate efforts to increase understanding of farm and farm related problems on the part of national and state legislators, "agriculture" could become complacent, special commodity groups could isolate themselves and the consequences of their actions even further than the situation which existed in 1965, and both urban and farm groups might not be any farther down the road of mutual understanding of one another's problems and opportunities.

Essentially, the 1965 Act carried forward many of the provisions of previous legislation in one form or another. Dairymen benefitted by being allowed a fluid milk base which permitted the reduction of surplus milk without damaging fluid markets. The Wool Act and feed grain program elements were extended through 1969. Cotton subsidy payments to textile mills and handlers were made unnecessary by lowering supports to 90 percent of the estimated world price. Cotton farmers received allotment compliance payments. The voluntary wheat certificate program was continued.

The Act established a Cropland Adjustment Program based on previous farm land retirement experience. Emphasis was put on long term (5 to 10 year) contracts with farmers for converting "unneeded" cropland to conservation, beautification, or recreational purposes.

Some of the disadvantages mentioned earlier were evident when Congressional and USDA minds turned to the task of introducing farm legislation to be effective after the 1965 Act expired. Labor interests because of the Food Stamp Program, urban interest in possibly inequitable payments to operators of large farms, and the Presidential election year all combined to cause a stalemate on a thorough farm legislation reappraisal. The result was a continuation of the 1965 Act *in toto* for one year, through calendar 1970. In 1969 and the spring of 1970 many of the forces described will be active again to enhance or detract from realistic farm legislation. The outcome is far from certain, particularly if one considers the relative and declining importance of farming in the total economy.

Parity computations

Parity means the concept of "fairness" and "equality." A parity price is one that will buy the same quantity of products in some future period as it does in some base period. It is a yardstick to measure what a "fair" price is for the commodities that farmers produce in relation to price of inputs they buy. The *parity ratio* is equal to the index of prices received divided by the index of prices paid by farmers times 100, both based on the years 1910 to 1914. The index of prices received is a composite weighted index of the prices of the commodities which farmers sell. The index of prices paid, sometimes called the parity index, is a composite index, including over 300 cost items to measure changes in the per unit cost of goods and services bought by farm families for living and food production. If the parity ratio is less than 100 it means that the prices which farmers are receiving for their products have increased less than the cost of producing the products, and hence they are getting pinched in what has often been called the price-cost squeeze.

The *old parity formula* was computed by multiplying the actual market price of the commodity in the period 1910 to 1914 by the current index of prices paid divided by 100. Essentially the reasoning behind it was that if the farmer's cost had gone up 50 percent since 1910 to 1914, then the parity price would be 50 percent higher than the 1910 to 1914 levels.

The *new parity formula* attempted to take changes in cost of production into consideration by relating parity prices to a more recent period. First, an adjusted base price is computed by dividing the average price of the commodity over the last 10 years by the average index of prices received for the last 10 years and multiplying the answer by 100. Then, the adjusted base price is multiplied by the current index of prices paid divided by 100.

The *support price* for a commodity is equal to the parity price multiplied by the support level.

Illustrations of Computing Parity and Support Prices

Given: Price of corn, 1910 to 1914—$.58/bushel
         Current prices-received index—240
         Current prices-paid index—290
         Current price of corn—$1.15/bushel
         Average price of corn (last 10 years)—$1.22/bushel
         Average index of prices received (last 10 years)—245
         Support level—90 percent

1. Parity Price (old formula)
$$\frac{\$.58 \times 290}{100} = \$1.68$$

2. Parity Price (new formula)
$$\frac{\$1.22 \times 100}{245} = \$.50 \times \frac{290}{100} = \$1.45$$

3. Support Price (old formula)
$$\$1.68 \times 90\% = \$1.51$$

4. Support Price (new formula)
$$\$1.45 \times 90\% = \$1.30\frac{1}{2}$$

5. Parity Ratio
$$\frac{240 \times 100}{290} = 82.7$$

23

Problems in resource development

Resource development in any area entails using resources more efficiently or more productively by shifting them to uses where marginal returns are higher or by using them more intensively. This approach allows for a more orderly and rapid pattern of growth than existed previously. It also permits a comprehensive approach to growth by integrating all the resources (human, physical, natural, social, institutional, political, etc.). Furthermore, this type of total growth situation encourages overall increases in farm and nonfarm income, as well as increases in employment of all kinds.

PROGRAMS IN RESOURCE DEVELOPMENT

This chapter will deal with three national programs of resource development sponsored by the federal government: the Tennessee Valley Authority (TVA), the Rural Development Program (RDP), and the Area Redevelopment Administration with the Rural Areas Development Program (ARA and RAD).[1] This emphasis does not imply that local com-

[1] Other major resource development programs of importance include those of the United States Department of Interior, the Army Corps of Engineers, and the Urban Renewal Administration. No attempt is made here to evaluate the alternative uses of government funds spent by the foregoing agencies, or invested in the resource development programs discussed in this chapter. However, cost-benefit analysis is a highly challenging area for economists, and all interested students should be encouraged to explore its opportunities further.

munities do not also have extensive resource development progress and activities. On the contrary, local communities are the backbone of local resource development in this country, as the case study included in this chapter will point out. County, city, and town planning commissions and boards, local development organizations of all kinds, as well as nation-wide private and public agencies, spend a great deal of time and money to achieve the development of local resources.

Passage of resource development legislation affecting economic development implicitly recognizes two things about the economic growth process: (a) Economic growth is a process which spreads unevenly across the country. There will be pockets of low income, underemployment, and unemployment within or close to areas of rapidly increasing incomes. These pockets will develop because of differences in natural and physical resource endowments, the ability of the area to combine its resources into salable products, its geographic location and transportation facilities, its accessibility to markets (either where it can buy its inputs or sell its output), and the technical ability of its people to engage in production. These factors tend to operate in a fairly independent manner for most areas. (b) Legislation recognizes that although there are some things about an area which cannot be changed, there are people within that area who may have a desire to change certain other things and can do so if they are provided the means to implement change.

The comparative production advantages of an area can be limited by many things. Differences in the adoption of technology, differences in transportation rates and in the costs of buying production inputs and selling output, and institutional barriers and the attitude of local people are factors which might limit the economic advantages of an area. However, inasmuch as the people can and want to change any of the factors above, they will change the rate of economic growth in the area. This is a highly important concept to understand because it is the basis upon which most of our economic resource development legislation is built. The values and capabilities of the people in the areas which are affected by resource development are the ultimate keys to the success of any enabling legislation.

OBJECTIVES OF RESOURCE DEVELOPMENT

The intent of most resource development programs is to permit the local people to change the rate of local economic growth either entirely by themselves or with the help of some public agency. In Figure 23-1 two rates of economic growth are shown; one is for an area with a poor resource base, the other is for an area with a relatively rich resource base. Initially, there is a difference between their rates of economic growth (see a, Figure 23-1). This is to be expected because of the differences in the resource base of the two areas. However, as time progresses the difference or the development gap between the two areas widens (see b, Figure 23-1). The purpose of a resource development program is to lessen the gap (see c, Figure 23-1), and achieve a more rapid rate of growth, as shown by the dotted line in Figure 23-1.

THE PROBLEM OF THE TENNESSEE VALLEY

The situation facing the Tennessee Valley region in the mid-1930's was one of declining farm income and few full or part-time nonfarm jobs of any kind. Off-farm jobs that were available paid relatively low wages. Floods were frequent throughout the Tennessee Valley, periodically destroying homes and farmsteads. And finally, nature had not been generous with the area in terms of its land and mineral resources.

The goals facing Congress in the midst of the Depression were to increase incomes, increase employment, and to do a better overall job of developing the country's resources. One of the problems facing Congress

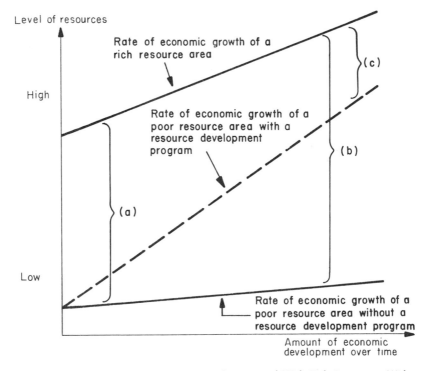

FIGURE 23-1:   Comparison of Areas With Poor and With Rich Resources, With and Without a Resource Development Program.

was, "What ought to be done to the Middle South to increase income and employment?" The alternative solution they chose was to create the Tennessee Valley Authority, a program of extensive and intensive resource development.

The Tennessee Valley Authority

The Tennessee Valley Authority (TVA) was established by Congress in May, 1933.[2] Initially a highly controversial subject involved in partisan politics, the Authority is now supported on a solid bipartisan basis. Its record of economic success has long since removed any "political experimentation" stigma attached to it in the minds of most people. The TVA was founded on the assumption that the living standards of people in a certain area can be considerably improved by the full development of the physical resources on which they depend for a living.[3] People employed by the TVA were given broad powers for implementing effective action in flood control, navigation development, generation of electric power, land use planning, reforestation.

The Tennessee Valley region covers 92,000 square miles, comprising the entire state of Tennessee and parts of six other states (Mississippi, Alabama, Georgia, North Carolina, Virginia, and Kentucky). There are 201 counties in the combined Watershed-Power Service Area. The watershed of the Tennessee River includes 125 counties; the TVA power service area includes 170 counties, 76 of which are outside the watershed.[4]

The land covered by the TVA is rough, ranging from the Appalachian mountains—about 6,000 feet high—in the eastern part, to low river valleys of altitudes of only a few hundred feet. More than half the land area is forested and is extremely rough, making commercialization difficult. The Valley's mineral resources consist mostly of coal and phosphate rock deposits, from which fertilizers are made. There is an abundance of surface water resources, but the soils in the area tend to be poor and highly susceptible to erosion.

The TVA is managed by a three-man Board of Directors, one of whom is elected chairman. There is also a General Manager who is in charge of all the operations of the TVA, including all of its divisions and branches. Congress gave the TVA an initial loan which is being repaid from profits from its various resource development projects. During the summer of 1960 the Board voted to sell bonds on the commercial capital

[2] Act of May 18, 1933, Sec. 23, 48 *Stat.* 69.
[3] John R. P. Friedman, *The Spatial Structure of Economic Development in the Tennessee Valley*, Research Paper No. 39, Department of Geography, University of Chicago, March 1955, p. 8.
[4] *Ibid.*, pp. 6-8.

market in order to finance further dam construction and power development expansion.

One of the principal functions of the TVA is to generate electricity which it then sells wholesale to various electrical utility companies, or retails to both private industry and public agencies, such as the Atomic Energy Commission which uses great quantities of TVA power. In cases where it markets wholesale power, the TVA retains a voice in the retail resale of the power to make sure that only a reasonable profit margin is received from their low-priced power. No power is sold by the TVA to private individuals or to households.[5]

The TVA has several different divisions and branches which handle hydro-power projects, agriculture and chemical developments, area development and regional analysis, reservoirs, dams and property developments, engineering projects pertaining to resource development, reforestation of the area, and recreation projects. Perhaps the most widely known TVA projects other than dam building and power generation are the manufacture of fertilizers (also munitions during World War II and the Korean War), the extensive research conducted and/or sponsored by TVA, and the educational activities conducted by its employees or consultants.

For example, within the Agriculture Division there are four branches: the Agricultural Economics branch, which does research on a variety of subjects; the Farm Test Demonstration branch, which acts in an extension education capacity for farmers on fertilizer application and total farm planning, including crop rotation, livestock and pasture programs, and woodlot management; the Distributor Demonstration branch, which extends research findings to distributors of fertilizer and to other farm supply industries; and the Agronomy branch, which conducts research necessary to service and stimulate the other branches. In addition to these activities there is much research of an agronomic-economic nature sponsored by TVA in cooperation with the Experiment Stations of various Land Grant Universities throughout the country. This research is an attempt to bring together people from many institutions who are interested in production economics and farm management, primarily response to fertilizer and the evaluation of the social and economic aspects of this increase in production. Research projects include the application of fertilizer in conditions of drought or through irrigation systems. The demand for fertilizer and the credit available for fertilizer application has been studied. Farmers' attitudes toward fertilizer, its

[5] During the fiscal year ending June 30, 1962, the TVA sold electricity to 102 municipal electric systems and 51 rural electric cooperatives which, in turn, sold power to 1,486,000 customers at standard TVA retail rates. See "Municipal and Co-operative Distributors of TVA Power," 1962 Annual Report, TVA (Knoxville, Tennessee: Nov., 1962).

technology of application, and the attitudes of dealers who sell fertilizer to farms have also been analyzed. Comparative production cost studies and the kinds of equipment needed to farm efficiently in the area are other examples.

Perhaps the largest single fact about economic development that the TVA has proven beyond doubt is that increased urban-industrial development also helps the farmers in an area. Not only does increased industrialization offer underemployed farmers jobs at higher incomes than they could earn on the farm, and provide additional markets through which farmers can market their produce, but it also provides an additional or increased source of income to the farmer. As a result, he need not be dependent solely upon the income from his farm for the purchase of all his farm inputs as well as for the necessities of his family. An increase in an area's total economic activity ultimately offers farmers more opportunity to buy more fertilizer and better equipment. Increased use of these inputs raises the farm production in an area and thereby also raises income from farming. Productivity per farm worker increases and, accordingly, the farmer is paid more. The spiral of increases in farm income and in nonfarm income results in more fertilizer and other technologies being applied to farm production. In this manner the economic development of a large area, initially poorly endowed with natural resources, can become stimulated and encouraged.[6]

THE RURAL LOW INCOME PROBLEM

The low income farm situation in the United States described by the 1950 Census of Agriculture was this: In 1950 1.5 million or 28 percent of farm operator families had net cash incomes under $1,000. Over half had net cash family incomes under $2,000. These low income farm families lived for the most part on small farms which were located in areas bypassed by current technologies and by the rapid urban-industrial development which characterizes most of the nation. With respect to agriculture, an important goal of Congress has been to provide better income opportunities for farm people on the farm and off the farm. The continuing problem facing Congress is, "What ought to be done about the low income farm families?" One solution was to establish legislation called the Rural Development Program (RDP). This program was to be administered by the Department of Agriculture through the Extension Service, but was also to rely heavily on local leadership.

[6] Publications explaining the progress of TVA can be received by writing the Division of Public Relations, TVA, Knoxville, Tennessee.

The Rural Development Program (RDP)

When President Eisenhower submitted his recommendation to Congress in January, 1954 he suggested that the Secretary of Agriculture should give special attention to the low income problems of small farmers. As a result of this directive the Secretary, in cooperation with other agencies and departments, prepared a report which outlined the extent of the low income problem in agriculture and made suggestions and recommendations to solve or alleviate these problems.[7]

This report was unique in several respects. First, it recognized that the solution to low income problems in farming needed to be a long-range program and could not be quickly implemented. Second, it separated the farm price and income policy problems (discussed in Chapter 22) from the low income problems in farming. And third, it recognized that to accomplish the desired goals of increased income for farm people the approach taken must be comprehensive and involve the total community and all of its resources.

The objectives of RDP were to increase employment opportunities off the farm as well as to show improvement in the kind of jobs available within farming, to raise the income level of workers on farms and off farms in areas of severe underemployment, and to involve local people at all stages in drawing up their own development plans and putting them into action. Because there were many elderly people in farming who were incapacitated for one reason or another, a further objective was to extend meaningful social security coverage to this group.

Approaches to attain these objectives included efforts to increase the productivity of those able to remain in farming, to improve the prospects for part-time farming and full-time nonfarm jobs, to increase the number of opportunities for training of all kinds, and to strengthen health programs and health facilities. The decentralization of industry and the widesperad distribution of defense contracts to some of these low income areas was also advocated.

The RDP program was formally initiated in 1956, with less than 25 rural counties involved. By June, 1960 there were 210 counties involved in 30 states and in Puerto Rico.[8] National meetings and regional conferences and workshops were held on an annual basis from the beginning of the program.

The structure through which this program was set into motion was

[7] "Development of Agriculture's Human Resources: A Report on Problems of Low-Income Farmers," Prepared for the Secretary of Agriculture, U.S.D.A., Washington, D.C., April 1955.
[8] 5th Annual Report of the Secretary of Agriculture on the Rural Development Program, Washington, D.C., September 1960.

based on "grass roots" interest and participation. Without local effort little could be done to bring about any effective long lasting change or improvement in the low income areas. Pilot counties were set up in several states. These counties were organized to experiment with different forms of community organization and different ways of servicing these groups. It was generally intended that as the pilot counties improved themselves other counties would learn from them and initiate their own programs of local development.

Most of the states involved in RDP formed state committees of various kinds. These organizations kept the local committees supplied with technical information and acted as a coordinating agency in many other respects. Membership on the state committees drew from public agencies of all kinds, private industry, commercial businesses, and individuals from all walks of life who had shown an interest and an analytical ability in the problems at hand.

The membership of local community development committees, or RDP Committees as some county groups called themselves, generally represented the county on four criteria: geographically, with all townships represented, occupationally, so that a broad cross section of business and job interest was represented, age-wise so that young and old people were placed on the committee, and by sex—both men and women were also members. Group size usually ranged from about 20 to 50 people. Some county groups had over 100 people involved. The number of people who participated in the program depended upon the judgment of the County Extension Agents who had been given the responsibility for organizing the committees and prompting interest in the country's problems. In some instances, the county RDP committee was both an analytical-educational group and an action-oriented group. In other cases, the committee analyzed the situation based on data gathered by consultants and resource people from the universities and other institutions willing to help, and turned their findings over to legally authorized county and state groups to put them into action if they saw fit.

All of the agencies in the U.S. Department of Agriculture contributed much time and effort through their field staffs. State and federal agency personnel also attended meetings whenever they were asked to contribute technical assistance or information. Technical assistance already provided to farms by the Federal Extension Service was stepped up, and special efforts were made to direct it more toward helping the low income farmers in areas in which they were concentrated. Some funds were also allocated through universities for research projects which explored the adjustments necessary for farm families if they stayed in farming under more intensive management, or if they moved from farming to some nonfarm occupation.

Appropriations for RDP were quite small compared to the price support and other government sponsored nationwide programs. Most of these funds were directed through existing agencies, and some were allocated to add personnel to handle RDP work either in the field or at the universities. Primarily, the monies appropriated by Congress were allocated for FHA farm operating loans for low income farmers. In general, these loans did not make significant contributions to farm income in low income areas because the size of enterprise they would permit was small and the management on these farms was often quite limited.

Low income farm areas are found scattered all over the country. However, at the time RDP started the majority of the areas were located in the southeast (north from the Gulf through the Mississippi Delta area into Arkansas and central Missouri, then east covering nearly all the area south of the Ohio River). Other areas include the northern parts of Minnesota, Wisconsin, and Michigan, northwestern New Mexico, and parts of the Cascade and Rocky Mountain areas in Montana, Washington, and Oregon. These areas were then characterized by rather dense rural settlements with high birth rates, few nonfarm jobs, and low levels of formal education. Topography, farmer attitudes, and credit limitations also restricted the use of modern farm machinery.

Three criteria were used through the RDP areas in the nation to denote the severity of the low income problem. These criteria were: (a) Less than $1,000 residual farm income to operator and family with level-of-living index below the regional average, and 25 percent or more of the commercial farms classified as "low production." (b) Level-of-living index in lowest fifth of the nation. (c) Fifty percent or more of the commercial farms classified as "low production." If all three of these criteria were met by an area, it was classified as a serious problem area. If two of the three criteria were met, the area was classified as having a substantial low income problem, and if one of the three criteria were met, the area was said to have a moderate low income problem. While the farms in these low income areas have many differences with regard to tenure, age of operator, and so on, they are also similar. They are all small farms with little capital investment. On the average, farm operators of the low income farms have completed only seven years of school and only one out of ten is a high school graduate. In contrast, farmers in the rest of the nation averaged 8½ years of school completed and one out of four is a high school graduate.

Credit for success of the program was often difficult to determine fully because of the large number of agencies, organizations, and individuals working in the program. Increased farm income, increases in the number of nonfarm jobs, the attraction of new industrial plants, clean-up campaigns, and "stay-in-school" promotions could quite easily be counted and assessed. But perhaps the more basic and lasting success of the program was that the local people learned to identify their own problems and to do something about them. There were subtle changes in personal attitude that would have lasting effects but could never really be identified and put in a report for congressional budget hearings. There were increases in self-respect and self-confidence that a job could be done to improve the community, and furthermore, that the job *was* well done. In retrospect, history may tell us someday that the educational, social, and psychological benefits of the RDP program were of equal or greater benefit than the immediate increases in income.

RURAL REDEVELOPMENT

The same situation that confronted the lawmakers at the time of the Rural Development Program legislation in 1956 still remained in 1961. The intensity of the problem had lessened somewhat due to the large numbers of farmers who had left farming. However, the low income areas containing many small farms with insufficient nonfarm job opportunities continued. Areas by-passed by urban industrial development still persisted. The goals of Congress were also the same, as the problem confronting Congress was much the same as it had been during the creation of RDP legislation. However, there was one major difference this time—a difference of money available for the job. The resulting law which resulted from congressional action was the creation of the Area Redevelopment Administration.

The Area Redevelopment Act (ARA) and the Rural Areas Development Program (RAD)

President Kennedy signed the Area Redevelopment Bill on May 1, 1961.[9] This new law replaced the old RDP program, and authorized $394 million in loans, grants, technical aid, and other benefits over a four-year period. A total of $100 million was specifically earmarked for low income rural areas.

The purpose of ARA was to create persistent and lasting employment in areas of unemployment and underemployment. The intent of the law was to improve income opportunities in rural and urban areas where a large number of people operate small farms or are out of work. As in the case of RDP, ARA work relied heavily on local initiative to find and develop new jobs.

In the late 1950's 22 percent or over a million farm families had money income from all sources (after farm production expenses were paid) of less than $1,000 and one third of the farm families were receiving

---

[9] Public Law 87-27, 87th Congress, S. 1, May 1, 1961.

under $1,500. In addition, over a million rural nonfarm families had incomes of $1,500 or less. In contrast, only three percent (600,000 families) of urban families were under $1,000 and only six percent under $1,500. These data indicate clearly that the poverty or low income problem in the United States is predominantly in rural arreas. Even if an allowance was made for higher living costs in the city the situation would not materially be altered.

All the counties that were under the RDP program were also eligible for ARA benefits. However, the criteria for new counties to become eligible under the law had shifted from low income criteria to specifications of unemployment. Thus, although part of the funds would go to areas counted as low income areas under the old law, the new areas would have to qualify on the basis of unemployment. Labor market areas were designated throughout the country and the Department of Labor was utilized to provide unemployment data to help determine eligibility. Newly designated areas had to have six percent or more unemployment for a specific number of months before they were considered eligible for ARA loan funds.

The $394 million authorized by Congress for ARA funds provided five broad types of assistance.[10] A $200 million loan and grant fund was established for industrial and commercial projects, including tourist facilities to be divided equally between rural and urban areas. A $100 million loan fund and $75 million in grants were set aside for the improvement of public facilities, such as water and sewage systems and power lines. Four and one-half million dollars were provided for grants in technical assistance to be obtained through federal, state, and private sources by all communities. These monies were available for surveys of resources and program planning. Ten million dollars were authorized for subsistence grants to workers out of jobs and small farmers while they were training for a different job or improving their skills. There were $4.5 million in grants allocated to finance retraining programs for persons qualified to use them. Also, there was an increased opportunity under the Federal Housing Act amendments to rehabilitate blighted industrial and commercial areas and to obtain urban planning aid in cities, small towns, and counties.

General administration of the ARA program was concentrated in a new Department of Commerce unit called the Area Redevelopment Administration. Under the law an Office of Rural Areas Development (ORAD) was set up in the Department of Agriculture to administer the Rural Areas Development part of the program (RAD). Loan funds were distributed to both urban and rural areas. This money was called 5a and

10 "Your Community and the Area Redevelopment Act," U.S. Department of Commerce, Washington 25, D.C., June 9, 1961.

5b loan money, which designated whether it was used for urban or rural purposes respectively. In general, both ARA and ORAD had to approve the projects for which 5b monies were loaned or given in rural areas. The 5a monies were allocated solely at ARA's discretion after consultation with various other agencies, such as the Small Business Administration.

The loan requirements stated that federal loans for private industrial and commercial projects were limited to 65 percent of the total cost; minimum state or local agency participation was required to be at least 10 percent of the total cost; and the minimum private participation allowed was 5 percent. The interest rate of the loan money was determined by the current cost of money to the government plus one-half percent overhead charge. The loans could extend up to 25 years. Federal loans for public facilities might cover 100 percent of the total cost, depending on state, local, and other private financing available. These loans would bear an interest rate determined by the current average rate of interest on the public debt plus one-fourth percent overhead charge. These loans were given for periods up to 40 years.

Within ORAD, as the organization worked itself from the federal to the state and local levels, several changes from RDP took place. Although the work was now carried forward under the banner of RAD, it was still essentially the same operational philosophy as RDP. However, there were three major differences between RAD and RDP. RAD had more money with which to work. Also, RAD had the added push of a legislative edict to get something done. The third change was that the Department of Agriculture had to organize ORAD so that the Federal Extension Service was no longer primarily in charge of the activity. Extension's job was to organize the state and local committees, but it was now at the same operating level as the Rural Electrification Administration (REA) which was given most of the responsibility in agriculture for industrialization, and as a Technical Panel, later changed to Technical Action Panel (TAP), which combined the resources of the Soil Conservation Service (SCS), Farm Home Administration (FHA), Rural Electrification Administration (REA), Forest Service (FS), Agricultural Stabilization and Conservation Service (ASCS), and Extension (FES). These organizations were to supply technical information to any and all public or private groups interested in the development of their local resources and areas.

In order to qualify for loans once the area or county was designated eligible under ARA criteria, the county had to compile an Overall Economic Development Plan (OEDP). "The basic elements of the OEDP include a description of the local organization that represents the area on redevelopment matters; a background picture of the area as a place in which to live and work; a summary of the factors basic to economic growth; the economic potentials in light of resources, markets, and labor skills; and a program of action for creating new employment opportunities or otherwise reducing unemployment and underemployment . . ."[11]

The ARA and RAD effort far surpassed that of RDP. By February 1, 1963 the ARA had designated 1,052 areas for redevelopment, 853 of which were rural counties.[12] These areas depended for the major part of their initiative on local leadership. In those counties which had previously been engaged in RDP work the transition was smooth and an OEDP was generally created easily from the basic analytical work that the county committees had done previously. In newer counties, where there was pressure to get an OEDP done quickly so that loans could be made, the local people often were deprived of the learning opportunity of making up their own OEDP, which requires considerable time.

Specific mention should be made of the occupational training and retraining provisions under ARA.[13] Individuals who want to qualify for training or retraining must live in designated redevelopment areas. They must also register with the nearest local office of the State employment service and must be willing to take tests or otherwise qualify to participate in a training program. The local employment office will refer individuals for training on a merit basis. If selected for training or retraining, the individual must attend classes regularly and perform to minimal standards.

Although subsistence benefits may be paid to people who are being trained, no one is permitted to accept unemployment compensation at the same time he receives subsistence payments. The aim of training programs is to develop useful skills and knowledge which people need to get jobs. This training can be of a refresher nature of supplementary training, or it may be entirely new occupational training.

Planning training programs for redevelopment areas requires careful consideration of the work experience, aptitudes, and other qualifications of the people who want training. The number of jobs available to the men and women after training must also be considered. The amounts and kinds of training needed and proved to be feasible, and the training facilities themselves, should also be noted and integrated into the overall planning and development process.[14]

During the 1960's, RAD efforts were expanded to many rural com-

11 "The Overall Economic Development Program," U.S. Department of Commerce, ARA, August, 1961, p. 1.
12 "Rural Areas Development Handbook," Agriculture Handbook No. 245, U.S.D.A., O.R.A.D., June, 1963, p. 9.
13 "Occupational Training and Retraining under the Area Redevelopment Act," U.S. Department of Labor, Preliminary, August, 1961.
14 The Manpower Development and Training Act of 1962 is supplementary to the occupational training provisions of ARA. The two pieces of legislation taken together present a broad attack on the problems of lack of training and education in our present labor force. See "An Explanation of the Manpower Development and Training Act," U.S. Department of Labor, Washington. Revised 1962.

munities. More loan funds and grants were authorized for increased development efforts in areas identified as not sharing equally in the nation's growing wealth and income opportunities. TAP (Technical Action Panels) committees have been set up in most of the country's counties. The purpose of TAP groups is to coordinate and stimulate growth by offering a "package" of resource personnel and talent from which local development committees and organizations can draw help.

The outlook for continued rural development efforts is good. The country is increasingly interested in rural areas, and how such places can be made more relevant to urban and suburban centers. The rural-urban fringe has brought about problems which call for large resource adjustments—new answers to old problems.

A CASE STUDY OF COUNTY RESOURCE DEVELOPMENT: CRAWFORD COUNTY, INDIANA

1958-1963

In order to provide a better understanding of resource development, Crawford County in Indiana is used as a case study. Crawford County rests on the bottom of Indiana's 92 counties when ranked by almost any economic criteria. However, the county contains some of the most determined, energetic, and hard-working people in the state. These people were responsible for the remarkable success story initiated by the Crawford County Economic Development Committee.

This Committee was formed in the early summer of 1958. Much previous work had been done by extension specialists in community development with the County Extension Agent who had to learn the problem-solving approach and apply it to his county's problems and resources. The overall County Extension Committee gave its approval for work in this area and thus legitimized the agent's work, which might have been considered out of bounds by the county's farmers. Coincident with training the Extension Agent, the Work Unit Conservationist of the Soil Conservation Service in the county was also briefed and was a tremendous help in getting the program on its feet. A list of people who might be placed on a development committee was drawn up with the help of the agent, the SCS man, a local farmer, and a local businessman. People from this list were invited to attend a meeting at which data were presented concerning population movements in the county, employment opportunities locally, and comparative incomes in farming and off-farm jobs both locally and in other areas of the state. The people decided that there were some problems evident from the data and voted to go ahead with another meeting to investigate the situation further. After the next meeting they voted to engage in county developmental work on a long-run basis and forced themselves to do some significant analysis.

The size of the group at this time was approximately forty. Membership included men and women, people who worked in town and on farms, people who commuted to work outside the county, and people who had never been far away from their home county. These people had been handpicked because they were the leaders and the policymakers of Crawford County. They represented the catalyst in the county, and if any development program was to get started these people would start it.

The group met regularly once a month. A chairman, vice-chairman, and secretary were elected. No treasurer was needed because at the beginning there were no funds to handle. This group of officers decided on an agenda for each meeting with the help of the entire group. Outside people were asked in if they had anything to contribute to the subject currently being discussed by the committee.

Extension specialists from Purdue University were used. However, their role was primarily one of group maintenance and stimulation. They made no decisions for the group. The group acted independently of any university, state, or federal agency or program. Their decisions were entirely of their own making and the priority of problems they discussed were entirely of their own choosing. The role this development committee played in the county was one of objective, impartial fact-finding and analysis. No other group in the history of the county had ever done this type of thing before, and as a result this group achieved a great respect and performed a service to the people in the county that no organization had offered. The people on the committee were there willingly because they were interested and had a stake in the future of the county, and any problems they considered important were taken up. There were no "right" or "wrong" things to be done, nor was there any particular value structure giving rise to any priority of problems other than that of the local committee.

The situation in Crawford County, Indiana was typical of other counties in Southern Indiana. They had a population of about 8,400 in 1959 and had undergone continued outmigration of population for almost 50 years previously. The main source of employment and income came from farming and there were approximately only 250 jobs in manufacturing in the entire county. Incomes from nonfarm employment were the lowest in the state at the time, while income per farm was also low.

When faced with this situation, one of the first things the people wanted to do was attract new industry. This would help employment, increase incomes, allow people to move off the farm to higher paying jobs, and improve the tax base to provide better public facilities of all kinds. Someone on the committee had read a recent article which stated that new industry needs to know the number, age, skill level, and health of its expected employees before it would seriously consider moving into an area. With these conditions in mind, the people decided that they wanted to survey the county population. With the help of specialists from the Indiana State Board of Health and from Purdue University, a questionnaire was devised that could fit individual and family information on 26 subjects all on one piece of paper. More than 300 persons carried this questionnaire throughout the county and obtained detailed information on 94 percent of the people living in Crawford County. This was done without charge to the local people involved and took only three weeks time. The State Board of Health said it established a national record for a volunteer organization in terms of population coverage, depth of questioning, and survey time elapsed. This effort is indicative of the interest and effort put out by the local people—a national record established by people who were materially from the poorest county in the state!

The information they obtained from the survey was analyzed, written up, and then printed by a local printer in the county, a woman intensely interested in getting factual information out to her readers. The uses to which this newly acquired information was put were many. First of all, it outlined the health picture of the county's inhabitants. Because there was no full-time doctor in the county this information was used to try to attract one. Special effort was made to begin a class for exceptional children in the county and for those who suffered from defective speech, hearing, or eyesight, epilepsy, or rheumatic fever. The State Department of Public Instruction was helpful in this endeavor.

The information was also used to establish labor force statistics compiled into a brochure for industrial promotion. A new school was being considered in one township because many of the people had heard about the population explosion and they thought they would need new facilities. When the survey showed that almost half the population was 65 years or older in that township, plans for the new school died a natural death. The survey also provided information useful in tax calculations because of certain county and state deductions made for age and health considerations.

Another project that the county group helped with was procuring an area forester for their county and two adjacent counties. He was needed to help do a better job of marketing the timber and to help with tree cultivation and woodlot management.

Working with the concept of an area approach, the group soon realized that there were some things that were better handled by cooperative action from several counties. Accordingly, they were instrumental in forming first a three-county group and later a four-county group. This area group met to discuss common problems of road building and maintenance, education, recreation, industrialization, and health. From this group of four counties sprang an action group called the Lincoln Hills.

This organization was dedicated to the promotion of the recreation industry in the area.

Southern Indiana has much scenery that has not been fully exploited. The Lincoln Hills group formed a Riverboat Festival and staged square dances and barbecues. The main objective of this area group was to attract tourists into the area. Once there, each individual county was free to try to attract them to their specific tourist attractions of historic spots, scenery, caves, and rivers. The group has printed attractive brochures outlining trips that might be made through the four counties, and each county also has a map or brochure that presents more detailed excursion routes.

There are many other things, large and small, that the Crawford County committee investigated and helped to implement. The material presented is merely representative of the things that local people can do when they are provided with relevant facts for analysis and with resource personnel to help with the technical aspects of the problems.

In order to qualify for consideration of ARA loan funds, the Crawford County Committee developed one of the first OEDP's submitted from Indiana. This OEDP was compiled almost wholly from existing reports developed from analysis done previously by the committee, the resource people it had requested, and various subcommittees. The OEDP report was readily accepted by both state and federal officials connected with the ARA-RAD program. So far there has not been any specific ARA money spent in Crawford County. All efforts to date have stemmed from the local people with the help of authorized state and county agencies who entered when called upon. However, there may come a time when the size of the project requires federal help. At that time Crawford County will be ready to use the monies effectively.

Other counties have utilized ARA funds. Below are a series of projects which have had federal assistance of some kind.[15] There are approximately 20 rural communities working on water systems that will service about 4,000 rural farm and nonfarm families in southern Indiana alone. Most of these plans call for ARA funds to cover at least a portion of the costs. One town in southern Indiana received a grant of $80,148 from Health, Education and Welfare (HEW) to help on a $449,000 sewer expansion and modernization program. Several industries have been helped. In some cases new plant locations and building facilities have been constructed. In other cases facilities have been replaced. In one instance a furniture plant burned to the ground. Over 150 jobs were lost in the community. Prompt action by the county RAD committee, helped by ARA funds, rebuilt the factory and there are now more people employed in the plant than before it burned. Recreation projects for fishing lakes and

15 ARA-RAD projects are scattered in almost every state. However, the authors draw upon their personal experience in Indiana to illustrate the program.

camping facilities have been approved and work has begun in an attempt to capture the tourist's dollar.

The development potential in southern Indiana is being realized for several reasons. The biggest reason is that the local people in the area recognized the economic and social facts of their current situation. They realized that if something were going to be done it was going to have to be initiated and kept going by them. In some cases local leadership and initiative was enough to get the job done. In other cases additional technical assistance or monies had to be called forth from state or federal sources. In all cases the enabling legislation of RDP and ARA-RAD was considered simply a means to achieve the ends of economic development. If the job needed help the tools were at hand for a community to use.

24

World trade of
agricultural products

WHY NATIONS TRADE

In the earlier chapters on the development of economic life, the importance of specialization of production and trade were emphasized as the basic contributors to the economic well being of a country. In the chapter on production principles the law of comparative advantage was formally stated and an example illustrated how two countries with differing physical efficiencies of production could benefit from trade. The fundamental reason, then, for maintaining and expanding foreign trade is to increase the economic strength and welfare of farmers and other citizens. In addition, foreign trade provides jobs in export industries and these workers purchase goods and services which in turn provide jobs for others. Through trade, a nation obtains the goods it imports with less effort and in greater volume by producing and exchanging export goods rather than by attempting to produce all the goods it needs by itself.

AGRICULTURAL TRADE AND ECONOMIC DEVELOPMENT

Size of agricultural exports relative to total exports

Ratios of trade to national income are strikingly similar for both developing and developed economies. However, agricultural exports constitute a larger part of total export earnings in the developing countries. For example, data developed by Tolley and Gwyer indicated that only 7 out of 23 developed countries derive more than 10 percent of national income from agricultural exports. In contrast, 16 out of 24 developing countries derived over 10 percent of national income from agricultural exports, which in most cases was over 80 percent of total exports.[1] In addition, most developing economies relied on but one or two products for most of their export earnings. For example, 85 percent of Ghana's total exports was cacao.

There are many and diverse views on the relation of trade to long-term economic development. If the law of comparative advantage is thought to be at the core, a national policy of specializing in agriculture would seem to benefit both trade and development if there is a comparative advantage in agricultural commodities. Clearly, Ghana has such a comparative advantage in cacao. Some view economic development as a process of diversification around some staple export base—for many countries, an agriculturally produced commodity. The proponents state that with the expansion of the export industry, increases in a domestic production of inputs used by that industry, processing of the export commodity and subsequent production of consumer goods for the people employed in the export industry will "kick off" a satisfactory growth rate for the economy. But the difficulty of this idea seems limited in looking at the developing economies of today. Again, Ghana has been exporting cacao for a long time and the alleged expansionary effects have not taken hold. Why?

More modern proponents of comparative advantage point to indirect gains from trade. Haberler puts forward the idea that trade may transmit experience and ideas, change attitudes, encourage competition, and open up channels for capital inflows, as well as provide the means to import capital goods for development.[2] For example, in the 1960's Thailand discovered a comparative advantage in producing corn for the Japanese market. In exchange, Thailand imported considerable capital equipment in the form of power machinery and transportation vehicles.

There are also diverse views on whether governments should try to achieve balanced growth between the agricultural sector and the industrial sector and within sectors, or whether unbalanced growth will actually spur a faster development rate. Hirschman stresses extreme concentration of investment in particular industries with deliberate neglect of

[1] G. S. Tolley and C. D. Gwyer, "International Trade in Agricultural Products in Relation to Economic Development," *Agricultural Development and Economic Growth,* edited by H. F. Southworth and B. F. Johnson, Ithaca, N.Y.: Cornell University Press, 1967, pp. 404-406.

[2] G. Haberler, "An Assessment of the Current Relevance of the Theory of Comparative Advantage to Agricultural Production and Trade," *International Journal of Agrarian Affairs,* 4:130-49, May 1964.

others.[3] The argument goes that leading sectors (those where investment is concentrated) will provide the impetus to growth through forward and backward linkages; i.e., by inducing attempts to supply the inputs for those sectors through domestic production and to utilize the outputs of the sectors in new activities. In this regard the agricultural export industry can be a leading sector inducing investment in agricultural processing industries (forward linkage) and investment in fertilizer, seed, pesticide, and agricultural machinery industries (backward linkage). Writers on balanced growth implicitly reject a role for the agricultural export industry by prescribing public planning for investment among industries in accordance with income elasticities of demand. Thus there is not unanimity of opinion as to the nature and importance of the role played by trade of food commodities in agricultural and overall economic development but clearly agricultural commodity exports are vital to some of the world's economies like New Zealand and Denmark. The rest of the chapter will focus on agricultural trade of the United States.

IMPORTANCE OF EXPORTS TO U.S. FARMERS [4]

Selling farm products in the world markets is a highly competitive and big business. World agricultural trade volume advanced to record highs in the 1960's with the United States contributing about 20 percent of the total. Although agriculture depends more on exports than does the rest of the United States economy, the share of total exports from the United States accouned for by agricultural products has fallen considerably from 80 percent during 1865-80. The share declined to a low of 9 percent between 1940 and 1941 but rose again to 25 percent by 1960. Since 1960 it has been relatively stable. In value terms, agricultural exports averaged below one billion dollars in the 1930's, but climbed to a record high of $6.8 billion in 1966 (Table 24-1). Much of the rise since World War II can be attributed to lend-lease and foreign aid programs.

In the period 1934-38, cotton and tobacco comprised 60 percent of all agricultural exports but in 1967 they made up only 16 percent. Tobacco was the principal export crop of Colonial agriculture but fell below cotton in relative importance after the Civil War. The three groups of wheat and flour, feed grains, and oilseeds including products each contributed about 20 percent of the total in 1966 and 1967 (Table 24-2). Soybean exports have expanded five times since 1950. Wheat and flour have held at a rather stable percentage (variation of only 18 to 26 per-

---

[3] A. O. Hirschman, *The Strategy of Economic Development*, New Haven: Yale University Press, 1958.
[4] Data from *Foreign Agricultural Trade*, U.S.D.A., E.R.S. (Monthly).

TABLE 24-1: Value of Agricultural and Total Foreign Trade, Selected Years, 1929-1967

	Domestic Exports		Imports	
Year [a]	Agricultural (Million $)	Agricultural as % of total	Agricultural (Million $)	Agricultural as % of total
1929–30	1496	32	1900	49
1932–33	590	42	614	53
1935–36	766	32	1141	52
1938–39	683	24	999	48
1941–42	1032	16	1503	49
1944–45	2191	17	1729	44
1947–48	3503	25	2826	45
1950–51	3411	27	5147	48
1952–54	2936	19	4176	40
1956–57	4728	23	3800	30
1960	4835	25	3894	26
1961	5023	25	3756	26
1962	5037	24	3898	24
1963	5584	25	4044	24
1964	6350	25	4090	22
1965	6229	24	4087	19
1966	6869	24	4491	18
1967	6388	21	4455	17

[a] Fiscal years beginning July 1 through 1956-57; calendar years 1960-67.

SOURCE: *Foreign Agricultural Trade,* U.S.D.A., E.R.S., January 1963 and "U.S. Agriculture and the Balance of Payments, 1960-67" E.R.S.-Foreign 224, E.R.S., April 1968, Table 1, p. 5.

TABLE 24-2: U.S. Exports: Percentage of Contribution to Total Agricultural Exports by Commodity Groups, Fiscal Year Averages 1955-59, and 1960-64; Annual 1965-1967.

	1955–59	1960–64	1965	1966	1967
	(percent of total agricultural exports)				
Animals and products	16.0	12.7	13.4	11.7	10.8
Cotton, excl. linters	17.9	13.9	9.6	5.8	8.0
Wheat and flour	18.6	23.2	20.3	21.0	19.4
Feed grains [1]	9.8	12.9	15.4	20.2	17.0
Milled rice	2.8	3.0	3.3	3.3	4.6
Oilseeds [2]	11.4	13.7	18.5	18.3	18.5
Fruits and vegetables	9.0	8.1	7.3	7.4	7.3
Tobacco [3]	9.0	7.5	6.5	5.9	8.1
Other	5.5	5.0	5.7	6.4	6.3
Total	100.0	100.0	100.0	100.0	100.0

[1] Excluding products.
[2] Including products.
[3] Unmanufactured.

SOURCE: Foreign Agricultural Trade, U.S.D.A., E.R.S., May 1968.

cent) since 1950. The value of agricultural products exported in 1966-67, Japan took about 15 percent of the total followed by India, Netherlands, West Germany, and United Kingdom (about 7 percent each).

Agricultural exports exceeded the value of agricultural imports in the periods 1914-23, 1942-49, and since 1956. Complementary product imports such as coffee, crude rubber, cocoa beans, bananas, carpet wool, tea, and spice make up 40-45 percent of total agricultural imports on a value basis. Coffee alone accounts for over half the complementary products import value. Imports from Latin American countries account for 40-45 percent of the total; Asia about 20, Europe about 15, and Africa 10.

IS FOREIGN TRADE POLICY A PROBLEM?

Commercial farmers have almost always operated in a situation where they enjoyed a liberal amount of export market sales. While the United States was a debtor nation up to World War I, farm exports played an important role in helping to pay our debts. During the 1920's however, the shift of the United States from a debtor to a creditor nation was not reflected in our trade policies. At the same time that the decline in foreign demand for food received the blame for depressed farm prices following World War I, tariffs were continually increased. This action to restrict imports in the face of a continued need for exports of agricultural surpluses was a self-defeating trade policy. Foreign trade was hampered further during the depression years of the 1930's when a wave of economic nationalism spurred efforts in many countries to increase self-sufficiency.

The scene shifted abruptly in the 1940's when World War II created concern about possible food scarcities to meet the war efforts. Through the lend-lease program the United States supplied friendly nations with a considerable volume of food and war materials without much concern over how payment was to be made. As a result, trade barriers lost much of their significance. Farmers responded quickly as prices increased by speeding the shift to mechanization and adapting improved technology. When European agriculture recovered after World War II, the volume of farm exports fell and the United States again found itself with surpluses of farm commodities. The Korean War interrupted this situation temporarily, but by 1952 stockpiles were again accumulating under the price-support program incentives.

Exports are not automatic

The initial reaction of many people to the surplus farm production problem is similar to that of the general opinion in the United States at the end of World War I: expand the demand for exports of food products in order to get out of the dilemma. This reaction is further strengthened by several misconceptions about foreign trade. One is that the foreign market is a bottomless pit ready to gobble up anything and everything that we may want to throw into it. Much of this illusion was built up during the two world wars when we exported considerable quantities of food to friendly allies. But these were artificial demands for food from the United States in that they represented physiological needs rather than economic demand. They did not represent true purchasing power on the part of the importing countries, and so these foreign outlets evaporated quickly at the end of both wars.

A second misconception is that millions of people are starving in the world. Although it is true that some two thirds of the world's people have less than adequate nutrition, most are not starving. A third misconception is that if we cannot sell our food surpluses we can give them away. Paradoxically, in some underdeveloped areas selling food is actually easier and cheaper than giving it away. While each country has some sort of distributive or marketing machinery through which food can flow, many of them lack distributive facilities and organizations through which donated food can be channeled to the needy. Food donations also have to be supervised carefully or other problems can arise. For example, it is often difficult to keep the food out of the black markets that exist in nearly all the countries of the world. When removed, food donations on a short-term basis can cause serious problems if the people receiving the food have geared their economic, social, and political decisions to be dependent on the donations. Feeding refugees may cause problems if, as a result, their diets are raised above those in the host country. These are just a few of the considerations which must be recognized. The problem of exporting food for commercial sale or of giving it away is more complex than meets the eye. Because the food needs are great in the world the doors of export are not automatically swung wide open.

What about imports?

Now let us turn to the other side of the trade coin and talk about imports. Trade is basically an exchange of goods and services. There is no international money as such and if the United States is to export and get paid, payment ultimately must be in the form of imports of goods and services. The fact that trade is really an exchange of goods and services shows that a trade policy that holds a tight rein on imports by means of tariffs and other barriers also limits the ability of other countries to buy from us, and thus limits the amount of goods we can export. This is the inconsistency that was noted particularly in the foreign trade policy of the United States during the 1920's. But what are these problems that imports bring to us?

Fear is an important obstacle to imports. Some countries look to the productivity of the American industrial giant and fear that they cannot compete successfully in our markets. And so they do not try. Americans also fear that bringing larger volumes of goods into this country at prices competitive with American goods will be harmful, and those who produce similar commodities here are vociferous about foreign competition. Cheaper labor abroad is often cited as the major factor which puts American producers at a competitive disadvantage. These charges are true to a certain extent. The law of comparative advantage does not dictate precise geographic areas where the most efficient production can take place. It also takes time for various regions to discover the items for which they have a clear comparative advantage in production.

But for the majority of products the fear of low wage competition is not well grounded. Look within the United States itself. Wage rates have consistently been much higher in the industrial areas of the Northeast than in the South. Yet the people in the North did not find that their incomes were lowered by trading with the South. The evidence actually indicates that trade was mutually beneficial. Those in the low income areas have been able to upgrade their incomes and become better customers. In addition, there is evidence that the highest wages are paid not by protected industries, but by the efficient industry operating free from trade barriers. Labor at a dollar a day may not be cheap labor. The real basis for comparison of labor costs should be the wage cost per unit of output, not wage rate per day or hour. However, if another country subsidizes exports in order to obtain dollars, this situation does present unfair competition for American producers. Countries discovering the products in which they have a comparative advantage will not need to resort to these tactics, which also tend to hurt international relations. We shall discover later that the United States has used this tactic.

Another argument for import restrictions is to protect infant industries. Protecting a new industry from foreign competition until it becomes strong will enable it to become stronger faster, and this is desirable for the industry concerned. Often, however, protection is continued because the industry lobbyists maintain that vested interests will be severely harmed if the trade tariff is removed.

Many people argue that the United States should be self-sufficient in order to lessen the intensity of problems in times of war or other national emergencies. These people feel that import restrictions would encourage diversification of enterprises and thus contribute to becoming self-sufficient. This is a valid contention, especially with regard to certain strategic materials. But the long-run result of this action could be a more inefficient use of our resources leading to a lower standard of living for us and for the countries with which we might trade. In addition, as the chapter on natural resources pointed out, the United States is virtually wholly dependent on other countries for such raw materials as tin. Although economic policy might tell us that free trade is good for us, domestic political considerations and international relations between non-Communist and certain Communist countries may well tell us not to trade.

In order to assure any success from farm price-support programs, it is necessary to put import restrictions on the commodities under the program. If this were not done the commodity would flow into the United States, seeking the artificially high prices. This would further complicate the problem of surpluses. A vivid illustration was the necessity to restrict potato imports from Canada under the potato price-support program several years ago in order to protect the government and citizens from even greater losses than were incurred. These are some of the arguments favoring restrictions on the importation of goods from foreign countries.

Objectives of trade policy

The objectives of trade policy and the uses to which it may be put might be listed as follows:

1. To increase the economic strength and well-being of the American people.
2. To foster international relations that will enhance the opportunity to remain a free and independent nation.
3. To aid underprivileged people for humanitarian reasons.

WHAT ARE THE ALTERNATIVES?

Self-sufficiency

One alternative is to become completely self-sufficient and shun participation in foreign trade. This would certainly be an extreme policy and no country and very few politicians would advocate such a position. In fact, for most countries self-sufficiency is not a real alternative. Even the Iron and Bamboo Curtains permit trade penetrations. Complete self-sufficiency would eventually bring a lower standard of living for the people. In order to produce some of the products for which the country was not adapted, a high cost of production and a corresponding inefficient use of resources would be required. National resources would tend to be depleted at a faster rate and if the country was lacking strategic materials necessary to produce military goods to protect themselves, the country would be an easy target for an aggressor.

Complete free trade policy

At the other extreme, a country choosing to adopt a completely free trade policy would eliminate all import quotas, exchange controls, and tariffs. But even such countries as England and the Netherlands, which once maintained a nearly free trade policy, now impose tariffs and import controls on many products. A completely free trade policy would generate severe competition for markets if all countries adopted such a policy. And for one country to pursue such a policy while others did not would put a severe strain on certain sectors of the country's economy.

Middle-of-the-road policy

Between the two policy extremes just discussed, trade policies could emphasize various degrees of self-sufficiency or free trade. Robinson has outlined two of these intermediate policies, one which he labels "protection" and the other "modified free trade." [5]

Protection. By protection is meant a trade policy which would maintain relatively high tariffs and import controls on selected commodities competing directly with commodities produced in the home country. A lower tariff with little or no control would be imposed on items not competing with home producers. Protection measures increase the share of a nation's resources devoted to producing the protected commodity. Protection, then, is an effort to increase the output level of an industry by restricting the trading opportunities that exist by guarding against competition from more efficient producers in other countries.

Tariffs are the most common form of a trade barrier to keep goods from being imported into the country to compete with home producers. Tariffs are a form of taxes, similar in nature to a sales tax which an importer must pay in order to bring foreign produced goods into the United States. A tariff may be a fixed amount on a particular item such as 50 cents a bushel or pound. Such a tariff is often referred to as a "specific customs duty." Another kind of tariff based on a percentage of the value or price of the item is referred to as an "*ad valorem* customs duty."

An import *quota* is even more of a restrictive barrier than a tariff. Quotas limit imports to specific quantities. If the quota is zero it is in effect an embargo. It means that none of the items may be imported into this country. An embargo is sometimes used to protect against the importation of plant and animal diseases. The *import license* by a government is another device to restrict trading. This device requires an importer to acquire a license before he can bring goods into the country. Also, our federal government is prohibited by law from buying foreign materials or

[5] Kenneth L. Robinson, "Alternative Trade Policies," *Increasing Understanding of Public Problems and Policies* (Chicago: Farm Foundation, 1952), p. 36.

commodities manufactured from foreign materials, unless these materials are not available in the United States or unless the prices of corresponding domestic items are priced unreasonably—meaning considerably more expensive (perhaps 25 percent). These are all examples of means which can be used to afford a high degree of protection if these are the wishes of those making trade policy.

For the past century and particularly up to 1934, the United States followed basically a trade policy of protection. The high point in import restrictions was reached in 1930 when Congress passed the Smoot-Hawley tariff bill calling for very high tariffs on many products. Following World War I protectionist sentiment was particularly strong in Congress and tariff increases were passed in 1922 and again in 1930.

Since 1934 our high tariff policy has been essentially reversed, but other kinds of barriers have been introduced. Quantitative restrictions and licensing requirements have been imposed on a number of agricultural commodities in recent years. Tariff quotas have been applied to such products as cattle, butter, potatoes, sugar, and wheat. Import licensing provisions have been used to restrict imports of fats and oils, rice, and peanuts. And with the passage of farm price-support legislation in the 1930's and 1940's, the federal government is authorized to impose restrictions on the entry of practically any product whenever import quantities tend to interfere with farm price-support operations.

What are the consequences of a protectionist trade policy? An almost immediate result of a high tariff wall is retaliation by other countries who move to restrict United States' exports to their counries. Following the Smoot-Hawley Tariff Act in 1930 some 25 countries retaliated within less than two years. This makes it difficult for the United States to sell its typewriters, fountain pens, electrical appliances, wheat, corn, rice, and many other products which are highly dependent on export sales. A loss of foreign demand would mean price-depressing surpluses of tobacco, wheat, and cotton and consequently an increase in the level of unemployment in the United States.

A reduction in the volume of imports would have very serious effects on the economies of countries such as Canada, England, Brazil, and Germany who need foreign trade in order to stay strong economically. Since these countries are our allies, a highly protectionist policy would tend to weaken them. This, then, might necessitate additional foreign aid from us if we felt it was desirable to keep them strong in order to repel the inroads of communism.

While an increase in tariffs would certainly benefit certain types of domestic producers—wool and sugar are two good examples—these benefits would come at the expense of consumers who would have to pay higher prices for the protected products. And we might just have to do without such products as fine woolens, china, and pottery.

A highly protectionist policy keeps the law of comparative advantage from working, and as a result countries are forced to forego the economic growth and prosperity that could otherwise be achieved by efficient use of resources in their most profitable production. This means a reduction in the amount of goods available. It also means higher prices and a lower standard of living.

Modified free trade. Modified free trade involves a policy where tariffs are low, little import licensing exists, and few if any market quotas are applied. Such a trade policy would most certainly increase the amount of foreign made goods that would come into the United States. This would tend to increase the number of dollars that foreign countries would have with which to buy American goods. With extra dollars, they would hopefully purchase more of our goods. A freer trade policy would mean that the law of comparative advantage would be able to work more effectively on an international basis, tending to make better use of the world's resources. Each country would be compelled to discover those products in which it had a comparative advantage. To the extent that a freer trade policy would increase the strength of our allies, it could reduce the burden of our foreign aid program.

Certainly free trade would make the going difficult for some American firms. Whether these firms would be forced out of business completely depends on their ability to adjust to the new situation. Shifting their production to a new line of products is one possibility. Government training and retraining programs help the workers put out of jobs by foreign competition to make an employment adjustment to other firms. In terms of the effect of a free trade policy on agriculture, Johnson concluded that it would have little or no net direct influence on the number of job opportunities in farming. It was his judgment that the job losses in sugar, wool, sheep (strongly protected products), and beef, butter, cheese, fats, and oils (mildly protected commodities), would be about offset by proportionate gains in cotton, tobacco, corn, and hogs.[6] Johnson is quick to point out, however, that the many variables in the situation make it extremely difficult to assess the impact of a freer trade policy.

A LOOK AT THE AGRICULTURAL TRADE PROGRAMS OF THE UNITED STATES

Reciprocal trade agreements

The first move to implement a freer international trade policy following the high degree of protectionism of the 1920's was the passage of the Trade Agreements Act of 1934. By this act the United States pledged its

[6] D. Gale Johnson, *Trade and Agriculture* (New York: John Wiley & Sons, Inc., 1950), p. 52.

efforts to work for a basic policy of freer trade between nations. The act gave the President the power to negotiate tariff reductions commodity by commodity, down to 50 percent of 1934 levels. In 1945 another 50 percent reduction was authorized for rates, effective January 1, 1945. As a result, total duties collected as a percentage of imports fell from 24.4 percent in 1934 to 12.2 percent by 1953.

A clause in the Reciprocal Trade Agreements legislation known as the "peril point concept" prevented trade commitments that would be seriously injurious to domestic industries. Under this provision the industry involved had the right to be heard by the Tariff Commission and the Commission had to turn its findings over to the President before he could act to reduce tariffs, and then not below the "peril point." In addition, the "most favored nation" principle was embodied. This means that a tariff reduction in a trade agreement with one country will be extended to all other friendly countries.

Prior to World War II all trade agreements were primarily between two countries or were bilateral in nature. Bilateral means one country negotiating with one other country as contrasted to multilateral, meaning negotiation among several countries. After extensive negotiations in 1947, 21 major trading countries provisionally adopted a General Agreement on Tariffs and Trade (GATT). By 1962 39 countries were participating in GATT. These countries had a combined trade account for 80 percent of the world total. All the participating countries espoused the "most favored nation" principle, and tariff schedules on some 60,000 items had been negotiated. In effect, agreements made by GATT are multilateral in nature—a less time-consuming and more efficient way to negotiate trade agreements than by bilateral means. GATT now serves as the mechanism by which the United States implements the majority of its trade policies regarding the level of tariffs.

To illustrate how GATT operates, the United States received trade concessions affecting imported agricultural commodities valued at $860 million (c.i.f.) during the Kennedy Round to be phased over a 4-year period. A few specific examples are: Japan agreed to reduce its duty on soybeans from 13 percent to about 6 percent (ad valorem equivalent). Soybean exports from the United States to Japan were valued at over $150 million in 1964. The United Kingdom agreed to eliminate its 5 percent duty on soybean imports placing United States soybeans on an equal competitive footing with oilseeds from Commonwealth suppliers. On the other hand, the United States granted concessions on oilseeds and related products (castor oil, cocoa butter, and sesame seed) affecting about $25 million worth of products. Brazil and Nicaragua will be the principal beneficiaries of these duty reductions.

Principal reductions in the livestock product sector as another example involved concessions by the United States on canned pork (about

$105 million), mostly hams from Denmark, Poland, and EEC countries and a 50 percent reduction of canned beef duties mainly from Argentina, Paraguay, and Uruguay. Concessions given to the United States included the EEC eliminating its 2 percent duty on inedible tallow and reducing the tariff on variety meats from 20 to 13 percent. Canada also reduced its duty on inedible tallow from 4 to 2.5 percent. There are many other examples and GATT negotiations will continue from year to year.

Trade Expansion Act of 1962

The Trade Expansion Act of 1962 espouses a liberal trade policy similar to the Reciprocal Trade Agreements Act of 1934. It provides general authority to reduce existing tariffs by 50 percent and to negotiate with the Common Market to reduce still further or to eliminate tariffs on those categories of products for which the United States and the Common Market together account for 80 percent of world trade. (The Common Market is known as the European Economic Community and includes Germany, France, Italy, the Netherlands, Belgium, and Luxembourg.) It provides for tariff reductions by categories rather than the item-by-item approach which was mandatory under former legislation. Where existing rates are five percent or less the new act would permit those products to move to the free list (zero tariffs). Provided the Common Market would take similar action, the Act also permits the elimination of duties on tropical products not produced in significant quantities in the United States. This would tend to help countries in Latin America, Africa, and Asia.

The "peril point concept" has been replaced with a "trade adjustment assistance program" aimed at assisting firms and workers in firms which find it difficult to adjust production in the face of import competition. A firm would be eligible for assistance if, as a result of a trade agreement on an article similar to, or directly competitive with, an article produced by the firm, the increase in import quantities would cause or immediately threaten to cause (a) significant idling of the productive facilities of the firm, (b) prolonged and persistent inability of the firm to operate at a profit, or (c) unemployment or underemployment of a significant number of workers of the firm to result. Firm assistance would take three forms: (a) Technical assistance to aid the firm in preparing a sound adjustment program in the form of information, managerial advice and counseling, training, research and development, market research, etc. (b) Financial assistance in the form of loans or guarantees of loans for construction, installation, modernization, development, conversion, or expansion of land, plant, buildings, equipment, facilities, or machinery. (c) Tax relief by allowing accelerated depreciation on capital items and/ or some other tax incentives directly related to plant modernization.

Assistance to a worker would include: (a) Readjustment payments in the form of a weekly unemployment allowance equal to 65 percent of his average weekly wage for 52 weeks or up to 78 weeks if the worker is undergoing approved training. (b) Training programs similar to those under the Area Redevelopment Act discussed in Chapter 23. (c) Relocation payments to finance expenses incurred in transporting himself and his family and their household effects to a new place of employment and, in addition, a lump sum equivalent to 2½ times the worker's average weekly manufacturing wage. Both these assistance programs for firms and workers who are hurt by the increased imports resulting from a freer trade policy are designed to lessen the economic impact on their incomes and aid the transfer of resources to other employment.

Food-for-peace programs

One of the objectives of our foreign trade policy is to safeguard and strengthen the community of trading nations in the West to provide a strong bulwark against the threat of communism. With the ability of the American farmer to produce food in amounts greater than both our domestic needs and that which can be sold in world markets, the question of using food to fight against communism in some way is logically raised. The question seems particularly appropriate in light of the fact that two-thirds of the world's people are undernourished. The motivation for helping underdeveloped countries is partly humanitarian in origin, partly to defend against communism, and partly economic. Hopefully, once the less developed nations get on their feet they will be able to purchase some of our products which will strengthen our economy. What role can food products play or what role should they play in this assistance?

The elements of economic development and the process of growth have already been discussed in detail. For example, let us take capital and see how food might serve to increase the rate of capital formation in a less developed country. To the extent that people are undernourished and not able to do physical work, food donations could increase the adequacy of their diet and enable them to have the physical strength to engage in roadbuilding and other projects. To the extent that people were undernourished and necessarily preoccupied with getting enough food to eat, food donations could relieve their worry and allow them to use their minds in formal programs of education. It is difficult to be interested in studying agriculture, history, or chemistry in school when you are hungry. To the extent that donated food would increase the health of the populace, it would again aid in increasing the returns from their work efforts. These are a few possibilities but let us not forget Malthus. In some areas of the world it appears that his theory is still correct: following an increase in the means of subsistence will be an increase in the death rate from starvation. This compels a country that starts to donate food to continue until the people have the ability to maintain themselves, which may be a long time. The logical conclusion would seem to be, however, that food can play a role in the development of human and physical capital in a less developed country and could certainly supplement other forms of technical assistance. For the relatively wealthy 20 percent of the world's people to carry a subsistence program which maintains a minimal consumption level for the other 80 percent would seem to be an impossible task. As a result, subsistence aid has been used only to supplement other developmental aid aimed at increasing a country's ability to increase its own productivity.

Public Law 480. Passed initially in 1954 as a surplus disposal program, Public Law 480 is by far the most important piece of legislation currently dealing with federal programs of food disposal. The "Food-for-Peace" program developed out of Public Law 480. Originally, it was designed to dispose of short-term food surpluses, but by 1959 it had been given a much broader framework.

The major activity falls under Title I of the Act, which permits the sale of food products for local currencies. For example, India can buy wheat and cotton and pay for them in rupees rather than in dollars. Since the rupees cannot be used in the United States, they are left in India to be used for various purposes. Some are used to pay the costs of our government expenses in that country, such as the cost of maintaining our foreign embassy. Some are loaned back to the government (India) which uses them for economic development projects. Other uses include lending the money to private U.S. firms in the recipient country to produce products for that country or to finance exhibits and trade fairs designed to promote farm products of the United States. Any money remaining merely remain in the United States' "rupee checking account" available for future claims. Thus, to a large extent sales made under Title I can be viewed largely as donations and evaluated on that basis. Of total export sales, P.L. 480 accounted for 75 percent of the total (Table 24-3).

Title II and Title III of P.L. 480 provide for donations, either direct to governments for local distribution or to voluntary agencies (church groups, CARE, or UN children's fund), for distribution to needy people in schools, orphanages, or through food packages. Title II has been used primarily to provide food to foreign countries faced with famine arising from natural disasters such as earthquakes and floods and for use in feeding school children, refugees, and other groups. This program is principally motivated by humanitarian values and is not intended to be a major contributor to the country's development. In 1967 Title II exports accounted for 1 percent of total exports and about 4 percent of the total under P.L. 480 (Table 24-3). Between 1954 and 1962 some $880 million

TABLE 24-3: Percentage of Agricultural Exports Aided by Government Programs (in percent), Years Ending June 30, 1955-67

Type of Export	1955	1956	1957	1958	1959	1960	1961	1962	1963	1964	1965	1966	1967
Public Law 480:													
Title I, sales for foreign currency	8	15	17	19	19	21	17	20	21	19	15	12	16
Title II, disaster relief	2	2	1	1	1	1	2	2	2	2	1	1	1
Title III, donations and barter	14	13	9	6	7	5	7	6	4	5	6	6	7
Title IV, long term credit sales	—	—	—	—	—	—	a	1	1	2	3	3	1
Total P.L. 480	24	30	27	26	27	27	26	29	28	27	25	22	25
Mutual security (AID), sales for foreign currency and economic aid	11	11	7	6	4	3	4	a	a	a	a	1	4
Total exports under government-financed programs	35	41	34	32	31	30	30	29	28	27	25	23	29
Total exports outside government-financed programs	65	59	66	68	69	70	70	71	72	73	75	77	71
Total exports	100	100	100	100	100	100	100	100	100	100	100	100	100

a Less than one-half percent.
SOURCE: Foreign Agricultural Trade, U.S.D.A., E.R.S., June 1968.

worth of commodities were supplied under Title II and the United States also supplied the transportation.

Under Title III donations of Commodity Credit Corporation stocks are authorized through agencies which have conducted relief programs for many years. In 1960 some 54 million persons were fed with U.S. foodstuffs donated through private voluntary agencies. The number increased by 10 million in 1961 and continuing gains are being made.

Barter exports also fall under Title III. These exports involve the exchange of surplus U.S. farm commodities for strategic or other materials needed by the U.S. government, or for materials which can be used in U.S. foreign aid programs. Wheat, cotton, and feed grains are the major commodities exported for barter. Between the fiscal years 1949 through 1961 surpluses exported under barter contracts totaled $1.4 billion in value. The value of strategic and other materials delivered to the CCC in exchange totaled $1.3 billion in the same period. Title III exports accounted for 7 percent of the total in 1967 (Table 24-3).

Title IV of P.L. 480, approved in 1959, provides for the use of surplus farm commodities in assisting economic development in friendly nations. Commodities may be delivered over periods of up to 10 years. The credit period may extend up to 20 years; principal and interest are repayable in dollars. The first three loan agreements under this title were signed in the latter part of 1961 with El Salvador, Portugal, and Venezuela. Others are in various stages of negotiation.

In summary, parts of P.L. 480 exports are little different from commercial sales where dollars are earned with which goods and services can be purchased. A large part, however, comprises donations or what amounts to the same thing. To the extent that local currencies earned under Title I sales can be used to buy goods the government needs in the recipient country, the United States is essentially getting goods and services in exchange. It is often difficult to tell whether exports are under subsistence aid or developmental aid. Much depends on how the products are used in the recipient country and on how the country in turn uses the loans which can result from Title I sales and certainly from Title IV sales.

Private trade activities

An increasing awareness of the importance of foreign markets to American agriculture has prompted private trade and agricultural groups to direct more attention and resources to maintaining and developing these markets. The interest is reflected in better regulation of export commodity quality control, salesmanship, catering to foreign market preferences, market surveys and analyses, and improved public relations with foreign trade and agricultural groups. Trade associations representing nearly every agricultural commodity have participated and their efforts have been closely coordinated with those of the federal government. For example, under international trade fair activities the Foreign Agricultural Service organizes and manages exhibits, provides space, furnishes supplies and equipment, and pays travel and administrative costs. Private industry groups participate by supplying exhibit ideas and materials and technical personnel to man exhibits and carry out other promotional activities in connection with the displays. This is just one of several programs where government and private industry work together to promote food sales abroad.

Conflict between price-income legislation and trade policy

The effect of price-support legislation is to raise domestic prices above the going world prices. Therefore, if American exporters had to buy commodities at the artificially high domestic prices they would be at a severe disadvantage in competing for sales in world markets. As a result, it has been the general policy of the United States to use export subsidies to maintain exports of agricultural products when the domestic market prices are above world prices. Export subsidies are the payments made to exporters to compensate for the difference between the two prices. While this procedure seems harmless and easy to administer, it creates several problems. For example, on a commodity like wheat, of which the United States contributes a significant amount to total world trade, the world price eventually becomes heavily dependent on the export subsidy rate. This leads Canada and other wheat exporting countries to the view that the United States policy of export subsidies makes for unfair competition, since the international market price is not the one at which the wheat producer is willing to sell. In this situation it would be possible for wheat to be sold at less than its cost of production.

Cotton is another example. To make our price-support program work and still sell cotton in international markets, export subsidies were paid on both cotton in raw form and on finished cotton goods. The result was that foreign mills could buy raw cotton, process it, and ship it back to the United States at prices well below those incurred by domestic cotton processors. In the case of cotton, not only did we experience animosity from other countries exporting raw cotton by depressing the world price, but we put our own processors at a severe disadvantage. It is clear that many complications can arise when a workable foreign trade policy is sought. The principal difficulty for the United States in recent years has been the extreme complexity in trying to move toward a freer trade policy and maintain domestic price-support programs at the same time. These two policy programs are simply of a contradictory nature.

Many countries face the same dilemma. Any government program which involves the stabilization and maintenance of domestic farm prices to aid home producers will result in a difference between domestic and world prices for the commodity involved. A major exception has been in England, where farmer income was supported by direct subsidies and domestic prices were kept at world prices. The inconsistency between agricultural price and income policy, and international policy also disrupts the economic law of comparative advantage and thus reduces the efficiency by which resources are put to use in the world.

Are international commodity agreements a possibility?

The main objective of international commodity agreements is to provide an orderly marketing method through which patterns of production and trade can best be adjusted to the requirements of world demand over time. If prices are to be stabilized, reasonable terms of trade secured and world production and consumption brought into balance, commodity agreements need to include provisions for coordination with the national policies of the countries concerned.

Since the end of World War II, international agreements have been concluded for wheat, sugar, coffee, tin, and olive oil. Most have been plagued with difficulties and only the wheat and tin agreements had operative provisions between exporting and importing nations having much impact on world trade.

Wheat. The International Wheat Agreement (IWA) of 1949 was of the *multilateral* contract agreement type. It provided for guaranteed quantities to be exchanged, a maximum price at which exporters agreed to sell a specified quantity and a maximum price which importing countries agreed to pay. For the first several years, world prices were running above the stipulated maximum of $1.80 a bushel which meant the IWA was operating entirely in the interests of importers. Upon renegotiation in 1953, the primary exporting countries were successful in bargaining for a rise in the maximum price to $2.05 a bushel; the minimum price was placed at $1.55. However, the United Kingdom withdrew (based on a correct assessment that wheat prices would fall) as did some other importers reducing the amount of world trade in wheat covered under the IWA to 25 percent; it had been 60 percent under the original agreements. By 1959 when the IWA was up for renegotiation again, the idea of guaranteed quantities was abandoned and replaced by a simple undertaking of member importing countries to purchase a minimum percentage of their commercial requirements from member exporting countries as long as prices moved within a stipulated range but without any obligation to buy guaranteed quantities at the minimum price. The exporters retained the obligation to sell a certain amount at the maximum price if called upon to do so. While this new agreement brought the bulk of world wheat trade under its wing, it was at the expense of diluting the prospects for achieving its original purpose of dampening down the sharp annual price variations in the world price of wheat. However, exporting nations have used it, to some extent, as a mechanism to fix prices and keep them from being too depressed. It was certainly not the intention of the agreement that it should be used to increase the long run average price level of wheat.

To the extent that prices negotiated under the agreement are higher than what the "true" level of a free world price would be, the agreement gives rise to problems similar to those which price-support legislation creates. In order to maintain prices above levels that would clear world markets, someone must take the job of handling surplus accumulation or supervise a production control program. The high prices tend to draw larger supplies into the world market, as would be expected. Largely by default, this responsibility fell to the United States government and the Canadian Wheat Marketing Board which accumulated surplus stocks in the late 1950's and attempted to channel them into trade as best they could. An international commodity agreement which results in maintaining an artificially high world price encourages increased output, which in the case of France contributed to its changeover from a wheat importer to a wheat exporter. Therefore, to be successful it would seem that an international agreement should be set up so that it would not allow prices to rise above the prevailing market and that some agreement be reached in allocating reasonable market shares and production rights to countries.

During the Kennedy Round of GATT negotiations, the major wheat trading members replaced the IWA with the International Grains Agreement (IGA) which included food aid provisions as well as basic price arrangements. The IGA is in effect for three years beginning July 1, 1968. A continuing major objective of IGA is to assume equitable and stable prices in international wheat trade. In an effort to improve on former IWA pricing arrangements, the IGA has established a series of minimum and maximum prices of 14 major wheats moving in world trade, based on differences in market value and quality at a common location. A Prices Review Committee has the power to adjust these prices in response to changes in competitive conditions. Minimum prices for U.S. wheat are about 20 cents higher than old IWA minimums.

The food aid provisions of the IGA commit member countries to contribute a total of 4.5 million tons of grain annually in food aid to less developed countries. These contributions may be wheat, coarse grains suitable for human consumption, or cash equivalent. (Japan retains an option to give other types of aid.) Grain purchases are to be from member countries and, in the use of monetary grants for grain purchases, priority will be given to grain produced in the less developed countries. Donor countries may select recipients and either administer their own programs or channel contributions through international organizations.

The minimum contribution of each donor country is fixed as follows (as a percent of 4.5 million tons): United States, 42; EEC countries, 23; Canada, 11; Australia, Japan, and United Kingdom, 5 each; Sweden, 1.2; Switzerland, Denmark, Argentina, Finland, and Norway, less than 1.

Other agreements. A second type of commodity agreement consists of the institution of an *international buffer stock* to stabilize price through obligations to buy whenever the world price falls below a certain minimum and to sell when the price rises above a certain maximum. This plan was attempted under the International Tin Agreement but has not been very successful. A third type of agreement is the *export restriction agreement* which provides for limitation of exports insofar as is necessary to secure some degree of price stability. Clearly, this could be successful only if nearly all of the exporting countries could be brought into the agreement. It was originally incorporated in the International Sugar Act of 1953 which was reasonably successful for three years before the Suez crisis. With further difficulties caused by the trade disruptions by the more recent United States–Cuba situation and the inability of participating governments to agree on the distribution of quotas, the agreement became inoperative in January 1962.

EFFECT OF THE EUROPEAN ECONOMIC COMMUNITY ON WORLD AGRICULTURAL TRADE

The development of the European Economic Community (EEC), most commonly referred to as the Common Market, has been described by many as one of the most significant events in the twentieth century. Because of its emerging importance and particularly because much of the exporting of food commodities from the United States goes to Common Market members, a brief discussion of it is included in this chapter on agricultural trade policy. Under the treaty of Rome, which went into effect on January 1, 1958, the six countries of West Germany, France, Italy, the Netherlands, Belgium, and Luxembourg agreed to create an economic community over a 12 to 15-year transition period. Each country committed itself to the common purposes:

1. To remove tariffs, quotas, and other barriers to trade within the Community by gradual stages;
2. To create a uniform external tariff between the Community and the rest of the world and to act as a unit in negotiating on external commercial policy with others;
3. To abolish restrictions on the movement of services, labor, capital, and business enterprises within the Community;
4. To allow colonies and associated territories of the Six (mainly in Africa) to link themselves to the Common Market, extending the

benefits of the Common Market to their exports while allowing them to maintain restraints on imports;

5. To prohibit private cartels and other restraints on trade unless they foster the improving of production or distribution or technical and economic progress;

6. To coordinate monetary and fiscal policies in order to promote balance of payments, high employment, and price stability in each member country;

7. To establish a common agricultural policy within the Community;

8. To create an Investment Bank for Europe and a Development Fund for Associated Overseas Territories to transfer capital to the less developed parts of the Community and to dependent or associated areas;

9. To equalize wages for men and women and harmonize methods of computing overtime; to undertake to improve and harmonize living and working conditions within the Community;

10. To create a Social Fund to finance retraining, resettling, or otherwise assisting workers harmed by liberalizing trade within the Common Market.[7]

More specific to agriculture, the objectives of the common agricultural policy of the EEC is to (a) increase agricultural productivity by developing technical progress and by insuring the rational development of agricultural production and the optimum utilization of the factors of production, particularly labor, (b) to insure thereby a fair standard of living for the agricultural population, particularly by the increasing of the individual earnings of persons engaged in agriculture, (c) to stabilize markets, (d) to guarantee regular supplies, and (e) to insure reasonable prices and supplies to consumers. These broad policies have been implemented by (1) control of farm products through common market authorities, (2) gradual establishment of common prices for some farm products and equalization of internal trading conditions for others during a transitional period, (3) control of imports through variable levies or fees together with stipulated minimum import prices; (4) use of funds derived from import levies and fees to finance improvements in agricultural production and marketing operations and domestic price supports, and to subsidize exports, (5) to establish common quality standards, and (6) to harmonize veterinary, plant health, and similar regulations.

Two countries, Greece and Turkey, have become associate members and 18 African countries became associated with the EEC Community in 1963 and the nineteenth, Nigeria, signed a treaty of association in 1966. A

---

[7] "The European Economic Community and the United States," Prepared by Robert R. Bowie and Theodore Geiger for the Subcommittee on Foreign Economic Policy of the Joint Economic Committee, 87th Congress, 1st Session, USGPO (Washington: 1961, p. 15).

number of other countries (mostly European) have shown an interest in joining the EEC.

Agricultural trade of the EEC members has increased substantially since inception. Total trade in agricultural products was up 46 percent over the period 1959 to 1964. In 1967, the United States exported agricultural products to the EEC with a value of $1.46 billion, 7 percent below 1966 but 27 percent higher than 1962. Thus, the EEC is the largest market for agricultural products of the United States accounting for about one-fourth of the total. Imports of food products from the EEC to the United States average about one-fifth the value of exports to the EEC from the United States.

Farming in EEC countries is generally less efficient than in the United States although relatively rapid gains are being made in yields and total output. Feed grain and wheat sales to the EEC members by the United States continued to record increases through 1966. In July 1967, the unified grain system went into effect in the EEC which permits movement of grain between the member countries without any restrictions. Such freedom of movement will encourage greater trade between the EEC countries and also encourage greater grain production. Intra-Community trade accounted for 18 percent of total feed grain imports in 1964. A strong farmer response to the anticipated price equalization would reduce the demand within the EEC group for U.S. feed grain exports. In oilseeds and cotton, the EEC is at a much greater comparative disadvantage.

Progress in carrying out the 10 objectives of the Common Market has been slowest in the area of establishing a common agricultural policy. The main problem of European farming is low income. Many people are living at low standards on inefficient small farms. The number of male workers engaged in farming in the six countries of the Common Market is about 12.5 million. These workers cultivate an area of about 70 million hectares, or about 14 acres per man.[8]

This is one-twelfth as much as each farm worker handles in the United States. Europe's principal problem, then, is one of moving large numbers of workers into secondary and tertiary employment. This migration will likely take a period of years to accomplish. While industrial jobs are being created at a rapid pace, there is no provision for migration on the scale necessary to solve the problem.

To aid the low incomes of farmers the Common Market countries all have price-support programs similar to that of the United States. Agricultural prices have been raised by restricting imports, and most of the governments participate in sales and purchases of food products to prevent wild price fluctuations. There are considerable differences within the

---

[8] A hectare equals about 2.5 acres.

countries with regard to the magnitude of price help. On the average German prices, which are the highest, exceed French prices, which are the lowest, by about 20 percent. The other countries are in between. Price supports for soft wheat in 1960 in West Germany were $2.97 a bushel as compared with the French price of $2.33. By comparison, the support price was $1.78 in the United States.

Although the EEC plans to follow the same general rules of removing tariffs and quotas for agricultural products as they now do for industrial goods, other measures of protection will stay imposed. For all practical purposes this action insulates the agricultural production in the EEC from world markets. Because of the magnitude of price differences among the EEC countries, illustrated above for wheat, it will take some time before agreement can be reached on how to establish the "European price." The effect of the Community's program for agriculture on other nations, including the United States, will hinge mainly on which European prices are fixed, how they are established, and at what level. If high prices are set, imports from the rest of the world will be reduced. Farming interests in the Community can be expected to press for European prices substantially above world prices and to resist expansion in imports from the outside. To the extent that each member of the Common Market realizes that slow progress with regard to agricultural policy will impede the Community's total growth, an early agreement will be stimulated. In any case it seems clear that farming will be a highly managed industry in the EEC for some time.

It appears likely that for the next few years the effect of the Common Market will be to reduce our total agricultural exports, particularly in the case of wheat and feed grains. But over a longer period, if the free world commits itself to freer trade and maintains such a policy, the comparative efficiency on American farms should tend to maintain our export levels. The rapidity with which agricultural technology is transported and communicated, however, makes prediction of comparative advantage for any and all commodities extremely difficult.

OTHER ECONOMIC TRADE COMMUNITIES

European Free Trade Association (EFTA) [9]

In 1960 the European Free Trade Association (EFTA) was formed with the original signatories being Austria, Denmark, Norway, Portugal, Sweden, Switzerland, and the United Kingdom. Finland was added in

[9] T. A. Warden, "EFTA's Agricultural Imports 1962-66," *Foreign Agricultural Trade,* U.S.D.A., E.R.S., November 1967, pp. 24-32.

1961. These countries agreed to eliminate (in stages) tariffs and quotas on industrial products moving between members, while retaining individual restrictions on imports from outside countries. This was accomplished three years ahead of schedule at the end of 1966.

Agricultural imports by EFTA countries were $8.6 million in value terms in 1966—two thirds accounted for by the United Kingdom. Agricultural imports (about one-fourth of the total) rose 22 percent in the period 1962-66 but total imports were up 40 percent. The U.S. share of EFTA's agricultural imports has fluctuated from 9-12 percent, trended downward from 1962-65 but rose again in 1966. In 1966, the United States supplied a little over half of EFTA feed grain imports, one-fifth of the wheat and flour, nearly one-third of the rice and 9 percent of the oilseeds.

Latin American economic communities [10]

Exports of United States agricultural products to Latin America have been quite stable over recent years even though total U.S. agricultural exports were rising. The often used assumption that less developed countries should supply mainly raw products to world markets in exchange for manufactured products from the developed countries has generally prevailed in the Latin American case. These countries have exported large volumes of coffee, sugar, and bananas, for example, and imported such finished items as chemicals, machinery and transportation equipment.

Economic integration is a primary economic change which was occurring in Latin America in the 1960's and the major as well as most small countries are members of some economic union whether it be the Central America Common Market (CACM), Latin American Free Trade Association (LAFTA), or the Caribbean Economic Community (CARIFTA).

The five Latin American countries of Guatemala, El Salvador, Costa Rica, Nicaragua, and Honduras ratified a general treaty forming the CACM in 1961 and have been experiencing a steady growth in per capita income. Their success has been aided by a succession of good crop years and their ability to move the increased production through world trade channels. As a whole, the region receives 80 percent of its export earnings from agricultural products and has increased the value of agricultural sales 60 percent from 1960-62 to 1965. Under the Sugar Act of 1948, the countries of CACM have been receiving an increasing share of the total

[10] Data taken from Norman R. Kaclemeyn, "Impact of Central American Integration on U.S. Agricultural Exports," Foreign Agricultural Trade, U.S.D.A., E.R.S., February 1967, pp. 46-53.

basic foreign allocations by the United States increasing from less than one percent in 1959 to 4.5 percent in 1966.

The United States was still the largest supplier of agricultural products to the CACM countries in 1965 but intra-CACM import trade increased from 25 percent of the total in 1959 to 36 percent in 1965. Imports of wheat and flour comprised the major agricultural import item followed by feed grains, dairy products, vegetables and products, live animals, cereal preparations, fruits and products, animal fats and oils, vegetable oils, and rice. The U.S. share of these imports has been declining except for live animals, animal fats and oils, and rice. It is likely that third country suppliers such as the United States will have to contend with a more restrictive CACM trade policy as more common external tariffs are consummated.

25

Persisting problems in agriculture

Throughout the history of agriculture and the sector's continual adjustment to economic, social, institutional and political pressures, one can find a series of persisting questions. Certain issues keep reappearing and each new generation must find its own answers to them. It is particularly noteworthy that although these questions involve essentially the same basic issues through time, the answers offered by the policymakers at each stage may change radically. For example, answers to questions such as, "How should agriculture best be encouraged to contribute to a growing economy?" range from a policy of free prices with no production controls or price supports to a fully planned economy in which agriculture is integrated into a broad scheme of centralized social and economic planning.

Solutions to persisting questions may last for a few years or many years, depending upon the pressures to which they are subjected, including the changing values of the people involved. Some of these continuing questions are discussed below. No attempt has been made to rank these questions. Each group of analysts must establish its own priorities.

EXPANDING TECHNOLOGY AND THE FAMILY FARM

For generations the family farm has been the epitomy of individual proprietorship operating as a small business in our private enterprise economy. There is constant concern that the family farm will be gobbled up by the huge corporations prevalent in the modern day business world. We have seen that the average size of the commercial family farm is growing as the substitution of capital for labor and the adoption of new biological and managerial technologies allow one farm operator and his family to handle more and more. We have also noted that more than half the land farmed is cultivated by part owners rather than full owners. What will changing technology and capital requirements call forth in the future?

The question of how expanding technology influences the organization of the farm business has been a particularly pertinent and important one for the last 200 years. Will it eventually eliminate the family farm? Will the size of the economic unit in farm production grow indefinitely, outstripping the financial resources that most families can muster or manage? Will it mean a change in the transfer of ownership from one generation to another? Will it mean that the farm will be operated with a large percentage of hired labor and will all farm labor be unionized?

Indigenous to the socio-politic mind of the typical family farm operation of colonial times was that proprietors deserve the right to make all the decisions with regard to the procedures for operating their business enterprise, and that the individual manager and his family alone are responsible for the economic security of the entire household. In colonial times any government intervention was deemed undesirable, as it would tend to impinge on the freedom and responsibility of the family as a producing unit. Individual thrift and industry took the form of accumulating land and capital and called for extraordinary effort in many cases. To come to old age without having sufficient security was considered a reflection of a misspent life and habitual distaste for the work-imperative ethic.[1]

Expanding technology has necessitated a reshuffling and rethinking of the ethics held dear by the concept of the family farm. Even in the mid-twentieth century the farm business unit could operate economically in the majority of instances with one man and his family providing both the labor and the management. The farming industry, which is now capable of using all kinds of machines, results in recombining the managerial and labor inputs in many ways. As farm boys left the farms, became the captains of industry (McCormick's, Deerings, Armours, etc.), and helped reshape older rural value judgments, socio-politic attitudes were modified. By the mid-twentieth century, with farmers eligible under Social Security and with burdensome surpluses at hand, opinions that farming was first a way of life and second a business have been reversed in the minds of

[1] See John M. Brewster, "Technological Advance and the Future of the Family Farm," *Journal of Farm Economics* (Volume 40, December 1958, Number 5, pp. 1596-1609).

many farm operators, particularly those with college training who seek their fortune in the farming industry. The great American dream may still be underlaid with the spirit of the work-imperative ethic, but with great advances in technology the sentiment of maintaining small, inefficient farm units gives way to the institution that will perform with superior efficiency in carrying out its functions of feeding the nation. This institution may or may not continue to be the family farm. Perhaps the sacred family farm cow will die an evolutionary death. The outcome depends on the ability of the family farm as an institution to adapt and change in the face of new developments.

Will advances in technology expand the economic size of a farm unit beyond the ability of a family to supply the majority of the labor and management?

Excluding boys 10 to 16 years of age and women, the average family farm has a work force of about 1.5 man equivalents. Hence, if family farms are defined as those farms where the operator and his family provide 50 percent or more of the labor, the upper limit by definition of a family farm would be a work force of 3.0 man equivalents. Using this approach McElveen calculated that larger-than-family farms accounted for only 31 percent of the total commercial farm output in 1954 as compared with 34 percent in 1944, and for only 26 percent of land farmed in 1954 as against 30 percent in 1945.[2] On this basis it would appear that the family farm was holding its own, although the concept of the family farm in the minds of many would restrict the nonfamily labor input to 30 percent or less of the total.

A USDA–ERS study on the extent to which corporation farming has made inroads into family farming was reported in 1969. It indicated that about two-thirds of the existing corporate farms were still family operations. However, it also showed a concentration of production and resource control on corporate farms: while this group numbered only about one-half of one percent of all commercial farms it accounted for about 8-10 percent of total farm output and about 4-5 percent of the nation's land farmed.

Much of the answer to the question depends on whether future technology is labor-saving or capital-saving. To date, the majority has been labor-saving in the form of new machines and equipment. If the farmer is able to utilize seasonal labor in peak periods of need and if farm operations continue to become more routinized as they are in some kinds of production, such as eggs and broilers, the farm operator and his family

[2] Jackson V. McElveen, "Family Farms in a Changing Economy," Agricultural Information Bulletin 171, U.S.D.A. (Washington, D.C., 1957, pp. 49-50; 54-55).

will be able to handle the work load and still operate an efficient economic unit for some time. The trend for market agencies closer to the consumer, such as the processor, to deal directly with the farm producer will also aid the situation as the farmer can get more help in moving the product off his farm and the scheduling of marketing can be arranged in advance.

Will the advance in technology likely expand farm investment beyond the ability of the farm family to acquire enough capital to give them major control of the business?

While capital needs are continually increasing per farm and per farm worker, it does not necessarily mean that a farm family cannot continue to operate and control larger and larger units. In terms of the number of farms operated by full owners (owners who farm only the land they own), the percent of total farms operated was 50.5 percent in 1940, 57.1 percent in 1950, and 57.6 percent in 1964. These data offer no evidence that family farms are declining in relative importance. However, the number of part owners as a means to enlarge farm units without the capital required to own the land is increasing. In 1940 only 10 percent of the farms were owned by part owners, but by 1964 this changed to almost 25 percent. A part owner is defined as one who farms his own land and rents additional land from others. This increase came at the expense of tenant-operated farms, which decreased from 39.5 to 17 percent in the same period (see Table 9-5). Thus, renting additional land is a very real alternative for farmers who cannot afford additional purchases. Any money available may be better spent in the purchase of machinery and equipment, livestock, or other items. Brewster concludes that "both empirical and conceptual evidence supports the view that the future of the family farm is in no way threatened by the expanding size requirements of the most complete mechanization conceivable. For the highest degree of mechanization and specialization are found on the wheat farms of the Great Plains and it is well recognized that no economies of scale are achieved through expanding such farms beyond the point where a family can do most of the work. Larger-than-family farms are least frequent in types of farming such as cash grain, where operations are most mechanized, and they are most frequent in types of farming such as vegetable production, where operations are least mechanized." [3] Brewster further states, however, that "biologically determined time intervals between many livestock and poultry operations are much shorter than those between crop operations. Consequently, certain specialized livestock enterprises may be reorganized off the farm in an approximate factory pattern,

[3] John M. Brewster, *op. cit.*, p. 1606.

as in dry-lot dairies, and some cattle feeding set-ups." [4] This situation can be noted in the table egg and broiler industries. This means that family farm operations in certain kinds of agricultural production are more valuable than in others.

Is technological advance in the agribusiness sector of agriculture likely to change the marketing which would spell doom for the family farm?

Market channels are becoming shorter for food products. For several enterprises, such as broilers and eggs, there is only one stop between the farm and the retail store. The impersonal selling techniques used in the modern supermarket require that the product be uniform both with respect to physical characteristics and quality. In order to assure this uniformity retailers are putting pressure back through whatever channel agencies are involved. The processor is often the key middleman between the farmer and the retail store. To assure adequate supplies of a uniform product, contracts may be used between the retailer and the processor or the processor and the producer. Market agency contracts with farmers do nothing to destroy the family farm as long as the agency does not extend any management influence over the production.

But in those production processes where management can be split apart from the labor input, as in the case of broilers, the family farm loses its identity rather rapidly. If the feed supplier or the processor makes the management decisions the farmer becomes a hired employee doing largely routine tasks in a "factory type" operation. To the extent that integration of producing and marketing agencies yields organizational economies, the family farm will tend to be eliminated. If the farmer is in a position where he does not have to bargain away his managerial prerogatives, fear of losing the family farm is lessened. This leads us to another problem area, that of bargaining power in agriculture.

BARGAINING POWER IN AGRICULTURE

The economic issue underlying the question of bargaining power is how the total income of agriculture will be divided with respect to distributing it to the owners of the factors of production. Each individual and business firm or group of individuals or business firms are interested in increasing their share, and increasing their share of bargaining power in the market is one move toward this goal. In Chapter 16 the difficulty that an individual farm producer experiences when approaching the mar-

[4] *Ibid.*, p. 1607.

ket was noted. In most cases the individual producer has no influence on market price. As a consequence the best he can do is to stay informed so that he can be assured of getting the market price. In other words, no one can take advantage of his lack of knowledge about what the market price is.

Over the years a principal weapon of the farmer to improve his bargaining power was the cooperative, a legal business entity whereby a group of individuals could collectively pool their efforts to bargain more effectively. Purchasing cooperatives are designed to pool purchasing power so that items can be purchased at lower cost. Marketing cooperatives attempt to increase the returns to the individual members by enabling them to bargain more effectively in selling a commodity. Service cooperatives attempt to increase the individual's return by providing services which would not be available if only one party were involved. They also attempt to improve existing services. Bargaining cooperatives are designed specifically to improve the price at which a commodity can be sold to the next market agency; dairy bargaining cooperatives are a good example. Organized efforts through trade associations is another example of collective action to improve bargaining power.

Improved bargaining power may be achieved in several ways. One is to favorably influence the terms of trade in day-to-day operations. This would require that the individual or group improve their ability to operate as a buyer and/or seller in the market. The first requisite would be to stay completely informed on market conditions. Another would be that the buyer and/or seller would also be a technical specialist with regard to the commodity involved so that the correct quality of the product could be judged and proper merchandising methods could be employed. These approaches articulate most of the collective bargaining concepts developed by nonfarm labor unions and management.

The most frequently mentioned mechanism for improving bargaining power is to withhold supplies from the market. For perishable agricultural commodities this procedure is difficult both for an individual and for a group of individuals. Although limited "test" livestock withholding actions by the National Farmers Organization (NFO) in the early 1960's were unsuccessful for several reasons, the milk holding action of 1967 was more organized and effective. The milk action held large amounts of milk off the market for about two weeks during which time the production and prices of manufactured dairy products were more effected than fluid milk. Some groups, such as the cranberry and walnut growers, may simply reduce the quantity of the product put on the market and enhance the price enough so that greater total returns are realized through price increases. To do this requires the allocation of market shares among the producers of the group, which is by no means an easy task. This method is restricted to products for which the market demand price is inelastic and where production is geographically localized so that effective control can be exercised over a major portion of the crop. It may also be effective for commodities such as fluid milk, where transport over long distances is costly and the boundaries of milk markets are defined and where Federal and State Milk Marketing Orders have exerted an attitudinal and operational influence. Market orders which were discussed in Chapter 10 are partially of this nature. The difference is that market orders stipulate conditions as to how the quantity produced will move through market channels in an orderly fashion. The objective is more one of stabilizing commodity prices and resulting incomes rather than of actually restricting production so as to increase price by reducing the total quantity on the market.

Another means of obtaining more market power has been called the "expanded" view. This would include the manipulation of other variables in the market, such as product development, grades, and quality standards, market information, market area and composition, technology, and government regulations that affect the trading environment.[5] Any influence exerted on these variables would probably require group action of some kind. Expanded activity by trade associations appears to be a good possibility. The larger agribusiness firms are able to carry on their own research and development in the area of product technology.

Product differentiation is another monopoly element which affords a chance to improve bargaining power. The individual farm producer is virtually helpless in differentiating his product, except as he attempts to produce for a highly specialized quality market. Research and development programs are necessary to get new products, and while the Agricultural Experiment Stations carry on some product technology research, the majority is done by the large agribusiness firms.

There are three possible sources of gains from activities which are generally associated with bargaining efforts: (a) through greater efficiency or increased productivity in purchasing and marketing activities, (b) from an outside group, such as consumers, from other marketing agencies, or from society in general, and (c) from the opponent in the bargaining transaction.[6] Thus collective bargaining can create wealth for farmers from: (1) capturing excess profits of processing and distribution firms, (2) forcing elimination of waste in parts of the input-output marketing system, (3) contributing marketing services, and (4) extracting monopoly profits indirectly from consumers through higher retail food

[5] For more detail, see Paul L. Farris, "Building Bargaining Power," Paper presented at American Institute of Cooperation Annual Meeting, University of Nebraska, Lincoln, Nebraska, August 5, 1963.

[6] These sources were identified in a report entitled "Group Bargaining Power for Farmers," Purdue University Agricultural Extension Service, Mimeo EC-214, April, 1961.

prices or some other means. The last source certainly offers the greatest hope of monetary gains for farmers.[7]

Gains from greater efficiencies may yield a mutual benefit to both buyer and seller. Any individual or group effort to improve product quality, develop better grades and standards, facilitate more rapid movement of the product, or develop a mutually beneficial contractual agreement can result in gains to both parties. However, gains in efficiency may not necessarily spread to both buyer and seller if through market imperfections the gain can be held for some time by one party.

Gains from government may come through lobbyists who influence legislators to vote for changes that will improve the trading environment. Gains from consumers may come from effective sales promotion and advertising or from multiple pricing. Gains from these sources may also be mutually advantageous to both buyers and sellers.

To make gains directly from the agency with which an individual or group buys or sells a product requires some condition giving extraordinary market power or coercive ability. Here a real conflict of interests is involved. Such a situation might exist if, for example, the producers in a certain area were the only ones whose product exhibited a particularly desirable characteristic needed by a certain processor. By banning together the producers might be able to bargain for a higher price.

The methods employed by any group in improving their bargaining power will depend to a large extent on the market structure of the industry and the way the firms conduct themselves (previously discussed in Chapter 16). The purely competitive nature of the farming industry prohibits individual producers from exercising any market influence. There are just too many firms and no individual firm produces enough of the total market supply. In the agribusiness industries the situation is different. In attempting to build market power a group will try to reduce firm numbers. They may also try to become the price leader in the industry and differentiate their product to reduce the number of substitutes for it and also to raise barriers of entry to the industry. Market shares may be increased by nonprice competition (discussed in Chapter 16). Building market power is probably more difficult than challenging the market power of existing competitors through sales promotion, new product variations, and price competition, which may be possible through introducing new efficiencies, particularly if the industry's performance is poor.

It seems clear that bargaining will increase in the future as more prearranged marketing occurs in the form of agreements between pro-

[7] See "Collective Bargaining for Farmers," J. D. Shaffer, Increasing Understanding of Public Problems and Policies, 1968, Farm Foundation, pp. 109-121. Also, "Farm Program and Farm Bargaining," Hearings before the Committee on Agriculture and Forestry U.S. Senate, April, 1968, USGPO.

ducers and market agencies. To exercise a large degree of bargaining power will require effective control over a major portion of the supply, which is difficult for nearly all agricultural products. Gains from increased efficiencies and outside agencies, such as the government and consumers, are easier than gains from one's opponents in a transaction. Cooperatives may have a resurgence in importance since the individual member can identify his business entity and importance more than if he were just a member of a trade association or large corporation. Organizational economies stemming from integration and other contractual arrangements will change market structure and have an influence on the bargaining position of the parties involved. The issue of how to cut the income pie is one that will certainly persist for all time.

WHAT IS ENOUGH REGULATION?

The complexity of the food business is growing each day. No longer, is it simply sweat and soil which produces our food but it is pesticides, additives, antibiotics and all sorts of chemical phenomenon used to increase production, to improve and to preserve our products. The two extreme goals within which compromise is necessary are complete protection for the consumer and maximum freedom for businesses to operate. Regulation is a costly business both to administer and sometimes for producers.

Two of the regulatory agencies that are constantly under fire are the Federal Food and Drug Administration plus its various inspection divisions, and the Interstate Commerce Commission. Thousands of decisions are required each year with one party in each case often feeling that he was treated unfairly. The validity of labels and advertising, the chemicals in food additives, and administering grades and standards are just a few of the regulatory activities. The wheels of regulation often grind slowly. Mr. Prince, Chairman of Armour and Company, related several experiences in a speech before the Agribusiness Education Symposium held at Purdue University in 1962. One example will suffice: Armour and Company submitted informally to the Food and Drug Administration (FDA) an "enzyme" used in the making of cheese. After certain tests were conducted by the Wisconsin Alumni Research Foundation from 1955 to 1958, the FDA was satisfied that it was not harmful to use, but it was not until March 1962 that clearance was finally given to use the additive.[8] Does this constitute too little, about enough, or too

[8] W. W. Prince, "The Role of Agribusiness in our Food and Fiber Industry—A Ten-Year Estimate," Symposium Proceedings, National Study on Agribusiness Education (Purdue University, September, 1962).

much protection for the consumer? Talk to three different people might get three different answers.

Freight rate regulation is another difficult matter. The rates that are set can influence the location of production for commodities, the location of the processing of the product, and many other aspects pertinent to the marketing process. It is virtually impossible for regulatory agency personnel to keep up with needed changes as technology continually brings about market disequilibriums and changes in the comparative advantages in production for various areas of the nation. Therefore, what usually takes place is that the firm or industry group that feels they are being treated unfairly asks for public hearings before the regulatory commission. These hearings take time and mean considerable lags in making needed adjustments to facilitate a relatively free enterprise economy.

Another difficult area is retail food pricing and the availability of certain food items in low income or ghetto areas. Retail food stores in these areas tend to be relatively higher cost, lower profit operations than in most white collar suburbs due to such items as higher rates of pilferage, wider use of credit, and higher insurance rates. Being small stores they must often buy older merchandise than other stores, and because of their low income customers the stores often do not carry many of the higher priced or delicatessen food items. Higher costs suggest higher prices in order to maintain a set rate of profit, even if it is not very high. However, such a pricing policy means that the poor pay more for a narrower choice of food items than do the more well-to-do families. What kind of pricing policy is equitable considering the social costs involved as well as the entrepreneur's costs?

There are many other aspects and kinds of regulation. Some examples, such as market orders and production control legislation, are discussed in detail in other chapters. One thing seems certain. As production and marketing of food products become more and more complex and as the adoption of new technology continues at a rapid pace, the regulation job increases at an equal or greater rate of complexity. Depending on what position one finds himself in—consumer, businessman, or politician—there will always be instances to which one can point and no doubt have a legitimate complaint.

ARE PROPERTY TAXES ON FARM LAND TOO HIGH?

Another persisting question is that of how much the land should be taxed and how much owners or controllers of this resource should pay. Property taxes are one of the oldest kinds of taxes. The amount of land a man owned has generally been assumed to be indicative of his income and therefore his ability to pay taxes. Local governmental units have depended upon property taxes for a major share of their operating funds almost ever since the first taxes were levied. Although taxes on real property have always been of concern to those who impose them and to those who paid taxes, the recent trend in many areas for the property taxes to rise faster than incomes has intensified the public's interest. Although taxes are a fixed cost in farm production and therefore do not directly influence the most profitable level of farm output, these "fixed" costs have risen significantly, tending to reduce profits. For example, average taxes per acre of farm real estate in the United States rose from 69 cents in 1950 to $1.89 in 1967 (a 174 percent increase).[9] However, average taxes per $100 of valuation on those same lands only rose 5 percent over this period, from $1.00 to $1.05—and the 1967 average tax was 47 cents less than it was in 1932! Average per acre taxes, in 1967, ranged from a high of $5.39 in the Pacific region to a low of 57 cents in the Mountain region. New Jersey had the highest 1967 average per acre farm land tax at $15,70, while New Mexico was low at 17 cents. Taxes levied on farm real estate provided an estimated $2 billion in 1967 compared to $742 million in 1950 and $461 million in 1932. These increases put farm property taxes in the category of one of the most rapidly increasing costs of producing farm products. For these several reasons some states are considering preferential tax treatment of some kind for farm and ranch lands.

A large percentage of property taxes have traditionally gone for financing local schools. With increased population, especially in the rural nonfarm classification, the number of pupils to be educated in local schools in rural areas has risen quite sharply in recent years, even though rural farm population is declining. School consolidations, the merging of entire school districts, and rising per pupil costs have all helped raise the property tax rates.

Land falls into a special category for tax purposes, since the tax cannot be easily shifted to someone other than the owner of the property. The landowner can never escape the tax by moving his land to some other spot. For this reason, one of the most common complaints concerning land taxes is that there is not a fair tax assessment made on the land. As long as farm property taxes are low it does not much matter if the properties are assessed on an unequal basis. However, when property taxes get to be a large expense to the farm business, there is considerable concern by the individual farmer that he does not pay more than his fair share. The farmer is concerned that there be an equalization of tax assessment within his own assessing district, and he is further concerned that there is equalization between districts. For example, if the assessment is to be 30 percent of the estimated market value of the property the farmer wants all properties to be assessed at that rate; he also wants the adjoining districts

[9] "Farm Real Estate Taxes," U.S.D.A., E.R.S., RET-8, December 1968.

assessed at that rate because of possible school mergers which may join two districts.

A good tax has the following characteristics which need to be present in the property tax: (a) *Stability*—the tax should not be affected by fluctuations in the level of income, rate of assessment, or method of tax collection. (b) *Predictability*—the tax should provide revenue that can be counted upon by local officials of local government and for which a budget can be written. (c) *Adequacy*—the tax should provide funds that are adequate to finance the project for which they are raised. (d) *Balance* —the tax should be complementary to other sources of taxes. (e) *Efficiency*—the tax must be easy to administer and collect. (f) *Popularity* —in order to survive, the tax must be popular enough with the people so that it is not rejected completely.

While there will undoubtedly always be a property tax, there is increasing concern about the proportionate share of the costs of local government that farmers and other property owners are paying. While the costs of government continue to rise and while the number and quality of services offered and demanded by the public continues to grow, some thought must continue to be put forward concerning the burden that farm land should carry.

PLANNING AND ZONING

There is a natural desire to protect against the risk and uncertainty associated with a dynamic society. Change is as certain as death and taxes; however, what it will bring is uncertain. A question asked by people through the ages is how much planning there should be to provide security but not take away too much freedom. There are many types of planning to be considered: economic, social, political, and institutional.

One type of planning considers regulations concerning the use of land. In the United States most of the planning concerning land use is done in the public interest (from the viewpoint of public health, safety, convenience, and welfare), and protects individual freedom while promoting security through the "due process" clause in the state and federal constitutions. The public interest is made up of a total of many individual freedoms and interests. Limiting the freedom of one or of a few individuals often increases the freedom of many more. For example, limiting a person's freedom to drive at any speed in town increases the freedom of others to walk or drive safely. Limiting the freedom of one person to use land as he wishes may increase the freedom of others to enjoy their land. The real problem in a growing society is to gain the most freedom by limiting as few as possible.

A common objection of many farmers and people living in rural areas is that they prefer not to have planning and zoning regulations because they feel that their individual freedoms would be restricted. "I don't want someone telling me what to do and the way I have to build my cattleshed!" might be a typical objection. However, without planning of some kind for land use in the future, any kind of land use may occur—one which may actually restrict other freedoms, including the right to sell property. Lower land values may be expected from certain unrestricted uses of land. An unsupervised dump or junkyard placed across from a beautiful farmstead will undoubtedly be an eyesore for the whole community. On the other hand, these enterprises carried on under the supervision of zoning regulations and periodic inspections with appropriate rodent control provisions will not be unsightly or restrict conditions of sale. A lowering of property value usually brings a lowering of tax revenues and eventually a decline in the kind and quality of public services financed by local property taxes.

As applied to land, most planning of land use utilizes the democratic process. The people involved assume a self-imposed regulation which is considered by them to be in their best public interests. The planning issue is discussed at open meetings to which the public may come. A vote is taken on the proposed plan and opportunity for appeal exists for whichever side is unsatisfied. Appeal also exists for those individuals who are adversely affected by the land-use planning. In planning, the people take on a managerial role which can be voted out or changed when the will of the majority will legally permit changes. Land-use planning is almost never a dictated instrument.

Planning and zoning are quite different. Planning refers to the blueprint which the citizens of a city, county, area, or metropolitan board decide they want. They decide what land they want to be used for residences and farms, which sites should be used or saved for industry and commercial enterprises, and where the parks, schools, and roads should go. There is no edict that tells people what specific things ought to be included in the plan. Each planning commission decides for itself what it wants to present to the public for a vote. Sometimes this process has been called an inefficient way to consider land use. Sometimes it is. But most of the time it accomplishes what needs to be done so that the people who live in the area derive greater benefits than those which existed under the previous land-use system. In addition, the local people have adopted the land-use plan themselves because they value it as a better use of their land resources.

Zoning is a legal instrument by which the plan is put into effect. Zoning describes regulations which affect the future use of land. Existing uses of land cannot be changed unless by certain special procedures, or if the use can be declared a "nuisance." Zoning regulations set out the minimum size lot on which one can build a house; they specify whether an enclosed sewerage system must be used or whether septic tank systems are permitted, whether city water or well water may be used, whether livestock may be housed on the property, how close to the road a building may be constructed, or whether the land can be used for farm, residential, commercial, or industrial use. In most cases, the zoning regulations are simply created to carry out the planning blueprint.

In some areas subdivision ordinances accompany zoning ordinances. These include building codes which prescribe the things that have to be done if one builds a house or a commercial building. Sometimes these ordinances also include items such as restrictions concerning the disposal of trash and the amount of floor space a house is required to have.

The jurisdiction of planning and zoning regulations is generally spelled out by state legislation. Usage of planning and zoning depends upon the experience, knowledge, and understanding of the local people involved. This situation means that there certainly will be some arbitrary planning and zoning, depending on the will and ability of those authorized to develop the regulations.

Planning and zoning will be a cost to the community so that they will have to be evaluated just like any public investment. A planning commission operates within a budget provided by the relevant legislative body, which may be a county council, city board, or state legislature. Money is appropriated for specific operations, such as personnel, office expenses, and professional services like mapping and surveying. Usually the costs are higher at the start because of all the technical services required in developing the new plans.

Evaluating planning and zoning regulations is sometimes difficult, especially when a plan is first proposed and efforts are made to motivate general understanding. Much misunderstanding is likely at this point because planning takes effect over time and in the beginning must deal with intangible things rather than tangible things. Another cause for misunderstanding is the fact that although planning and zoning are good examples of the economizing process, they are really nonmarket allocations of resources. In other words, they do not rely on the market price mechanism to determine building and placing of schools, hospitals, and roads. Although market prices are considered in these endeavors, particularly once the decision about the land use is made, they are not generally a great influence in determining whether or not there will be a park or a museum.

Land use regulations can be credited either by explicit laws or may simply by adhered to and followed through custom and tradition. Sometimes the simple preference of the majority involved determines what is to be planned, including the jurisdiction involved, how the plan should be presented, who will administer the planning, and when the job is expected to begin and end.

NONMARKET ALLOCATIONS OF RESOURCES AND THE NEED FOR INCREASED PUBLIC UNDERSTANDING

Increasingly society has influenced the allocation of money expenditures and revenues, as well as physical resources, on the basis of criteria quite different from those associated with traditional market price, productivity, supply and demand factors. For example, the "public" has initiated space research programs, defense expenditures, pollution and poverty programs, water and sewer grants, and other investment in social capital within a structure expressly excluding individual market considerations. Increasingly resources are being allocated more on the basis of institutional arrangements and identifications than according to active markets in the resource fields. These nonmarket allocations are usually of a public or quasi-public nature and often involve an international as well as a domestic posture.

Agricultural policy as it has evolved in this country is not synonymous with commodity programs, and food and fiber production and marketing. It is much more. A limited perspective is the main reason why more people must more fully comprehend the breadth and scope of agriculture if the nation is to continue to construct and negotiate better policies relating the farm and nonfarm sectors. The structural, foreign, regulatory, developmental, facilitating and educational elements of agricultural policy are bridges to a continually better nourished country and world economy. We cannot allow ourselves the luxury or arrogance of being nearsighted.

Summary

There are many other persisting questions which have endured the centuries but have not been discussed. The issues that confronted landowners and farmers during the reign of the Pharaohs in Egypt still confront today's landowners and farmers. The only differences between those times and our times is that the social perspective and burden of power and control have changed. These changes necessitate different answers by the different generations. Certain topics will continue to haunt our society and will constantly call forth new analytical efforts on the part of policymakers.

Index